In memory of my mother and father

The Ottoman Renaissance

A Reconsideration of Early Modern Ottoman Art, 1413–1575

Metin Mustafa

Blue Dome Press

New Jersey

21 20 19 1 2 3 4

Published by Blue Dome Press
335 Clifton Ave.
Clifton, NJ, 07011, USA
www.bluedomepress.com

ISBN 978-1-68206-023-0

Library of Congress Cataloging-in-Publication Data Available

Cover photo: Iznik tile panel from the entrance to the mausoleum of Sultan Selim II, Hagia Sophia Museum, Istanbul, Turkey, completed by Mimar Sinan in 1577. Photograph by Metin Mustafa.

ACKNOWLEDGEMENTS

This book is dedicated to the memory of my parents who valued education. It grew out of my doctoral thesis. I am grateful to Dr. Karen McCluskey and Associate Professor Mehmet Özalp for their guidance and ongoing feedback during the writing of my thesis. It was extremely helpful, insightful and very much appreciated.

I would also like to express my sincere thanks to the following institutions and persons who have made this project possible: Topkapı Sarayı Müzesi Kütüphanesi: figs. 2.1, 2.6, 2.7, 2.8, 2.9, 6.7, 7.3, 7.5, 7.6, 7.7, 7.8, 7.9, 7.10, 7.11; Türk ve İslam Eserleri Müzesi: fig. 2.2; Ankara Üniversitesi: fig. 4.23; Rustem Pasha Mosque, Istanbul; Süleymaniye Mosque, Istanbul; Hagia Sophia Museum, Istanbul; Çinili Köşk, Istanbul; Selimiye Mosque, Edirne; Üç Şerefeli Mosque, Edirne; Yeşil Camii, Bursa; Yeşil Türbe, Bursa; Muradiye Mosque, Bursa; Karatay Madrasah, Konya; National Gallery, London; Harvard University Art Museum; Los Angeles County Museum; M. Aksoy: figs. 4.6, 4.7, 4.13, 4.14, 4.16, 4.18b, 4.26c, 4.26d, 4.27b, 4.27d, 4.27e; T. Hosaran: fig. 4.27c; O. Ibrahim: fig. 4.18; S. MacCallum: fig. 4.21; G. Elgar: fig. 4.22b; H. Lower: fig. 7.1c; N. Shield: fig. 7.3b.

Of course, such work cannot be possible without the support from one's family and loved ones. My warmest thanks go to my sister Neşe Sözen, nephews Kaan and Korhan for their support over the years. I also would like to thank my brother-in-law Volkan Sözen for accompanying me on my research field trip to Turkey, Russia, Poland, Hungary, Israel / Palestine, and Egypt.

Contents

PREFACE

The Ottoman Renaissance, which took place during the fifteenth and sixteenth centuries in Bursa, Edirne and Istanbul, produced an extraordinary array of artworks in the form of monumental architecture, Iznik tiles, calligraphy and illustrated manuscripts. Notwithstanding the exceptional artistic production, Ottoman art and architecture have not received the same attention in historiography as, for instance, the celebrated Renaissance of Italy. Drawing upon notions of rebirth characteristic of renaissances more generally, this study seeks to situate early modern Ottoman art within a more global Renaissance context. The study recognises the cultural interaction and sharing of values across the Mediterranean basin that characterised the period yet examines Ottoman artistic expression through specifically Ottoman conceptions of rebirth. Ottoman ideas of rebirth although built on the classicism of Greece and Rome moved well beyond these legacies. Indeed, this work uniquely contends that the Ottomans were much more focused on their Eastern (Turkic, Timurid, Persian) and Islamic heritage, than that of the classical world which features in the West. Additionally, both the ancient and recent past provided inspiration on which to build a cultural identity specific to the Ottoman experience. In order to fully understand the shared values of the early modern Mediterranean and critically engage in different interpretations of rebirth, the study explicitly compares the works of three Renaissance contemporaries: the Italian Giorgio Vasari and the Ottoman Mustafa Ali and Mimar Sinan.

This study argues that the unique geographic position of the sultans of the Ottoman court allowed the artists of the Ottoman Empire to capitalise on the inherited legacies of both the Islamic–Timurid–Turkic–Persian East and the Latin West. The result was a synthesis of Eastern and Western exemplars which ultimately produced a rebirth in the arts distinct from their early modern Italian and European counterparts. This work traces this Renaissance from its beginnings in 1413 through to its triumphant phase in the Süleymanic Age (1520–1575). In its examination of the empire's monumental architecture, decorative tiles, calligraphy and miniature paintings, the study contributes to current scholarship in the field which seeks to assess the Renaissance from a more complex, multi-focal and multinational perspective. Furthermore, it reinforces the idea that many renaissances arose concurrently in the Mediterranean basin in the fifteenth and sixteenth centuries.

INTRODUCTION

CONTEXTUALISING THE RENAISSANCE

> Underlying all these [early modern achievements by the cultures of the world] is a need to synthesize new global experiences into a structure that would bind individual fragments into a collective unity. To comprehend the world thus required deft oscillation between local details and global frameworks and a reconfiguration of the particular against the universal.[1]

In 2005, the celebrated Ottoman historian Gülru Necipoğlu published a groundbreaking study on the Ottoman Renaissance architect Sinan.[2] In the text, she analysed the great buildings of Sinan by placing his accomplishments fully within his own historical period. She noted his adherence to past models (Turkic, Islamic, and Roman), as well as his Sufi humanist values. In short, she deftly scrutinised Sinan's works within a broader framework that connected the past to the present and the local to the global. In doing so she presented an inspiring model for future Ottoman Renaissance scholarly, calling for "a 'fresh narrative' [to] rescue [Ottoman arts] from the clichés of orientalist theories and to set it into a more universal historical perspective."[3] This book is a response to that call.

This study takes a novel approach to early modern Ottoman art and architecture. It situates the development of Ottoman art during the fifteenth and sixteenth centuries within the broader current of Renaissance experience, defined most unambiguously by its chief attribute of cultural rebirth. In this way, it makes a significant contribution to global Renaissance studies—a constructive trend in early modern scholarship that seeks to reshape our understanding of this period by approaching it with a more inclusive and global lens. This study is careful, however, not to fuse the Ottoman experience with that of the celebrated Italian Renaissance, as doing so would obstruct one's ability to understand Ottoman art history on its own terms. Indeed, such an approach smacks of the Eurocentrism which has traditionally characterised Renaissance studies. This study aims instead to examine notions of rebirth more broadly, beyond the Western prerogative founded upon the glories of ancient Greece and Rome. It is innovative in that it engages with contemporary *Ottoman* notions of rebirth, which intersect with civilization's ties to both East and West and to both the ancient and recent past, all of which combine to build a cultural identity specific to the Ottoman experience. As the examination of literature throughout the study shows, a comprehensive reassessment of Ottoman art as a Renaissance experience has not yet been accomplished. Although there is a growing body of scholarship which acknowledges a common Renaissance experience within the Mediterranean region,[4] this study places early modern Ottoman art and architecture within a global context of cultural rebirth by reaching beyond the West.

Like many cultures of the period—from that of the Timurids in the East to those of the Florentines and Burgundians in the West—the Ottomans sought justification, even legitimisation, and identity in their glorious past.[5] While the Greco-Roman past was securely part of the renewed Ottoman narrative, it formed only a small part of a greater whole. Ottoman history was more firmly attached to its Turco–Mongol, Turkic–Timurid, Iranian, and Islamic legacies, which proved even more consequential to its nascent Renaissance identity. Revisionist in its approach, this work therefore aims to place the Ottoman narrative of the fifteenth and sixteenth centuries into "a more universal historical perspective," but one which captures the nuances of the Ottoman experience.[6] It is this archaeological approach to history which ultimately led to the development of a distinctly Ottoman artistic and cultural efflorescence that characterised Ottoman art from the Bursa tradition in the early decades of the fifteenth century to that of the Süleymanic tradition in the sixteenth century. Renegotiating the Renaissance narrative to include the Eastern "other" is ultimately at the core of this book and furthers current scholarly interest in the global nature of the Renaissance.[7]

As Stephen Greenblatt has eloquently argued, the Renaissance of the fifteenth and sixteenth centuries was a period of intense self-fashioning.[8] Both individuals and states took pride in constructing their public and global presence. Almost without fail, it was the past that defined their subjective present, representing a conscious attempt to link themselves and their state to a greater legacy and thus to justify their place in the world. In the same way, key elements of Ottoman history were strategically shaped to define a burgeoning Ottoman identity.

The link between historical context and identity is essential to fully understand the formation of a Renaissance identity. Thus, by placing Ottoman art in its own historical context, the book offers a culturally contextualised, broader definition of the global Renaissance. In this way, the critical emphasis of this study shifts away from the Italo-centric narrative of the Renaissance, and instead focuses on how the Ottoman court presented its own, distinctly Ottoman narrative of rebirth.

Historical consciousness of the Ottoman dynasty played a crucial role in the self-fashioning of the ruling sultans. The Ottoman court's artistic expressions ensured the propagation of the Ottoman sultanate's legitimacy in the Islamic East and Latin West. For the Ottoman rulers, the past served as a justifiable and valid "example" to guide the self-fashioning of the sultans. This understanding of temporality, or the relationship between past, present and future, affects the self-fashioning of Ottoman sultans, pashas and viziers and the formation of their political and cultural identity.[9] By understanding and manipulating the past, the Ottomans merged the real and the fictional to construct a new, historically sound and modern identity.

According to Jörn Rüsen, "history is . . . an internal and external synthesis, of the real and the fictional, of the objective and the intentional, of the empirical and the normative."[10] This approach to history making in which the past informs the present is typical of the self-fashioning of the Medici in Florence, the Burgundian dukes in northern Europe, and the Timurid sultans in Samarkand.[11] As Rüsen argues, this theory is not specific to one cultural group but rather universal. Without understanding the Ottoman context, it is impossible to fully appreciate the nature and complexity of Ottoman identity and its projection in artistic works produced between 1413 and 1575.[12]

Ultimately, the revisionist approach aims to shed light on the many regional expressions of Renaissance, and reflects more accurately the fluid, interactive experiences of the larger Mediterranean world in the fifteenth and sixteenth centuries. Revisionist historians Jerry Brotton and Matteo Burioni recognise the many "Renaissances throughout the regions, each with their own highly specific and separate characteristics" and acknowledge "a wider variety of instances of rebirth."[13] Similarly, for Gerald MacClean, the period under discussion "often encouraged us to forget just how many of the artistic, social, religious, philosophical, scientific, technical and cultural developments that distinguished the period depended upon the movement and exchange of ideas, skills and goods between what came to be thought as separate spheres: East and West."[14] MacClean's point underscores the cultural fluidity of the early modern Mediterranean. His emphasis on the interconnectedness of the cultures of the early modern Mediterranean reinforces the dissolving of cultural barriers in this period. Like MacClean, Heather E. Grossman and Walker state that "[t]he term 'Mediterranean' makes possible an alternative framework that offers a more open and fluid field within which to situate the disparate objects, monuments and cultures that were networked with one another in real ways, even if these connections were contingent and constantly changing."[15] The interconnectedness of cultures in the early modern Mediterranean basin through exchange of material goods and ideas became one of the defining features of the Renaissance. These cultural connections and influences "disrupt notions of static cultural identity" and "challenge the political, economic, geographic and religious boundaries that are traditionally employed to define, categorise and interpret the art of this period."[16] Similarly, for Jack Goody this revolution could not have happened without non-European influences.[17] This is the approach taken by this work, which in its thematic focus on Ottoman art contributes a novel perspective in the field of global Renaissance studies.

More specifically, this book argues that through visual analysis one can come to understand the power of art in fashioning Ottoman imperial identity, and in conveying the power and magnificence of the house of Osman to greater numbers of people across Istanbul, the Empire, and beyond. For this work, primary visual sources range from architectural works to the fine arts of calligraphy, miniature painting, and tiling. Some of the major visual data used in this study includes fifteenth-century buildings from Bursa, including the Yeşil Camii (1413–21) and Yeşil Türbe (1413–21) of Mehmed I, and the Üç Şerefeli Mosque (1438–78) of Murad II in Edirne. These complexes are explored in Chapter Four. Chapter Four also focuses on the post-1453 imperial architecture from Istanbul consisting of the Fatih Camii of Mehmed II in 1471 and the Çinili Köşk (Tiled Pavilion) of 1473. From the sixteenth century, two monumental complexes of the imperial architect Sinan, the Süleymaniye (1557) and Selimiye (1575) mosques, form the primary analysis of Ottoman architecture in Chapter Five. The critical re-evaluation of Ottoman fine arts in Chapter Six includes the Iznik tiles that decorate the Rustem Pasha Mosque (1560–61); finally, Chapter Seven elaborates on the illuminations and calligraphic works of the sixteenth-century artists Kara Memi, Ahmet, and Hasan Karahısarı, respectively; and Arif Çelebi's representation of the life of Süleyman the Magnificent in the illustrated history *Süleymanname* (1557).

In addition, this study draws on contemporary textual sources to give voice to contemporary early modern ideas and ideals—both Ottoman and Western. Primary sources considered in this study include transliterations of written sources, including the works of three sixteenth-century contemporaries: the Florentine Giorgio Vasari's *The Lives of the Painters, Sculptors, and Architects* (1550/1568), his Ottoman counterpart Mustafa Ali's *Epic Deeds of Artists* (1587) and *The Essence of History* (1591–99), and the imperial architect Mimar Sinan's autobiographies dictated to the poet-painter Mustafa Sa'i Çelebi (d. 1595–96). Although Ali and Sinan are unique voices in the Ottoman world, these sources are, like Vasari's, highly subjective. Although geographically dispersed, all three artists perceived their historical epoch as one of cultural significance, as one in which many of its merits were measured by or based on the emulation of precedents. It is clear from their writings that they were all highly self-aware and held a sharp sense of historical consciousness. In addition to Ali and Sinan, seventeenth-century Ottoman traveller Evliya Çelebi's (1611–82) *Seyahatname* (*The Book of Travels*) similarly boasts of the grandeur of the Ottoman past and the surpassing of that past in his own time. Other travel accounts of Europeans to the Ottoman Empire, such as *The Travels of John Sanderson in the Levant, 1584–1602,* are analysed to access contemporary European perceptions of Ottoman cultural rebirth and the self-fashioning of its rulers. Although subjective in nature, these sources provide useful historical, social and cultural contexts for defining Ottoman notions of rebirth.

Approaching this data from a revisionist perspective that emphasises the visual impact of the works themselves and the historical self-consciousness that gave them their form allows this study to assess Ottoman art from its own historical position. As Karl Popper states, "each generation has a right to look upon and re-interpret history in [its] own way . . . there can be no history of 'the past as it actually happened': there can only be historical interpretation, and none of them final; and every generation has a right to frame its own."[18] Popper's view here rejects the mono-cultural approach to a given historical period and supports a more inclusive approach.

Appreciating Ottoman attitude to rebirth is integral to understanding a more global perspective of the Renaissance period. Like their Renaissance counterparts in Florence, Venice and other regions in Italy and Europe at the time, the Ottomans, too, looked to past exemplars to forge a powerful identity. They, too, experienced a rebirth—but with a difference. The Ottomans not only propagated the classical heritage of the West, which they inherited at the conquest of Constantinople in 1453, but they also exploited the powerful and enduring imperial legacy they shared with their Islamic, Turkic, and Perso–Timurid cousins. Within the context of this strategic appropriation of both Eastern and Western legacies, the work argues that the Ottomans fashioned a distinctive cultural rebirth. By interrogating the product of this synthesis, the study makes an original contribution to global Renaissance studies. This study expressly tests the question: did the Ottomans have a Renaissance? Further, it inquires about the dominant characteristics of that Renaissance: how does the Ottoman Renaissance compare to other renaissances, especially the Italian Renaissance? Through establishing the nature of the Ottoman Renaissance, can we assert the existence of a global Renaissance?

In order to place Ottoman art of the fifteenth and sixteenth centuries within a legitimately global context, the next chapter examines the historical context of the Ottoman Renaissance experience, which will set the foundation for the rest of the study.

CHAPTER ONE

HISTORICAL CONTEXT OF THE OTTOMAN RENAISSANCE

Ottoman ideas of rebirth share many characteristics with other regions, both Eastern and Western. However, because such discourses are inseparable from their historical and cultural contexts, there are several departures that distinguish the Ottoman Renaissance from those regions. These contexts are exemplified through the Ottomans' historical connections to its Turkic kinsmen: the Turco–Mongols and Timurids of Central Asia, the religion of Islam and philosophy of Sufism, and empire building and expansion. In addition, the Ottoman Empire acknowledged a shared heritage with Mediterranean centres including Latin and Orthodox Christendom, as well as the historical empire of Rome. Further characterising the period is the Ottomans' struggle for Islamic ascendancy against their Muslim adversaries to the east in Safavid Iran (Persia). All of these factors impacted, to greater or lesser degrees, on artistic expression and official Ottoman self-fashioning.

In his *Essence of History*, Mustafa Ali cites key historical moments as catalysts for Ottoman greatness in the sixteenth century, including the rebirth of the arts.[1] For Ali, the rebirth phase is long and gradual, lasting from 1413 to 1517. He traces the beginning of this phase to the re-emergence of the Ottoman Empire after the Battle of Çamurlut in 1413, which ended the political interregnum following the Timurid invasion of Anatolia in 1402. Ali then cites the conquest of Constantinople by Mehmed II in 1453 and his occupation of the Crimea in 1478 as a further impetus of the rebirth. For Ali, the rebirth phase ends in 1516–17 with the conquests of Selim I through his acquisitions of the three Holy sites of Islam—Mecca, Medina, and Jerusalem—and the conferring of the title "caliph" onto the Ottoman sultans. In 1534, Süleyman added

Baghdad to the Empire. With this addition, the Ottomans brought all the significant past Islamic religious and historic sites of early Muslim achievements since the Umayyad period in the seventh century under its rule. As inheritors of such a rich cultural heritage, the patronage of sixteenth-century sultans contributed to the surpassing of past accomplishments. Consequently, the "subsequent triumph" phase (1520–95) in Ali's text coincides with his own time and that of the three sultans Süleyman, Selim II, and Murad III. For Ali, their reigns exemplify the glory of Ottoman political and cultural greatness and the mature phase of the empire. Each of these significant moments in the history of the empire, Ali argues, prompted the self-fashioning of the ruling sultans as "Alexander, Cengiz Khan and Timur" through art and architecture—a strategic move that reinforced their global sovereignty.[2]

These three figures appear in Ali's assessment of the history of the Ottoman sultans. However, only Mehmed the Conqueror, Selim I, and Süleyman attained "sahib-kıran" status—that is, master of an auspicious conjunction—signifying that of a world conqueror who establishes a universal dominion on a par with Alexander, Cengiz Khan, and Timur.[3] Through Alexander, Cengiz Khan, and Timur, Ali was able to create a traceable legacy, one that made historical sense to him through understanding the cultural achievements attained during his lifetime. Ali demonstrates a clear awareness of the sultanate's self-fashioning around these historical figures to legitimise its universal claim in its ever-expanding empire. For this reason, it is important to establish the historical context of the pre-Ottoman world to determine the complexity of Ali's belief that the Ottomans sought to forge links to many cultures to establish a distinct cultural identity. As the empire expanded from 1453 onward, major historic areas including Mecca, Medina, Jerusalem, and Baghdad came under Ottoman rule. For the Ottomans, this created a sense of historical destiny through which they could understand themselves as the inheritors and custodians of these places that had once been the centres of pre-Islamic and medieval Arabo–Turkic–Persian–Islamic civilizations.

The expansion of the empire eastward in the fifteenth and sixteenth centuries required serious consideration by the dynasty to justify its legitimacy over its Muslim subjects. Founded in the late thirteenth century around Bursa by Osman's tribe after the disintegration of the Seljuk

Sultanate of Rum in Anatolia (1077–1317), these "new" torch bearers set upon conquering their neighbouring Turkish principalities in the rest of Anatolia. Linguistically, culturally and ethnically connected to their brethren in Anatolia and Central Asia, Osman's tribe transformed the region in the subsequent centuries through a rapid expansionist policy. This expansion would ultimately see the Ottomans control the former territories of the medieval Umayyads and Abbasids, and Islam's three most holy sites: Mecca, Medina, and Jerusalem. The Mamluks and Seljuks, as ancestors of the Ottomans, seamlessly amalgamated local Arab and Persian culture, language, and aesthetics into their societies As heirs to these regions, the Ottomans quickly staked a claim to rulership and inheritance of the whole region.

The Ottomans' political and cultural connections to the regions date to the ninth century through their ethnic and cultural links. The emergence of Turkish-speaking kingdoms in the Islamic East assured the Turks' historical place as inheritors of Abbasid, Persian and Central Asian heritage. According to Aydın Sayılı, Lamaan Ball, and Salim Ayduz, "[f]rom the eleventh century on . . . Turks could be expected to be encountered in any part of the Islamic East."[4] As early as the ninth century, independent Turkish kingdoms began to emerge in the Islamic East, including the Mamluk Tulunids (868–905) and Ikshidids (935–69) in Egypt; the Seljuks (1037–1194) who ruled from Isfahan in Iran; the Qarakhanids (999–1211) who ruled in Samarkand; and the Ghaznavids (977–1186) who dominated large parts of Iran, much of Transoxiana in Central Asia and North India, assimilating with the Perso–Arab Muslim cultures. The Ottomans were descended from the same people as the Mamluks and Seljuks and all Turkic tribes. Thus, their eventual rulership can be seen as a renewal or rebirth of those Turkic lines. The Ottomans forged direct links to the Mamluks and Seljuks who, between the ninth and eleventh centuries, increased their presence in the region by undermining the weakening authority of the Abbasids. First as mercenaries, and later after their conversion to Islam, the Mamluks and Seljuks became the Abbasids' defenders and eventual rulers. By the eleventh century the Great Seljukid Empire (1037–1194), founded by Tughrul I (990–1063) who ruled on behalf of the Abbasid Caliph al-Qa'im, cemented their political power in the region. As Marshall Broomhall explains, "the Turks . . . soon became the bodyguard of the Caliphs, until in the end the

[Abbasid] Caliphs became the helpless tools of their rude protectors."[5] Thus, forging links to the various cultures in the region was important for the Ottomans' in efforts to seamlessly integrate their rule and justify their authority through conquest and pre-existing cultural associations.

Despite various levels of assimilation, each of these diverse groups retained some of their native Turkish characteristics and saw themselves as essentially Turkmen. As the protectors of the Abbasid caliphate, the Mamluk and Seljuk Turks became inheritors of their cultural and literary achievements, and protectors of the medieval Arabo–Islamic civilization to which they made their own contributions. Indeed, one can argue that the very early beginnings of the rebirth of Turkish civilizations can be seen during the Mamluk period in Egypt. As the Abbasid power waned, Turkic groups led by the Tulunids (868–905) seized authority in Egypt. Through the adaptation of Abbasid works, Tulunids' contributions to the cultural expressions of Mamluk Egypt signify the birth of an emerging cultural identity. The ninth-century Ahmad Ibn Tulun Mosque (868–84) in Cairo is one such example. It is constructed around courtyard galleries decorated with carved stucco, with a covered hall on each of the four sides, the largest being on the side of the *qibla* facing towards Mecca. As the first building of its kind to use stilted columns to carry the arcades and roof, the building is unique for its time.[6] With its distinct spiral minaret emulating the Abbasid Samarra Mosque (851) in Baghdad, the Tulun Mosque marks the Mamluks' strategic plan to emulate a visually meaningful past in order to signal the birth of the new Turkish kingdom of Egypt and the self-fashioning of their new cultural identity.

The waning force of the centralised power of the Seljukid Empire in Iran and Egypt saw the emergence of separate Turkish kingdoms in the region, including in Anatolia with the founding of the Seljuk Sultanate of Rum in 1075. By the eleventh century, Turkish and Iranian cultures had become inextricably intertwined, in both Anatolia and farther east. Three official languages became the norm: Turkish, Arabic, and Persian.[7] Persian served the literary and intellectual domains of society and Arabic the religious, while Turkish dominated the administrative and political spheres. This interchange between languages continued throughout the Ottoman period with Ali noting that sultans and patron-pashas composed in "eloquent . . . Persian and Turkish."[8]

Persian calligraphic works were highly esteemed for their artistic sophistication in the Islamic world, and emulating them became a challenge for the Ottomans. In direct competition to surpass their Persian counterparts, the artists of Rum invented *ihtira* (new styles). Artistic competition as a Renaissance trait seen in Italy and echoed in Vasari's *The Lives* is similarly reiterated by his Ottoman counterpart here. Stretching from Anatolia in the west to Egypt, Iran, and Central Asia in the east, these inextricable political, linguistic, and cultural connections made the Turks an integral part of a multifarious entity. By the fifteenth and sixteenth centuries their descendants, the Ottomans, inherited this rich heritage, which they used to exploit their political advantage, manufacture a new identity, and historically legitimise their position. To demonstrate their continuity, this legitimacy required not only the emulation of past rulers to demonstrate their continuity, but also to publicise that they came from the same lineage.

By the fourteenth century, Timur, another Turkish ruler aiming to re-establish the universal empire of Cengiz Han, entered the scene in Central Asia. As attested by Ali in *The Essence of History,* Timur is one of those world sovereigns whom the Ottomans set out to emulate through cultural symbolism. In both *The Essence of History* and *Epic Deeds of Artists*, Ali consistently references "the courts of Fatih Sultan Mehmed and [the Timurid] Sultan Husayn Bayqara as the paradigmatic models of statecraft . . . [and] literary patronage."[9] Such comments demonstrate Ali's awareness of relevant models for Ottoman magnificence. He acknowledges that from "[t]he Timurid dynasty and Cengizid house . . . bloomed those praiseworthy ones who are the Ottoman House."[10] Ali's comment is significant: he makes explicit the Ottomans' ties to their Turkic predecessors, linking Ottoman cultural greatness in political, literary, and artistic spheres to their Eastern heritage in the way that Vasari positions ancient Rome for Tuscan triumphs. Ali's attitude is more than just a rhetorical art tool; it is a belief system which encapsulates the Ottoman mindset of the early modern period. For Ali, the Ottoman rebirth was a continuation of the achievements of the 'Timurid Renaissance' (c. 1370–1507) achievements that began in Central Asia and attained perfection in Anatolia with the help of Timurid and other Muslim artists working at the Ottoman court.[11] For Ali, the Timurid Renaissance of the fifteenth century under Timur and his successors continued to develop in the sixteenth century, producing cultural change in distant places like Bursa, Edirne, and Istanbul.[12] Thus, for Ali the Ottoman narrative of rebirth required constantly looking back to their shared Eastern heritage.

In *The Essence of History,* Ali justifies the Ottomans' claim to universal sovereignty. He relies on Turco–Mongol and Timurid precedents as historical examples against which to measure the achievements of the Ottomans.[13] Although these examples represent mainly administrative and political borrowings by the Ottomans in their governance of the empire, they form, nonetheless, significant elements of the Ottoman mindset and contribute to our understanding of the rebirth of the arts as a means of representation of sovereignty, dynastic power and legitimacy. Following Timur's defeat of Bajezid I and the dismantling of the first Ottoman Empire in 1402, the Timurid influence on the rebirth of the second Ottoman Empire in 1413 by Mehmed I (1389–1421) is profound and is constantly referred to by Ali in *The Essence of History.* He refers to Sultan Husayn Bayqara (1438–1506) of the Timurid court as "a model of cultural greatness and political wisdom," praising the sultan's patronage of the arts in Herat and Balkh in Afghanistan.[14] By emulating the Timurid court after its defeat in 1413, official fifteenth-century commissions in Bursa and Istanbul symbolise the resurrection of the Timurid legacy through the new masters—the Ottomans.

This sentiment is clearly expressed by Mehmed I in 1416, three years after the reunification of the Ottoman Empire. In a letter to Timur's son and heir Shahrukh in 1416, Mehmed I recognises the universal sovereignty of the Mongol world order represented by Timur and Shahrukh by acknowledging them as "*güregen*" (sons-in-law of Cengiz Han). While recognising this, however, Mehmed I asserts the rebirth of a new political entity in Anatolia, "the rise of the dawn of the Ottoman State" (*Dawlat-i 'Osmaniyye*), which is taking charge and fighting Christendom in the Balkans. Mehmed I thereby asserts the legitimacy of his state as *the* emerging world force beyond the Timurids.[15] It is for this reason that Mehmed I, to commemorate the momentous occasion of the political rebirth in 1413 and to broadcast a symbolic link to the Timurid past, looked to emulate the aesthetics of Timurid Central Asian with the commissioning of his mosque and mausoleum in Bursa. While proclaiming his sovereignty as the champion of Islam against Christendom, Mehmed I's assertive tone forges the beginnings of a distinct Ottoman identity and mindset that will become more solidified in the following century. Ali's repeated references to the Timurid court thus reflect the importance of a relatively modern Eastern heritage in the Ottoman conception of rebirth. This unification of the empire saw the influx of an international team of Timurid artists and artisans from Tabriz and other parts of the Islamic world. These artists would transform the architectural landscape of the two cities, marking the Renaissance of the Ottoman arts with the Yeşil Camii (Green Mosque) and Yeşil Türbe (Green Tomb) of Sultan Mehmed I, and the Muradiye Mosque (1435) and Üç Şerefeli Mosque (1438–47) of Murad II.

Despite this initial phase of rebirth, Ali argues that the conquest of Constantinople in 1453 provided a paradigm shift in Ottoman self-consciousness. Conquering the capital of the Eastern Roman Empire known as Constantinople or New Rome—a rule over the city that lasted from 330 to 1453—the Ottomans ironically did not put an end to the legacy of the Roman Empire. Instead, they saw both the momentous conquest and themselves as inheritors of an ancient Roman legacy. The capture of the city gave the Ottomans a new global vision and outlook. The city's transformation and rebirth as Istanbul by Mehmed II would serve as the capital of the Ottoman Empire for the next four and a half centuries. Thus, the fallen city was to be reborn under Sultan Mehmed II's patronage to rival the glory of its heyday. Ali asserts that the imperial status of the Ottomans had been established by the conquest of Constantinople, and that under Mehmed II's guidance "the future" had been "planned well."[16] Claiming the title of "caesar," the sultans began to rule vast regions of the former Eastern Roman Empire and the Islamic East both as "caesar" and "sultan," respectively.

The transition from a principality to a state centred on Bursa and Edirne, and from there to an imperial universal status in 1453, allowed for a paradigm shift in the Ottoman psyche. As Cornell Fleischer notes, for Ali, the reign of Mehmed II represented "the hey-day of patronage and the flowering of the cosmopolitan literary . . . political, [and cultural period] of the post-Mongol Islamic period."[17] In this way, according to Ali, the reign of Mehmed II that followed the conquest of 1453 marked the beginning of the Ottomans' attempt to surpass the Mongol Islamic legacy by creating a more culturally assertive Ottoman identity, further legitimising their claim to universal sovereignty in both the Turkic and

Muslim worlds. Propelled by Mehmed II's artistic stimulus, this planning signalled the power of the rebirth phase in the Ottoman artistic legacy. Although the Ottomans could not claim direct lineage to the Greeks and Romans, their possession of the lands of the Caesars including Constantinople, the former capital of the Eastern Roman Empire, placed them in an historical position from which they could lay claim to this heritage and see themselves as legitimate heirs to Roman/Byzantine emperors after 1453. The humanist George of Trebizond acknowledges this in his 1466 Latin treatise *On the Eternal Glory of the Autocrat and His World Dominion,* which was dedicated to Mehmed II. In this work, George refers to Mehmed II and his successors as the "Emperor of the Romans."[18] This new ownership of the Western classical legacy and the continuing engagement with the Roman-Byzantine past, thrust the Ottomans onto the Western stage and into direct dialogue with Europeans.

Although Ali does not refer to it explicitly, Mehmed's Islamisation of the former Christian city begins by emulating the Roman/Byzantine structure—the Hagia Sophia. Mehmed II's dialogue with the ancient Roman past through the Hagia Sophia begins with the commissioning of the first imperial mosque in the new Ottoman capital of Istanbul. The Hagia Sophia became a model to be imitated, leading to the Ottomans' first attempt to replicate and surpass it. The Fatih Camii (Conqueror's Mosque) achieved this in 1471. In terms of Ottoman architectural development, Mehmed II's imperial mosque shifted the paradigm of Ottoman rebirth towards the West. To demonstrate his connection to his ancestral roots, two years later in 1473 Mehmed II constructed a tiled pavilion, the Çinili Köşk, in the Timurid style in the Topkapı Palace gardens. Construction of the Çinili Köşk showed Mehmed II's interest in the artistic and architectural interplay between East and West, and reinforced his universal sovereign.

Mediating between East and West, Mehmed II's interest in emulating Alexander is well documented. Franz Babinger, a twentieth-century biographer of Mehmed II, notes:, "[t]he oldest treatments of Alexander legend in the Persian language . . . passed into east Turkish and Ottoman Turkish . . . for certain . . . he was familiar with the classical accounts of Alexander's heroic deeds . . . the one written in Greek by Flavius Arrianus, was among the Conqueror's books in the Istanbul serai."[19] Another example of Mehmed II's interest in Alexander is the illustrated copy of *Iskendername* (Book of Alexander) housed in the scriptorium of the Topkapı Palace. The *Iskendername*, written by the fourteenth-century Anatolian poet Ahmedi, is one of the earliest surviving examples of an Ottoman illustrated manuscript that celebrates the conquests and feats of Alexander.[20] Ownership of such manuscripts and attempts to shape himself in the image of Alexander as the ruler of the East and West illustrate Mehmed II's interest in reaffirming and perpetuating his own image as a world conqueror and imperial sovereign.

Mehmed II's expansionist policy of empire building coincided with such representations of the Ottoman dynasty, ensuring that the dynasty advocated its universal legitimacy by linking its lineage to its Turco–Mongol past. Mehmed II's 1478 conquest of the Crimea, whose rulers traced their heritage to Cengiz Khan and to the Mongols of the thirteenth century, meant that he now possessed the land of his Central Asian ancestors. Mehmed II's conquest of the "Cengizid Giray Hans of the Crimea" served as a symbolic reminder of the Ottoman dynasty's Turco–Mongol heritage and the once great Mongol empire that stretched from the Pacific to the Black Sea.[21] For Ali, this symbolic connection reinforced the lineage of Ottoman rulers like Mehmed II and Süleyman whose mothers were descendants of Crimean Tatars. By connecting the heritage of the steppes of Central Asia to the sultanate, Ali makes a direct link between Ottoman greatness and the successes of the Turks under the Ottomans. Ali's analysis is reflected in Fethullah Arifi Çelebi's 1558 *Süleymanname* ("Book of Suleyman"), an illustrated manuscript and carefully constructed visual history of Süleyman that highlight's the monarch's Mongol heritage. An example of the 'triumph phase' of Ottoman rule can be found in the *Süleymanname's* depiction of the sultan's reception of the Crimean Khan Devlet Giray, the nephew of Süleyman's mother. Inclusion in folio 519a of the scene of the sultan's reception of the Crimean Khan Devlet Giray in *The Süleymanname*, the nephew of Süleyman's mother, celebrates one of the moments of the "triumph" phase of Ottoman rule.[22]

However, as the Ottomans emerged as the dominant force of the region in the sixteenth century, they would also be challenged on religious and geopolitical grounds as legitimate rulers of the Islamic East. The Ottomans perceived themselves as champions of Sunni Islam over the Shi'a Safavids of Iran; however, they could not claim direct descent from Muhammad. Their Safavid Shi'a adversaries confounded the Ottomans with their claims of being the "true" heirs, or *seyyids* (direct descendants of Prophet Muhammad), of the Islamic world.[23] The tenuous link to Muhammad through the appropriation of ancient and medieval Islamic structures allowed the Ottomans to reign supreme over these largely foreign cultures.

The Ottomans challenged their Safavid adversaries. This was done in two ways: first in 1516 when the campaigns of Selim I brought Islam's three holy sites (Mecca, Medina, and Jerusalem) under Ottoman control, Selim I assuming the title of "caliph" in the name of all Muslims; and second when, following this triumph;[24] and seeing themselves as legitimate successors to medieval Islamic civilization, art and architecture became the medium through which Ottoman sultans could further assert their religious legitimacy publicly and in grand form. Challenging Safavid Shi'a claims to their inheritance of Islam, the sultans Ottomanised past Islamic structures in Mecca, Medina, and Jerusalem. Süleyman and his sons were particularly active in the refurbishment of Islam's three holy sites. Some of their modifications include: the semi-domical and minaret revamps at the Ka'ba in Mecca by Sinan and completed in the reign of Selim II in 1571 (fig. 1.1); Süleyman's embellishment of the holy precinct by commissioning a marble inlaid *minbar* (pulpit) which was used until the early decades of the twentieth century (figs. 1.2 and 1.3); a single Ottoman minaret known as the al-Süleymaniye built on the northeastern wall and *mihrab* additions to the Prophet's Mosque in Medina, completed in the reign of Murad III in 1589 (figs. 1.4 and 1.5); and the Iznik tile embellishments of the Dome of the Rock in Jerusalem in 1545 (fig. 1.6).[25]

The Ottomans' reliance on using past exemplars from medieval Islamic and Eastern imperial styles and techniques contributed to their ever-increasing cultural awareness. The extant imperial mosques and palaces spread throughout an ever-expanding empire from East to West. The refurbishments of past medieval Islamic structures, serve as a testimony of the legacies of patron sultans, underpinning their self-fashioning and cultural assertiveness as legitimate rulers of the Muslim world. At the annual *hajj* pilgrimage these visual embellishments reinforced and legitimised the image of the sultan-caliph to the entire Muslim world. With the addition of the Süleymaniye Mosque (1557) in Istanbul, the physical and symbolic constructs of these structures proclaimed Ottoman custodianship over the past and supremacy over Safavid claims as *seyyids.* Hence, Rüsen's argument that "[t]he past provides the paradigms which one can adhere to if one is to overcome the present and shape the future" is consistent with the Ottomans' sense of self-consciousness and the idea of rebirth that clearly dominated their self-fashioning.[26]

Furthermore, in the illustrated history, the *Süleymanname,* the oscillation between the steppe and sedentary traditions became consolidated in a symbolic sense during the reign of Sultan Süleyman. This work depicts the monarch in a variety of settings—on the nomadic steppes, as a warrior, a dispenser of justice, a religious leader—and as the executor of building programs in Istanbul, Mecca, Medina, and Jerusalem. All these symbolic representations augment the prestige of the Ottoman dynasty as the leaders of the Muslim world. As David Lowenthal claims, "[t]hose who magnify their past are especially prone to amplify its age."[27] Using the past to justify their present state, the Ottoman sultans in the fifteenth and sixteenth centuries continually and actively sought to enhance their universal power, prestige, and authority through artistic and architectural expressions.

This relationship to the distant and recent past, both East and West, is essential to the Ottomans' historical consciousness. This view resonates in Ali's works and is an integral element of the Ottomans' cultural achievements and narrative of rebirth, where meaningful pasts and the present are brought into equilibrium to assert a Renaissance ideal.[28] In order to examine the nature of cultural rebirth from the Ottoman point of view, understanding of the complexity of Ottoman history is essential. To fully understand the Ottoman experience, art historians must look beyond the confines of an Italian Renaissance shaped by classical Greece and Rome. This book thus integrates the specific history and attitudes of Vasari's Ottoman contemporaries into the Renaissance narrative to ultimately gain access to a multifaceted, multilayered, and distinctly Ottoman interpretation of the Renaissance. In this way, this work approaches early modern Ottoman art from a "more universal historical perspective" and demonstrates not only that there was a rebirth in early Ottoman art, but also that this rebirth was different from (but no less important than) other contemporaneous Renaissances around the globe.[29]

CHAPTER TWO

THE REBIRTH PARADIGM: ITALIAN AND OTTOMAN PERSPECTIVES

With the hindsight of the twenty-first century, reframing the definition of Renaissance is a high priority not only for Western scholars but also for non-European scholars, especially for those in the Mediterranean basin, which share a historical legacy with their European counterparts. Directly engaging with a revisionist approach, this study reshapes the notion of Renaissance by looking at Ottoman, rather than Vasarian, understandings of rebirth, specifically through analysing the contemporary works of Mustafa Ali and Mimar Sinan.

The Vasarian paradigm

The Renaissance is traditionally associated with the revival of classical Greek and Roman literature, philosophy, and art and the aesthetic and intellectual innovations they inspired. The Renaissance is also typically associated with the Florentines of the late fourteenth to mid-sixteenth centuries. Giorgio Vasari's *The Lives of the Painters, Sculptors and Architects*, published in 1550 and again in 1565, was the most authoritative written articulation of Renaissance. [1] The Vasarian *rinascita* saw ideals of progress and perfection as its key qualities.[2] Indeed, within his Tuscan-centric vision, Vasari argued that "perfection" had been attained by Tuscan artists alone. These artists occupied a privileged position in history, appointed by God to revive and indeed surpass the arts of the ancients and to launch their contemporaries into a bright future entirely embedded in a Christian framework. Vasari's narrative exerted influence well into the twentieth century, being the most influential Renaissance text composed in the West.

In its literal translation, the verb *rinascere* means "to be born again." In his *Lives,* Vasari uses the term specifically to characterise the stages of art development up until his own day. For Vasari, the perfection of the classical arts in his own time took centuries to attain, suggesting that it was an evolving process: " . . . the rise of the arts to perfection [the classical past], their decline [the Middle Ages] and their restoration or, to say it better, renaissance."[3] Vasari unambiguously introduces the notion of *rinascita* into the discourse of the period. For Vasari, this rebirth of the arts was a gradual process that took approximately three centuries, beginning with the works of Cimabue (1240–1302) and "improving little by little from a humble beginning, and finally . . . arriv[ing] at the height of perfection"[4] via Michelangelo (1483–1520) in Vasari's own time. This slow trajectory towards perfection evolved through distinct stages including *imitazione* (imitation) and *adeguazione* (adaptation), both of which were necessary to surpass classical models and achieve *perfezione* (perfection) in Vasari's temporal present.

Vasari's narrative is imbued with a humanist impulse typical of his day—the close imitation of the classical past and the astute adaptation of those models in the present. Emulating ancient classical authors like Aristotle and Pliny, the *Lives* is a biographical celebration that links Vasari's temporality to both past and future, yet maintains a focused relevance to his contemporary day. Such imitation of the past was part and parcel of Vasari's characterisation of the Medici rulers to whom he had dedicated his work. In part three of the text he praised their contributions to the city of Florence in a true Aristotelian manner, signifying the permanence of their magnificence: " . . . men of rare and beautiful genius, from whom the world receives such beauty, honour, convenience and benefit, deserve to live forever in the minds and memories of mankind."[5] This panegyric, delivered through congratulatory rhetoric and self-aggrandisement to promote the excellence of Florence, has at its core a desire to claim uncontested superiority.

Leonardo Bruni's *Panegyric to the City of Florence* (c. 1401) is a fine precedent to Vasari's civic self-fashioning. In humanistic style, Bruni wrote in imitation of Aelius Aristides's *Panathenicus* (*Panegyric to Athens*, 117–81). Hans Baron argues that Bruni cast his work on the classical model because it spoke directly to contemporary Florentines in the fashioning of their cultural identity. Indeed, Bruni ascribes to Florentines all the virtues associated with Aristides's Athens (well-known even in Vasari's day as the cultural capital of the Greek world) in an attempt to identify Florence as the new Athens of its time.[6]

Yet by Vasari's time the path of emulation and imitation was already well-trodden. From as early as the eleventh century onwards, Vasari informs us, artists began adapting and imitating classical remnants. For example, in the 1016 Duomo of Santa Maria Assunta in Siena, the Pisan architect Buschetto relied on " . . . endless quantity of spoils brought by sea from various distant parts, as the columns, bases, capitals, cornices and other stones . . . of all sizes, great, medium, and small . . . Buschetto displayed great judgment and skill in adapting them to their places . . . the façade . . . consisting of a great number of columns, adorning it with other carved columns and antique statues."[7] The adaptation of classical remains went hand in hand with the imitation of past precedents. By the fourteenth century Tuscan architect, Andrea Taffi, was imitating classical doors, windows, columns, arches and cornices " . . . with the same Greek manner, but indeed much more beautiful in the church of San Giovanni in their city."[8] In the Church of Santa Maria della Spina in Pisa (1323), Giovanni Pisano's works of sculpture "brought ornaments in that oratory to that perfection that is seen today."[9] For Vasari, Pisano demonstrated "grace," "style," and "excellence" of invention, which he saw as prerequisites for distinction.[10]

To surpass the greats of the antique past required skill. For Vasari, this meant the artist had to demonstrate precision, intellect, and patience. According to Vasari, Michelangelo was one such man who "gave his attention only to the perfection of art" to attain a higher "degree of refinement," which could be only realised through devotion to "minute" and "delicate" details.[11]

Michelangelo's *David* (1501–4), clothed in God's glory, epitomises His perfection and the Christian message of man's triumph. This first revival of the ancient male nude who stands over four metres tall in monumental form depicts its subject patiently waiting for battle against the giant Goliath. As a Christian hero writ large, *David* overshadowed any extant antique sculpture of comparable character. This Renaissance representation of the figure of David is appropriated from the ancient Greek statue of a standing heroic male nude, the *Doryphorus* of Polykleitos (450–400 BCE), which is thought of as a distinctive style of antique sculpture for its solidly built, well-muscled standing warrior. The nudes of Greco-Roman art are conceived of as perfected ideals of heroic qualities, and *David* epitomised the rebirth of the "perfect" Renaissance Christian hero.

Both the *Doryphorus* and *David* statues are in the same *contrapposto* pose. The right leg carries the weight with the left leg positioned slightly behind it to suggest movement. Both have their weapon of choice on the left arm. Although the spear is no longer there, it too would have rested on Doryphorus's left shoulder. Like *Doryphorus*, the sculpture of *David* effectively conveys the feeling that David is in motion, an impression heightened by his *contrapposto* stance, the twist in his body heightening the figure's animation. In the biblical context of Michelangelo's *David*, David appears to take a moment between conscious choice and action—a man of logical thinking and reason—a Renaissance trait that characterised humanist thought of the time.[12] His facial expression looks drawn, and his neck tense and the bulging veins on his right hand reflect this. Like his classical hero counterparts, *David* stands ready to face his giant enemy Goliath, to demonstrate his heroic qualities, his "perfect" form clothed and protected by God; it is only through this perfection that he can truly defeat his adversary.

Michelangelo achieves this impression of perfection by foreshortening the body and sacrificing perfect proportions to accommodate the viewer's intended position below the sculpture, and enlarging the hands and eyes for effect. By adjusting the "perfect" Greek model for dramatic effect, Michelangelo's *David* becomes a Christian hero, for which he ultimately is more perfect than the statues of pagans celebrated since antiquity. With *David*, Michelangelo's work reflected the rebirth of the classical beauty of the human body as well as the Christian God's handiwork. In Vasari's words, *David* surpassed the ancient nude: " . . . [w]hen it was built up, and all was finished, he uncovered it, and it cannot be denied that this work has carried off the palm from all other statues, modern or ancient, Greek or Latin."[13] According to Vasari, Michelangelo's genius makes him unparalleled: " . . . no one . . . has ever equalled him in perfection of finish [and] that, wherever he turned his thought, brain, and mind, he displayed such divine power in his works, that, in giving them their perfection, no one was ever his peer in readiness, vivacity, excellence, beauty, and grace."[14] For Vasari, the perfection in art attained by Michelangelo solidifies his triumph over the past. This surpassing of the past further echoed Vasari's Florentine panegyric of Tuscan cultural achievements. Vasari's classical paralleling is explicit. Indeed, he modelled his art history on the Pliny the Elder's *Natural History* (77–79) but, of course, in Vasari's humanist adaptation of it, Florence and its artists were considered a superior version of the ancient world because of their Christian underpinning.

Vasari's narrative of rebirth took place within a Christian framework, thus offering a convincing argument for Florence's singular superiority in the arts. As part of his Christian worldview, Vasari understood Tuscan achievement in cosmological and eschatological terms, with Florence (and Florentine artists) at the centre of the earth and indeed central to God's greater salvific plan. It was through their deeds and skill that the mysteries of the divine plan were revealed to humanity. In a neo-Platonic way, they stood as imperfect signposts of the perfection of God. According to the Vasarian narrative, perfection in art in the sixteenth century was only possible through a Christian "spark" where the truth of the Creator's greater cosmos—its perfection, longevity, and existence beyond time—was being slowly revealed to man through engagement in creation. Such a privilege was exclusive to Christians. Thus, the great artists of Greece and Rome would always be subordinate, never attaining Vasarian perfection. As Vasari states in *The Lives*:

> Thus the first model from which the first image of man arose was a clod of earth, and not without reason, for the Divine Architect of time and of nature, being all perfection, wished to demonstrate, in the imperfection of His materials, what could be done to improve them, just as good sculptors and painters are in the habit of doing, when, by adding additional touches and removing blemishes, they bring their imperfect sketches to such a state of completion and of perfection as they desire.[15]

This Platonic concept of the Prime Mover as craftsman or *artifex maximus* recalls Christian evocations of God as Deus Faber, the divine craftsman and creator of the world.[16]

The Vasarian notion of historical consciousness interprets these ontological phenomena of the starting point of the world as, according to Ulrich Libbrecht, a "real but imperfect becoming."[17] From the humanist perspective, the man-artist is a shadow of the perfect Deus Faber. Thus, all man-made precedents imitating nature represent the imperfections of reality. These imperfections are in constant need of refinement or revision. The humanist project of "imitating" and "restoring" the great but imperfect ancient art forms was essential to attaining a state of near "perfection" which, in Vasari's view, was most diligently expressed in the art of his own time and city. For Vasari, "our art consists entirely of imitation, first of Nature, and then, as it cannot rise so high of itself, of those things which are produced from the masters with the greatest reputation."[18] Because of their Christian beliefs and God's alleged partiality for them, Florentine artists in particular saw their role as the privileged recipients of God's cosmic message, and it is they who constantly strived through the process of imitation to reach perfection. The Vasarian *rinascita* paradigm thus became essentially self-aggrandising in its aim, glorifying Florence as the pinnacle of God's creation as witnessed through the "perfection [of] the art . . . among the Tuscans."[19]

This construct of progress in the arts allowed Vasari to construct a powerful cultural discourse. In keeping with Rüsen's idea of historical understanding, in order to make sense of the rebirth of the classical arts in his own time Vasari needed to convincingly connect the past with the present.[20] His narrative relies on contemporary historical consciousness to make the claim to the cultural triumph of his time—that is, to identify Florence as the pinnacle of artistic evolution.

Vasari's definition of *rinascita,* therefore, is multidimensional. First, he argues that the rebirth of art was a slow evolutionary progression that was clearly discernible in the arts of painting, sculpture, and architecture. The perfection entailed engaging in a number of developmental stages: *imitazione* and *adeguazione* of the past in order to reach a state of perfection in the sixteenth century. Surpassing the past, the final stage of the *rinascita*, was tied inexorably to God's cosmic plan for the world which He, in Vasari's view, invested in the wholly Christianised Republic of Florence. From this viewpoint, it is, therefore, natural to broaden the term beyond the confines of the Italo-centric narrative to include the Ottoman art of the early modern period. Indeed, by interrogating the Ottoman voices from the sixteenth-century historical context—Mustafa Ali and Sinan—the need for this broader understanding becomes even more apparent.

Taqlid, tecdid, nezāket and *zuhūrat* in Ali's *Epic Deeds of Artists*

In his work *The Epic Deeds of Artists* (1587), Mustafa Ali provides an account of the lives of the artists of the East (that is, of the Muslim lands including the Ottoman world) and the part they played in the formation of the fine arts in the sixteenth century. Unlike Vasari, Ali does not explicitly use the term "rebirth" but conveys the idea through comparable expressions and sentiments. The Ottoman man of letters used terms such as *taqlid* (imitation) and *tecdid* (to make new, restore, or renovate) to describe early modern Ottoman cultural achievements, thereby reflecting the broader Renaissance attitude to "rebirth" discussed above.

Ali spent a year in Ottoman Baghdad from 1585 to 1586 as financial advisor to the Ottoman Governor. The setting inspired in Ali a new worldview which offered three significant insights into ideas about political and cultural rebirth. First, from 750 to 1258 Baghdad served as the centre of the Abbasid Caliphate to which the Ottomans considered themselves heirs. Second, the Mongols destroyed the city in the thirteenth century and converted to Islam. They then became the champions of Islamic civilization through their descendants—the Timurids—to whom Ali recognised as Ottoman ethnic connections. Third, the collapse of the Mongol Khans from the mid-fourteenth century and the rise of the nomadic Turkic tribes from the steppes, created a new political context which, according to Fleischer, "is marked by a process of amalgamation between the political ideals of the steppe and the sedentary values and institutions of the Irano–Islamic high cultural traditions to which the conquerors had fallen heir by confession."[21] Here, Ali's acknowledgement of the triumph of the Turkic tribes after their conversion to Islam serves as another factor in the way the past shapes the present. As an historian, Ali was able to see the achievements of the Ottomans through their cultural ownership of their Eastern legacies. In this way, the past served for Ali as a signpost to make sense of the sixteenth-century Ottoman world.

Ali's sojourn in Baghdad enabled him to formulate his understanding of Ottoman cultural and artistic achievements in his time. He observed how the Ottomans absorbed and adapted both visual aesthetics and learning from the medieval Islamic civilization of the Abbasids, the efflorescence of the Timurids, and the political ideologies of steppe heritage. Despite the devastation it had suffered at the hands of the Mongols three centuries earlier, sixteenth-century Baghdad continued to attract an array of visitors from merchants to philosophers from the East. This reflected its cosmopolitan makeup as a city where sharing ideas and developing new ones recalled the heyday of its medieval glory.

Furthermore, Ottoman Baghdad gave Ali an opportunity to be at the centre of Islamic medieval knowledge. In the West, Vasari turned to " . . . notes and memoranda, which I had prepared ever from my boyhood, for my own recreation, and because of a certain affection which I preserved toward the memory of our artists, every notice respecting whom had always been most interesting to me."[22] In the same way, Ali was in a unique position to scan the entire Islamic world—from Herat in the east, to Safavid Persia and Egypt, the Arab worlds, and his own artists of Rum (i.e. Ottoman) in the west. He had the opportunity to immerse himself in the artistic and intellectual Persianate milieu and Safavid culture. He observed the rich interconnections and legacies forged there.[23] He could converse with storytellers like Yazdi, and Qutb al-din who wrote a biographical treatise on calligraphers and painters, a copy of which Ali read during his service there.[24] Indeed, like Vasari, Ali recorded his impressions in a text specifically focused on the artists: *The Epic Deeds of Artists* (1587). Like Vasari, Ali had first-hand knowledge of the artists he wrote about. Communicating with local peers, enthusiasts, and other Muslim artists about the artistic world of the East, as well as consulting the written sources that he had collected over time, allowed him to compose his own art treatise. This work not only showed the achievements of Muslim artists, but also, more importantly, emphasised the successes of Ottoman artists in particular.

As a literary source, *The Epic Deeds of Artists* is composed in Ottoman Turkish with Persian and Arabic interspersed throughout. Ali demonstrates his full grasp and appreciation of this literary genre of biography of artists. Like Vasari, one of Ali's goals in composing this work was to create an uninterrupted linear progress (*silsile-i celileye ihtisasla*) in the history of Muslim art, which he understood to be an integral part of a civilization's progress.[25] Such an understanding would enable him to construct his framework for Ottoman cultural rebirth. In his text, Ali recounts the lives of about 270 Muslim artists, beginning with the third-century Chinese painter Mani (216–74 CE) before jumping into the Islamic period. He ends his treatise by praising the achievements of contemporary Ottoman court painter Nakkaş Osman (d. 1600?) who worked in the ateliers of Murad III.

As an art history treatise one of the drawbacks of *The Epic Deeds of Artists* is that, unlike Vasari, Ali does not establish any set criteria against which to make judgements about style. By providing the reader with information only on the origins, personalities, and virtues of the artists, his discussion about their art is limited. The constraints of Ali's approach make interpretation of his treatise problematic, as his message is not always clear. He does, however, make some broad references to the main area of the artists' specialisations, such as Master Uthman's (i.e. Nakkaş Osman's) fascination with detail in *şebih* (human portraiture), or Şah Kulu's mastery in the *saz* style of serrated leaves. But Ali does not develop an account of their specific themes or individual works. Ali's omission of architecture and ceramics from the treatise weakens his work and limits its claim to be a true representation of Ottoman fine arts.

Other limitations in Ali's treatise lie in his visual analysis and in the structure of the text. His analysis of the originality of past and contemporary Islamic art works is problematic. Without establishing any set criteria, he uses ambiguous terms like "original," "pleasing styles," "inimitable," and "impeccable" to describe artistic achievements. Additionally, he devotes four out of five chapters of the text to the art of calligraphy and merely one to painting. Clearly, such an arrangement signifies his bias towards the art of writing of which he was a master. As God's Word was recorded in the Qu'ran, the word was more highly prized than the image, with calligraphy becoming the most sacred of art forms.[26] However, despite its limitations, *The Epic Deeds of Artists* is the only existing text from which we can learn about sixteenth-century Ottoman attitudes towards the arts, and for this reason alone it is an essential source for this study.

Ali stresses the point that his main objective in *The Epic Deeds of Artists* is to promote the art and artists of Rum (that is, the Ottomans). Just as Vasari saw that it was his "genius" to recognise the need to record for posterity the Tuscan patrimony of art, Ali also wished to draw attention to new works by lesser-known artists. In so doing, Ali's focus turns almost exclusively to the East. He makes comparisons between Turkic and Central Asian Timurid–Persian artists' styles and those of the Ottomans to reinforce the Eastern influence on the nature of Ottoman cultural expression. Just as the Tuscan vision of rebirth looked to Greece and Rome, the Ottoman orientation towards the East defined its period of Renaissance. Ali provides an insight into the practices of a culturally dynamic and creative international atmosphere by including foreign artists from the East working in conjunction with the local *nakkashane* (atelier) masters at the palace ateliers.[27] For Ali, this international collaboration of artistic activity at the Topkapı Palace, as well as in Bursa and Edirne from 1413 onward, contributed to producing works that, stylistically, became synonymous with early modern Ottoman visual expressions. Ali's emphasis on the East suggests that modern Renaissance scholars need to do the same.

Like Vasari, Ali does not explicitly refer to "rebirth"; he implies it. Like Vasari's emphasis on *imitazione*, *adeguazione*, and *perfezione*, Ali too praises those artists who resort to *taqlid* (imitation), *tecdid* (restoration), and *nezāket* (refinement) of artworks to attain *zuhūrat* (perfection). His inclusion of Eastern artists in *The Epic Deeds of Artists* who flourished during the Timurid Renaissance from Samarkand to Herat, and Tabriz to Bursa is crucial. Ali suggests that the Timurid achievements found perfection in his own time through the patronage of the Ottoman sultans.[28] Ottomans are historically and ethnically connected to these cultural accomplishments of their brothers in the East and in his biased tone, like Vasari, Ali elevates the achievements of his own time as being superior to past and present exemplars. He writes of Ottomans mastering earlier Persian calligraphic styles by way of *taqlid*. He acknowledges the artists creating a distinctly Ottoman calligraphic mode by *nezāket* or refining the original script in form and style.[29] In the fine arts of illumination and book repair, Ali speaks of "Monla Sharaf of Yazd [d.1454] [who] was his time's outstanding master of excellent refinement."[30] In the area of gold sprinkling Qadi Ahmed was "a remarkable master."[31] For Ali it is through *taqlid*, *tecdid*, and *nezāket* that the arts of old are brought back to life, renewed, and perfected in an original form, or *sūret*.[32] Ali praises "men of refinement and learning" who, through the craft of calligraphy, "embellish the pages of time," restoring and repairing past works.[33] He highlights that, by learning from the past, "men of refinement" perfect or *zuhūrat* the art of the Word through their "elegant penmanship" or *qat'-i qalem ve nezāket -i raqam*.[34]

Ali's analysis of the rebirth of calligraphy begins with the thirteenth-century chief calligrapher of the Abbasid court, Yaqut al-Musta'simi (d. 1298). Ali praises Yaqut al-Musta'simi for reviving the esteemed art by perfecting it, writing "*Yaqut zuhūr eyledi*" (Yaqut perfected it.)[35] While the original *kufic* art of calligraphy had not been forgotten since the earliest recording of the Qur'an in the late seventh to early eighth centuries, Ali emphasises that it had become stifled and in need of rejuvenation. He makes this point clear when he underscores the linear development (*silsile-i celileye ihtisasla*) of style: "It was Ibn Muqla [886-940] who first Arabicised the *Kufic* style, then Ibn a-Bawwab [d.1022] refined it, and then Yaqut al-Musta'simi [d.1298] perfected it and he standardised it by listing all its regulations."[36] The closest Ali comes to paralleling Vasarian discourse is in implying the *ihya* or rebirth of calligraphy through the progression of historical figures. Also like Vasari, Ali recognises the importance of past art forms and addresses their significance to the progress of civilization. He acknowledges the ninth-century calligrapher Ibn Muqla for creating a unified sense of cultural and religious consciousness through "Arabicizing" the original *kufic* style. A century later the *kufic* style was further refined, *i'rab* (made clear) by Ibn Bawwab. Yaqut's style was emulated and modified by calligraphers for centuries to come. Ali mentions Yaqut's "pearls of rules of calligraphy" having been reborn by the master: *usūl* (fundamentals), *terkīb* (ligatures), *kurrās* (support), *nisbet* (i.e. interrelation or harmony of design in relation of the script to the white space on the paper), *su'ūd* (upstroke) and *teşmir* (extension), *nüzūl* (downstroke), and *irsāl* (flourish).[37] Like Vasari's veneration of Tuscan artists, Ali extols the artists of Rum (i.e. the Ottomans) for their *taqlid* and *tecdid*. He acknowledges that their improvements on early Persian models ultimately bring in new "*ihtira sūret*" (original forms or style).[38]

Ali skips a few centuries to bring his discussion up to the achievements of the Ottomans in his own time. One needs to be aware of the ways in which he prioritises Ottoman greatness over other Eastern accomplishments. He praises the progress made in calligraphy during the fifteenth and sixteenth centuries at the Topkapı Palace by the calligraphers Sheyh Hamdullah (1436–1520), Ahmed Karahısarı (1486–1556), and Hasan Karahısarı.

The Ottomans' modifications of the canonical script used in religious works of art, created their own distinct *Ottoman ta'liq* style. According to J. M. Rogers and R. M. Ward this style "had been developed in the Timurid court of Tabriz, Shiraz and Herat in the early fifteenth century" and became a favored style at the court of Süleyman the Magnificent.[39] Sheyh Hamdullah's copies of the Qur'an transformed the rounded scripts to suit Ottoman taste. Ottoman calligraphers learned from predecessors like that of Yaqut's 1282–83 Qur'anic verse written in the *muhaqqaq* style. The thirteenth-century calligraphic work was later decorated in the sixteenth-century by Ottoman artists and is now housed at the Topkapı Palace. Such works provided Sheyh Hamdullah with a prototype that marked the revival of the Turkish art of calligraphy (figs. 2.1 and 2.2). He became the first Ottoman calligrapher to consolidate the canonical Arabic "six scripts" that calligraphers are required to employ when copying the Qur'an. This principle, established by Yaqut al-Musta'simi, meant introducing the additional styles *nasta'liq, jele, nesih, kufi, tevki, divani, jele-talik, jele-divani*, and *jele-thuluth*, as seen in figure 2.2 of Sheyh Hamdullah's "Murakka Calligraphic Album" at the Museum of Turkish and Islamic Arts in Istanbul.[40] These new styles were combined with the *nezāket* (refinement) of the art of *tughra*, which by the sixteenth century had become the symbol of Ottoman religious and secular power and the authority of the sultan. Together these developments marked the epitome and surpassing of the past in a uniquely Ottoman calligraphic *sūret* (style) (see fig. 2.3). The art of *tughra* in particular continued to evolve with each subsequent sultan signifying both his religious and secular functions as ruler. At Sheyh Hamdullah's death, Ali wrote the following panegyric:

> Ever since the calligraphy of Hamdi son of Shaykh appeared
> The writings of Yaqut has surely vanished from the world.[41]

This verse reflects the Ottoman refinement of the art[42] and further reinforces Ali's acknowledgement of the progression and development of calligraphy, not only in books, as with the copies of the Qur'an, but also as decorative artwork in mosque architecture.

Ali mentions two figures who excelled in using calligraphy in the interior decorations of mosques: Ahmed Karahısarı's (1486–1556) Süleymaniye Mosque (1557–58) and his adopted son Hasan Karahısarı's Selimiye Mosque (1575). According to Sinan's autobiographies Hasan Karahısarı "became a second Yaqut in the world," implying a "high Renaissance period" in Ottoman–Turkish calligraphy under the patronage of the Ottoman sultan.[43] As a calligrapher, Ali's bias for this art form dominates all others. For Ali, the *thuluth* inscriptions of Ahmed Karahısarı on the domes of Sinan's mosques are "[t]he glory of [the art of] of writing."[44] In this description he implies that Ahmed Karahısarı has surpassed the thirteenth-century Abbasid calligrapher Yaqut al-Must'asimi and attained the ideal of perfection at the court of Süleyman the Magnificent (figs. 2.4 and 2.5). With the monumental inscriptions introduced in imperial mosque architecture by Ahmed and Hasan Karahısarı, the art of calligraphy reached a new height. Structurally, by placing their achievements at the end of his work, Ali is symbolically situating them as inheritors of all the artists who came before. In this way he, like Vasari, boasts of the attainment of the perfection of the arts under Ottoman patronage in his own time.

While calligraphy dominates four out of five chapters of his treatise, the art of painting is covered in the last section of Ali's work. Ali's brief descriptions of painters make it difficult for art historians to reach an accurate assessment of his intentions. Focusing on Persian, Timurid, and Ottoman painters from the fifteenth to the sixteenth centuries, Ali ends his chapter by praising the Ottoman artist Nakkaş Osman for his portraits of the sultans at the court of Murad III. He emphasises Osman's fascination with detail in şebih (human portraiture), and Şah Kulu's mastery of the *saz* style in serrated leaves. Ali does not develop an account of their specific themes or individual works. The omission of architecture and ceramics from the treatise weakens his work, limiting its claim to be a true representation of Ottoman fine arts.

In his assessment of Ottoman style and rebirth Ali does not ignore the contribution of Italian artists. He recognises the achievements of past palace artists from the time of Mehmed II, Süleyman the Magnificent, and Murad III, including the fifteenth-century painter Sinan Bey "who appeared at the paradise resembling palace (harem)" as the portrait painter of Sultan Mehmed II.[45] He acknowledges that Sinan

Bey was a pupil of a "Frankish master named Mastor [Maestro] Paoli who flourished in Venice and became a most exalted artist in his field."[46] Ali's praises also includes Sinan's pupil Shibilzada Ahmed, a "native of Bursa," although Gülru Necipoğlu acknowledges Costanzo da Ferrara as his master (fig. 2.6).[47] Figure 2.6 is the only three-quarter profile of Mehmed II and is attributed to either Sinan Bey or Ahmed Shibilzada of Bursa. The picture clearly demonstrates the influence of the Italian Renaissance. Such a larger-than-life representation of any figure had never been attempted before by any Ottoman painter. Although Ali provides only brief statements, his acknowledgement of Western contributions to the Ottoman artistic *oeuvre* endorses looking beyond the East to create something new and unique in the Ottoman artistic tradition.

Furthermore, the transference of the legacy of the West to the Ottoman artistic *oeuvre* reinforces the cultural exchange of ideas that characterised the Mediterranean basin. Ali writes, " . . . the talented Re'is Haydar . . . known as Naqqas Haydar or Nigari, he was a person whose artistry and talent in human portraiture, especially in depicting the portrait of the late Sultan Selim (II)."[48] Nigari was a mid-sixteenth-century portrait artist in the tradition of Sinan Bey who had been trained by the Venetian Gentile Bellini a century earlier. His paintings became available to Italian artists.[49] For example, in his portraits of Sultan Süleyman, and in one of two portraits of Selim II, Nigari's Western influence is seen in his use of shading techniques, his figures always set against a dark background (figs. 2.7 and 2.8). His figures are posed in a style that evokes both the Islamic miniature painting tradition and European-style portraiture. His depiction of Süleyman, especially in his old age, in unpretentious attire, strolling in a garden accompanied by his attendants, standing alone, lost in thought, his back bent and, his face lined and gaunt, is emotionally moving and representative of the monarch's ill health in the latter part of his life. The availability of Nigari's work to Italian and French artists makes this cultural exchange even more pertinent because it reflects the humanist interest in coming to terms with one's mortality irrespective of social status. For Ali, the training provided by Bellini and others represents a shared cultural heritage where the transference of classical Western modes to Ottoman portraiture creates authoritative guidelines recognisable in both East and West. Equally, this cultural exchange demonstrates that the Ottomans had indirect access to the classical ideals of the Roman Empire.

Perceiving Ottoman rebirth as an integral part of a shared cultural heritage, Ali's notion of Ottoman artistic achievements is unique. With his vision firmly set on the East, Ali provides twenty-first-century scholars with a broader historical framework and an alternative paradigm from which to revise Renaissance discourse—one that breaks from an orientalist perspective and integrates the East into the narrative. More significantly in the context of this discussion, however, Ali's reference to the transference of painting techniques from the West to the East contributes to the broader legacy of the classical arts while adapting the Islamic–Turkic *sūret* and giving it its own unique *ihya* (rebirth) with a distinctly Ottoman flavour, as seen in the sitting pose and the bent knees of the sultan in *Mehmed II Smelling a Rose* (fig. 2.9). Thus, the fluidity of the Renaissance narrative reinforces Brotton's and Burioni's understanding of the diverse characteristics of cultural rebirth. Finally, in keeping with Rüsen's argument, Ali demonstrates that "[h]istorical consciousness belongs to the elementary cultural achievements of his life, through which he organises his temporality for and through himself, the objective and the subjective, through which internal and external time are brought into equilibrium, that enable man to interact as a being directed at the future and influenced by experience, with his world and himself."[50] In short, Ali's experience at Baghdad provided him with the intellectual understanding to bring into "equilibrium" the linear progression of past to present, thereby offering a context for understanding the Ottoman artistic experience as a cultural rebirth. Ali notes this understanding only very briefly (when he reviews the development of style in the history of painting at the Ottoman court). While Ali's sentiments of Ottoman rebirth in the art of painting may be limited in comparison to his discussion of calligraphy, his complete omission of architecture in *The Epic Deeds of Artists* is problematic. This is where the imperial architect Sinan's *Treatise on Architecture* fills the gap.

Sinan's *'azim* (magnificence)

According to Soyini Madison, cultural appropriation "involves an intertextual process of creating or revisioning an object, idea, or subject from another object, idea, or subject to create another or different version."[51] Cultural appropriation does not intend to imitate or mimic, "or to necessarily make it known that appropriation has even taken place or to reveal that in creating this new form something has been borrowed."[52] In the context of Ottoman architecture, sixteenth-century imperial architect Sinan boastfully states in his autobiographies that he triumphed over the Roman/Byzantine Hagia Sophia by creating the largest dome the world had ever seen at the time, clearly demonstrating the competitive spirit of the age and the creation of a new, distinct artistic medium.[53]

Like his Renaissance contemporaries, Sinan composed his treatise " . . . in order that a memorial and record [of his artworks] endure through the pages of time."[54] The treatise lists all his works—mosques, hospices, madrasas, bridges, palaces, fountains, and countless other structures—as a testimony of the decades of learning and adapting of the old into something new in the creation of a distinct Ottoman style. Sinan states: "I acquired a sought-after bit of wisdom from the crenellation of great ancient remains and a provision of knowledge from every ruined monument."[55] Having learned from the ancient ruins around him by *tecdid* (restoring, renovating and renewing), he refined his *sūret*, üsl'ub (style) and gave birth to the old.[56] Sinan attained *'azim* (magnificence), *nezāket* (elegance, refinement), *cemile* (beauty), and *zuhūrat*, literally meaning perfection, through stylistic progression in his buildings leading to his distinct new *sūret*.[57] Like Vasari and Ali, Sinan saw a linear progress in his work. "Day by day many types of buildings [are created], and refinement increased," he writes, signifying the progression of art through the ages and its culmination in "complete realization."[58] Praising his 1548 work, the Şehzade Mosque, in the style of the Hagia Sophia in Istanbul, Sinan confirms, "such artistry had not been previously accomplished by any master," as previous works imitating the *Ayasōfya tarzı*[*nda*] (Hagia Sophia style) "did not possess elegance."[59] Sinan informs the reader that the Roman/Byzantine structure of the *Ayasōfya tarzı[nda]* became the inspiration for his works and that these works in return became a *nümūne* (model) for the Süleymaniye Mosque (1557–8): "this servant perfected the noble Friday mosque of Şehzade Sultan Mehmed . . . in the style of Hagia Sophia . . . which was the model for the model building complex of His Majesty Sultan Süleyman Khan."[60] To signify the rebirth of the classical past exemplified in the Süleymaniye Mosque, Sinan refers to "four marble columns" used in the construction of the building.[61] Like St. Peter's "stone columns" coming from Roman antiquity "the mold of Hadrian" according to Vasari, each of Sinan's four marble columns came from different parts of the empire.[62] He states:

> Each of its variegated marbles was removed to the horizon and came as a token from a different land. According to most historians they were left from the palace of His Majesty Solomon's Belkis [Queen of Sheba] . . . Also another brought from Alexandria with a base . . . another column [i.e. from the remnants of the old Byzantine Palace] was found standing ready in the imperial palace [Topkapı Palace], [and the] Maiden's Column [from the Church of the Holy Apostles in Istanbul].[63]

The symbolism surely was not lost on Süleyman. The columns alluded to the following: biblical figure Solomon, the namesake of Sultan Süleyman, ancient Egypt, the Eastern Roman emperors, and Christianity, demonstrating the Ottoman dominance of these civilizations under Süleyman. According to Selen B. Morkoç, the use of marble columns from Istanbul and other parts of the empire alludes to "[. . .] distinct royal connotations even if they appeared to be identical."[64] Combined with the Hagia Sophia style, this gave birth to the classical past within an Islamic monument that embraced all the civilizations that had come before it, which allowed Sinan to claim that "[t]he arts manifested in it."[65] Under his guidance the old model of the Hagia Sophia was transformed into a distinctly new Ottoman form in the Süleymaniye and embodied the "'*azim*" of Ottoman cultural greatness.

Sinan's self-aggrandising tone in relation to his achievement in the Süleymaniye reflects the spirit of the Renaissance. It also embodies his claim that such monumental representation was a reflection of a global ruler like Süleyman. As David Lowenthal claims, "[a] magnified or invented antiquity also aggrandizes localities and individuals."[66] The visual metaphor of the Süleymaniye Mosque established the universal status of Süleyman, while the city of Istanbul gained the crowning glory of Ottoman imperialism. Necipoğlu asserts that the Süleymaniye complex "[. . .] demonstrate[s] that culturally recognized symbolic and ideological [political and religious] associations . . . constitute[s] a significant aspect of the Süleymaniye's multilayered architectural discourse."[67] By resurrecting these four columns of antiquity within the context of the sixteenth century, Sinan emphasises the early modern nature of Ottoman historical consciousness. For Sinan, the structure makes sense of Ottoman cultural rebirth through the convergence of Roman/Byzantine with the Islamic–Timurid–Perso–Turkic historical memory and the creation of the new in the present. This understanding resonates with Rüsen's theory of the lasting legacy of historical consciousness: "Historical consciousness specifically does not reduce the meaningful and sense bearing time to just the past, rather . . . historical memory will always and fundamentally have a perspective of the present and the future." [68] Vasari had noted that Florentine artists in 1013 learned from classical works by imitating "the good ancient order in the doors, windows, columns, arches and cornices, which they perceived in part in the very ancient church of San Giovanni."[69] In the subsequent centuries, their art reached its status of *perfezione*, that is, its "great" and "truly extraordinary beauty" with Michelangelo. Similarly, Sinan, like his Italian counterpart, attained *'azim* (magnificence), *nezāket* (elegance, refinement), and *cemile* (beauty). Each of his art works—mosques, minarets, mihrabs, minbars, fountains—were like the Tuscan creations, "each of them matchlessly furnished" having "attained perfection" in the years after the Abbasids.[70]

This attainment of *'azim* strongly reflects the influence that the humanist interest in ancient Greece had on the Ottomans. For example, the idea of magnificence, imbued in the architecture of Sinan, aligns with Aristotelian notions of magnificence expressed in the *Nicomachean Ethics*. Here, "the greatness implied in the name of the magnificent man . . . will produce a more magnificent work of art."[71] Like Aristotle's notion of magnificence, Sinan's *'azim* also attains an aesthetic dimension.

Sinan further expressed his Sufi ideals in his esoteric work in the Rustem Pasha Mosque (1560–61), through the use of the floral naturalism of Iznik tiles. By 1575 the rebirth of the classical arts enabled the Ottomans to *a'zam* (surpass) the past and declare to the world a high Renaissance through the Selimiye Mosque: "Never would a dome like Hagia Sophia's be built, the world wagered. This exalted dome exceeded that [and this mosque] is worthy of the admiration of humankind."[72] For Sinan, this state of *zuhūrat* (perfection) and *a'zam* came to fruition in his own lifetime and under his own artistic guidance, recalling Vasari's claim that (European) art reached perfection in his own time.

Sinan's dialogue with the sixth-century Roman/Byzantine Hagia Sophia resonates throughout his *Treatise on Architecture.* The references to Ayasōfya suggest that Sinan was a man of intellect and curiosity, a man who not only studied this building closely throughout his career as imperial architect of the empire but who also restored it (*tecdid*), strengthening the massive dome on the orders of Selim II in 1572–73 to prevent it from collapsing.[73] In his autobiography Sinan states that, "a few years after its completion, the dome collapsed" but was later "rebuilt by the . . . architect–engineer with various apologies."[74] Sinan's point here is that although ancient works are worthy of being studied and emulated, they are not without defect.[75] The implications of the Ottoman-Turkish words used by Sultan Selim II and Sinan are significant. The words *ihya*, *tecdid* and *zuhūrat* literally translate as "rebirth," "bringing back to life anew," "restoring," "resurrecting," and finally bringing something original into existence through perfection.[76] With the transformation of the Hagia Sophia into a distinctly Ottoman–Islamic monument, its Christian origins dissipated. It was reborn in a new form. This important project, however, is omitted from Sinan's autobiographies. Although he does not specifically use the word *ihya* in his work, one does, however, learn of the court's intentions from imperial edicts addressed to Sinan personally. The sixteenth-century historian Selaniki notes that the Sultan was informed of the Hagia Sophia's structural weakness and of its imminent collapse.[77] Sultan Selim II therefore issued an order: "It is my request to give rebirth to the noble Friday mosque as my own imperial monument."[78] The sultan's *firman* or edict orders a massive renovation project that involves strengthening the buttresses and building a minaret on one of them. Selaniki informs us that the Hagia Sophia has not witnessed such *ihya* (rebirth) in more than a millennium. Most significantly, however, is that the formal imperial ownership of the newly Ottomanised Hagia Sophia solidifies the Ottomans' legitimacy as the "true" heirs to the Eastern Roman legacy. Changes to the structure began with the single minaret additions of Mehmed II, Selim I, and Süleyman. Selim II's fourth minaret gave Justinian's building its present look. Just as "Michelangelo had given life to the building [i.e. St Peter's]" as noted by Vasari, Sinan too gives life to the Hagia Sophia "which is there at the present day."[79] Combined with its internal Islamic additions of a *mihrab*, *minbar*, and sultan's loge, the transformation of the Christian Hagia Sophia into an Islamic building was complete.

This project as well as Sinan's work on previous buildings in the Hagia Sophia style constituted a learning process from ancient structures. At the hands of Ottoman artisans, the Hagia Sophia underwent many renovations: "building a minaret above the reinforcement . . . building [new] buttresses and water channels in the thirty-five-cubit-wide open space, repairing . . . all necessary places at the interior and exterior . . . reusing . . . stones and bricks for the renovation of essential places."[80] This reborn building is celebrated in the c. 1581 miniature painting from Seyyid Lokman's Şahname-i Salim Khan with new Ottoman additions including the mausoleum of Selim II on the sacred grounds.[81] Folio 190b of the 1582 miniature painting in the *Surname-i Humayun* manuscript depicts a model of the Süleymaniye mosque paraded in front of Sultan Murad III. The model of the Süleymaniye carried by Sinan himself reflects an Ottoman Renaissance attitude of cultural greatness in the Süleymanic Age in the latter decades of the sixteenth century. This suggests that Ottoman artists eventually ceased using Hagia Sophia—which had long dominated the discourse until the building of the Süleymaniye—for their architectural inspiration. Instead, they created their own original and creative masterpieces. The float of the Süleymaniye dominates the entire folio 190b and signifies a shift in Ottoman vision for the future architectural aesthetic.[82] By this stage, Sinan's distinctive architectural style had entered into discourses of Ottoman art, signalling the confidence in the Ottomans' own cultural achievements; at this point, the past was left behind because it had done its job to define and shape its present.

In *The Formation of Islamic Art*, Oleg Grabar acknowledges that Islamic cultural appropriation of past exemplars demonstrates "the conscious attempt to relate meaningfully to the conquered word, by Islamicizing forms and ideas of old."[83] According to Grabar, cultural appropriation was important to demonstrating Islam's dominance as a burgeoning culture and religion, through which it took aspects of older cultures and made them *Islamic*.[84] By appropriating the historical and religious significance of the site of the seventh-century Dome of the Rock in Jerusalem, and borrowing motifs from Sassanians and Byzantines in Islamic decorative aesthetics, Grabar argues that Muslim architects created a monument that not only demonstrated Islam's political dominance in the region but also its religious and cultural.[85]

Ottoman restoration of ancient Islamic sites further reinforced this notion of rebirth. Beginning with Süleyman and continuing into the reigns of his son Selim II and his grandson Murad III, the three Holy Sites of Islam, Mecca, Medina, and Jerusalem underwent massive restorations. Overseeing the restoration of the ancient Islamic site of the Ka'ba in Mecca, Sinan reflects the Ottomans' ongoing dialogue in mediating between two classical civilizations. In 1551 he "repaired the defects of . . . the Ka'ba" (*tecdid etmiş*).[86] Twenty years later he restored the Holy Shrine, the Ka'ba, in Mecca 1571–84 "according to its old form" suggested by the decree of Sultan Selim II.[87] This signifies the renewal of the legacy of this ancient Holy House with some Ottoman refinements or *nezāket*. Like the Hagia Sophia, the Ka'ba had not been revitalised since the Umayyad renovations of 693 by Caliph Abdul Malik bin Marwan, directly pitting the Ottomans with the past. Beginning with the construction of the dilapidated roofs of the Haram [i.e. Holy Precinct], the Ottoman artisans added minarets, creating a domical arcade with 360 domes around the Ka'ba, supported by new stone pillars.[88] According to Necipoğlu, "[s]ince the old foundations were incapable of bearing the load of stone domes, new foundations were laid . . . [where] these domical arcades visually Ottomanised the Haram."[89] By Ottomanising the holiest site of Islam, the Ottoman sultans were also legitimising their caliph status in the Muslim world.

Like Vasari, the sole purpose of both Ali's and Sinan's works is to promote the arts of the Ottoman world. Ali's self-aggrandising endorsement reflects the achievements and superiority of Ottoman artists to their Eastern counterparts. Similarly, with their predominantly boastful tone, Sinan's autobiographies promote a lasting legacy in which his works will be the subject of much discussion and admiration. His tendency to boast about his architectural achievements and decorative aesthetics led him to claim that he had created "magnificent" (*'azim*) works of art by studying and learning from past exemplars. Like Vasari's elevation of Tuscan artists above others, Sinan's boasts work to promote his achievements over that of his contemporaries as well as his predecessors.

In conclusion, through the works of Ali and Sinan the sixteenth-century understanding of Ottoman notion of rebirth emerges. This understanding expresses a sense of Ottoman historical consciousness and identity in an expanding empire which sees cultural rebirth as part of its self-fashioning and worldview. For Vasari's Ottoman contemporaries, rebirth coincided with a political impetus mediating between East and West. In his political history *The Essence of History*, Ali connects the Ottomans' Eastern heritage to Turco–Mongol, Timurid, Persian, and Islamic elements, which he sees as signalling the Ottomans' dynastic and religious legitimacy over the Muslim world. Ali's analysis demonstrates that, for the Ottomans, looking to the past meant making sense of their cultural revival within the context of global sovereignty. This legitimacy is reinforced in Ali's art treatise *The Epic Deeds of Artists*. Ali's notion of artistic rebirth converges with Vasarian views of *rinascita*, where stylistic evolution from past exemplars helps shape progress made in the present. This reinforces the Vasarian idea of the Tuscan *rinascita* as "seeing past events as present."[90] Calligraphic works and paintings from Abbasid and Persian exemplars, together with European interactions, led to a sharing of values and ideas. This interaction prompted the Ottoman artists to create new styles (*ihtirā sūret*) through *nezāket* (refinement) and, finally, *zuhūrat* (perfection of the old).

Sinan, in his architectural treatise, *Risāletü'l-Mi'māriyye*, similarly informs the reader that Ottoman rebirth has links to the past. His confession about learning from ancient ruins to create works of *azim* (magnificence) with *nezāket* (elegance) and *cemile* (beauty) that finally *a'zam* (surpass) the past clearly resonates with Vasari's notions of rebirth. Sinan's dialogue with the Roman/Byzantine Hagia Sophia aligns Ottoman art with that of the West by using it as a model (*nūmūne*) for his works. Sinan acknowledges that through cultural appropriation his works are the result of learning, experimenting, and restoring the old (*tecdid*), finally creating distinctly Ottoman masterpieces like the Süleymaniye and Selimiye that are "worthy of the admiration of the humankind."[91] Furthermore, his restoration of ancient buildings like the Ka'ba in Mecca mediates Ottoman rebirth with the classical Islamic past, signifying a more meaningful and specifically Ottoman definition of Renaissance. By placing these Ottoman voices within the context of a global Renaissance narrative, this work fills a yawning gap in the scholarship of early modern Ottoman studies. Before exploring these artistic links to the Timurid–Persian–Islamic-Turkic and Roman/Byzantine past and their influences on Ottoman art beginning in Bursa and Edirne in the fifteenth century, it is pertinent to focus on the impact of Sufi Humanism on Islamic art in the following chapter.

CHAPTER THREE

SUFI METHODOLOGIES

Islamic art provides the observer with a larger view of the Qur'anic paradise through the prism of Sufi mysticism. As Seyyed Hossein Nasr states, "[. . .] Islamic art [i]s the manifestation in the world of forms of the spiritual realities (*al-haqa'iq*) of the Islamic revelation itself as coloured by its earthly embodiments."[1]

To gain a closer relationship with God, in Sufi philosophy, a number of key themes including: theophanies (visible manifestations of God to humankind), a world which access is given by means of esoteric knowledge through symbols (*ta'wil*), *tawhid* (Unity of God), *ittihad* (Union with God), and the creative imagination are fundamental in understanding the nature of Islamic art aesthetics.[2] Islamic art embodies these key Sufi elements. According to David P. Brewster, "[. . .] it is . . . true to say that Sufism, together with Islamic Art and Architecture, represents one of the more 'immediate' and accessible aspects of Islam [. . .] to Western students [and scholars]."[3]

Tawhid and *Ittihad*

Understanding Islamic art requires understanding the idea of *tawhid*, the belief and acknowledgment in the Unity and Oneness of the Indivisible God is paramount. In the Qur'an, God says, "Do not set up besides God any other deity" (17:22). *Ittihad,* on the other hand, means to be one with God. According to Nasr,

> Islamic art is the result of the manifestation of Unity upon the plane of multiplicity. It reflects in a blinding manner the Unity of the Divine Principle, the dependence of all multiplicity upon the One, the ephemerality of the world and the positive qualities of cosmic existence or creation about which God asserts in the Quran, 'Our Lord! Thou creates not this in vain' (111:191). [4]

For the Sufi, the comprehension of the *tawhid* and its dependence upon multiplicity requires silence and contemplation. In order to achieve this,

Nasr states, "[t]his art makes manifest, in the physical order directly perceivable by the senses, the archetypal realities and acts, therefore, as a ladder for the journey of the soul from the visible and the audible to the Invisible which is also Silence transcending all sound."[5] Thus, in a sacred space like the mosque, the experience of silence and contemplation of the observer activates the senses to perceive the "archetypal realities" and serves as a stepping-stone for the soul to comprehend the Unity of God.

For the observer the spiritual experience the soul undergoes in a sacred space surrounded by decorative aesthetics becomes an inner link to his spirituality. As Nasr explains, "[. . .] this art plays in the induction of *hal* or spiritual state, which is itself a grace from Heaven, and in the attitude of those closest to the heart of Islamic spirituality to this art in its manifold manifestations."[6] Islamic art as all art plays on one's senses and emotions, for it places emphasis on the "origin of the inward in the outward and reduces sacred art with its interiorizing power to simply external."[7] It is noteworthy to mention the connection of St. Thomas's dictum "*ars sine sciential nihil*" (the art without science is nothing) to Islamic art is based upon the "science of nature."[8] This science is not concerned with the outward appearance of things, but with their inner reality. The visual vocabulary of Iznik naturalism, for example, serves to unlock and stir the inner realities of the self and Hidden One (i.e. God), for art itself is the manifestation of the Beauty of God and His Creation.

In a similar way, to understand Islamic fine art one must also tap into his own spirituality in order to seek *Ittihad*—Union with God. As Şefik Can notes, "[t]he level of *Ittihad* is superior to the level of *tawhid* because in the former there is only the notion of God as one, while in the latter there is the notion of being one with God."[9] Can, a Sufi scholar, further explores this concept by indicating that to become one with God, one must enter the path of God to cleanse his lower self (*nafs* of the ego) through "self-mortification," "good deeds," and "worship."[10] As Ayla Esen Algar states, "[t]his Sufism is meditative and ethical. The vision of God is insight into reality; it yields understanding of the self and the place of the self in the world and brings into harmony inner character and outer behaviour."[11] It is through these actions that the individual can demonstrate his obeisance to the One. In doing so the individual submits his free will to God alone—the individual then according to Can, has attained God.[12] On this matter Rumi elaborates further: "If you kill your desires and do away with your human attributes, the sea of secrets carries you over its head."[13] For the Sufi, the individual's attainment makes him *insan al-kamil*—the ideal human being. According to Rumi,

> I do not know how I have become effaced; is it due to that wine of divine love / Or where I am due to that Beauty of Nowhere? I arrived at such a place that I do not fit into that world / Now I do not suit anyone other than Unique Beloved who is not associated with a place / You are telling me: "Why aren't you coming to yourself [to your senses]?" You show to me myself and who I am, and I shall come to myself. You are the light, you called out to Moses, "I am God, I am God!"[14]

However, becoming one with God, the individual cannot stay in that state indefinitely because he cannot carry the heavy burden. According to Rumi, "I cannot sit with You [i.e. God] as much as I want as long as Your love does not empty myself from myself and as long as I do not give up on myself, my anachronism."[15] As for *tawhid*, according to Rumi, it is attainable in the silence: "In disciplined silence it opens. With wandering talk it closes."[16] Sixteenth century Ottoman imperial architect Sinan demonstrates this in his mosques, none more so than in the Rustem Pasha Mosque. It is in the silent ambiance of the mosque interior surrounded by the art of Iznik tiles that one experiences this spiritual awakening that is further elaborated on in Chapter Six. However, this spiritual awakening cannot happen without Sufi esotericism and the allegorical interpretation of the Qur'an (*ta'wil*).

Ta'wil and esoteric knowledge

The Sufi interpretation of the Qur'an is also known as the esoteric interpretation of the Revelation. For the Sufi, the esoteric interpretation of the Qur'an establishes a symbolic connection to God and the imagined world—paradise. Through this mystical elucidation, God's Signs (*ayah*) in Nature serve as symbols to attain spiritual knowledge. It is here that the naturalism of Islamic aesthetics becomes a tool for the observer to gain knowledge of the self (*nafs*) and reach a higher plane of spirituality in his quest for *tawhid* and *ittihad*. For this reason, Nasr states, "[t]o grasp fully the significance of Islamic art is to become aware that it is an aspect of the Islamic revelation, a casting of the Divine Realities (*haqa'iq*) upon the plane of material manifestation in order to carry man upon the wings of its liberating beauty to his original abode of Divine Proximity."[17] In order to reach the "original abode" esoteric interpretation of the scripture requires theophanic understanding of the symbolisms attached to the message it is intended to convey. The symbolisms associated with the material manifestations of God's Beauty can be seen in the Islamic garden imitating the Garden of Eden on earth. This is expressed in the Qur'an where the righteous will have gardens beneath which rivers flow (18:31). In a similar way the symbolisms linked with the multitude of flowers in Islamic naturalism allows the individual to:

> [. . .] see through the phenomena of the natural world in all its intimate glory to the underlying truth: Nature, as a sign of God, both veils and reveals. So the beauty of the natural world is one of God's greatest symbols and through meditation on its glories we can, as with all true sacred art retrace a back to Truth.[18]

For the observer, to make sense of the deeper meaning of his life requires self-reflection, prayer, and meditation. The sacred space is one such place providing this theophanic experience through the symbolisms associated with objects—in this case—floral representations of paradise.

Sixteenth-century Ottoman Renaissance thought and art are influenced by Sufi humanism and the classical ideals of Plato. Rumi's influence on Ottoman literati is immense. Having lived and preached in Seljuk Konya in the thirteenth century, Rumi's work the *Mesnevi* (*Mathnawi* in English) is a spiritual text of 25,000 verses teaching Sufis how to attain their goal of uniting with God and being truly in love with the Divine. This mystical and esoteric understanding of Islam influenced his contemporaries including the Sufi poet, Yunus Emre (1238–1320). Throughout the Seljuk and Ottoman periods, Rumi's teachings also influenced calligraphers, miniature painters, mosque lantern makers, weavers of prayer rugs, tile makers, musicians and other artisans at the dervish lodges, usually built either adjacent or nearby to public and imperial mosques such as the Süleymaniye Mosque or the Atik Valide Mosque (Mosque of Nurbanu Sultan—1583, the wife of Selim II).[19] Sufi calligraphers and painters created expressive artworks using Arabic script for drawings as well as floral designs and personal insignias (*tughras*). Of Sufi calligraphy, Jurgen Frembgen writes,

> Characterized by the harmony of their lines and the magic of their beauty, many of these works exhibit a special aura: decorating the walls of aesthetically designed rooms in dervish lodges *(khanqah, tekke)*, they create not only an important visual dimension in veneration and contemplation of God or charismatic Sufi saints, but also in concrete practices of ritual recollection of God.[20]

Such works of art that decorated the lodges underpinned the Sufi *tasavvuf* philosophy of exemplary behaviour and closeness to God. Combined with their proximity to public and imperial mosques, the *tasavvuf* philosophy became ingrained first in Seljuk, and then in the Ottoman spiritual and literary consciousness.

Like Sufi art, such literature contributed to further understandings and remembrances of God. Sufi literary greats including Letafi (d. 1582), Nef'i (d. 1635), and Ismail Rusuhi (d. 1630) are among the followers of Rumi during Süleyman's rule.[21] Reverence for Rumi and his Sufi order by the Ottoman sultans in the sixteenth century can be seen through the sultans' restoration of the Sufi master's his tomb. As Mehmet Önder states,

> During the reign of Süleyman the Magnificent, Sinan, the leading architect of the day built a semahane [assembly hall for whirling ceremonies] and a mescid [chapel] in the complex on imperial orders. The domed dervish cells were surrounding the mausoleum were built during the reign of Murad III [d.1595], on his orders, and the monumental fountain – şadırvan – in the courtyard was built during the period of Selim the Grim [d.1520].[22]

Such restoration of works signified not only reverence for Rumi but also conveyed the continuity of the royal connection to the mystic great through Mehmed I (d. 1421), whose father Bajezid I (d. 1403) married Devlet Hatun (d. 1414), whose mother Mutahhara Hatun was the granddaughter of Rumi.[23]

It remains unknown whether Rumi had read the works of Plato, but with the existence of medieval Arabic translations of classical works circulating in the Islamic world there is a chance that he may have done so. Rumi, like Plato, sought to find and understand, and make others understand, the Being who created the universe. This role of God is echoed in the Qur'an's descriptions of His attributes: *Al-Khalik* (the Creator,

6:102, 13:16), *Al-Musawwir* (the Fashioner of forms, 59:24) that manifest in nature, and His ever-forgiving attribute, the *Al-Ghaffar*.[24] Both masters declared that everything living must have origins. Both agreed that our spirits dwelt in some place before our existence on earth. Plato calls this the "World of Ideas" and the "World of Examples," while Rumi calls it the "World of Spirit." According to Rumi, "our real motherland is that universe which is the 'World of Absolute Beauty.' We are strangers on earth. All human beings are strangers in this world . . . We have been exiled from that world into this one."[25] From this philosophical viewpoint, because humans have been exiled to earth, the yearning for beauty and perfection is an innate human trait. We are continually in search of these qualities.

Rumi reminds one that everything is not perfect and is subject to permanent change. He reminds one that the beauties that perish or decay in this world should not trouble him, offering,

> The original of every substance, or every picture you see in this world is in the World of the Spirit. Do not worry that this picture is gone. Do not be troubled that every pretty face you have seen, every subtle saying you have heard has vanished since the truth does not consist of what you see and what you know in this world.[26]

From this perspective, the individual has been given responsibilities to seek the world to come, the Hereafter, to find salvation and mercy. For this reason, the anagogical and eschatological readings of the Mosque of Rustem Pasha require critical examination in Chapter Six.

For the Sufi, the self's continuous striving for contentment begins with ongoing reflection on one's shortcomings. Influenced by Sufi mysticism, Islamic art and more specifically the Iznik aesthetic echo Rumi's famous words: "Come, come, whoever you are. Wanderer, worshiper, lover of leaving. It doesn't matter. Ours is not a caravan of despair. Come, even if you have broken your vows a thousand times. Come, yet again, come, come."[27] In other words, hope and salvation come with the sincerity and true intentions of the believer who submits to the One, even after a thousand sins. This yearning to seek the One, according to the Andalusian Sufi and mystic scholar Ibn Arabi (1165-1240), is where "[. . .] the Active Imagination [of the individual] carries out the divine intention, the intention of the 'Hidden Treasure' [i.e. God and His Beauty] yearning to be known [. . .]" because, like the observer seeking, He, too, desires to be discovered.[28] The individual ponders on this from the moment of entering a sacred space like a mosque.

Creative Imagination as theophany

The "Imaginal World" (*mithal*) and "World of Souls and Lights" (*malakut*) are totally unconnected to matter and the mundane physical reality in the peripatetic sense. For Islamic art, from monumental architecture and miniature paintings to tiles, characteristic of Ottoman, Persian, and other Islamic art of the East, according to Nasr is an "[. . .] echo of the joy of paradise serving as reminders of a reality which transcends the mundane surroundings of human life."[29] It is only through esoteric knowledge and theophanic experience that man is able to penetrate into the meaning of other realms.[30] Concerning this Imaginal World, Suhrawardi's (d. 1191) commentator Qutbuddin Shirazi (d. 1311) says,

> It is there that the various kinds of autonomous archetypal Images are infinitely realised, forming a hierarchy of degrees varying according to their relative subtlety or density . . . The pilgrim rising from one degree to another discovers on each higher level a subtler state, a more entrancing beauty, a more intense spirituality, a more overflowing delight. The highest of these degrees borders on the intelligible pure entities of Light and very closely resembles it.[31]

This, according to Ibn Arabi, requires the use of the Creative Imagination.[32] For the observer in the sacred space searching for meaning and self-transformation, wandering, contemplation, and self-reflection act as prayer. For Ibn Arabi, prayer "[. . .] is the expression of a mode of being, a means of existing and of *causing* to *exist*, that is, a means of causing God who reveals Himself to appear, of 'seeing' Him, not to be sure in His essence, but in the form which precisely He reveals by revealing Himself by and to that form . . ."[33] In this way, prayer becomes the highest act of the Creative Imagination.[34] Through this the individual begins to tap into the visible manifestations of God to humankind. According to Ibn Arabi, "His [i.e. God's] unknowness" aspires "to be known."[35] Prayer/reflection/meditation, then, "accomplish this theophany because in it and through it the 'Form of God' (*surat al-Haqq*) becomes visible to the heart."[36] The eyes then begin to see His Signs as symbols and reminders of His Beauty.

Theophanic perception is attained in the imagination—"*alam al-mithal*." Ibn Arabi states that "Imagination is the organ of theophanic perception . . . capable of transmuting sensory data into symbols and external events into symbolic histories."[37] For Rumi, these symbols reveal the spiritual worlds above, where they become transparent and reveal meaning of the beyond, the higher order of reality, and finally the Ultimate Reality.[38] Concurring, Ibn Arabi affirms that the imagination "guides . . . [and] molds sense perception; that is why it transmutes data into symbols."[39] This way the Hidden One becomes transparent and "known" to the observer.

In Islamic fine arts, the reliance on naturalism to evoke God's creation serves to highlight the experience of theophany. To appreciate the Beauty of Creation in the Natural world, as presented in Islamic fine arts, the artist attempts to recreate it in various mediums using vibrant colours and variety of floral ensembles. To imitate or recreate the creation according to Ibn Arabi "[...] is essentially the revelation of the Divine Being" and "[...] the creation signifies nothing less than the Manifestation (zuhur) of the hidden (batin) Divine Being [...]."[40] Such views inspired modern writers, philosophers and scholars.

The nineteenth century German writer and statesman Goethe (d. 1832), whose interest in Islam contributed to the publication of work on Sufism. Goethe wrote on literary and aesthetic criticism; and treatises on anatomy, botany, and colour. His immense philosophical interest in Islam and Sufism, and as a scholar, saw the publication of his *Der west-östliche Divan* (The West-Eastern Divan) in 1819. The work represented his homage to the peerless Persian Sufi poet Hafez (d.1390). Furthermore, in his treatise on the vibrancy of colours used by the artist to stir the soul, Corbin cites Goethe:

> The perception of color is an action and reaction of the soul itself which is communicated to the whole being; an energy is then emitted through the eyes, a spiritual energy that cannot be weighed or measured quantitatively . . . the eye at this point produces another color, its own color. The eye searches at the side of a given colored space for a free space where it can produce the color called for by itself[41]

For colour, according to Goethe, "[. . .] is not a passive impression, but the language of the soul."[42] In the colourful imaginary garden of mosque aesthetics like that of the Rustem Pasha Mosque, the observer seeks salvation because the garden of paradise is for "those who have believed and have done good works" (2:25; 4:57), for "those who are God fearing" (3:15; 44:51; 52:17; 78:31), for "the true servants of God" (37:43; 38:49), and for "those who believe in Our Signs and are submissive" (43:69). However, hope and salvation are not lost on the observer who is questioning his belief, for God says in the Qur'an, "Say: O my servants who transgressed against their souls! Despair not of the Mercy of God, for God forgives all sins, for He is Oft-Forgiving and Most Merciful" (39:53). This hope urges the individual to strive to become the ideal human being—*insan al-kamil* as intended by God.

Islamic art leaves to the imagination and the conscience of the observer to contemplate the world to come. The mosque as a religious space and place of worship enriched with visual aesthetics remind the viewer of God's immeasurable Mercy and of the hope for an eternal blissful Hereafter as reflected in the Qur'an. From a Sufi humanist perspective, Sinan's omission of the imagery of Hell[43] allows the viewer in the midst of the temporal paradise he created in his mosque aesthetics to enter a state of self-reflection. Rumi writes, "I am the foundation of both reason and ecstasy. Now we realize that the beauty which we saw in forms and fantasies was the reflection of our beauty."[44] In other words, the beauty that the soul experiences in the "World of Spirits" reflects the Beauty of God in human form.

Sufi philosophy is expressed in Sinan's writings that invite the observer on a journey of theophanic experience to witness his art as an expression of the visible manifestations of God to humanity and ponder his salvation. Sinan alludes to the metaphysical nature of his art by comparing it to the Prophet's ascension (*mi'raj*) to different levels of heaven and finally meeting God at the "Utmost boundary" (53:14).[45] Muhammad's witnessing of the Imaginal World of Angels and other spirits by complements the Qur'anic message of hope for an afterlife. This message further inspired Muslim artists, including Sinan, to evoke through art the transcendental experience of the world to come. This transcendental experience provides hope and salvation for the individual seeking *ittihad* through the intercession of the Prophet. In his autobiographies Sinan states, "And because that Beloved of God was the cause of all Creation, on the Night of the Prophet's miraculous ascent to the Throne of God, [that] seal of the seal ring, signet of intercession, and joyful crown was exalted and celebrated with the jewelled ornament [. . .]"[46] References to ascension, jewels, ornaments of paradise, and the Throne of God stimulated the artist's imagination to create works of art that evoke this Imaginal World. Sinan then continues to allude to his works in Istanbul as being "lofty like the heavens," similar to the paradisiacal wonders experienced by Muhammad.[47] Within this context, the works of the artist enhance the theophanic experience for the observer.

For Sinan, Ottoman Renaissance art came to represent the Ottoman paradise on earth as a signpost of the next life. He compares his art to "nightingales" inviting all to the "rose garden," the "celestial throne," and the "Milky Way."[48] Entering a mosque built by Sinan is like entering a "rose garden" whose doors "are like those of Paradise" where the seeker can wash his sins away from the "pool of Kevser, that matchless fountain to be."[49] Like the whirling dervish and the pilgrim circumambulating the Ka'ba during the *hajj* pilgrimage and seeking union with God, Sinan, too, affirms that the observer will find salvation, mercy, and be absolved of his sins by "Circling the rose garden of the sanctuary . . . [and] [c]om[ing] there [his mosques] to win God's blessing" and be "free from hellfire secure."[50] For Sinan, Ottoman Renaissance art exemplifies the renewal of this classical mindset. In the following chapters, Ottoman artists and architects of the fifteenth and sixteenth centuries provide the visitor glimpses of the hereafter and the Qur'anic paradise through a theophanic and esoteric experience.

CHAPTER FOUR

LINKS TO THE PAST: TIMURID–PERSIAN–ISLAMIC-TURKIC AND ROMAN /BYZANTINE INFLUENCES ON OTTOMAN ARTS

In the previous chapter, Renaissance was defined as a cultural rebirth which begins by appropriating the past in order to create or revise a contemporary identity. A key factor in this identity making is an acute sense of historical consciousness; an awareness of one's relationship to the past. The Ottomans drew inspiration from two meaningful pasts to which they were linked in real or imagined ways. They looked first and foremost to the East, to the thriving civilizations in which they found their historical and cultural roots: the Timurid–Persianate–Islamic–Turkic. After 1453, the Ottoman sultans became heirs to the Roman/Byzantine world, prompting them to exploit both Eastern and Western cultural models in their paradigm of rebirth.

The Ottomans' engagement with the past begins in Bursa in the fifteenth century. The unique geopolitical positioning of the Ottomans in Istanbul, the former Roman/Byzantine city of Constantinople, contributed to the creation of a unique form of Ottoman artistic expression. The Greek and Roman aesthetics made their impact on the early fourteenth century Ottoman visual expressions in Bursa. According to Suna Çağaptay, "[...] the Ottomans transformed the existing urban order by adding new structures and reviving elements of the ancient Greek, Roman and Byzantine layers [i.e. ancient remains]."[1] The transformation of the Greek Orthodox Church, the St. Sophia in Nicea in Bursa environs in 1331 and the Orhan Ghazi mosque in Biga in the mid-fourteenth century reflect the Ottomans' early engagement with the Roman/Byzantine past.[2] For Çağaptay, the fifteenth-century Bursa builders "Ottomanised the past as they built their capital city into a metropolis."[3] This was significant because, as Robert Ousterhout states: "[t]he Ottoman appropriation of the past may be understood as a part of their symbolic control of the land

and as an attempt to position themselves within the larger context position of world history as the rightful heirs of the Roman/Byzantine Empire."[4] For post-1453 Ottoman rulers, however, this geopolitical centre was precarious because the sultans were not European, nor did they have a direct lineage to the Prophet Muhammad. This meant that they could not legitimately declare themselves as either a European power or as the leaders of the Islamic world. Thus, art came to be used as a visual means of fabricating a distinctly Ottoman dynastic identity through negotiating across two different worlds. Prior to 1453, however, the legitimacy of the Ottoman dynasty was firmly focused on their Eastern Turkic origins. For this reason, there appears a strategic emphasis on emulating their Turkic counterparts and casting themselves as heirs to that legacy—especially, but not only, the Timurids of Central Asia. This signalled their sense of identity and consciousness of the sultanate as an emerging power.

Timurid–Persian–Islamic legacies and the rebirth of Ottoman art in Bursa and Edirne

Despite the influence from the Latin West following the capture of Constantinople, the lure of the East remained a dominant influence on the sultanate's representations of its legitimacy and authority. A dynasty of Turkic–Mongol origin descended from the conqueror Timur and was recognised for its brilliant revival of artistic and intellectual life in Central Asia and Iran. Linda Darling describes the Timurid civilization and its lasting influence in the following words:

> The Timurids . . . followed the same pattern of kingship as the Mongols ... combining military activity with artistic patronage to such a great effect that the fifteenth century came to be known as the era of the Timurid renaissance, a match in glory (if not in transformation power) for the Italian Quattrocento . . . For the Ottomans, Safavids, and Mughals . . . the Timurid florescence had a continuing development in the sixteenth century, producing cultural change in distant countries.[5]

As Darling asserts, the internationalism of the Timurid Renaissance influenced artistically the neighbouring regions, integrating local aesthetics into distinct visual forms reaching as far west as Bursa. This revival of the arts in the Timurid period (1370–1526), with its major cities of Herat (Afghanistan), Samarkand, Bukhara (Uzbekistan), and Isfahan (Iran), was characterised by the work of the finest artists, architects, and craftsmen from all over the East. The Timurid rulers were builders of major monuments rivaling those in the West.

Incorporating Iran into the Timurid Empire stimulated a revival of interest in classical Persian art. Monumental building projects in the fifteenth century including mausoleums, madrasahs, astronomical observatories and advances in mathematics attracted more attention. During Timur's reign, the Summer Palace or "White Palace" in Shahrisabz and the Mosque of Bibi Khatun were constructed in Samarkand, inspired by Persian aesthetics. The Timurids brought this golden age to fruition through cultural amalgamation with Iranian civilization, eventually spreading westward into Ottoman territories.[6]

The descendants of Timur were also builders. Timur's grandson Ulugh Bey (1394–1449) embodied the intellectual as well as the artistic spirit of the period: he served as sultan, as an astronomer at the observatory he built in Samarkand, and as a mathematician who revised earlier Arab works on trigonometry.[7] Timur's invasion of Ottoman Anatolia in 1400, and his subsequent defeat of the Ottoman sultan Bajezid I in 1402, brought the two cultures into direct contact. Although subdued by Timurid overlords in Anatolia, the nascent Ottoman state remained strong in the Balkans and, eleven years later under Mehmed I, reasserted its power over the Timurids. The Ottoman Empire was then reborn under a single ruler. Rather than cast aside the Timurid link, Mehmed I sought to incorporate its rich legacy into a renewed vision for the Ottoman Empire. Sharing an ancient Turkic ancestry, the integration was seamless. Mehmed I looked to the Timurids for dynastic legitimacy and identity and emulated elements of Timurid court culture and its prized artistic achievements.

Despite the dominance of the Timurid aesthetic, other eastern Turkic tribes played a part in these renewed visual statements as well. Although the Timurid influence was most powerful, the Ottomans of Anatolia were beholden to an earlier Turkic tradition which previously held regional domination: the Seljuks of Rum. The Seljuks ruled Anatolia from 1075 to 1307. Like their Ottoman successors, they also saw themselves as successors to the Romans, hence their use of the term "Rum," as they had occupied the former territories of the Eastern Roman Empire from the Byzantines. Their sultanate stretched from Konya in central Anatolia to Erzurum and Sivas in the east. During their 232-year rule, they established their own distinct art forms.

The Turks' interaction with the past is further evidenced by the Seljuks. Appropriating ancient Roman buildings in the thirteenth century in the Seljuk city of Antalya underpins the Turks' ongoing engagement with the classical past. As Scott Redford notes, "At Aspendos [in Antalya] the Seljuks converted the stage building of the second century A.D. Roman theater into a palace. To the outside of the stage building, Seljuk builders attached an arched portico made of brick, reused stone, and rubble. A tall, buttress-like support was also attached to the stage building to the left of this entrance."[8] In Sinop, on the Black Sea coast, the Seljuks' encounter with the classical past is seen in the building of the city's walls following its conquest in 1241. Appropriating the Roman past into the Seljuk historical consciousness affirms their inherited legacy of the classical past, justifying the forging of imperial identity creation of the Seljuks as Rumis or Romans.

However, the flavour of Central Asian and Iranian aesthetics set a precedent and model for the new Ottomans following the demise of the Seljuks. Thus, the importance of both Timurid and Seljuk influence in the newly triumphant Ottoman state after the interregnum in 1413 signalled the continuation of Central Asian and Iranian aesthetics. Timurid architecture was distinguished by large dimensions, naturalistic tiles, and *thuluth* calligraphic decorations, which employed the *cuerda seca* technique that would be reflected in the rebirth phase of Ottoman art."[9] The interior decorative aesthetics included the *iwan* (an open and vaulted rectangular space) scheme and *muqarnas* pendentives. The new Ottoman ruler, Mehmed I, set out to use the most efficient propaganda of its age—art and architecture—to commemorate, according to Mehmed I, "the rise of the dawn of the Ottoman State."[10]

Timurid-inspired minarets, domes, portals and *iwans* were absorbed into the new Ottoman style of fifteenth-century Bursa. Interior and exterior decorations of wall surfaces included the characteristic Timurid colours of turquoise, blue, black, white, and yellow with red geometric and floral patterned tiles.[11] As the main component of their decoration, the technique and colour variations of Timurid tiles were more advanced and refined than the Bursa decorations of this period. Timurid techniques provided the Ottomans with an opportunity to express their own imperial identity after the interregnum period. For this reason, looking to past Timurid exemplars served ideas of political unity and proved to be a seminal moment in defining the Ottoman Renaissance.

The complex sense of cultural exchange in early Ottoman art can be seen in a number of key monuments in Bursa and Edirne. The new sultan's patronage of architectural works began in Bursa. The influence of Timur's Eastern legacy on Ottoman art can be seen in the Yeşil Camii (Green Mosque) and Yeşil Türbe (Green Tomb) of Sultan Mehmed I (figs. 4.1 and 4.2) built in Bursa between 1413 and 1421. His successor Murad II continued this tradition of patronage with the commissioning of the Muradiye Mosque (1435) and Üç Şerefeli Mosque (1438–47). The Muradiye Mosque continued the Timurid–Bursa tradition, while the Üç Şerefeli Mosque signals the beginning of a break from Central Asian conventions and tapped into the Roman/Byzantine tradition (figs. 4.3, 4.4, and 4.5).

The Bursa Tradition: the Yeşil Camii (1413–21) of Mehmed I

As a grand visual gesture to commemorate the restoration of Ottoman rule under his sultanate, Mehmet I constructed the Yeşil Camii. Furthermore, he sought to clarify his inheritance of the Timurid legacy by deliberately emulating the iconography of Timurid Renaissance masterpieces in Samarkand, such as the Gur-i Amir, Timur's mausoleum (1401) and the Registan observatory (1417–21) (figs. 4.6 and 4.7). It is here at the Yeşil Camii complex that extensive tile decorations in the Timurid tradition make an appearance for the first time, marking their revival in Ottoman art.

A complex consisting of a tomb, a madrasah, and a hospice surround the Yeşil Camii built by Mehmed I. Construction began in 1421 and was completed after his death in 1424 by his son Murad II. The mosque is the most ornate of the reverse T-plan in Bursa (fig.

4.8), which included an imperial mosque with three *iwans* (rectangular halls, usually vaulted) and four rooms attached to the corners for the Sufi dervishes. This was important as each sultan belonged to the Sufi brotherhood and had his own spiritual dervish.[12] The mosque is built entirely of hewn stone and marble. The carving on the stalactite marble portal is covered with ornate ornamentation and inscriptions. The marble windows are carved in the same style as the portal, giving a sense of unity to the whole structure. Only the console of the portico was laid, and it was clear that it was to have five sections. When the sultan died, it was assumed that work on his private mosque would stop. Over the portal is an inscription signed by the Grand Vizier architect Haci Ivaz Pasha giving the date of completion as 1419: "He who planned and designed this mosque is the most humble servant of the patron, Haci Ivaz bin Ahi Beyazit."[13] The inscription draws attention to the self-fashioning of fifteenth-century artisans by leaving their names on the works they created. The decoration of the interior was completed on the orders of Murad II in 1424 following his father's death.

Following the political interregnum, to project this new identity, the newly-emergent Ottomans, sought inspiration from many cultural traditions. The early influence of the Timurids and Seljuks underscored the shared cultural heritage of the Ottomans. However, the cultural rebirth was much more complex. At its inception in Bursa, the Grand Vizier, architect Haci Ivaz Pasha, invited foreign artisans to the Ottoman court. These artisans were from Central Asia and Iran and were known as "Masters of Tabriz." Upon their arrival in Bursa in 1419 they introduced their techniques to the Ottoman court. In particular, they introduced *cuerda seca*—monochrome glaze and underglaze on painted blue and white tiles, first in the Yeşil Camii and then in the Tomb of Mehmed I. This transference of Timurid aesthetics to Bursa contributed to the Ottomans' sense of cultural renewal and reinforces the historical consciousness of an emerging dynastic identity. In fact, so important were these artists to Ottoman style that when the capital officially moved from Bursa to Edirne under Murad II, the Tabriz artists and craftsmen followed.

Similarities with the Timurid aesthetic and the Bursa tradition

The Timurid-inspired elements of the Yeşil Camii reflect the early modern Ottoman historical self-consciousness. This self-consciousness is important to the Ottomans' emerging sense of self-fashioning.[14] Visually, the building needed to project grandeur; symbolically, it needed to represent the power of the new sultan as a unifying figure like his Central Asian counterparts. The entrance to the mosque is like the sultan's palace with its galleries below and an imperial gallery above, as well as women's galleries and two balconies that open to the outside. In the first section of the central area, which is roofed by two domes similar to the Timurid tradition, there is a pool containing two carved marble fountains. The central hall of the mosque consists of an inner vestibule with two *iwans* in the Timurid tradition of the Bibi Khatun Mosque (1404) in Samarkand. The Yeşil Camii has one on the left and one on the right entrance facing the *qibla* wall. The majestically tiled *mihrab* represents the gardens of paradise (figs. 4.9, 4.10, and 4.11). The second section is on a higher level and can be reached by steps. Here there is a splendid tiled niche 10 metres high. The interior walls are tiled to a height of 2 metres with hexagonal tiles, while the walls and ceilings of the imperial and palace galleries are entirely covered with coloured glaze tiles. One wall in each of the side rooms is ornamented with a plaster chimneybreast and shelf niches. By emulating the aesthetics of Timur's capital Samarkand, the building reflects Mehmed I's vision for attaining cultural greatness at his capital of Bursa—the city that represents the rebirth of the Ottoman state. The rebirth phase experienced in Bursa speaks to Rüsen's claim that "identity is shaped by the affirmative adaptation and imitatory emulation of pre-given [or existing] cultural definitions [or experiences]."[15]

The variation in the intensity of the *cuerda seca* technique demonstrates the sophistication of the technology of tile making. The *cuerda seca* technique now makes its debut in Bursa. The transference of this technique not only reflects a shared cultural heritage, but its movement from east Asia to west Asia also reflects the universal appeal of this aesthetic in Muslim court culture, including that of the Ottomans. The universal appeal of this art form is important for the Ottomans' sense of identity as it reflects imperial status and unity, as well as continuity. As

Patricia Blessing states, "With their varied techniques, color schemes, and visual references, the tiles signal the extent to which Ottoman visual culture in the early fifteenth century mirrored the constant renegotiation of power, rule, and representation that involved the sultan, his historians, and his builders."[16] The two large *iwans* recessed on each side of the vestibule are tiled from top to bottom. As Godfrey Goodwin attests, they "[. . .] are richly tiled mahfils in the centre of whose ceilings are wheels of roseate arabesques of fantastic complexity. The wainscot tiles of the eyvans [iwans] are simpler although their original deep green hexagons were gilded after firing and gold traces lie over the cloudy surface like a fragile veiling."[17] Drawing on Gillian Rose's understanding of "audiencing," in which the viewing of objects is manipulated by people's perceptions, the mosque at first appearance does not represent the typical Ottoman building. Its initial appearance is very Eastern, as indicated by the *iwans* and *mahfils*. To understand the building's role in the rebirth paradigm the viewer must pay attention to details or adopt, as Rose puts it, "a way of seeing . . . differently."[18] According to Doğan Kuban, the inner vestibule walls are covered with deep "green hexagonal tiles, with large circular rosettes decorated with elegant *rumi* motifs in white, [arabesque] yellow and blue."[19] While the dark of the *rumi* floral ensemble inspired by Timurid–Persian heritage heightens the visual intensity of the interior, the arabesque-like cut-tile mosaics are adapted from earlier Seljuk techniques. The dominance of the Timurid colour green is significant beyond simply giving rise to the name of the mosque and mausoleum. The dominant colour of dark green, as in Timur's mausoleum the Gur-i Amir in Samarkand, establishes Ottoman identity in relation to the previous Timurid ruler. As noted by Blessing, "The Yeşil Kulliye was a focus of Mehmed I's patronage . . . [who constructed a] . . . deliberate dialogue with both the Anatolian heritage of the Seljuk architecture and the broader Persianate culture of post-Mongol Iran and Central Asia."[20] This demonstrates Ottoman ascendency over the old rulers as it uses their style both to tap into their heritage and to signal Ottoman dominion over it.

While the small floral motifs tend to lose themselves in the predominantly green composition, they still, however, draw the viewer in to take a closer look at the natural world. This closer look leads the viewer toward a sense of comfort and beauty where, according to Rose, "particular ways of spectating mediate the visual effects of . . . images."[21] The natural beauty of the floral motif is further complemented by the inclusion of the marble ablution fountain in the centre of the interior, located between the two *iwans* at the entrance. The symbolism of the continuously flowing water suggests the life-giving force and continuity of the "green paradise" in the mosque's structure, thus guaranteeing—with God's help—the safety, security, and the rebirth of the sultanate under his rule.

Differences between Ottoman and Timurid aesthetics

Mehmed I's Yeşil Camii did not merely reawaken the Timurid aesthetic in Bursa, it also introduced new stylistic developments. This reawakening signals the initial step towards a distinct Ottoman Bursa tradition. The unique architecture of the central prayer area is situated on a raised platform and is a break with the Timurid tradition. As figure 4.8 shows, it faces the two loges on either side of the anti-*qibla* wall, both separated by the newly designed Bursa arch. The new or *ihtirā* Bursa arch, with its wide flat crown and rounded corners in the Yeşil Camii, represents the emergence of the distinct Ottoman style.[22] In this way, according to Rüsen, "historical consciousness plays off the one [i.e. past] against the other [i.e. present] in order to create a new constellation of relationships between them."[23] This break from the Timurid tradition signals the emergence of a distinct Ottoman aesthetic. Architecturally speaking, as a new arch form it offers the viewer a triumphant welcome and encourages the confident embrace of a new era.

Figures 4.9 and 4.10 showcase how the highly ornamental and intricately designed *mihrab* stands as the crowning glory of this mosque. The building of the Green Mosque in fifteenth-century Bursa signals the foundational stage of Ottoman *ihya* in the influence of the Timurid artisans. It stimulated the shaping of a distinct Ottoman style and of its burgeoning imperial identity. Standing majestically as the centrepiece of the mosque, the *mihrab* is a unifying feature of the building and reflects the patron's political role and reasons for commissioning it. In all its glory, the *mihrab* of the Green Mosque dominates the prayer hall with its moulded tile frame and niche and its twelve rows of elevated stalactites, concluding in a six-ribbed shell. As Goodwin explains, "[the tiles'] intricate three-dimensional work . . . is achieved by the potter applying the *cire perdue* technique of a sculptor to his tiles. In the firing, at the point when the glaze begins to set and the clay harden, the molten wax vanishes away to leave an effect of fretwork behind . . . The four or five colours are separated by a thread which turns to ash in the firing, the *cuerda seca* technique."[24] The three-dimensional interplay and the use of colour are characteristics of the type of decoration used to consciously emphasise the symbolism of the *mihrab.* Colour is a crucial component of the work. Studies on the use of predominant colours such as yellow and blue seem, according to Rose, "to have quite high value . . . because they are often where the light falls into the [work]" and draw our attention to it.[25] Furthermore, the three-dimensional effect of the *cuerda seca*, combined with the colours yellow and blue, "heightens" the "sense of its realism."[26] Despite the attractive quality of the final product, however, a closer examination reveals the matte, non-glossy quality of the work, a technique that would not be mastered for another century. Politically, the *mihrab* is a reflection of order and unity and of a return to stability, represented by its dominance and grandeur in the centre of the *qibla* wall. Aesthetically, however, the *mihrab* of the Yeşil Camii is a product of the shared visual aesthetics between the achievements of the Timurids in the East and Ottoman Bursa in the West, giving birth to an early modern Ottoman artistic tradition.

The *mihrab* rests in the centre of the *qibla* wall and is reached by steps leading to the raised central prayer hall that is supported by a giant Bursa arch. This innovative design accentuates the prominence of the *mihrab* as its focal point. The flat surface of the *mihrab* is full of Timurid-inspired chinoiserie flowers and interlacing stems. These signify not only the gate of paradise, but also the blessed reign of the sultan and the restoration of the state from the turmoil of the past. Two cages on the either side of the *mihrab* represent the sun and the moon and herald the return to the rule of law and order.[27] In this way, the *mihrab* is also reflective of Mehmed's triumph over disunity. His triumph over disunity is the rebirth of the Ottoman state.

The spiral arabesque design of the *mihrab* interspersed with Qur'anic calligraphy in *cuerda seca* is typical of tile decoration in the Timurid period and reveals a connection to the medieval Islamic past. The *kufic* (i.e. seventh-century Arabic script of the Qur'an) inscriptions are frequently used on *mihrab* niches. These early attempts at using calligraphy as a decorative motif were limited in their design, relying in large part on the original style of the Qur'an that was mostly used at the Timurid court, a style the Ottomans now adopted. The adoption of the seventh-century *kufic* exemplifies the interplay between distant and recent pasts and accentuates the historical consciousness of the Ottomans' nascent identity. Figure 4.12 shows the mirror image of *Allahu Akbar* or "God is Great" written in the centre of the *mihrab*. This calligraphy is scarcely visible and is integrated somewhat less harmoniously in the midst of the surrounding tiles. This reflects the re-emerging identity and the confidence of the Ottoman state. However, the *mihrab* achieves its purpose of representing the Ottoman power unified under a single ruler through the continuous and unbroken lettering in Arabic calligraphy of "God is Great" in the centre of the *mihrab*. The repeated message draws the attention of the viewer. This unified lettering is representative of the sultan's rule, signifying that it is one of security, law and order under God's protection. At the same time, the lettering demonstrates that by emulating Timurid aesthetics a new Ottoman art aesthetic is being reborn under the auspices of the inheritors of the Timurid legacy.

Aside from the commissioning of the Yeşil Camii and the Yeşil Türbe, an indication of the historical significance of the unification of the empire under Mehmed I, is the rise in status of the artists that constitutes a part of Ottoman rebirth. This correlates with the significance of the artists in Vasari's *The Lives*. As Stefanos Yerasimos notes, "During this same period, artists began to be recognized as individuals; they no longer remained invisible but signed their work with confidence," reinforcing Mustafa Ali's comments on raising the status of artists and giving them a voice.[28] The artists who signed their names to the artwork of tiles, plaster, and woodwork are Muhammad al-Macnun, Ali ibn Ilyas Ali, and Ali bin Haci Ahmed of Tabriz respectively. Ottoman biographer Taşköprülüzade states that the court designer Ilyas Ali supervised the works. Ilyas Ali, a native of Bursa, was taken in 1402 by Timur to Samarkand where he was trained in the Timurid–Persian artistic tradition. Alongside builders from Tabriz and Damascus, Ilyas Ali had worked on the Sha-i-Zinde, a necropolis in Samarkand, which was considered to be a Timurid "masterpiece of ceramic art that combines Persian, Arab and Chinese influences" (figs. 4.13 and 4.14).[29] Taşköprülüzade also informs us that Ilyas Ali became the first artist to introduce the Timurid mode to his homeland after Timur's grandson Ulugh Bey permitted his and other artists and craftsmen's return to Bursa in 1411 on the invitation of the sultan to work on his buildings.[30] Ilyas Ali now bore the title Nakkaş ("the Decorator"). He left his signature on a title above that of Mehmed I's loge: "The decoration of this blessed building was carried out by the most humble of all human beings, Ali bin Ilyas Ali, who completed his work in the last days of the Holy Ramadan of the year 827 [August 1424]."[31] Another artist signed his mark on the sultan's loge: "The work of Mehmet, the eccentric."[32] Other artists followed, leaving their marks in an inscription in white letters on a blue ground beside the *mihrab*: "Work of the Masters of Tabriz." The sixteenth-century historians Nesri and Ashıkpashazade credit Haci Ivaz, the first grand vizier-architect, as the person responsible for the construction of the mosque and the one inviting skilled Eastern artists to the Ottoman court. [33] This invitation introduced the universal appeal of Timurid aesthetics to the Ottoman court.

The Yeşil Camii heralds the shared cultural heritage of the Ottomans and Timurids and signals the dawn of the distinct Ottoman culture. The rebirth of the empire under Mehmed I was consciously constructed by looking back to Timurid heritage to mark the event and to signify the Renaissance of its arts. And, like the Yeşil Camii, the mausoleum of Mehmed I also confirmed the rebirth of early modern Ottoman art. Under Sinan, the tile decoration in Ottoman architecture will gradually achieve the status of mural painting, quite independent of architecture in the sixteenth century. Under Sinan's supervision this unique art form signals the technical and aesthetic maturity of Ottoman Renaissance art in the Rustem Pasha Mosque 1560–61.

The Bursa tradition: the Yeşil Türbe (1413–21) of Mehmed I

Both the mosque and tomb were built and decorated by the same architect and craftsmen from Tabriz. The tomb, like the mosque, commemorates Mehmed I, who succeeded in reuniting the Ottoman state following a bitter struggle with his brothers over the throne after Timur's departure from Anatolia with the captured Ottoman sultan Bajezid I.

The *türbe* has a burial chamber on the ground floor and is a continuation of the traditional Timurid and Seljuk styles found in Anatolia and Western Iran. Like the Yeşil Camii above, the connection to past Eastern models is highly discernible in this mausoleum. As noted by Rüsen, these connections assert the nascent identity of the ruling dynasty. There is a strong resemblance between the Yeşil Türbe and the tomb of Shirin Bika Aka, Timur's sister, (c. 1440–50) in Samarkand. The similarities in the portal decorations of the curvilinear *muqarnas* and the reliance on the single-centred arch with a high crown make it difficult to differentiate between the two structures. This indicates not only the parallel between Timurid and Ottoman Bursa structures but also suggests, more significantly, the Ottomans' desire to look to ancestral lands to signify the rebirth of the Turkic empire under a unified sovereign (figs. 4.15 and 4.16*)*.

The Yeşil Türbe demonstrates architectural parallels with its Seljuk and Central Asian nomadic forebears and, at the same time, aesthetically competes with the tomb of Timur, the Gur-e Amir, in Samarkand. The Yeşil Türbe achieved a dome height of 25 metres above floor level with a diameter height of 10.6m, compared to Timur's 30m above floor level, with a dome diameter height of 15m by 12m.[34] In this case study, architectural continuity with Timurid aesthetics appears more evident than through distinct "Ottoman" forms that occurred later. The octahedral base of the exterior of Gur-e Amir is decorated with jade green, yellow, and black geometric tiles against a background of terracotta bricks. The upper cylindrical part of the base supports the azure fluted dome, accentuating the cupola. It is adorned with bright blue tiles with deep rosettes and white spots. Architecturally, the Yeşil Türbe deviates slightly from its Timurid model and connects more with its Anatolian and nomadic Turco–Mongol ancestors. According to Goodwin, "[the türbe] is much nearer to the Selçuk [octagonal] type than that of the earlier Ottoman sultans and, through the Selçuks, is nearer to the Iranian *kumbets* and the fragile *yurts* or tents of the people living in Central Asia."[35] From the exterior, the tomb has a tent-like structure, with eight sides built mainly from brick and stone and painted green, culminating in a dome with a slightly pointed profile like that of a Mongolian *yurt*. The columns on each side are placed within a brick marble frame with a pointed arch. Although the exterior is closer in design to the Seljuk tombs of Emir

Saltuk in Erzurum (c. 1190) and Doner Kumbet in Kayesri (1276), the octagonal style of the Yeşil Türbe deviates from the Anatolian Seljukid two-storey tombs. Instead, it follows the Central Asian Seljuk design from western Iran and Timurid styles of a single-level structure. This emulation in the new Bursa tradition suggests the legitimacy of a stronger and more powerful ruler as universal sovereign, like Timur or Malek Şah (1055–92), the Seljuk sultan of Anatolia, Iran, and Central Asia. Although the Yeşil Türbe cannot claim the grandeur of Timur's tomb, its interaction with past Seljuk architecture and Central Asian nomadic tent structures asserts the formation of an Ottoman imperial identity.

While architecturally Mehmed I's tomb could not compete with Gur-e Amir in grandiosity, it does compete on a smaller scale through its tiling aesthetic. Timur's tomb's interior has a high chamber with highly-decorated niches at the sides. The walls are covered with onyx slabs and painted plaster. High-relief papier-mâché *muqarnas*, gilded and painted, decorate the arches and the interior dome, imitating the starry night sky. The dominance of the colour gold interspersed with blue and green highlights the majesty of the royal tomb. In an anticlimactic manner, the absence of a highly-decorative sarcophagus for Timur suggests that the limelight is on the architecture itself and not the individual buried inside.

The inclusion of a *mihrab* in the tomb not only draws attention to God and salvation, but also accentuates the focus on the structure of the building itself. However, as in the Green Mosque, the colour glaze and mosaic tiling decorates the mausoleum. The use of hexagonal dark green tiles in the interior arch of the entrance portal shows its Arabic–Umayyad origin. The arch's use of tiled mahfils—unique in Ottoman architecture—shows Mehmed I's integration of past medieval Islamic style into this complex to connect with an inherited legacy (figs. 4.17 and 4.18). As Rüsen notes, "historical consciousness seeks to set aside the dominant historical patterns of signification of current life practice to make room for . . . different perspectives [or visual mediums]," signalling the slow progress of rebirth of early modern Ottoman art and the growing self-fashioning of the ruling dynasty.[36] The facades are covered with panels of turquoise tiling. In contrast to the Gur-e Amir, the Yeşil Türbe includes a highly-decorated *mihrab* and a sarcophagus that are entirely covered with tiles of floral bouquets with Qur'anic inscriptions in *cuerda seca* yellow on blue background. This form of decoration, which grew out of stylised vegetation, has affinities with Chinese motifs and reinforces a link to the far-Eastern past. Like the Yeşil Camii *mihrab*, it also lacks luster and vibrancy due to its matte finish; however, the interlaced chinoiserie floral composition makes up for what it lacks in vibrancy of colour.

Triple frames border the *mihrab*. This is followed by an elaborate pattern of stars. Enclosed within a multifoliate arch reminiscent of the Islamic Umayyad period (650–750) is a complex garden of hyacinths, carnations, marguerites, and roses blooming in paradise. On either side, decorated candles burn in gold bell-bottomed candlesticks inscribed with the names of Allah and Muhammad respectively. A pair of ceramic columns guards the stalactite niche and the central panel, signifying the strengthened empire under the rule of Mehmed I who ushered in an era of peace and stability. The columns symbolise the pillars of strength and the stability on which the new empire is built under his rule.

A similar message is also alluded to in the calligraphic inscription on the sarcophagus. The highly-decorative sarcophagus makes its debut in the yellow *cuerda seca* style, symbolising the sun's radiance and the rebirth of a new "prosperous" era: "This shining sepulchre, this couch saturated with perfumes, is the tomb of the very great Sultan and very honoured sovereign, pride of the sultans of the universe, supporters of the servants of God, he who has made prosperous the land, who has fought against injustice and corruption . . . may God . . . grant him eternal rest in the gardens of Paradise."[37] As in the Yeşil Camii *mihrab* above, colour is a crucial component of the composition of the sarcophagus. The dominant yellow of the Qur'anic inscriptions, combined with its central location on a raised platform in the tomb, draw attention to and reflect the dawning of the new era for the Ottomans that occurred under Mehmed I's reign. His intention to build a complex, thus, commemorates the end of the political instability of the interregnum period following the Battle of Ankara. The mosque and the mausoleum are two symbols commemorating that rebirth. Mehmed I's sarcophagus makes a political and artistic statement absent from the more austere sarcophagus of Timur, implying that the Ottomans are ready to assert a distinct cultural identity of their own and which reflects their new geographical and imperial contexts (figs. 4.18a and 4.18b).

The artisans of Bursa are certainly inspired by the mystical interpretation of Rumi, the Sufi mystic (d. 1273) who arrived in Anatolia from Balkh (Afghanistan). Rumi describes the outward garden (both natural and artistic) as a reflection of the spiritual garden in order to see with purer vision the eternal Garden and cypress plot of the Hereafter.[38] From a Sufi perspective, the imagery of the sarcophagus highlights Mehmed I's attainment of paradise after his triumph on earth as a unifying force for his people. Thus, the outward visual expression of paradise so vividly portrayed in the mausoleum and the sarcophagus reflect the peace the sultan brought to his realm. This represents the ease with which Mehmed I will make his spiritual journey to the Hereafter and suggests that his final resting place will be one of complete rest. The significance of this style of tiling at the Green Mosque and Green Tomb represent an artistic legacy that spread from Central Asia and Iran to Ottoman Bursa. This cultural legacy highlights the slow but continuing maturity of early modern Ottoman art that instigated the rebirth of Ottoman cultural transformation in a different historical context.

The mausoleum is an extension of the Yeşil Camii of Mehmed I and serves as his resting place in the grounds of the mosque complex. As the patron of the mosque and the mausoleum, Mehmed I will be forever remembered as the ruler who unified the empire politically and embarked on an artistic program to demonstrate his political power. With the transfer of the capital to Edirne by Mehmed I's successor, Murad II, this nascent cultural reawakening continues to develop further, and the imitation of Timurid visual vocabulary slowly begins to lose its appeal. This signifies the strengthening of Ottoman culture's self-consciousness as it begins to be attracted to another cultural aesthetic. By commissioning the use of Timurid art as representations of power and stability, Mehmed I conveyed the legitimacy of the rebirth of his new state and his sovereignty as a stable ruler. Thus, the growing self-consciousness of the Ottomans for the time being relegates the Timurid and Eastern models to the background before its resurgence again during the post-1453 reign of Mehmed II. For now, however, Edirne architecture demonstrates a muted Timurid style with a move toward the West. Therefore, Edirne, as the second capital of the Ottoman state demonstrates the continuity of the evolutionary progress made in the development of the rebirth phase of its architecture.

The Edirne tradition: the Üç Şerefeli Mosque (1438–47)

The unification of the empire under Mehmed I in Bursa and Murad II's relocation of the capital to Edirne in the early decades of the fifteenth century were accompanied by the emergence of a different style that, for the first time, oriented Ottoman architecture to a central-domed structure. This orientation resonates with the rebirth paradigm and reflects the progression of architectural *sūret* or style in the Üç Şerefeli Mosque (1438–47). Before this, however, the Timurid aesthetic makes its appearance in Edirne in the Muradiye Mosque of Murad II, although with less intensity and robustness than in the Yeşil Camii in Bursa.

During the sultanate of Murad II, the son of Mehmed I, the capital of the empire was transferred to Edirne. The Masters of Tabriz followed Murad II to Edirne when the new sultan established his new capital there.[39] He commissioned two mosques in Edirne, the Muradiye (1435–36) and the Üç Şerefeli (1438–47). The *mihrab* of the former complex closely resembles that of the Yeşil mosque, evoking a visual continuity with Bursa. Necipoğlu notes that "it has underglaze painted blue-and-white insets forming a unified group with the underglaze hexagonal tiles decorating the dadoes."[40] The interior of the tiles depicts blue floral motifs on a white background. Necipoğlu also argues that the tiles were simultaneously produced at the local kilns, as the technology used for making *cuerda seca* and underglaze blue and white by the Masters of Tabriz in the Muradiye Mosque was similar to that of those in Bursa.[41] In this mosque the Masters of Tabriz also refined their ceramic techniques by providing underglaze ceramic tiles with the introduction of two new colours. There are two inscriptions using ceramic covering of the pediments of the windows on both sides of the entrance to the courtyard opposite the *qibla* wall. They have not only the traditional Bursa underglaze white and blue decoration, but, for the first time, glazed turquoise and purple (fig. 4.19). These colours would not to be seen again in Edirne until Mehmed II's construction of the Çinili Köşk in 1473.[42]

In the meantime, in Edirne, a shift occurred in Ottoman architecture in the fifteenth century with the Üç Şerefeli Mosque. After Bursa, having provided the architectural and artistic "rebirth," Edirne would be the next Ottoman city to introduce Timurid–Persian style into its artistic repertoire, but this time the architect of the Üç Şerefeli Mosque, Muslihiddin, would orient himself more to the Hagia Sophia for inspiration as demonstrated in figure 4.5. This attempt to integrate the Roman/Byzantine tradition into Ottoman architectural technique marks the beginning of a long technological and engineering challenge for the Ottomans to achieve an uninterrupted space under a single dome. This challenge was not mastered until Sinan's Selimiye Mosque, also in Edirne, in 1575.

In 1437, Murad II began the construction of the Üç Şerefeli mosque in Edirne. This mosque marks the next step in the evolution of Ottoman architecture. The dome became central to Ottoman architectural consciousness because the Ottomans needed to create a unified prayer space for the worshippers. In Islamic prayer rituals the worshippers need to stand shoulder to shoulder facing the *qibla* wall. For this reason, it is important not to have columns or barriers preventing the flow of the lines of worshippers. Therefore, the unity of the interior architecture must be in unison with the unity of the worshippers. As with earlier mosques from the time of Orhan, Bajezid I, Murad I, Mehmed I, Murad II, and others, it had been architecturally problematic to create a unified prayer space under a single dome. While the *ablaq* style of the mosque's portal in contrasting marble is inspired from Mamluk aesthetics, for its domes the architect looked to the Roman/Byzantine tradition to create a more unified interior. From the Roman/Byzantine model, Muslihiddin discovered the significance of semicircular domes in distributing the weight of the central dome outward onto supporting piers. First he added nine smaller domes on the north portico or *revak*. This was followed by seven higher domes. Finally, he added two lesser domes on each side of the great cupola of the mosque.[43] By combining these structures with two of its minarets and four of its eight flying buttresses, Muslihiddin achieved the first monumental pyramid mosque structure with the great dome as its pinnacle.

The Üç Şerefeli Mosque, with a dome of 24 metres in diameter and a height of 28.5 metres, was set apart from its Eastern neighbours and paved the way for the Ottomans to push the boundaries of engineering further. The dome rests on a hexagon supported on one side by the *qibla* wall and the other by the façade of the courtyard. The remaining sides are made up of arches resting on two centre piers. The mosque for the first time attempts to find a solution by separating the side aisles from the central space, similar to the Roman/Byzantine tradition. All of these domed structures underscore the sacred prayer space of the mosque. However, once inside the observer experiences a sense of heaviness from the almost equal length of the height of the dome from the floor level with its diameter. This feels like a weight pressing on one's shoulders. It was another century before developments in Ottoman architecture rectified this. According to Yerasimos, the mosque "remained unequalled until the construction of the court mosque of Mehmet II from 1463 to 1470 in Istanbul."[44] Thus, the dome of the Üç Şerefeli Mosque was groundbreaking in its architectural engineering. It set a precedent and posed a challenge for future Ottoman architects to perfect its design. For Goodwin, the complex, which was completed prior to the conquest of the Byzantine stronghold of Constantinople, "was a prelude to a struggle of a century to excel the dome of Hagia Sophia" and Kuban notes that "the spatial effect of the great central dome . . . open[ed] the way towards Istanbul architecture."[45]

The defining stalactite domes of the Üç Şerefeli Mosque tapping into Umayyad and Abbasid aesthetics came to express the new dome shape of Ottoman architectural style. Six years after its completion and with the conquest of Constantinople, the architecture of the sixteenth-century Ottoman court would align more powerfully with that of the West, while its fine arts aesthetics, more specifically the Iznik tile, underwent complete transformation by being reborn anew and with more elegance or *nezāket*.

At the next capital of the Empire, Istanbul, the Ottoman rulers continued to merge and amalgamate the Eastern and classical Roman/Byzantine traditions. Fusing the two played a crucial role in the consolidation of the distinct Ottoman style, while the fine arts of tile making, illustrated chronicles, and illuminations were further refined to form a whole new dimension of their own. The Ottomans continued to gain inspiration from the Timurid East and were newly influenced by the Renaissance in Italy. Addressing both Eastern and Western audiences through artistic representations, Mehmed II assured the legitimacy of his universal sovereignty as the "ruler of the East and West," reinforcing Mustafa Ali's assertions in *The Essence of History*. By appealing to different audiences, Mehmed II ensured that the propagation of his image appealed in different ways to both sides of the cultural divide, a significant gesture post-1453.

The patronage of Mehmed II witnessed the creation of cross-hybrid works influenced by both the East and West. Once again the Eastern influence was very influential in underpinning Ottoman visual tastes, but Mehmed II's astuteness and cultivated personality ensured that the influence of the Renaissances of the Timurids and of Italy would contribute to an intercultural synergy. In Spiro Kostof's words the Ottomans were now in a position to "stage their own renaissance."[46]

1453 Istanbul and beyond: the East-West legacy of Mehmed II (1451–81)

The Ottoman dynasty's fascination with classical antiquity to justify its universal sovereignty began just before the conquest of Constantinople in 1453. Bajezid I, Mehmed II's father, demanded a ransom of figural tapestries from Arras in exchange for return of the captive Prince Philip the Bold, son of the Duke of Burgundy, after the Ottoman victory in 1396 over the crusader armies at Nicopolis.[47] Bajezid sent to France a Turkish-speaking messenger, Jacques de Helly, to negotiate the ransom. De Helly reported that the sultan would be greatly pleased to receive tapestries from Arras depicting "appropriate ancient histories" representing "the history of King Alexander [the Great], with the major part of his life and his conquests."[48] According to Tahsin Öz, the Topkapı Palace Treasury inventory, dated 1505, cites a *frengi muşavver perde*—"European figural tapestry."[49]

This broadening of Ottoman worldview by tapping into the shared classical heritage of East and West is evident in the inscription at the gate of the new palace Mehmed II the Conqueror built on the shores of the Bosphorus, which refers to Mehmed II as "the ruler of the two seas and the two continents."[50] Although the Ottomans were not directly related to Europeans, after their conquest of Constantinople in 1453 they deliberately portrayed themselves as heirs to the great empire of Rome and the legacy of the classical West. The sultan's Greek biographer Kritovoulos portrays Mehmed II as the neo-Alexander who is enacting ancient Troy's revenge upon the West. He addresses Mehmed II as the "Lord of Land and Sea, by the will of God."[51] The author explains that he wrote this work to immortalise Mehmed II's heroic deeds, so that his Greek-speaking subjects and all philhellenic "Western nations" would know that Mehmed II's accomplishments were "in no way inferior to those of Alexander the Macedonian."[52] Mehmed II's own endowment deed, written in Arabic during the last years of his life, also compares him to Iskender (Alexander) in terms of his justice, mercy, wisdom, and learning.[53] His posthumous biography written by the Ottoman historian Tursun Beg (c. 1490–95) introduces Mehmed II's heroic deeds with the Qur'anic reference to Alexander, who is presented as an Islamic role model for the divinely appointed Ottoman *pādişāh-ı cihān* (world emperor):

> And they will ask you of Dhu'l-qarnayn [i.e. Alexander], the two-horned. Say: I will recite to you an account of him.[54]

Tursun Beg continues to compare Mehmed II to Alexander the Great, pointing out that his conquest of twenty kingdoms makes him more deserving of the title "world emperor" than Timur.[55]

Mehmed II's collection of classical manuscripts in Greek and Turkish found in the Topkapı Palace library sheds new insights on his engagement with the Hellenic and Islamic intellectual traditions that conditioned his receptivity to Western humanist ideas.[56] A Greek copy of Arrian's *Life of Alexander* was read to him every day, along with the works of Laertius, Herodotus, Livy, Quintus Curtius, chroniclers of the popes, emperors, the kings of France and the Lombards because, according to Lauro Quirini (d. 1479), he wanted "to become and be proclaimed sovereign of all the world and all the people; that is, a second, Alexander."[57] In addition to Greek and Latin texts, works in Arabic and Persian included: "Blessed Book of Aristotle on Politics concerning Advice to Dhu'l-qarnayn, and Aristotle's Epistle to Alexander on Matters of Sovereignty"; an Arabic epistolary novel including a biography of Alexander, letters he exchanged with Aristotle, and the discourses of his court philosophers, titled "Book on the Vicissitudes of Alexander, Traditions on [His Life], and the Traditions of Wise Men in the Age of the Aforesaid Alexander."[58] Additionally, *Alexander Romance* (*Iskendername*), an Ottoman manuscript composed in Turkish by Ahmedi (d. 1413) and illustrated during the reign of Mehmed II, reinforces the paradigm shift of the empire's universal ambitions. It cements the connections between Mehmed the Conqueror as a Muslim Iskender and the contemporary ruler of East and West. Mehmed II Islamicised Alexander by wearing

Ottoman costume when riding with the janissaries to the Dome of the Rock in Jerusalem after having completed the hajj pilgrimage in Mecca. In this way he justified seeing himself as the second Alexander executing an ecumenical mission (fig. 4.20a). Mehmed II's behaviour also signifies his belief that a wise ruler was directed by the teachings of classical Greek and Islamic philosophers, as reflected in Ahmedi's miniature painting depicting Alexander seated on a throne conversing with his court intellectuals (fig. 4.20b). Strategically situated at the juncture of Europe and Asia, Mehmed II's court was therefore positioned at the ideal centre for a world empire that sought to merge Turco–Mongol, Persian–Islamic, and Roman–Byzantine traditions into a universal sovereignty.

Moreover, Kritovoulos records Mehmed II's brief sojourn in Athens in 1458. His visit to the Acropolis demonstrates his inquisitive intellect and deep connection to classical antiquity fostered by his study of the classics. Kritovoulos states, "He saw it, and was amazed, and he praised it, and especially the Acropolis as he went up to it. And from the ruins and the remains, he reconstructed mentally the ancient buildings, being a wise man and Philhellene and as a great king, and he conjured how they must have been originally."[59] Mehmed II's connection to the classical antiquity is reflected in his interest in the patronage for the arts.

By looking to both the East and West, the Ottomans were now in a position to manufacture an identity. Necipoğlu states that Mehmed II negotiated "the western and eastern cultural horizons of his rapidly expanding domains through visual cosmopolitanism, a process of creative translation and fusion that contributed to the construction of a multifaceted imperial identity."[60] By setting the standard for future development, Mehmed II merges the East with Roman/Western aesthetics. This complex imperial identity continued under Mehmed II's successors. From thenceforth their art would come to reflect this multi-faceted cultural self-identity by emulating, adapting, and restoring different visual expressions from cultures past and present to form a uniquely Ottoman manifestation. According to Rüsen, this lure to the past and yet also be different "imbues historical consciousness with potential for hope."[61] The hope engendered by the patronage of Mehmed II energised and rejuvenated the arts through its return to the past.

This was similar to Florence's claim to be the new Athens (c. 1400) when the encroaching power of the Duke of Milan led Florentine artists to look to the past as a hope for the future. Several visual languages from architecture to the decorative arts were synthesised in a celebration of an "intentional hybridity," a literary term defined by Mikhail Bakhtin as the conscious fusion of different visual mediums, set against each other dialogically.[62] As Marwan Kraidy states of this hybridity, "[i]ts intentionality increases the possibility that it will become a process of othering, where identities are projected by powerful social agents onto others who are [deemed] less powerful."[63] Thus, the Renaissance of the arts through the shared Eastern and Western heritage came to represent the universal sovereignty and power of Mehmed II. This signalled the rebirth of the Ottoman sultanate as the new caesars of the Eastern Roman Empire and even surpassing the achievements of the Timurid sultans. This political and cultural resurgence emphasised the new identity of the dynasty that ruled over many ethnic nationalities on different continents from both the East and West.

More than any other sultan, Mehmed II played a crucial role in mediating between the two worlds of East and West. As Necipoğlu notes, the patronage of Mehmed II after 1453 allowed "[a] paradigmatic shift by incomparably extending the Western horizons of the post-Mongol Islamic artistic tradition, previously characterized by a predominantly Eastern gaze focused on China."[64] Through multi-faceted art genres: miniature paintings, portraiture in traditional Renaissance oil painting, bronze medallions, tiles, calligraphy and architecture, the sultan, therefore, actively engaged with diverse artistic traditions while fashioning his public and dynastic image on the reconstructed stage of his new imperial capital. Like his Central Asian predecessor Timur, Mehmed II achieved this, firstly, by encouraging foreign artisans to come to his capital—not only from the East but from the West as well. This suggests that not only the Timurid Renaissance but also that of Italy would become catalysts for the further development of the Ottoman Renaissance.

Just as his Turkic predecessor Timur had transported artisans from conquered territories in Azerbaijan, Iran, Egypt, Syria, Anatolia, and India to Samarkand, so too did Mehmed II, mirroring his grandfather's practice. This included inviting artists from Italy and Flanders. Muslims, Christian converts to Islam, and talented individuals from East and West flocked to the city. They came willingly or by force or invitation after their territories fell to the Ottomans. Mehmed II also took a considerable interest in his dealings with the cultural elements of Latin Europe, communicating with rulers, scholars, artists and engineers. These included the Florentine Medici family and Leonardo da Vinci who worked on the initial designs of the Galata Bridge project on the Bosphorus. Mehmed II also built up a collection of Western engravings, statues, and paintings and employed Gentile Bellini and Constanza da Ferrara in Istanbul from 1479 to 1481.

Mehmed II equally supported the influence of the East, employing Mamluk scholars from Egypt and Syria and paying a pension to the foremost Persian poet Jami (1414–92) of 1000 gold pieces each year. Mehmed II also supported artists and intellectuals from the Timurid Sultanate in Persia and Central Asia. From Tabriz, he brought Mufti Fahred-Din to be appointed as Sheyh ul-Islam, the chief of religious affairs, and the scholar Hussain. The scholar Ali el-Fenari who trained in Herat (Afghanistan), Samarkand, and Persia followed. In 1472, Mehmed II also brought to Istanbul the Sufi master Alaed-Din et Tusi from Khorasan (Iran), and Alaed-Din Ali, who was the astronomer and mathematician to Ulugh Bey (Timur's grandson). Alaed-Din Ali arrived with a retinue of 200, from the court of Uzun Hassan of the Aq Quyunlu Turkmen (the "White Sheep Turkmen"), paving the way for the intellectual and artistic revival of the Ottomans.[65] These individuals left not only written works but also illustrated scrolls in the palace library collection, thus influencing the *nakkashane* artists in the Timurid–Persian tradition. Circulation of such works signifies "social, economic or political processes [that] are shaping that movement."[66] This view is further supported by Necipoğlu's and Payne's assertion that circulation of objects mediates "transcultural exchanges" and "decorated artifacts often become extensions of selfhood."[67] In the context of Mehmed II's Renaissance self-fashioning, the availability of these works contributed first by augmenting his political image as a universal sovereign to different audiences in the East and West. Second, their circulation contributed socially by bolstering his image at home as the all-powerful Muslim ruler of the dynasty. Finally, the works contributed to his goal of self-aggrandisement.

The patronage of Mehmed II

Both local and foreign artists played a crucial role in articulating Mehmed II's vision of his world empire. The cultivation of heterogeneous visual mediums—Ottoman, Timurid–Turkmen, and Roman–Byzantine—resonated with the cultural pluralism of the sultan's imperial capital Istanbul. Thus, the two worlds of East and West met at the ateliers of the Topkapı Palace, forging and reshaping the imperial image of the post-1453 Ottoman world. The availability of numerous works at the sultan's scriptorium provided the artists with the impetus needed to propel this budding cultural rebirth into its next phase.

Mehmed II's interaction with the Timurid East did not completely dissipate, however. He would use this as well as the techniques learned from the Italian masters at court to create distinct Ottoman hybrid works of art, including portrait painting and bronze medallions, to bolster his image among both Eastern and Western audiences.[68] On the one hand, Mehmed II needed to project himself as the powerful Turkic leader to his kinsmen in the East to bolster the cultural greatness of his dynasty. On the other hand, he needed art to propagate his image in the West to legitimise his position as the "caesar" of the Roman Empire.

To achieve his objectives, Mehmed II firstly relied on Eastern forms of visual expression to represent himself as an "ideal" Turkic ruler like Timur. A Timurid illustrated genealogical scroll (c. 1405–09) at the Topkapı Palace served as a model for the *nakkashhane* artists. The scroll contains depictions of enthroned royal men and women. These images depict the individual Timurid royals in various three-quarter views, portrayed either cross-legged, kneeling sideways on both knees or, in other portraits, with their feet on the floor. Some of the figures are shown holding or wearing emblems of power and authority: handkerchiefs, flowers, a dagger, sword, shield, bow, quiver, arrow, mace, belt, and various headgear.[69]

One of the rare miniature paintings that merges Timurid and Italian conventions depicts Mehmed II smelling a rose. The painting, dated c. 1480 and attributed to Sinan Bey and his assistant Sibilzade Ahmed, demonstrates the undeniable influence of the Timurid style on Ottoman sultanic portraiture. Mehmed II was a contemporary of Sultan Husayn Mirza Bayqara of Herat, a Timurid ruler from 1469–1506, and Mehmed

II's portrait bears a resemblance to representations of his Central Asian counterpart produced in the Timurid iconographic tradition. Painted around the same time, Mehmed II is shown holding a handkerchief in his left hand and smelling a rose with the other. On the little finger of his right hand he is wearing a stone-mounted ring which is complemented by an archer's thumb ring. This detail bears similarities to a portrait of Sultan Husayn by Bihzad (c. 1480–90), a contemporary central Asian artist. In Bihzad's portrait the sultan is also depicted holding a rose in one hand; in another representation the monarch is seen wearing a thumb ring. The ring is an allusion to the military achievements of both sovereigns. Mehmed II's portrait) shows him in a wrapped turban, typical of scholars, unlike Husayn Bayqara's portrait in which the sultan is seen without the royal aigrette (figs. 4.20c-d).[70] This genre of Ottoman portraiture continued well into the sixteenth century and beyond. This reflects the desire of the Ottomans to connect to the Timurid legacy by appropriating the Central Asian tradition, further solidifying his legitimacy and sovereignty.

Furthermore, Italianate influence is also marked in Mehmed II's portrait commissions. Mehmed II brought Gentile Bellini of Venice and Costanzo da Ferrara from Italy to paint his portrait in the Renaissance style and create bronze medallions of him in the style of ancient Rome medallions.[71] Both the princes of Italy and the Ottoman monarch demonstrate a penchant for adopting this ancient custom (fig. 4.21). Mehmed II's attempt to create culturally hybrid art works is evident by examples of Timurid miniature paintings on paper that also employ conventions of Italian realism. The sultan's face resembles Bellini's oil painting, while his seated body conforms to the Timurid iconographic tradition. Such hybrid elements represent the desire of Mehmed II and subsequent sultans to articulate a unique Ottoman idiom in portraiture painting that would stand out from both Timurid and Western prototypes. These portrait paintings of Mehmed II were executed at the Topkapı Palace towards the end of the sultan's reign by both the invited Italian artists and Ottoman court painters trained by their Western counterparts. The portraits speak to both Eastern and Western audiences, although, as Rose points out, "different audiences interpret the same visual images in different ways." [72] Bellini's use of Latin inscriptions in the painting made it more accessible to European audiences, augmenting the sultan's image in the Latin

West. Sinan Bey and Ahmed's portrait of Mehmed II smelling a rose, on the other hand, appealed to the Ottoman court elites who had access to it at the palace and reinforced the self-consciousness of the dynasty in bolstering its image as the "ideal" Turkic ruler by depicting him sitting with his knees bent.

Cultural hybridity did not work in just one direction. The sultan's message had consequences in Italy, too. Duke Federico III of Montefeltro of Urbino (1442–82) specifically asked his Dalmatian architect Luciano to emulate the grand style of the Topkapı Place.[73] As a Renaissance humanist who kept a private scriptorium and had copyists and editors, the Duke also represented justice and stability for his small state. By emulating Mehmed II's palace, the Duke was associating himself with the symbolism of a sultan whose similar interests in the classics and Western aesthetics were known in Italy. Figure 4.22a depicts the similarities in the arcaded courtyards of the Topkapı Palace with that of the Palazzo Ducale in Urbino. Both colonnaded central courtyards are a triumph in the revival of classical architecture of the middle to late fifteenth century (figs. 4.22a-b). Similarly, Mehmed II's Topkapı Palace in Istanbul "[. . .] . . . was closer to the modular planning of courts in contemporary Italian designs [. . .]" where "[t]he buttressing is also shown on an elevation drawn on Italian Renaissance designs."[74] Çiğdem Kafesçioğlu notes that the Ottoman ruling elite's preoccupation with the classical past signalled the emergence of an imperial identity.[75] She asserts that Mehmed II's New Palace (i.e. Topkapı Palace), situated in a prominent position of the peninsula with its courtyards and kiosks, is assimilated into the classical environs of the Hagia Sophia and the Roman/Byzantine Hippodrome, thus introducing the new imperial Ottoman visual vocabulary and merging it with its shared classical heritage.[76] Furthermore, she stresses that, "[i]f architecture was part and parcel of the making of the imperial state and the site from which it ruled, simultaneously entailing the appropriation . . . of the Byzantine past, so too the construction of a new image of Constantinople was an essential aspect of the making of the imperial capital."[77] Moreover, to bolster his claim as the ruler of the city, Mehmed II's building of the Rumeli Fortress at the narrowest point of the Bosphorus during the conquest of Istanbul in 1453 served as a strategic point, according to Kafesçioğlu, "indicat[ing] that Constantinople was now completely under the command of its new rulers."[78]

These Renaissance intercultural exchanges created hybrid art works that connected the Ottomans to the Latin West. They added weight to the influence of cross-cultural activities and the legacy of Ottoman cultural revival, thus contributing to the fluidity of the age. Although Mehmed II's Western-facing aesthetic is more powerfully articulated than that of any previous Ottoman ruler, driven by his self-styled identity as a new Roman, his attachment to his Eastern heritage and the traditions begun at Bursa and Edirne were nurtured as significant elements of his self-fashioning.

As a patron of the arts Mehmed II also left a powerful architectural legacy. In 1471 he commissioned the first imperial mosque, the Fatih Camii, in the style of the Hagia Sophia but with the hope of surpassing it. According to the fifteenth-century historian Tursun Beg, " . . . he [Mehmed II] built a great mosque based on the design of Hagia Sophia *(Ayasofya karnamesi resminde),* which not only encompassed all the arts of Hagia Sophia, but in addition incorporated modern features constituting a fresh new idiom *(tasarrufat-i muta'ahhirin uzre nev-i sive-i taze)* unequalled in beauty *(husn).*"[79] Tursun Beg's account suggests that the Fatih Camii was a modernised reinterpretation of a sixth-century Byzantine model whose selectively repeated features were amalgamated with Ottoman and Islamic forms. Such innovative practices as the symmetrical layout of the complex were, according to Necipoğlu, "[. . .] inspired by Italian Renaissance theories of ideal planning."80 Tursun Beg's statement resonates with Vasari's description of Bramante (1444–1514) as an architect who translated the past into modern idiom through new inventions: "While the Greeks invented architecture and the Romans imitated them, Bramante not only added new inventions, but greatly increased the beauty and difficulty of the art, to an extent we now perceive."81

Mehmed II sought to take the achievements made in Edirne with the Üç Şerefeli Mosque to the next level. With the Hagia Sophia now firmly in his possession, the structure could be closely studied and scrutinised by his engineers. His Fatih complex consisted of eight madrasahs, the prayer hall, a courtyard and a garden, his mausoleum and a 26-metre diameter dome with a height of 44 metres, surpassing that of the Üç Şerefeli Mosque.82 Mehmed II's patronage of the Fatih Mosque complex had its connections to Renaissance urban architecture. Kafesçioğlu states that Mehmed II's patronage of building projects following the conquest of the city in 1453 demonstrates the "[. . .] interaction between the Byzantine and Ottoman urban and architectural traditions, on the one hand, and the Renaissance ideas of ordering the urban environment, on the other."83 Furthermore, by the end of Mehmed II's rule in 1481, ". . . the space of the city was transformed through a large-scale urban project that had its roots in Ottoman, Byzantine, and Italian urban practices [. . .]."84

Unfortunately, not being able to surpass the dome of the Hagia Sophia's 31-metre diameter dome with a height of 56 metres, the efforts to surpass the past had to wait until the engineering achievements of Sinan a century later. The attempt, although unable to surpass the past, nevertheless reflects the sultan's Renaissance mindset. Such efforts show his desire to push technological boundaries to attain the "ideal" by attempting to surpass past exemplars. Mehmed II's efforts reflect Andrew Glencross's observation that "history challenges the present's ability to represent the past by seeking to uncover the signs, symbols and even language that enable us to make sense of the past in its own terms as well as how these same elements have been used to represent a particular version of the past."[85] Although the dome of the Fatih Mosque did not match the size of the Hagia Sophia—a sore spot for Mehmed II—for one hundred years its dome remained the largest ever built by the Ottomans and stood as a testament to Mehmed II's power and wealth.[86] The original mosque was badly damaged in the 1506 earthquake and was then finally destroyed in the earthquake of 1766. Thus, the sixteenth-century engravings of Melchior Lorichs provide important evidence regarding its design, indicating a drum carrying a dome[87] (fig. 4.23). Cornelius Gurlitt considered the mosque a monument with a Renaissance spirit built at a time when no such grand structures were constructed in Italy.[88] Despite Mehmed II's disappointment with his mosque, it must be stressed that the fifteenth-century building represents the first monumental central-plan structure constructed after Roman/Byzantine structures in Istanbul. With this complex, Mehmed II, according to Necipoğlu is "credited with launching in Istanbul a renaissance of antique architecture parallel to that of Rome."[89]

In 1473 Mehmed II turned his attention to other works. He embarked on three simultaneous building projects in the gardens of the Topkapı Palace, which he had just completed. These projects would see his vision of universal rule come to fruition and represent, through architectural symbolism, the cultural cosmopolitanism of his empire. His desire to unify the cultures of East and West would see him build three pavilions in different styles: classical Greek, Timurid–Persian, and Turkish.[90] Following the conquest of Otranto (Italy) in 1480, Mehmed II also planned to build a European style pavilion to commemorate this event, "which he believed was only the overture to the conquest of Italy," and invited Venetian and Florentine painters to assist Gentile Bellini who was staying at the Topkapı Palace at the time.[91] Mehmed II's death the following year, however, prevented this from coming to fruition. This desire to unite the cultures of the world under the Ottoman banner resonates in the biography of Mehmed II written by Greek biographer Kritovoulos, who wrote that Mehmed II saw himself as the next Alexander the Great who would unite the peoples of the East and West.[92] Constantinople was already his, a powerful trophy. As Warwick Ball rightly acknowledges, "No other city in world history has bridged so many civilizations, nor has brought so many cultures together."[93] With an imperial capital in his possession, Mehmed II needed to reflect through his patronage the elevated status of his dynasty.

Unfortunately, of the three pavilions only the Çinili Köşk in the Timurid–Persian style survives (fig. 4.24a). The significance of this building demonstrates the importance of Timurid visual tastes once again in the Ottomans' representation of imperial power. This is more significant at this stage of the expansion of Ottoman power, when they had come into possession of the former Roman city of Constantinople. Ownership of this city reinforces not only the continuing imperial legacy of the Romans, but also that of the Timurid imperial legacy of the East. With the other two lost works, the combination of the three pavilions would come to symbolise Mehmed II's rule over the two continents, as well as express that the Ottomans' Iranian and Central Asian heritage was as important as the much-trumpeted connections to the Latin West. The synthesis of these allegorical readings complements the accolade for which Mehmed II is renowned—the Fatih or the Conqueror.

The architect Kemal ed-Din, whose ethnicity is unknown, had been trained in the Timurid–Persian architectural style designed and built the pavilion on the grounds of the Topkapı Palace. Mehmed II set out to consciously construct his "utopian" vision through his new palace overlooking the Sea of Marmara and the Bosphorus. By positioning his palace where two continents meet, Mehmed, like Alexander, would seek to unite the cultures of the world. The new palace was within a short walking distance of the Old Palace that had served as the residence of the Roman/Byzantine emperors. To achieve Mehmed II's vision, the palace was to involve three different construction styles. A closer look at the design and decorations of ceramic tiles in the Çinili Köşk or the Faience (Tiled) Pavilion reveals it is in the Timurid–Persian style. The Çinili Köşk consists of a square plan, with stairs to the lower floor, open *iwans,* and royal apartments and a central throne room.

The Köşk served as a palace pavilion and the residence for both the Sultan and the Grand Vizier when not on campaign. It was built before the main royal entrance to the Topkapı Palace. The Çinili Köşk is built on two levels; the Sultan occupied the upper floor, the Grand Vizier the lower level, demonstrating a clear hierarchy of power. A staircase on either side allowed access to the two floors. Built from stone-framed brick in the traditional Eastern manner, it measures 32 by 34 metres and its facade is lined with a row of 14 polygonal pillars with Timurid-style pointed arches. Under a tiled arch is the massive entrance door of the *piano nobile* which leads to the vestibule and then to the covered court, beyond which is the central room of the royal apartments (figs. 4.24b-c). From the exterior, the physical structure of the building looks Timurid in style, but there are subtle elements that make it uniquely Ottoman. For example, the balcony railings at the base of the columns on the second floor and the arches of the first floor supported by square columns are decorated in the distinct Bursa arch style.

The decorative aesthetics of the building further demonstrate a connection to the earlier Bursa tradition. This is visible in the inscriptions at the entrance to the pavilion. While the high crown arch dominating the entrance is decorated with large *kufic* inscriptions, the framed white Ottoman *thuluth* inscriptions above the entrance door resemble those of Tabriz and Samarkand. The seventh century *kufic* lettering and the contemporary Ottoman *thuluth* styles mediate between past and present. The inscription in cut tile work in the ceiling of the *iwan* is written in Arabic in *Haliki* script and reads *tawakkaltu 'ala'llah* (I place my trust-reliance in God). These inscriptions are mirrored twice on either side. The inscriptions around the outer face of this *iwan* repeat the name "Allah' 'Akbar" (God The Great) seven times and Muhammad and Ali four times, all in Arabic and *Makili* script. There are two interspersed cartouches containing the Muslim profession of faith "*Lailahe illa'llah Muhammed Resul Allah*" (there is no god but God and Muhammad is His messenger) in *Jeli-thuluth* script, one on either side of the *iwan*. The long inscription in Persian that runs above the door is in two parts and written in two different scripts, *Muhakkak* and *Jeli-thuluth*. The first inscription compares the Sultan's kiosk to the "Gate of Heaven," "as honorable as the Kaaba," its entrance "auspicious," and the pavilion is the "adornment of the earth."[94]

The second part of the inscription provides significant insights into the Ottoman understanding of astronomy and astrology and their symbolisms to define and represent the authority of the sultan. The inscription reads:

> The building of this palace pavilion was constructed so beautifully that, due to its quality, it seems to surround the waist and belt of Gemini. The lowest part bestows honour to the top of Ferkadan (The stars Ursae Minoris) and to the roof (the celestial sphere) of Saturn. The dome of emerald (Heaven's mansion and the dome of the Köşk) has become precious (decorated) with the constellations of the stars. Its floor, which looks like turquoise, like the gardens of paradise, with its various types of flowers and scintillating embroidery of designs. With the power of the Sultanate's good fortune and highness (authority) and with the mighty help and augury of God, this building has the honour of being completed at the end of the year 877 (1472/3), as buildings always record the help of their patrons (constructors).[95]

These two Persian inscriptions, characteristic of many building inscriptions, in their allegorical form and style, draw our attention to the pavilion as symbolic of the celestial spheres, of the Moon, of Saturn, and of the constellations. Mehmed II, as the patron of the building, seeks to articulate and reinforce that his authority and legitimacy in this world come from the Almighty Creator. He does this in part through the use of astronomy and astrology and in part through the religious inscriptions on the façade of this harmoniously balanced and highly symbolic palace pavilion. The pavilion, then, is the microcosm of the macrocosm—Mehmed II is God's legitimate ruler on earth.

While Turkish remained the language of government bureaucracy and the vernacular of everyday use, the reliance on Persian inscriptions reflects the literary significance and sophistication of the language at the court of Mehmed II. Like the use of Latin in the West, the use of Persian in scholarship and decorative art retained its prominence in the Islamic world. As Persian was also the court language of the Seljuks and the Timurids, from the universal ruler's point of view, the reliance on Persian in literary and artistic creations suggests its collective appeal to Eastern imperial court cultures, including the Ottomans, allowing Mehmed II to legitimise his rule and to integrate the East into his realm from the symbolic location of Istanbul.

The tiles of the Çinili Köşk, however, differ from those of the styles and the *cuerda seca* technique introduced by the "Masters of Tabriz" in Bursa and Edirne. The absence of the *cuerda seca* in the Çinili Köşk suggests the tiles are related to the fifteenth-century Chinese blue and white porcelain in pottery, suggesting different artists' crafts at the Köşk and a slow progression in the rebirth phase in early modern Ottoman art. The colours green, turquoise blue, and black in tile revetments reappear from the Bursa and Edirne traditions. In keeping with those traditions they are made up of hexagons and triangles. The evidence of connections with past traditions as well as openness to new visual mediums produce a unique aesthetic in the Çinili Köşk. The structure indicates the slow transition from the rebirth phase to a more distinct Ottoman visual vocabulary, much bolder and more emphatic. The grand main entrance is decorated in blue and white tiling with Qur'anic inscriptions, further denoting Mehmed II's grand ambitions. Whereas his grandfather Mehmed I's legacy was only of uniting the Ottomans, Mehmed II aimed at world domination, where all cultures lived under his rule. And as the ruler of both the East and West, the sultan wanted to replicate the Roman and Cengiz Khanid concepts of a universal state. For Mehmed II, the Çinili Köşk represented the power of the Ottoman state in its absolutist form. This absolutist ideology—that God conferred on the dynasty its universal sovereignty and authority—reinforces Mustafa Ali's idea in *The Essence of History* when Ali describes absolutism as a Turco–Mongol belief. This belief is reinforced by the Qur'anic inscriptions at the entrance.[96] The art and architecture of the Çinili Köşk evoke these Renaissance mindsets.

The geometric patterns emerging from the circle are the triangle, square, and hexagon, thus forming the three fundamental figures of Islamic art. Their symbolic meaning dates to pre-Islamic traditions found in Hinduism, Buddhism, and Judaism. The hexagon became the manifestation of paradise and its reflection on earth. That is, it represents the divine and its reflection in creation, and of the connection between heaven and earth, between the macrocosm and the microcosm, and between spirit and matter. The allegorical reading of the pavilion's geometric aesthetics connects science, astronomy, cosmology, astrology, and religion. They symbolise Mehmed II's desire to unify diverse cultures of the world under his domain. The Çinili Köşk, therefore, metaphorically becomes Mehmed II's earthly paradise. However, his emulation of Timurid aesthetics also proclaims a much larger political message. Echoing Ali's continual praise of the greatness and magnificence of the Timurid court, the Ottoman rulers sought to imitate this in order to augment their power and prestige in the Turkic and Islamic world. Mehmed II's predecessor Mehmed I had proclaimed the rebirth of the Ottoman state to Timur's son and heir Shahrukh, and had commissioned his mosque and mausoleum in Bursa in the Timurid style. In the same way, through the Ottoman hybrid work in the Çinili Köşk with its emulation of the Central Asian model, Mehmed II declared to the world in 1473 from his imperial capital in the Eastern Roman Empire that he alone was the "universal" ruler and representative of the Turkic and Muslim peoples of the East.

Furthermore, the symbolism of the geometric patterns at the Çinili Köşk allow for an alternative reading. The triangular tiles represent the harmony and unity established by Mehmed II after his conquest of Constantinople, and the hexagon signifies his universal sovereignty of the two continents (fig. 4.25). These tiles are stencilled with flowing gold patterns of interlacing leaves and blooming flowers, with clouds bordered by a cartouche-filled floral garden. As Titus Burckhardt argues, "[i]nterlacement represents the most direct expression of the idea of Divine Unity underlying the inexhaustible variety of the world."[97] The floral imagery is an early Ottoman representation of paradise in Istanbul. These esoteric expressions of paradise would manifest in the artistic explosion of the sixteenth century during the Süleymanic Age under Sinan.

Çinili Köşk is clearly an adaptation of recent past precedents of the Seljuk–Timurid–Persian and even Mughal traditions. Following the traditional Timurid centralised plan, dome and *iwan,* the Çinili Köşk is decorated in Persian *saz* scroll style, also known as the *resm-i sazi* style. This is applied to the arched spaces of the domed chamber, the *iwan*, and to the passages. In its centralised plan, the *iwans* and the decorative motifs of the Çinili Köşk present a uniquely Ottoman style, although adapted from the East. This Ottoman pavilion inspired from the Timurid aesthetic style of architecture looks to the great Seljuk period of the eleventh to the thirteenth centuries, where excavated buildings at Merv in Central Asia show a similar architectural style carried into Anatolia by the Seljuks. The geometric patterns, including hexagons and triangles of the tile décor, is reflected in buildings found in central Anatolia and in Samarkand: in the Karatay Madrasah of 1251 in Konya, central Anatolia, as well as in those completed in Samarkand in 1404 by Bibi Hatun (wife of Timur) and the Koca Abdi Darum mosques (figs. 4.26a-d). W. R. Lethaby has suggested that this centralised plan is also seen in Fatihpur Sikri, the city of the Mughal ruler Akbar, where the sultan's throne is placed in the centre of the four cardinal points to symbolise Akbar as the Vicegerent of Vishnu. The octagonal dome of the throne room represents the wheel of the Law of Akbar.[98] Later examples that continue this Central Asian–Timurid–Persian tradition and demonstrate Çinili Köşk-inspired features include the Hoca Ahrar Mescit at Samarkand of 1640 (rebuilt in 1910), the Safavid Chilhil Sutun or "The 40 Columns" at Isfahan, Persia of 1647, and two eighteenth-century mosques, the Khidr Mosque in Samarkand and the Hoca Zayned-Din Mosque in Bukhara. The latter's square central domed plan, ten slender columns and frontal *iwans*, clearly resemble elements of the Çinili Köşk (figs. 4.27a-e).

In conclusion, the conquest of Constantinople by Mehmed II in 1453 encouraged the sultan's desire to unify the East and West. His patronage of architecture and decorative arts included the Çinili Köşk (1473) in the Timurid–Persian style. Looking west, the sultan brought Gentile Bellini and Costanzo da Ferrara from Italy to paint his portrait and create bronze medallions of him. By training the *nakkashane* artists at his court in the "Renaissance" tradition, the Italian masters contributed to the palace artists producing portraits that fuse Eastern and Western traditions, making them uniquely Ottoman in style. The result of these two shared traditions in the post-1453 period emphasises Mehmed II's symbolic political message that he was the legitimate leader of both the Islamic East and Christian West, governing from the former capital of the Eastern Roman Empire, Constantinople. Furthermore, drawing on Rose's notion of the social modality of audiencing, it can be argued that through the circulation of these transportable visual productions Mehmed II was able to manipulate different audiences and their perceptions of him.

These complexes and artworks are thus among the first to demonstrate the combined influence of Timurid–Persian and Western influences on Ottoman art as it moves towards a unified articulation of style in the triumphant phase of the next century. The significance of the impact of these works is the culturally inclusive nature of the evolution of Ottoman visual tastes before the sixteenth century. By laying claim to the Timurid legacy from his own imperial capital that geographically and historically united East and West, the patronage of Mehmed II forged a more culturally inclusive style of Ottoman art in the second half of the fifteenth century. Tapping into the Ottomans' shared Eastern and Western cultural heritage, Mehmed II's patronage paved the way for its triumphant phase in the coming century. Mehmed II's patronage, which mediated between the two worlds, recalls Lowenthal's words: "We shape our heritage to make it attractive in modern terms; we seek to make it part of ourselves, and ourselves part of it; we conform it to our self-image and aspirations."[99] From 1413 the Ottomans embarked on an artistic transformation to mold and shape their culture to suit their self-image. From a minor principality on the northwestern shores of Anatolia in the thirteenth century they established three capitals: Bursa, Edirne, and Istanbul. By looking to the past for inspiration from both the East and West, they created innovative artworks, sometimes similar, other times more refined, culminating in a distinct narrative of the Ottoman Renaissance. Their ability to borrow from other cultures and conform to their self-image and aspirations triggered their own symbolic rebirth, which began in fifteenth-century Bursa and Edirne.

The art works in the traditions of Bursa, Edirne, and early Istanbul have shown that these creations are not mere cultural borrowings. In this nascent revival the Ottomans not only saw the East as their connection to their ancestral past but also claimed a Western legacy as well. Artists in the Latin West related their rebirth to claims of a cultural legacy with ancient Greece and Rome. Similarly, the Turks saw their cultural Renaissance as dating back beyond classical antiquity. From their origins in the nomadic steppes and throughout their history, they moved westward, adapted to historical conditions, converted to Islam and assimilated into different cultural groups from Iran and the Arab world, until they finally settled in the former lands of the Romans. Historically speaking, the experiences of the fifteenth century demonstrate "[the] critical articulation of historical consciousness [that has] contribute[d] to the skill of demarcation and the assertion of [the Ottomans'] own interests."[100] This articulation demonstrates the inevitability of a Renaissance of a different kind, one that conflated both East and West in ways that exemplified the specifically Ottoman experience.[101] It is to this multifaceted period that the Ottomans looked for artistic inspiration, and for defining the legitimacy of their power, and to which sixteenth-century Ottoman historians and intellectuals like Mustafa Ali and Sinan refer. Both Ali and Sinan reject the idea of Ottoman artistic expression as merely imitating the past. Reinforcing Madison's words, they are "revisioning an object, idea," and creating a different version from the original under a different historical, political, and geographical context.[102] These visual expressions signify Ottoman receptions of cross-cultural practices. Appropriation constituted not only a challenge but also a culturally compatible point of intersection for highly diverse discourses that both defended and confirmed distinctly harmonious modes of representation. Fifteenth-century cultural practices from Bursa to Istanbul, and the sixteenth-century reception of Sinan, provided the circumstances for the cultural appropriation of Timurid–Persian–Islamic and Roman/Byzantine artistic conventions, epitomising the strength of the links between the past and reinvented present.

In this way, the trajectory of style envisioned by Vasari manifested in sixteenth-century Ottoman art during the Süleymanic Age, as Sinan and his artists learned to accomplish ideal beauty by refining the deficiencies of previous models from the Roman/Byzantine tradition. By appropriating the Christian Emperor Justinian's basilica, the Hagia Sophia, into an Ottoman–Islamic setting, Sinan created a distinctly Ottoman Renaissance architectural medium in two of his monumental works: the Süleymaniye and the Selimiye imperial mosques.

CHAPTER FIVE

OTTOMAN ARCHITECTURE: SURPASSING THE PAST

The idea of progress is identifiable in Sinan's autobiographies, wherein he sees architectural history as a mirror of the development of civilization.[1] Participating in Renaissance discourses of stylistic development, Sinan praises his own creations, talents, and the greater aesthetic refinement, which he sees as culminating in his own works.[2] Sinan describes his works as featuring more stable domes built in a shorter period of time reflecting the magnificence of the Ottoman dynasty.[3] Sinan's aim was to improve on past exemplars, such as the sixth-century Hagia Sophia in Istanbul and the fifteenth-century Üç Şerefeli Mosque in Edirne. Sinan's engagement with the past is apparent in his words: "I acquired a sought-after bit of wisdom from the crenellation of great ancient remains and a provision of knowledge from every ruined monument."[4] This dialogue with the past is a hallmark of the Renaissance and reflects Sinan's concern with finding a solution to structural problems; he refines past models with the aim of creating an architectural idiom that represents the sultanate. Sinan's quest to surpass the past is best seen in his two major accomplishments of the period: the Süleymaniye Mosque (1557–58) in Istanbul and the Selimiye Mosque of Selim II (1575) in Edirne. These constructions demonstrate the Renaissance ideals of *tecdid*, *ihtira*, and *sûret*. Furthermore, in line with Vasari's ideas of stylistic development, Sinan set out with his competitive spirit to surpass the works of the past and, in the process, created an original architectural synthesis of Roman/Byzantine and Islamic, that can be interpreted as distinctly Ottoman.[5]

After the conquest of Constantinople, the distinct style of Ottoman architecture was slowly consolidated, particularly in the cases of the Süleymaniye Mosque and the Selimiye Mosque. In these works, mosque architects adopted the vocabulary of Roman/Byzantine architecture and modified it to suit Islamic prayer practices by producing a centralised planned structure. To develop a centralised plan, buildings isolated in the centre of a town square were raised on a platform to elevate their majesty. Sinan utilised these Renaissance architectural and aesthetic rules to define his distinctive style.

As mentioned in the previous chapters, the fusion of Eastern and Western stylistic elements after 1453 was an essential ingredient of Ottoman self-fashioning. Focusing only on the similarities between Ottoman and Roman/Byzantine architecture, especially on the reuse of half domes in the Hagia Sophia, nineteenth- and twentieth-century scholars saw the work of Sinan, the chief imperial architect, as mere imitation of precedent.[6] Other early twentieth-century architectural historians denied the influence of Byzantine precedents on Ottoman architecture entirely, citing instead its original Turkish style.[7] However, what is missing from these competing viewpoints is the recognition that the Ottoman Empire was not only heir to past Islamic civilizations of the East, but also to the Eastern Roman Empire after the capture of Constantinople in 1453.

A century of experimentation by Ottoman architects that began in Edirne had, by the middle of the sixteenth century, created a distinctly Ottoman style. In his autobiographies Sinan mentions over four hundred works constructed under his guidance within an expanding empire. Through these, Sinan transformed the early modern Ottoman architectural idiom. These works also show Sinan's progressive and global perspective. He was on the verge of looking not only for excellence but also something original that surpassed the past. Interpreting Ottoman mosque architecture from an understanding of the definition of the Renaissance allows for clarification of the originality of Ottoman style without ignoring the influence of Roman/Byzantine heritage. Analysing the spatiality of the Süleymaniye Mosque and the Selimiye Mosque allows us to better understand the Ottomans' historical consciousness and self-fashioning. This chapter will argue that Sinan used past precedents to reinforce the sultan's emergent global identity. One element of this progress is, as in the Florentine or Roman Renaissance narrative, using burgeoning ideas that originated in Edirne with the Üç Şerefeli Mosque and surpassing the past (both ancient and recent). In this way Sinan's imperial mosques project a powerful identity onto the empire of Süleyman the Magnificent.

For Mehmed II, Süleyman the Magnificent, and Selim II, respectively, emulating the Hagia Sophia meant legitimising their imperial status. For these three rulers, the architecture of the Hagia Sophia signalled their visions of imperial, universal power. Emulating the Hagia Sophia—a structure that represented the past and present for the Ottomans—was a statement of their victory over Christianity and the West, especially for Mehmed II who claimed to have inherited the Roman heritage of the caesars. The synthesis of Roman and Islamic styles allowed these sultans to straddle both regions and declare themselves universal rulers. The Ottoman sultans became self-conscious of their approach to self-fashioning in order to demonstrate the greatness of the Empire and the magnificence of the court. This construction of sultanic identity manifested in Mehmed II's projects, especially in the appropriation of the new and distinctive (foreign) Roman past in a post-conquest context. Furthermore, Süleyman, building on his great grandfather's successes, saw himself as a messianic savior of the world. In this way the legitimacy of his self-fashioning as the new "Emperor of Rome" from his capital, the "New Rome" (Istanbul), would be cemented. Selim II could not match the political and military achievements of his father (Süleyman the Magnificent) and great grandfather (Mehmed II).

Selim II desired to represent himself apart from the shadows of these two great Ottoman rulers and so built his imperial mosque in Edirne. Even for a weak ruler like Selim II, emulating the Hagia Sophia was equally important because, perhaps even more than his predecessors, he needed to justify his claim to universal sovereignty. But he wanted the buildings of his era to be distinct from the structures built by his post-1453 predecessors in Edirne at that time. Thus, the Hagia Sophia aesthetic was useful, giving birth to a new style of Ottoman imperial mosques that expressed visually a dialectic connection between the past and present through a unique stylistic synthesis.

As a result, the imperial symbolism of the Roman/Byzantine tradition and the physical significance of this building continued to drive the historical consciousness of the Ottomans. The fact that they did not destroy the Hagia Sophia after 1453 reaffirmed Ottoman claims that they were the "true" inheritors to the Roman legacy. The conversion of the Hagia Sophia into a mosque by Mehmed II in 1453 equally served as a reminder of Islam's triumph over Christianity. This dialogue with the classical Roman past became an integral part of Sinan's intent to surpass the ancient masterpiece. If the Hagia Sophia were surpassed, this would confirm not only the superiority of Ottoman civilization over Roman civilization but also symbolise the superiority of Islam over Christianity. This way of framing the world was common in the pre-modern era.

Furthermore, as Vasari, Ali, and Sinan each attest, per the Renaissance mindset artists are seen as being singularly chosen by God to reveal snippets of the Hereafter to humanity. Influenced by Platonic ideals, both cultures perceived the mysteries of God's cosmos as being slowly revealed to humanity through (near)-perfect works of art. Both Augustine in *City of God against the Pagans* (426) and Rumi in the *Mesnevi* (1258–73) compare the idea of earthly life to a pilgrimage. For Augustine, God's perfection is seen in His eternity and timelessness, just like the works of art created by man: "It is the common judgement, then, of all creatures that live by reason that God is eternal. So let us consider the nature of eternity . . . Eternity, then, is the complete, simultaneous and perfect possession of everlasting life."[8] Similarly, for Rumi, the pilgrimage of life is an invitation to transcend beyond the ephemeral existence and realise what one's destination truly is.[9] Since the Eternal God is complete, works of art inspired by Vasari's "Divine Artist" and Sinan's "Peerless Artist" represent a minute component of that Eternity. Therefore, artworks as hints of cosmic perfection reveal to the earthly pilgrim the perfection of God.[10] Furthermore, from a Platonic perspective, these works of art demonstrate that the signs of God is not only ethical and rational in nature but also aesthetic. As a result, "[t]he Good, the True, and the Beautiful are effectively united in the supreme creative principle, at once commanding moral affirmation, intellectual allegiance, and aesthetic surrender."[11] Such works of art thus function as reminders that the ultimate goal of man is union with the Godhead in the hereafter—"to overcome the separation from the divine and become one with it."[12] From this Renaissance perspective, Sinan acknowledges the Divine inspiration in his works: "Think not that a word's effect derives from you! It derives from the One who made you speak that word."[13] Thus, the Süleymaniye and Selimiye mosques stand as signposts of the world to come.

The Hagia Sophia (537) and the Süleymaniye Mosque (1557)

Sinan's close relationship with his patron Sultan Süleyman is mentioned in his autobiography, *Tezkiretü'l-Bünyān*, written by the scribe-poet Mustafa Sa'i. Sinan's patron, who is idealised as the "Solomon of the age," commissioned five of the six major projects Sinan completed.[14] The architect proudly mentions his personal interactions with the sultan who honored him with private conversations at his workshop: "The felicitous padishah arrived while this humble servant . . . was in the marble workers' workshop designing and laying out the noble mihrab and exalted minbar."[15] Such conversations and visits suggest that Sinan would have gained real insight into both the Sultan's global aspirations and his need for the architectural projects to reflect this. Chosen as the chief architect to build Sultan Süleyman an imperial mosque, Sinan's autobiography describes this experience through a conversation that takes place in the setting of the Third Hill of Istanbul: "One morning, the idea of setting about the construction of an exalted Friday mosque entered the noble, auspicious heart of . . . His Majesty. He summoned his servant . . . to consult about the noble mosque, and the design of the building was settled upon and its location determined." [16] Here, the architectural dialogue with the Hagia Sophia and the Süleymaniye begins with the sultan's wishes to construct his mosque on the plan of Justinian's basilica.[17] According to Kuban,

> the half dome/central dome/half dome arrangement may be attributed to the Sultan's desire to create a mosque in the style of Ayasofya, which had never lost its importance in the eyes of the Ottoman sultans as a symbol of an ideal sovereignty. If it had been lost, it would have been demolished. The Sultan's wishes must have acted as a spur to Sinan, as architect, to rival an ancient masterpiece.[18]

This reflects the lure and magnificence of the Hagia Sophia and the Renaissance desire to surpass it. In this way the unique integration of past and present, East and West, and Islamic and Christian is born in the newly-emergent Ottoman design.

Sinan sets out to achieve this task by using the Hagia Sophia as a *nūmūne* (model) to create an original imperial mosque structure that would visually articulate his patron's greatness. Sinan saw building in the "Ayasōfya tarzı[nda]" ("Hagia Sophia style") as not merely an imitation of Roman/Byzantine structures but instead as a challenge to rival it.[19] He acknowledges being inspired by Roman/Byzantine structures and their large domes. In his autobiography Sinan states that "Ayasofya . . . [became] the model for the noble building complex [and mosque] of His Majesty Sultan Süleyman Khan—may he rest in peace."[20] After completion of the Süleymaniye, Sinan claims his work to be "superior to these [past] examples," and that the new mosque will serve as "a model for the world" to emulate and admire.[21] Like the Italian Renaissance architect Leon Battista Alberti's argument in his treatise *On the Art of Building* (1452) that, "Inspired by their example, we should strive to produce our own inventions, to rival, or, if possible, to surpass the glory of theirs [i.e. past exemplars]," Sinan eulogises his own inventions by proclaiming to the world his triumph over the past.[22] Furthermore, Sinan's competitive dialogue with the past is not unlike that of his Florentine counterpart Michelangelo who was employed to construct St. Peter's Basilica in Rome (1506–1626). He, like Sinan, was engaged in the reinterpretation of the past models such as the Pantheon temple in Rome.[23]

The close relationship between patron and client provided Sinan with access to not only the resources necessary to construct his monuments but also to the vast literary sources housed in Süleyman's scriptorium. This included the ancient Roman Vitruvius's *De Architectura* (original 31–15 BCE; 1521 Italian version translated by Cesare Cesariano), which inspired Italian Renaissance architecture. The Duke of Milan originally sent a Latin copy of this work to the Hungarian King Mathias Corvinus in the closing decades of the fifteenth century. After the Ottoman conquest of Hungary in 1526 the book entered Süleyman's library at the Topkapı Palace.[24] Although there is no direct evidence to suggest that Sinan read these texts, its probability cannot be discounted.[25] It was in the context of such works, the ancient ruins around Istanbul and Justinian's Hagia Sophia, that Sinan set out to transform Ottoman art with the aim of creating a new imperial identity.

Past domes as precedents

Sinan's desire to equal or even surpass the dome of the Hagia Sophia may have first taken shape in Edirne with the Üç Şerefeli Mosque and continued under Mehmed II in Istanbul in the fifteenth century. However, the fascination and preoccupation with domed architecture dates back to the Turkic beginnings of Central Asia. Domical buildings and structures had been integral elements of the Turks' architectural legacy. The Ottoman Turks, whose ancestors were the Oghuz Turks of Central Asia, believed that the round tent used in their nomadic culture symbolised heaven.[26] The description of heaven as a "canopy" became associated with domical structures. According to Theresa Grupico, domed structures such as the seventh-century Dome of the Rock (691 CE) in the Islamic tradition and the Church of the Holy Sepulchre (c. 325 CE) in the Christian tradition represented paradise, and are borrowings from earlier Persian models: "The Pantheon was itself the culmination of still earlier traditions. The dome, along with its more transient precursor the tent-canopy, was associated with the heavens in both the Hellenistic-Roman and Ancient Persian worlds."[27] With the birth of Islam in the seventh century and its expansion in the subsequent centuries to Christian geographical areas, the dome was assimilated into the vocabulary of Islamic religious architecture. In fact, throughout Islamic history, from the seventh-century Prophet's mosque in Medina to the Umayyad to the Abbasid periods (661–1258), many Islamic architectural structures adopted the square- and rectangle-based Abbasid model, including the Great Mosque in Khairouan (670 CE) in Tunisia, the Umayyad Mosque (715 CE) in Damascus, and the Ahmad Ibn Tulun Mosque (879 CE) in Cairo. Furthermore, the dome built on eight squinches is part of classical Islamic architectural practice and is seen, for example, in the Dome of the Rock in Jerusalem and in the Seljukid imperial tombs in Kharaqqan, Iran in 1067. Muslim architects also adopted Christian and other architectural variations of the dome, making the dome an integral element of their religious and political expressions. One example of such cultural fusion is the eighth-century Great Mosque of the Umayyad dynasty in Damascus, converted from a Christian church, which retained its typical Greco-Roman façade and its Byzantine dome. The history of the dome in the Roman and Islamic traditions indicates continuity in its development, which culminates in sixteenth-century Ottoman mosque architecture.

Sinan notes the significance of the symbolism of the dome and his desire to surpass past exemplars. For him, the "canopy-shaded" mosque and "pillared throne is a keepsake of a skilful master . . . Among the revolving spheres its like has not been seen nor shall it be seen."[28] The dome, suspended like the heavens, symbolised the divine right of the sultan's universal rule with God's guidance. For Sinan, the sultan was "a wise spiritual guide" and "heaven-dwelling hero" aided by God to vanquish his enemies in the East and West.[29] The "heaven-dome, sultan-dome" duality noted by Kuban reinforces Sinan's acknowledgement of Süleyman as " . . . the felicitous padishah, refuge of the world . . . like the sun that illumines the world."[30] Moreover, the sultan as the caliph figure (God's representative on earth and leader of the faithful) became more closely associated with the symbolism of the dome.[31] Thus, to reflect this imperial and religious status of the sultans, achieving a greater dome than that of the Hagia Sophia was paramount in Ottoman historical consciousness.

Importance and influence of the Hagia Sophia dome

During the Ottoman centuries the horizontal façade scheme was abandoned in favor of a vertical structure rising into the sky. The adoption of a domed roof, sometimes with a number of small half-domes, ascended to the central dome, producing a unique, sanctified space. The Hagia Sophia further influenced this development. Its ancient architects, Anthemius and Isidoros, combined a massive centralised space with a basilica plan in order to accommodate the Christian rites. The innovative style of the Hagia Sophia resulted in an enormous elliptical inner space featuring a main dome, which measures almost 31 metres in diameter, and two half domes whose diameters are almost equal to that of the central dome.

Consequently, the Hagia Sophia, whose inner space was greatly extended by the use of half domes, influenced the Ottomans in their experimentation with domical structures. When the Hagia Sophia fell to the Turks in 1453, its imperial and universal significance only strengthened the Ottoman Turks' resolve to first experiment with it and then surpass it. This demonstrates "the competitive attitude" of Ottoman architects and the inspiration it found in the Roman/Byzantine building.[32] According to Ihsan Mungan, the dome of the Hagia Sophia perplexed Ottoman architects. Apart from being impressed with the concepts of engineering and building such a structure, they showed a rather "skeptical approach to its antisymmetry in the substructure carrying the central dome" because, "[I]n the Turkish tradition[,] the dome had always been supported axisymmetrically or at least uniformly by means of four arches of the same rigidity in two perpendicular directions."[33] For this reason, Mungan continues, the Ottomans adopted the semi-dome "with highest caution and only gradually,"[34] reflecting the slow architectural progression that took over a century to accomplish.

The Süleymaniye complex

The Süleymaniye Mosque complex (*kulliye*) is more than a place of worship. The complex also includes a hospital, *imaret* (soup kitchen), library, and *madrasah* (college). Here, the *ulema* or learned men taught religion, mathematics, astronomy, medicine, and other subjects.[35] The complex reflected the imperial majesty of Süleyman. Its location augmented his status in the minds of both his subjects and foreigners who visited the city and gazed at the monumental structure that dominated the Bosphorus, where East meets West. In this way the new Ottoman style exploited the special geographical setting of the Bosphorus on which the Süleymaniye was built to convey to both the East and West that the sultan ruled both Asia and Europe.

Location

The Süleymaniye majestically dominates the highest hill of Istanbul, overlooking the Golden Horn. Built on the Third Hill of Istanbul, Sinan took advantage of the site to create an imperial mosque on a monumental level which, according to Godfrey, is the "dominant aim of Ottoman architecture." With Süleymaniye, "the master architect establishes himself as a personality emergent from the anonymity of the Middle Ages" by continually pushing technological boundaries in order to surpass the achievements of the past and perfect his art.[36] In the context of a sixteenth-century audience, the mosque's symbolic location on the European side of the Bosphorus, overlooking the straits facing East, reflects Süleyman's status as the preeminent ruler of the Muslim world and his role as representative of Sunni Islam over the Shi'a Safavids of Iran. By rivalling the Hagia Sophia, the Ottomans' real triumph over the Latin West is symbolically announced.[37]

The imperial architecture of the Süleymaniye reflects a monumental scale the power and prestige of the ideal Muslim sovereign in Süleyman himself. The pyramidal effect visible at close range enables the viewer to be wholly absorbed into the mosque's grandeur and monumentality. It is as if the viewer is standing in the shadows of both Süleyman and Sinan, feeling a sense of awe at their greatness (fig. 5.1). While this pyramidal composition dominates the city of Istanbul from a distance, for the individual viewing it up close it achieves the same effect, thereby creating a visual dialogue between the individual and the mosque's location. The location of the mosque does not escape Evliya Çelebi's description of the courtyard and the view of the city:

> On this side [east], the courtyard is not enclosed by a wall but by a low parapet so that one can view Istanbul. The entire congregation stops here to enjoy a panoramic view of the imperial palace, Uskudar . . . Galata . . . views of the Golden Horn and the Bosphorus, with thousands of ferries and caiques plying the waters and other boats unfurling their sails.[38]

The location of the Bosphorus played a significant role in the visual aesthetics of the mosque and in representing Süleyman's power and majesty to the world.

Surpassing the past: style

Entering the main courtyard of the complex from the north, the visitor encounters the layered domical "superstructure" of the Süleymaniye. This is delineated from the lower walls by stone railings. In this way Sinan is able to dissolve the cubical base of the Hagia Sophia's dome by harmoniously integrating "curvilinear forms."[39] According to Kuban, the arrangement of the layered façade structure at different levels below the main dome "reveal[s] a movement like that of waves rising and falling around a rock."[40] Goodwin argues that Sinan shows his genius by distorting the domes on the left and right of the north door of the lateral porticoes by using elliptical shapes. For Goodwin, this is rather "fascinating" because it shows that "once an architect with a fertile mind seeks to introduce movement into a static classical concept, baroque forms will emerge."[41] This, Goodwin claims, reinforces both the dynamism and individualism of Sinan's architecture; unlike the dominant horizontal buttresses of the Hagia Sophia, those of the Süleymaniye are partly hidden within the walls. This effect accentuates their profile and is in architectural harmony with the layering of the domes.

The buttresses divide the mosque into three facades and the double-storey middle portico has porphyry roundels. At each end of the facades there are three triple-domed porticoes reached by steps, allowing the visitor to access the mosque from the side. Uneven columns with *muqarnas* capitals support the nine-arched lower portico, while more elegant columns featuring lozenge capitals support the upper porticoes. As the visitor enters the forecourt he is faced with a massive pyramid domical structure that symbolises the grandeur and power of the mosque's patron. Visually, the domical layers reaching the apex of the dome suggest imperial confidence, self-awareness as a universal ruler, and cultural greatness. Just as the exterior played a significant role in the visual aesthetics of the mosque and in representing Süleyman's power and majesty to the world, so the interior space served as an architectural challenge for Sinan in demonstrating Islam's engineering triumph over Latin Christendom.

Competing with the past: centralised space under a single dome

In the Süleymaniye Mosque, Sinan overcame the structural deficiencies of the Hagia Sophia and found a solution to creating an original stylistic expression for an Ottoman imperial mosque. He adopted the plan of a central dome with two half-domes, with the central dome resting on four massive square pillars, making it almost identical with that of Hagia Sophia. However, while the Hagia Sophia's central dome dominated the interior, the aisles and galleries flanked the central space on its northern, western, and southern sides, interrupting the flow of the unified space desired in Muslim worship.

Sinan placed the central dome on two tympana, while the main arches provided the support that emulated the Hagia Sophia. This way the load of the dome is transferred to the four piers. Following the Hagia Sophia style, Sinan's use of the exedras in the Süleymaniye contributes to carrying the weight of the central dome, allowing him to find a solution to creating a unified space under the central dome. He distributed the weight of the central dome by placing the load on the arches. This lightened the supporting role of the tympanums and contributed to an outward expansion of the upper part of the dome. Sinan integrated the four buttresses into the walls of the mosque, half protruding inside and half protruding outside. Concealing the projections by building colonnaded galleries supported by columns at the east and west sides, Sinan achieved the space required under a central dome, thus, achieving the desired effect for the time being.[42]

Here, Sinan deviates from the Hagia Sophia and transforms the Christian basilica into an Islamic mosque by achieving the unity of space under the central dome. Further, the use of colonnades in the Hagia Sophia between the piers and the upstairs galleries provides the appearance of directional movement in the interior, while Sinan's restrained reliance on columns and galleries in the Süleymaniye has the opposite effect, creating a sense of unity between the nave and the aisles. Sa'i describes the galleries of the Süleymaniye in a Platonic manner, as "the halting place of the lovers of purity" where only individuals with pure hearts reflecting on God at this place can attain understanding of the One.[43] The addition of the galleries inspired by the Hagia Sophia is, furthermore, an indicator that Sinan was abandoning the Timurid–Persian *iwan* as seen in the Yeşil Camii at Bursa in the previous century and was striving to create something different.

Choosing more modest dimensions than the Hagia Sophia (73.5 x 69.5 metres), in the interior space for worship Sinan achieved an area covering 58.5 x 57.7 metres. The central dome has a diameter of 26.5 metres with a height of 53 metres (fig. 5.1a). By opening up the enclosed and relatively dark interior that had characterised the Hagia Sophia, Sinan's Süleymaniye offered an original design that surpassed the Roman/Byzantine style (*sūret*). Although he could not manage to create the completely unified space he desired, both structures bare remarkable similarities in achieving the massive inner space (figs. 5.2 and 5.3). The

Süleymaniye as a building demonstrates a leap forward in architecture: a mosque under a single large dome with a massive interior space for worshippers, surpassing not only Roman/Byzantine precedents but also the Bursa and Edirne mosques of the fifteenth century, including that of his great grandfather Mehmed II's Fatih Camii in Istanbul.

In order to accommodate the sultan's imperial aim, Sinan needed to build a structure that not only surpassed the size of the central dome of the Hagia Sophia but that also accommodated its interior to suit Islamic rituals and practices (figs. 5.4 and 5.5). Focusing on the structural and aesthetic functions of the mosque, he set out to correct the defects in the works of ancient masters, in particular the Hagia Sophia's dark interior which "did not possess elegance."[44] Aesthetically speaking, Sinan's triumph speaks of his achievements in the Süleymaniye:

> [. . .] the ornamented windows, which are without like or equal, resemble the wings of Gabriel. When they are illuminated with the sun's radiance, they are like an embellished rose garden of the springtime, and the rays of the azure vault reveal their chameleon-like iridescent designs. Ruby, cinnabar, lapis, and verdigris were lavished on this transcendent exemplar of ornament and design, and beautiful, heart-attracting designs were fashioned, the elegance of which confounds the eyes of those with sight.[45]

Acknowledging his triumph over past examplars in designing a mosque worthy of admiration, Sinan recognises that the Süleymaniye is "a beautiful building."[46]

Unity and harmony of inner and outer space

The major theoretical principle underlying Sinan's aesthetic decision to create an uninterrupted Islamic prayer space was based on the *tawhid*—the unity of the one God. This principle encompassed all the structural and aesthetic elements of the mosque. In keeping with Islamic tradition, Sinan makes a conscious and innovative decision to unite the inner space with the outer space to create a both visually and spiritually reflective medium in which the interior is seen to extend outward. This becomes one of the most common characteristics of Ottoman mosques. This Islamic tradition of inner and outer sacred spaces of mosques originates in the seventh-century mosque of the Prophet in Medina, which had an outer courtyard that Sinan would masterfully refine to its ideal form within the distinct context of sixteenth-century Ottoman architecture.[47] By fusing the two traditions, Sinan achieved a distinctive imperial aesthetic. Sinan achieves this dual harmony with the three wide arches of the central-domed baldachins, also visible from the exterior, supported by massive square columns. The unity between the interior and exterior allows the visitor to visualise the interior prior to entering the mosque.

Muslims pray in tight rows without furniture. Both the need to be close to the first row and the feeling of oneness with the congregation are important during congregational prayer times and contribute to the central aim in constructing a Muslim prayer space: that it should be a unified uninterrupted floor space. In Sinan's mosque columns do not break up the rows of worshippers facing the *qibla* wall. From a Platonic perspective, attaining spatial unity for meant, for Sinan, not only creating a space for Muslim worship, but also, on a symbolic and philosophical level, validating the universal order of God and that of the patron—the sultan himself.

The dome as an architectural symbol that connects past, present, and future in an uninterrupted space acts as a unifying factor for the worshippers with the promise of eternal life. Gathering in the open space reminds the congregation that not only do they pray for salvation for all humanity in the hereafter but that the individual must also be mindful of his/her earthly purpose and cannot disassociate from that responsibility. The unity of the exterior and the interior are further emphasised when the mosque is at full capacity during Friday prayers and holy days, when the congregation fills the forecourt and the interior. Moreover, the 248 windows in the Süleymaniye achieve the visual continuity of the interior and the exterior and flood the interior with light, unlike its predecessor, the Hagia Sophia.

Light symbolism

In the Hagia Sophia the divine space is secluded from the outer world through the role played by light. In the Roman/Byzantine structure the light that enters from the openings in the wall of the aisles barely makes an impact on the central inner space. The church remains very dark and has a subdued atmosphere. For both the Sufi humanists and neo-Platonists, this darkness prevents the attainment of the spiritual enlightenment one seeks and thus distances the seeker from the Truth and Good.[48] The columns also play a role in preventing light from penetrating the nave space and aisles. The upper openings of the drum, half domes, tympanums, exedras, and wall galleries provide most of the lighting entering the inner space. This creates a sense of isolation between the sacred space and outer world.

In contrast, light plays a significant function in Sinan's mosques, contributing to their overall aesthetic and spiritual effects. The openings of the Süleymaniye Mosque, in the upper part of the drum, half domes, tympanums, and exedras, are uniformly distributed so that nothing prevents the light from entering from the openings. Seyyid Lokman, the coordinator of the palace artists, describes the spatial effect of the lighting where "Space and Time is exposed" through the multiple layers.[49] As Mio Takikawa states,

> a transparency appears in the mosque's whole space, and when we enter the inner space, we feel the centrifugal, outward expansion, which may be called an expanding effect. Yet, this effect of centrifugal expansion is not the only effect created by the inner space. Contradictory as it may sound, the space also creates a centripetal, attracting effect that leads the attention toward the top.[50]

This uplifting effect draws the individual towards the central dome and provides a sense of spiritual elation, connecting heaven to earth. Plato repeatedly linked light, truth, and goodness. In Platonic philosophy, as Tarnas claims, " . . . his discovering that luminous knowledge . . . brings harmony between the human soul and the cosmic order of archetypes, an order governed and illuminated by the supreme Idea of the Good."[51] In other words, by flooding the interior of this sacred space with light, Sinan's didacticism enhances both the sensory and spiritual experiences between the viewer and his/her relationship with God. Charles A. Martin, however, disagrees with this view and suggests that the profusion of light in Sinan's mosques deters the religious spirit required for a place of worship.[52] However, Martin misunderstands the Islamic concept of God and His nature expressed in the Qur'an—"Light upon Light"—and that this needed to be expressed both aesthetically and architecturally in mosques to achieve the desired effects.[53] Grabar concurs that the issue is not so much the physicality of the hundreds of windows but the symbolism associated with light in Islamic art.[54] For example, the arches of the central dome are lightly pointed and effortlessly transfer the vertical lines of the four piers from the bottom to upper regions, taking the visitor along for a spiritually uplifting experience into the "light." "4000 candles" used to light the interior reinforced the Qur'anic verse: "Allah is the Light of the heavens and the earth . . . Light upon light."[55] Flooding the interior with the light from 248 windows and thousands of candles augment Süleyman's role as God's representative on earth (Caliph of the Faithful) who illuminates the world and reinforces his triumph over Justinian's Hagia Sophia.

The New Solomon of his time

The design of the Süleymaniye also plays on Süleyman's self-conscious cultivation of himself as "the Solomon of the age," cementing his historical legacy and religious authority over his empire. Through clever manipulation, Süleyman used the past to amplify the age in which he ruled. He did this in part through allusion to his biblical namesake, Solomon, and by citing Justinian's references to the original Temple of Solomon in Jerusalem upon the completion of the Hagia Sophia. Justinian's claim, "Solomon, I have surpassed thee!" concretised Süleyman's aspirations to build his imperial mosque in the Hagia Sophia style to not only engender his messianic image but to surpass his Roman predecessor with a new structure.[56]

This attainment of perfection reinforces both Vasari's and Ali's understandings of "rebirth." Evliya Çelebi (d. 1682), the seventeenth-century Ottoman traveller, also makes reference to the Hagia Sophia. He asked "ten Frankish infidels with expert knowledge of geometry and architecture who were touring this light-filled mosque" how it compared with the ancient structure.[57] The Europeans, most likely Venetians, responded by acknowledging first that the ancient structure was much larger and well-built for its time. However, they were amazed at the "finer construction in terms of grace, elegance, and beauty" of the Süleymaniye and felt it could not be compared with the Hagia Sophia.[58] They admitted to Evliya Çelebi that, "In all of Frengistan [i.e. Europe] we have not seen an edifice built to such perfection as this," acknowledging the Ottoman architectural triumph over Latin West.[59] Evliya Çelebi's exaggerated tone here need to be noted. Noting the different audiencing of the Süleymaniye by the Franks, Evliya Çelebi's remarks in his travel accounts constitute a sense of Ottoman cultural awareness, and historical consciousness of the achievements of the Süleymanic Age.

The Süleymaniye, similar in its magnificence to the preceding structures, asserts Süleyman's historical importance as both a political and spiritual leader. The Süleymaniye expresses the vibrancy and dynamism of the cultural expressions of Ottoman Istanbul of the sixteenth century, whilst the Hagia Sophia articulates the bygone glories of the Eastern Roman Empire. The sixteenth-century traveller John Sanderson implicitly expresses this interplay between the Hagia Sophia and the Ottoman's competitive desire to surpass it:

> The sixth hill hathe the marvailouse church and sepullcer of the triumphant and invisible Sultan Solimen; a worthy of sutch a monarke, in the best and most frequented place of the citie, which passeth his greatnes, wourkemanshipp, marble pillars, and riches more than kinglie, all other churches of the empirorshis predecessors; a wourke which merith to be matched with the 7 Wonder of the World.[60]

Sanderson's observation that the Süleymaniye mosque should be included among the seven wonders of the world is significant. It illustrates how the magnificence of the architecture and the impact of its beauty transcend the boundaries of religion and culture. Sanderson's impression of the mosque is transferred to the greatness of Sultan Süleyman and the Ottoman civilization. For Sinan, the Süleymaniye became "his direct answer to the challenge of Justinian's masterpiece" that won him the accolade and praise he deserved from foreigners of the time.[61] By challenging the past through the intentional integration of the plan of the Hagia Sophia, Sinan achieved the original expression of great Ottoman mosques. He demonstrated that a "competitive discourse . . . can really occur once there has been a clearly defined break with the past."[62] Thus, the Süleymaniye, through its "subtle symbolic transformation of Hagia Sophia," introduces "a new interpretative language."[63] That language is the birth of the distinct Ottoman style through the innovative interpretation and adaption of the past. By reinterpreting the Hagia Sophia for Islamic worship Sinan avoided imitating it and instead created a building that represented the desires of his own age.

In his autobiography Sinan proclaims to the artisans of the whole world his engineering success in completing the Süleymaniye Mosque:

> To the engineers of the age and overseers of auspicious monuments it is manifest and apparent that although [formerly] buildings constructed in the style of Hagia Sophia did not possess elegance, this servant perfected the noble Friday mosque of Şehzade Sultan Mehmed—may God illumine his tomb—which was the model for the noble building complex [and mosque] of His Majesty Sultan Süleyman Khan—may he rest in peace. Subsequently, in this lofty edifice [i.e., the Süleymaniye complex] various beautiful works of art were created, each of which took form with elegance.[64]

Speaking on behalf of the "engineers of the age," Sinan links himself to Renaissance architects of the Latin West. He considers himself one of the Renaissance architects of the period and places himself in direct competition with them. His criticism of previous structures emulating the Hagia Sophia in the previous century, namely the Üç Şerefeli Mosque in Edirne (1447) and the Fatih Mosque in Istanbul (1471), reminds readers that through those buildings the Ottomans were still striving for perfection. He sees his accomplishment in the Süleymaniye as a triumph for art. The linear progression in attaining the "elegance" (*nezāket*) to which Sinan alludes occurred through a process of continual experimentation. He acknowledges this process in the Şehzade Mehmed mosque he built in 1548 a decade earlier and which served as the model for the imperial complex. The "elegance" of the Süleymaniye surpassed previous structures built by the Ottomans in the style of the Hagia Sophia. This reflects a sense of accomplishment and cultural confidence. Thus, Sinan did not see his role as merely that of chief architect but also that of a major contributor to art and architecture of his time.

At the mosque's inauguration in 1557, Sinan's patron Süleyman elevated his architect to the status of "most deserving" and "worthy," according him the honor of opening the gate of the imperial structure.[65] However, Sinan's ultimate triumph in surpassing Roman/Byzantine architecture had to wait until 1575 with his masterpiece, the Selimiye Mosque.

The Selimiye Mosque 1569–75: a High Renaissance masterpiece

Built between 1569 and 1575 for Sultan Selim II, this imperial Friday mosque in Edirne was seen by Sinan himself as both a personal and architectural triumph. Historically speaking, however, the choice of Edirne as the site for Selim's mosque has raised questions. In particular, why did the sultan not build his imperial mosque in Istanbul? According to Evliya Çelebi, Selim II decided on Edirne on the eve of the conquest of Cyprus to redeem himself after the disaster of the Battle of Lepanto (1571).[66] According to Necipoğlu, another reason why the Sultan failed to build his mosque in Istanbul is that he had failed to fulfil the Holy Law or that he had not successfully led a campaign against the Christians.[67] Selim II could not live up to, yet alone compete with, his father's achievements both on the battlefield and in terms of cultural refinement. The Süleymaniye occupied the best possible position in Istanbul. According to the English traveller Sanderson, the "somptiouse" Selimiye was built in Edirne because of the "want of place" in Istanbul.[68] Another reason that may explain the site chosen is that as a prince, Selim had served as governor of Edirne and developed a liking for the city. He also spent most of his sultanate years in Edirne, hunting and away from the politics of the palace and the harem. Edirne provided Selim the opportunity to establish a loyal following there and wished to make his mark in relation to those people.

In the *Tezkiretu'l-Bunyan* (Record of Construction) in Sinan's autobiographies, the architect portrays his masterpiece in these words: "In truth it [Selimiye] is a matchless marvel! Its like does not exist! The Tunca river is the pride of the city of Edirne, but this high-domed mosque is its crown."[69] The visual aesthetics of the Selimiye described in Sinan's autobiography encapsulate the architect's pride at having produced "a matchless marvel," where the mosque's dome crowned the city of Edirne as an imperial city just as the Süleymaniye had done in Istanbul.

Within a generation the Ottomans felt the same sentiments about the Selimiye as Sinan. Çelebi states that he heard from his father that Sinan contended: "The Şehzade is my apprenticeship work, the Süleymaniye my work of a journeyman, and the Selimiye my work as a master."[70] Sinan's remarks about his "masterpiece" point to the architectural progress he made and its culmination in the imperial mosque of Selim II. In this imperial mosque Sinan utilises all the Ottoman arts, from monumental architecture to the sophistication of Iznik tiles, Qur'anic calligraphy, and painting to attain "complete realization" of Ottoman and Islamic arts.[71]

Vasari describes the achievements of Leonardo da Vinci as driven by "the purpose of giving greater relief, and of discovering and attaining to the ultimate perfection of art." [72] Similarly, Sinan boasts about his attainment of perfection and illustrates Renaissance ideals: historical self-consciousness, progress, and improvement on past precedents. With the same Renaissance spirit as da Vinci, Sinan triumphed. Mustafa Ali's description of the triumph of early modern Ottoman art in the sixteenth century also encapsulate Sinan's achievements: "impeccable," "inimitable," "the most illustrious," "exalted," and "world-adorning" architectural wonder.[73]

Like Sinan, Le Corbusier (1887-1965), the Swiss-French architect, in his travels to the East in 1911 also compares the Selimiye to a crown: "Adrianople is like a swelling on this vast plateau, culminating in a magnificent dome . . . Sultan Selim gives the city a tiara of great splendour."[74] As one approaches Edirne from Greece, Bulgaria, or Istanbul, the main entry to the city converges at its one central meeting point: the Selimiye. From a distance its dome and slender minarets echo Le Corbusier's words above. This view similarly resonates with Rüsen's idea that art enables others "to understand the self-understanding of others."[75] Le Corbusier's view expresses the perceptions of a very different audience in regard to the Ottomans' cultural greatness and evokes the sense of pride Sinan felt in this accomplishment. Le Corbusier could see, like the Ottomans, that the imperial mosque accentuates the power and status of the sultan for both the inhabitants of the city and foreigners alike.

With its 70-metre high minarets the Selimiye dominates the skyline of the city (fig. 5.6). In another passage Sinan speaks of the Sultan's gift to the city, declaring it an unrivalled monument of world architecture:

> Because he [Selim, who was] felicitously settled upon the throne of fortune, had for the city of Edirne the highest affection and esteem, he gave an imperial command that a Friday mosque be built, the like of which had never been built before. This humble servant pre-

> pared such a [wonderful] drawing for a sublime Friday mosque in Edirne, that is worthy of the admiration of humankind.[76]

Sinan's humanist claim that the monument is worthy of humankind epitomises his competitive and creative spirit, as well as his willingness to push the boundaries of art. This resonates with Giorgio Vasari's and Mustafa Ali's ideas of art as progress and of art's symbolic import for the present in its surpassing of the past. Sinan elevates his task: it is not that he simply built a mosque for his Sultan, but that he produced a monument as a testament of human artistry and as a gift to humanity for posterity. In the same paragraph Sinan acknowledges that his construction surpasses the models built by his predecessors. He makes a reference to earlier artistic traditions established in the Ottomans' second capital Edirne in the fifteenth century. Sinan compares the "elegance" and "beauty" of the Selimiye with the Üç Şerefeli Mosque of Murad II built between 1438 and 1447. Sinan describes Murad II's mosque as lacking grace and refinement:

> Its [Selimiye's] four minarets are situated on the four sides of the dome. All of them have three balconies and three staircases, and the staircases of the two of them are separate from one another. [The minaret] of the previously built Üç Şerefeli [Mosque] is like a tower. It is very thick.[77]

His critique of past Ottoman achievements demonstrates that here, in the Selimiye, the art of the Ottomans under his guidance have been perfected and have attained a state of artistic sophistication. This triumph is eulogised by none other than Sinan's scribe Mustafa Sa'i:

> In truth, beneath that unsupported dome [of heaven], that dome was suspended like an orb . . . from the mosque of the Spheres with the Milky Way . . . Never would a dome like Hagia Sophia's be built, the world wagered. This exalted dome exceeded that . . . A dome such as this on earth never was nor ever will [again] be built.[78]

Sa'i gives God a voice in reply to this achievement:

> The Divine Voice heard of its completion and composed a date: "At this moment, the exalted dome was secured and completed."[79]

This Divine confirmation of Sinan's work echoes the Platonic idea discussed earlier in which the mysteries of God's great cosmos are slowly revealed to humanity through this (near) perfect work in the Selimiye. God's affirmation of the Selimiye thus bolsters the mosque's spiritual and political status, legitimising Selim II as His rightful caliph of the faithful against the "heretic" Safavids.

Sinan commenced collecting materials for the mosque between 1568 and 1569. As noted in Chapter Two, in addition to the ancient materials Sinan collected from abroad and used in the construction of the Süleymaniye, he also relied on materials from across the Mediterranean. The Genoese diplomat Battisto Ferraro reports from Alexandria in 1569 that several Ottoman galleys were loaded with "large columns" and loaded off Rodosto to be transferred to the construction site in Edirne for the sultan's new mosque.[80] Also in 1569, Marcantonio Barbaro, the Venetian *bailo* (ambassador) to the Ottoman Empire, sent a report from Pera in Istanbul to the Venetian Senate reporting of men searching for "antique remains" across different parts of the eastern Mediterranean to be used in the building of the new imperial mosque.[81] Like his father, Selim II wanted to connect with the legacies of past civilizations in an effort to legitimise his universal rule. This time, however, unlike his father's mosque built in the Hagia Sophia style, Selim's new imperial mosque would surpass the past with a completely new or *ihtira* style. Although Sinan does not mention surpassing the Süleymaniye, he does state in his autobiographies that a dome like that of the Selimiye "had never been built before."[82] This suggests he not only surpassed the Hagia Sophia but was also in competition with the Süleymaniye, confirming Evliya Çelebi's earlier statement that Sinan was continually striving to perfect his previous works.

Structure

By July 1572 Sinan had erected the eight piers of the Selimiye Mosque. This is twice as many as those found in the Süleymaniye. The piers support the large main dome and are united with the walls. However, the boundary separating the piers and the walls seems ambiguous. The piers in the Süleymaniye are independent of the walls and maintain their form as columns. By contrast, in the Selimiye, the upper parts of the piers merge with the walls and accentuate the uninterrupted unity of the internal space.

The dome and unity and harmony of space

The dome rests on an octagonal foundation, diverging from the square dome of the Hagia Sophia and the Süleymaniye. In terms of their visual spatial effects, the inner spaces between the Süleymaniye and Selimiye mosques are similar. The Selimiye has a dome of 45 metres above the ground and covers a worship space of approximately 40 x 45 metres.[83] The dome sits on eight immense, independent supports (fig. 5.7). The supports do not include capitals. Instead, Sinan uses squinches to accentuate the arches growing out of the piers.

Sinan continues with the past tradition of using the Islamic muqarnas-corbelled squinches from Timurid–Persian–Seljukid traditions. In doing this he departs from the classical Greco–Roman spherical pendentives and previous square baldachins arrangement of imperial mosques in Istanbul. This is specifically seen in the mosques he built for Süleyman's wife, Hürrem Sultan, in Istanbul (1539), and daughter, Mihrimah Sultan, at Üsküdar (1548) and Edirnekapı (1565). At this momentous juncture in Ottoman architectural history, Sinan makes a conscious decision to fuse the Hagia Sophia-inspired dome of the Selimiye with medieval Islamic-inspired muqarnas-corbelled squinches. This endorses the synthesis of the East–West dialogue in early modern Ottoman art and stresses the special characteristics of its rebirth through a more perfect version of the past. By creating a circle with the eight piers under the large dome in the interior, Sinan creates a smooth transition from the octagonal baldaquin in which the dome sits. This innovation creates the illusion of a weightless dome suspended on the interior, captured in Sa'i's description of an "unsupported dome . . . suspended like an orb."[84] The result is an uninterrupted triumph of space which dominates the interior.

This aesthetic effect enhances the massiveness of the space through the smooth form of the building. The piers have perpendicular lines running along them with a pointed arch between each pier. This pulls the viewer's eyes to the central dome and links the realm of the human to the divine. The structural strength of the Selimiye as compared to the Süleymaniye is demonstrated in the tall openings on the drum and the tympanums. As Mio Takikawa notes, "These repetitions of the effects create a still stronger orientation to the top—to the center of the dome."[85] The vertical shapes created by the numerous windows reinforce the structural strength of the mosque.

Just as viewing the mosque above ground level gives the visitor an elevating experience, so too does the interior. The visual narrative created by Sinan here is one of elation, where the observer is immediately drawn upwards to the brightly lit dome and then admires the rest of the interior aesthetics. This upward pull accentuates particular a sensory experience within the mosque. As Nina Ergin states, "Sinan's mosques had a direct sensuous appeal and gave great pleasure to the users [which] can be deduced from contemporary descriptions that use expressions such as glittering with light, joy-giving, and heart-captivating."[86] The viewer is mesmerised by the combination of light entering from the dome's windows with the massive white Qur'anic calligraphy of Ahmed and Hasan Karahısarı describing God as "Light upon Light," set on deep blue at its centre and enveloped by Islamic geometric patterns reflecting the incomprehensibility of the Divine. In the Platonic sense, the "audiencing" effect here assumes deeper metaphysical and spiritual dimensions. The reflection of natural light illuminates the dome's calligraphic inscriptions. When the viewer tilts his head up, mesmerised by the dome, he and the large inscriptions become connected as if in a dialogue. As Geir Hellemo states, "[t]he Qur'anic inscriptions appear as a visible representation of a divine reality. They reveal the word of God in the guise of human speech. In this light, the appearance of the written word must be seen as a perceptual glimpse of the divine."[87] For the Renaissance mindset, the spiritual elation achieved in the largest dome that had even been built in Islamic lands realises Sinan's aim to perfect the interior space for worshippers through his continuing dialogue with, and surpassing of, past precedents.

Surpassing the past: the dome in competition with Christianity and with the Hagia Sophia

The dome played a crucial role in Ottoman architecture. Sinan's ongoing dialogue with the Hagia Sophia is well documented in his mosques and autobiographies. In his autobiographies, *Tezkiretu'l-Bunyan*, Sinan tells us that Christians attest that Muslims cannot build a dome larger than the Hagia Sophia (fig. 5.8). His writings indicate that this challenge weighed on his conscience for some time and that he strove to show the world his genius as an innovator. In his autobiographies Sinan addresses his Latin counterparts, arguing that once and for all he will put a stop to criticism of Muslims: "those who passed for architects among the sinning unbelievers [who] used to say, "the construction of a dome such as that is very difficult. Were it possible to build one like it, the [the Muslims] would have done it."[88] But finally, Sinan triumphantly declares that this spurred him on:

> [their comments] pained and endured in the heart of this humble servant . . . and, with the help of God, the Lord, the Judge, showed my capabilities during the reign of Sultan Selim Khan and made this exalted dome to exceed that one [Hagia Sophia] by six cubits in height and by four cubits in circumference.[89]

He answered the Christian call by showing that it was not "beyond human capability" to build a "dome as large as that of the Hagia Sophia . . . in the lands of Islam."[90] Necipoğlu, however, notes:

> The architect's claims to have surpassed the dimensions of the Hagia Sophia's dome has puzzled architectural historians because the diameter of Selimiye's dome (31.22m) approximates that of Hagia Sophia (ranging between 30.90m and 31.8m), and is considerably lower. Sinan does not, however, say that he surpassed the diameter (commonly referred to as *kutr* or *cap*) of Hagia Sophia's dome, but rather its circumference (*devr*).[91]

Nevertheless, Sinan's triumphant tone exemplifies this new self-awareness and sense of the greatness of Ottoman achievements compared to their Latin counterparts. It also acknowledges a dialogue between East and West, one that really acknowledges the Renaissance spirit of competition. The Selimiye's 31-metre dome sustained by a buttress system and surrounding an octagonal central baldaquin thus came to symbolise the Ottomans' architectural triumph of Islam over Christianity. This bolstering of self-consciousness epitomised an empire that stretched from the borders of Vienna in the northwest to Yemen in the southern tip of the Arabian Peninsula, confirming and solidifying its legitimacy as a global power.

Unity of space enhanced

The remaining architectural additions to the mosque interior further elevate the spatial unity created by the dome. Sinan claims in his autobiographies, "I strove to perfect my art."[92] As in the Süleymaniye Mosque above, in striving for perfection he abandons the Timurid–Persian *iwan* here as well and instead aims to utilise galleries to maximum architectural and aesthetic effect. Inspired by the Hagia Sophia, this time Sinan adds U-shaped upper galleries to the Selimiye to create the feeling of continuity in the inner space beyond the large dome. This further refining of the Süleymaniye, the Selimiye galleries, gives a sense of freedom from being confined in a fixed space. As Goodwin states, "[t]he manipulation of these galleries and their arcades beneath, so that interior and exterior are used as the reversals of each other, gives the deep satisfaction that the perfect solution of an intractable equation offers."[93] In this way Sinan achieves harmony between the interior space and the upper level. However, while there is a sense of freedom expressed in the interior, Sinan employs a drastic strategy to alter the viewer's emotions. This strategy has the potential to change his sensory experience and way of viewing the Selimiye. Here, Sinan conforms to the Platonic rule that the finest harmony is composed of elements that are in tension with one another. This tension is seen in the muezzin tribune's location in the interior.

Uniqueness of *muezzin* tribune and effect

When the viewer enters the sacred space, the centrality of the muezzin's tribune may at first seem intrusive (fig. 5.9). For Goodwin, the location of the tribune "punctuates the central space," suggesting the opposite of Sinan's claim that his work had attained completeness.[94] Various writers have commented on Sinan's radical actions with this piece of liturgical furniture. One interpretation is that such a radical move clearly depicts the artist's genius and expresses his creativity and uniqueness. For example, Günkut Akın writes, "[t]he conspicuous central location in the Selimiye therefore represents a bold innovation, just at a time when the quest for an efficient central and total space had attained its goal."[95] Akın argues, however, that the muezzin's tribune is functional because of its optical and acoustic position. For Akın this innovation "seems an effective architectonic solution, as well as one very much in line with Sinan's creativity."[96] By placing the tribute right in the centre of the prayer hall Sinan manages to create a "beautifully balanced" sense of infinite space under the dome, "just as the sphere of heaven must be, yet with that definition which all space requires."[97] Tanju Cantay writes that by positioning the tribune directly under the central dome that Kuban identified as "heaven-dome, and sultan-dome."[98] Sinan represents the Ottoman's centralised and absolutist empire, which at the end of the sixteenth century attained its farthest geographical extent.[99] Lastly, Thomas Barrie notes that the size of the muezzin's lodge is similar to the Ka'ba at the Great Mosque at Mecca, which, along with its central location, suggests circumambulation.[100]

This is exactly what the visitor does when approaching the tribune from the entrance. After the initial pull upward to the dome, the visitor's gaze descends back to earth, circling the tribune and noticing the intricately painted flowers, tulips, carnations, and hyacinths with *saz* scrolls in gold, green, and pink. The floral ensemble is painted on a red background supported by Chinese clouds in the panel above. At the same time, through the open *mahfil* arches of the tribune the visitor admires the white marble pool underneath it, teased by the glimpses of the colourful Iznik tiles decorating the *mihrab* wall. Reaching the *mihrab* wall the viewer is faced with vertical Iznik floral panels supporting the horizontal banding of the tiled Qur'anic inscriptions of a white on blue background. The interior thus becomes one unit to be perceived in its entirety and in harmony with the architecture. As J. G. Davies notes, "Plenitude of space . . . majestic space . . . continuous space . . . *tawhid* (the consciousness of divine Unity) made visible."[101] Therefore, instead of punctuating the interior as claimed by Goodwin, Sinan instead cleverly manipulates the viewer. He leads viewers to immerse themselves in admiration of his masterpiece so that they too acknowledge that all of the Ottoman arts have become complete and realised in this unique structure. Thus, according to Thomas Barrie, the placement of the muezzin's tribune along the central axis of the complex is highly effective: "[it] mitigates, but does not obviate, the orientation of the space toward the *mihrab*. Its location also creates a rectangular prayer space in front of the *mihrab* apse that reinforces the cross-axial direction established by communal prayer."[102] Thus Sinan's interior aesthetic is in complete harmony with its architectural norm, where the visual and spatial directions are delicately balanced. This realisation of artistic harmony can be interpreted as exemplifying both Vasari's and Ali's ideals of the stylistic progress made in the sixteenth century, where art reached the state of "perfection."

Symbolism of the tribune

The tribune is set above a shallow marble pool in the form of an octagon inscribed in a square. Its wooden ceiling is decorated with a "painted whirl motif representing the wheel of heaven," cleverly positioned directly under the central dome to signify paradise (fig. 5.10).[103] This was not a mistake or lapse in judgement on the architect's part, although Sinan never repeated this element. By the time the Selimiye was completed, Sinan was already 89 years old. He spent the remaining ten years of his life renovating the Topkapı Palace by expanding the private quarters for Murad III and his family. The pool in the centre of the area below the platform is not for ablutions but for drinking. While this diminishes the importance of its function, it serves as an affective device to clarify to the faithful in a tangible way how paradise will be: refreshing, with cleansing water. It thus gives a literal taste of what is to come in the Hereafter. The water in the pool is symbolic of the water in Paradise shown to the Prophet by God and is expressed in the Qur'anic verse: "Indeed We have granted you, (O Muhammad), al-Kawthar" (one of the rivers of Paradise).[104] Sa'i makes a reference to this river and compares it to the pool under the tribune: "You would think a pool of Kevser (i.e. al-Kawthar) that matchless fountain to be."[105] Thus the river/pool is associated with abundance and acts as a reminder to the faithful to not abandon hope of a better life in the Hereafter. Combined with the uninhibited space enveloping the individual, the pool achieves a sense of spiritual connection with the divine. This connection to the Divine resonates further in Sinan's autobiographies.

The Selimiye: an Islamic exemplar

Sinan's aesthetic legacy in the Selimiye resonates with Islamic mysticism. He calls it "an exemplar of the nine spheres."[106] According to Sufi belief, "all works of art are the works of humans who carry the Divine Entrustment and are subject to Divine Grace . . . exhibiting in the masterpieces that they produce themselves, their humanity, their feelings, and their thoughts."[107] This Sufi humanist mindset is also a Renaissance way of looking at art and is similar to the neo-Platonic idea that everything is subject to permanent change, and nothing in the world is perfect or faultless. In a gesture of humility Sinan demonstrates this belief by carving an upside-down tulip on the northwest pillar of the muezzin's tribune, showing that even the masterpiece created by this mortal knows that his work cannot compete with the Work of the "Peerless Artist"[108] (fig. 5.11). As an earthly pilgrim seeking to represent God's Beauty in his works, Sinan realises that his work is only a fragment of the Great Master's perfection.

Sa'i then extends his praise of the Selimiye, comparing it to the Dome of the Rock in Jerusalem (the Aksa Mosque) and the Ka'ba in Mecca: "May God be exalted! What is this beautiful place, [this] this sublime mosque, This Aksa Mosque, the like of the exalted Ka'ba?"[109] Both the places Sa'i celebrates are places of pilgrimage in Islamic history and exist to draw the individual on earth closer to God. Similarly, as works of art they are reminders of union with God. Sa'i's connection to these past Islamic structures exemplifies the triumph of Ottoman rebirth that culminated in the Selimiye. The connection Sa'i makes between the Aksa Mosque, the Ka'ba, and the Selimiye is significant. First, Sa'i makes this comparison because the Al-Aqsa's, like the Selimiye's, rests on an octagonal structure. The significance of the octagon in Islamic tradition is connected to the eight gates of paradise attributed to the sayings of Muhammad and to the references to gates made in the Qur'an.[110] This scriptural link bolsters the Selimiye's status as the place from which the believers will enter paradise. Second, in Islamic iconography the Aksa Mosque represents God's throne descending from heaven to the sacred rock on Judgement Day.[111] As the new Aksa Mosque, the Selimiye built in Edirne makes the city into the New Jerusalem; the mosque becomes the place where God's throne will descend on the Last Day.

Sa'i accentuates his claim that the Selimiye is the new Aksa Mosque through his many references to the Biblical and Qur'anic prophets: Noah, Abraham, David, Jesus, and Muhammad.[112] Comparing the Selimiye's beauty to the prophets, he strengthens his claim about the mosque's eschatological status in the Muslim world. In the process he also reinforces the sultans' legitimacy as the true heirs of Islam. From a neoplatonic viewpoint, Sinan has created the most fitting earthly throne in preparation for both the artist and humanity to seek union with God. Sinan's interpretation of the world from a neoplatonic viewpoint during the Renaissance exemplifies the Ottomans' intellectual understanding and historical consciousness of the period. The Selimiye is an "admiration of humankind." This new pilgrimage site is alluded to by Sa'i: "[a]ll the world comes there to win God's blessing."[113] The site thus draws Muslims from all over the empire and the East, bolstering the Ottoman sultans' claim to the rights of universal rule and the Islamic religion.

The mosque becomes the Ka'ba, augmenting its status as a pilgrimage site like the annual hajj pilgrimage to Mecca. The Ka'ba has a cubic structure, with its many corners symbolising the different parts of the globe. The Selimiye's spiritual, religious, and political symbolism as the centre of the Islamic world becomes complete and legitimises the Ottomans' claim as the true inheritors of the Islamic religion, thus challenging the Shi'a Safavids of Iran. As the Ka'ba represents for Muslims God's House on earth, Sa'i sees the Selimiye as "Ka'ba of the heart."[114] In this way, the Sufi humanist perspective, like the neoplatonic ideal, stresses the Selimiye's importance as a place leading to spiritual enlightenment, and where God can be found under the "unsupported dome ... suspended like an orb."[115]

Sa'i takes this hyperbole to the next level by making a reference to a symphony of prophets and angels singing. They sing in the Ottoman–Turkish classical compositional modes of *neva* and *pengcah,* reaching a crescendo to form paradise on earth:

> When the beautiful cherubim with David-like voices are assembled And take shelter like the turtledove atop the cypress trees
> Continually from the four minarets, in the *neva* and *pengcah* [modes]
> They like nightingales, the world to this rose garden invite.[116]

In describing this paradisiacal symphony where the singing "nightingales" invite the visitor to this earthly paradise, Sa'i provides the reader with an insight into the Ottoman psyche of how the outside world perceived its cultural marvels:

> The luster of its golden crescent-finial, which sends forth to humankind light / Is luminous; the world thinks this the dawn's brightness.[117]

In reinforcing the rightful inheritance of the Islamic religion, Sa'i conveys that with the Selimiye the Ottoman cultural accomplishment epitomises the "dawn's brightness." His verse implies the monument's symbolism as the zenith of Ottoman High Renaissance. This structure is therefore not only a product of rebirth but also an expression of the triumph and ideal beauty echoed by Vasari and Ali.

The Selimiye, like all the other imperial mosques, symbolises the power of the Ottoman Empire and its representation of Islamic civilization, in which mosques play a key part in structuring the city and the society. The Selimiye's location outside Istanbul represents the Ottomans looking to Europe and their symbolic claim of triumph over the Latin West. Sinan draws on the architectural vocabulary developed in Istanbul in the 1550s to describe the Süleymaniye in Edirne, the second capital of the Empire's rebirth. In his refining of the Selimiye, Sinan was affirming the cultural achievements of the Ottomans. This progression in architectural development reinforces Vasari's and Ali's idea of stylistic development through the ages and the claim that this style found perfection in the sixteenth century. For Kuban, Selimiye is a synthesis in which the Mediterranean and other Eastern architectural traditions unite and reach their culmination. This progression for Kuban, "presents Ottoman architecture as an intermediate world between East and West, with styles based on the Sassanid oriental tradition of domed structures or on the styles of the Mediterranean tradition …" including the sixth-century Roman/Byzantine basilica, the Hagia Sophia, and the seventh-century Islamic structure, the Dome of the Rock. [118] Therefore, looking back to the achievements of past cultures from East to West confirms the unique status of Ottoman architecture and its distinctive Renaissance narrative.

Architectural historians hold divergent views on Sinan and his Renaissance contemporaries. Necipoğlu argues that "[a] cross-cultural comparative perspective [with Renaissance Italy] has not yet emerged" in order to evaluate Sinan's architecture.[119] Necipoğlu argues that Sinan's contributions to architecture with centralised domed baldachins pushed the boundaries of structure, space, and light but that this is rarely incorporated into Eurocentric narratives of art history whose exclusions have only recently been revised.[120] Goodwin also sees a connection between Sinan and "Renaissance" architects of Italy. For him, the similarity between Alberti and Sinan is that they both inherited the Eastern concept of the dome, seeing God as the centre of the circle and the symbol of the universe.[121]

Architectural historian Muzaffer Özgüleş argues that there was a separate evolution of the single-domed structures based on cultural and religious requirements. This resulted in the Ottomans' divergence from the Italian Renaissance architects. It led to the creation of Sinan's individual and distinct style, separating him from the likes of Brunelleschi. For Özgüleş the fusion of the Islamic dome with Roman precedents such as the Pantheon and Hagia Sophia inspired the creation. However, he argues that Sinan's achievement of uninterrupted space under a single dome diverged from the approach of his Latin counterparts because the solution for this problem "is only for Sinan's architecture in totality, which is a comprehensive system of the domed structure."[122] Separating Sinan from his Renaissance contemporaries and placing him in a category of his own, as one who staged the Ottomans' separate and culturally distinct Renaissance, Özgüleş endorses Brotton's and Burioni's ideas of cultures with their own highly specific instances of rebirth.[123]

Most importantly, irrespective of cultural divergence or convergence, Sinan's imperial mosques, especially the Süleymaniye and Selimiye, represent a competitive dialogue with the Roman/Byzantine Hagia Sophia. Instead of imitating the past Sinan forged ahead to create something original and distinct—an Ottoman style born out of the remnants of the ancients. An artist like Sinan knew when he created something more sophisticated and refined than the works of the ancients. He knew when his creations represented "various beautiful works art . . . each of which took form with elegance."[124] He also knew how to recognise a masterpiece, as in the Selimiye, and when to acknowledge that he had created the "ultimate" realisation of art that underpins the claim of a cumulative growth that results in the perfection of art.

By pushing contemporary engineering boundaries, Sinan further stimulated notions of renewal and "rebirth" in Ottoman architectural consciousness. The accomplishments of Sinan as an artist are captured by Vasari's words, "[i]nspiration demands the active cooperation of the intellect joined with enthusiasm, and it is under such conditions that marvelous conceptions, with all that is excellent and divine, come into being."[125] Similarly, Sinan's architectural "wonders" reinforced his awareness of his own creative genius and prompted him to continue perfecting his art and pushing boundaries. In his autobiography Sinan states, "They say talent is a gift from God. I strove to perfect my art."[126] This reflection echoes Vasari's and Ali's notions of art as progress and the creative spirit of the artist.

Sinan's innovative response to the engineering challenges in his Selimiye masterpiece brings the Ottoman artistic period of the sixteenth century to a close. The successes achieved in the Süleymaniye and the Selimiye represent an historical continuity that began with past precedents in antiquity and in the medieval period and which came to fruition in the present. According to Rüsen's idea of historical consciousness, these structures "empirically expose the classical characteristics of a beginning, middle and an end."[127] After a millennium separating the Hagia Sophia from the Süleymaniye and the Selimiye, the leap forward made in architectural engineering put an end to the great achievements made in the Roman/Byzantine structures of the sixth century. The Ottoman technological response to the Hagia Sophia constitutes a period during which boundaries were pushed through both adaptation and appropriation. The outcome was the birth of a distinctive Ottoman artistic explosion, which built on the cultural awakening a century and half earlier in Bursa.

Conclusion

The rebirth of Ottoman art and architecture began in Bursa, Edirne, and Istanbul in the fifteenth century. In the last quarter of the sixteenth century Sinan returns to Edirne, and in his achievement of the Selimiye Mosque brings Ottoman rebirth into its triumphant phase. Choosing to locate the Selimiye within walking distance of the Üç Şerefeli Mosque signifies historical continuity in the evolutionary progress of art from Ottoman rebirth to its aesthetic triumph. This way the Ottomans did not compromise their cultural tradition; instead, they amalgamated existing aesthetics with traditional norms creating a distinct style. Through continuous experimentation that lasted well over a century, the Ottomans' progress in engineering allowed them to achieve a unified space under a central dome.

This idea of progression and experimentation as characteristics of the Renaissance is echoed in the words of figures such as Vasari and Ali. Vasari's idea of Renaissance as progress through the ages echoes Ali's understanding of artistic progress through the linear progress of history. As two monumental works, the Süleymaniye and the Selimiye are products of an age in which the idea of surpassing the past was established as the total of all virtues. That is to say, the Ottomans, as inheritors of past legacies, established a new self-awareness and cultural self-assurance by rebirthing a more "perfect" version of the past through the Süleymaniye and the Selimiye, buildings that reflect the Ottomans' new identity.

This interplay between past and present resonates with Rüsen's theory that "memory will always and fundamentally have a perspective of the present and the future."[128] Sinan's works reflect the idea of using the past to shape the present and leaving a legacy behind for the future. Sinan's use of the past as a foundation for creativity established innovative practices to suit the context of his time. He introduced domical layering, multi-level porticoes, U-shaped upper galleries, and effective interior lighting, to name a few. Through his abandonment of the Timurid–Persian style of the *iwan* and his engagement with the past Roman, Islamic, Seljukid heritages, the works of Sinan surpassed their central domed predecessors. As imperial monuments, they reflected the power and universal sovereignty of their respective sultan–patrons. Built in two different Ottoman cities, the two structures symbolically legitimised each individual sultan's rulership over an expansive continent and varied peoples, more specifically representing the sultanate as the unifying force of the Sunni Islamic world against the Safavids of Iran. However, in a period of unparalleled productivity and as a man endowed with talent, Sinan demonstrated his creative zeal a decade prior to the completion of the Selimiye and soon after the Süleymaniye mosques.

Two years after the completion of the Süleymaniye in 1560–61 Sinan took Ottoman art to a transcendental level with his first and only experimentation in the use of the fine arts of Iznik tiles in the Rustem Pasha Mosque. While the purpose of the mosque is for the patron Rustem Pasha's soul, at the same time Sinan expresses the paradisiacal garden created on earth by Sultan Süleyman. The following chapter focuses on an alternative reading of the decorations of the interior of the mosque, providing art historians a more accurate approach to the nature and character of the Ottoman Renaissance.

CHAPTER SIX

OTTOMAN FINE ARTS: WORD OF GOD, ART OF MAN

The Mosque of Rustem Pasha (1561-62) is unique in the history of early modern Ottoman art. It is in this mosque that, for the first time, the artistry of the Iznik çini (tiles) is reborn and makes a technological leap forward. The innovations include variation in design and the use of a new range of colours and floral motifs. Most importantly, the tiles demonstrate a stylistic and technological progression from the Timurid-inspired Bursa tile tradition of the previous century. The tiled walls, galleries, and pendentives of the main dome and spandrels of the main arches constitute a triumph for the Ottoman fine arts tradition, surpassing earlier exemplars. Although only a fraction of the Süleymaniye Mosque in size, the Rustem Pasha Mosque applies Iznik tiles far more successfully, integrating classical floral motifs and Eastern and Islamic designs into its narrative. By focusing on the aesthetic qualities of the tiles, the patrons of the mosque were able to make their mark in expressing the sultan's absolute authority. The narrative of the tiles first and foremost expresses Sufi humanism and its integral role in Ottoman ideas about cultural rebirth.

Sinan uses Iznik tiles in the Mosque of Rustem Pasha in Istanbul within the context of the Renaissance paradigm. This chapter discusses first the technological achievements of the Iznik tiles in Sinan's Mosque of Rustem Pasha. Carefully prepared by Sinan, the narrative of the tiles celebrates God's artistic mastery of the natural world, "[w]hose works in this world are exemplars of the next."[1]

The poems of Süleyman, composed while the mosque was under construction, are also valuable here, as his words reflect the visitor's own experience there. In the context of the mosque's aesthetics, the transformation of Süleyman also came to be reflected through his poetry about his personal and spiritual anguish, from his early to later years. Losing his wife Hürrem Sultan in 1558, and the decision to execute his first-born son and heir to the throne, Mustafa, on the grounds of treason, must have weighed heavily on Süleyman's conscience. Becoming more ascetic in his later reign, Süleyman's poetry reflects his anguish and inner turmoil. The anagogical and eschatological readings of the mosque also echo this personal angst. Furthermore, as there is no evidence to suggest otherwise, Süleyman must have visited the mosque at its inauguration to congratulate Sinan on his accomplishment, just as he had at the opening ceremony of his imperial mosque, the Süleymaniye.[2]

Straddling different cultural legacies, the imperial rulers—who presented themselves as the rulers of true Islam—were influenced by Sufi humanism. The Sufi humanist narrative of Rumi and Süleyman's poetry are associated with the mosque's aesthetics. In the words of Ayesha Ramachandran, the creative aesthetics of the Renaissance reflect the idea that "the invention of the [early] modern world owed much to theology and the spiritual practices of imaginative identification; [and] creative faculties of the intellectual imagination."[3] The creative aesthetics, then, provides a detailed anagogical and eschatological reading of the motifs of the tile designs with respect to the Qur'anic allusions to Paradise and salvation. This "intellectual imagination," combined with technological advancements, produced a vibrant period, pushed Ottoman artistic boundaries into a new sphere and reinforced an early modern Ottoman cultural identity. As it is beyond the scope of this book to examine every wall panel of the mosque, only the entrance portico panel, the *qibla* wall, and the *mihrab* will be closely analysed.

The Iznik tiles of the middle to the latter quarter of the sixteenth century represent a completely new genre of Ottoman art. The uniqueness of the tiles is expressed in the *vakıf* document or endowment deed of Rustem Pasha Mosque where the tiling is described as "a rarity of the period, and encompassing all kinds of creativity and artistry."[4] In this era, Iznik kilns were refired for the first time since the medieval Islamic era, prompting a renewed interest in the art of tile making. Sinan's use of Iznik tiles in the Mosque of Rustem Pasha, however, is no longer an imitation and adaptation of the Bursa–Timurid–Persianate–Seljukid traditions of the previous century. Instead, it is a leap forward in technological and aesthetic refinements from *cuerda seca* to underglaze productions than those created in the Bursa and Edirne mosques and mausoleums. In this context, Sinan created something new and original, that identified with the Ottoman court. In a figurative and technological sense, the Iznik tiles came to represent, like the mosque's architecture, a distinctly Ottoman artistic innovation or *ihtira*. Perhaps limited by the budget, the size of the mosque did not allow for innovation in architecture; however, the mosque's relatively small size allowed Sinan to try something no other architect had attempted: to cover the interior walls entirely with tiles.

The unique Mosque of Rustem Pasha, Istanbul was designed and built by Sinan in the name of Süleyman's Grand Vizier—who twice served the Sultan in the highest office of the Empire during 1544–53 and 1555–61. The mosque was the first major decorative Iznik tile project to be undertaken in Ottoman art history. Despite this fact, the Mosque of Rustem Pasha has not received scholarly attention since 1971, when Walter B. Denny's *The Ceramics of the Mosque of Rustem Pasha and the Environment of Change* identified the tiles, motifs, designs, and technical aspects of Iznik craftsmanship.[5] Denny focused predominantly on the production method of the tiles and the progress made in tile making during the Süleymanic period. Subsequent research, such as that of Michael D. Willis (1987) and Fatih Cimok (2001), has also relied largely on Denny's interpretation.[6] While this study also utilises the past works of Denny and Cimok, the scope of the argument moves beyond the technical mastery of the tiles. The achievement of Iznik tiles in the sixteenth century set a meaningful precedent in quality, design and symbolism. The Iznik achievements exemplify Vasari's, Ali's, and Sinan's ideals of rebirth. For the three contemporaries, the artistic quality which marked their age was achieved slowly through imitating and adapting old ideas and remaking them anew. Ali praises Ottoman artists' "pleasing styles," "much-admired [stylistic] innovations," and their "impeccable" and "inimitable" achievements, writing that Sinan's *taqlid* (imitation) and *tecdid* (restoration) ultimately bring into existence new *ihtira sūret* (original forms).

A description of the mosque

This Renaissance mindset is reflected in the self-fashioning of the patrons of the mosque, Rustem Pasha and his wife Mihrimah Sultan. In the *vakfiye* (endowment) documents after the death of the pasha in 1561,

Sultan Süleyman on February 20, 1562 acknowledges the purpose of the mosque—to perform the Friday prayers, pray for the "soul" of Rustem Pasha, and for the "continuation" of his (i.e. the sultan's) reign.[7] The document suggests that the site for the mosque was chosen after the death of the pasha and that its purpose was for prayers to be recited for his soul as well as to glorify Süleyman's reign and propagate his patronage. Thus, the mosque served to augment not only the image of the former pasha but also the sultan himself. Rustem Pasha belonged to the *devshirme* and was taken by the janissaries from either Bosna (Bosnia) or Hırvat (Croatia) as a child, before his rise to power in the Ottoman political hierarchy. He first became Süleyman's son-in-law by marrying the sultan's only daughter Mihrimah Sultan. He subsequently became the sultan's Grand Vizier.

Standing at Tahtakale in Istanbul on the Golden Horn, the Rustem Pasha Mosque is situated within the economic hub of the city. Right next door is the spice bazaar where merchants buy and sell their goods. The location of the mosque therefore reflects the pasha's own business ventures. The mosque is built on top of warehouses and shops in Tahtakale, and the rent from these businesses was used for the upkeep of the mosque. This is noted in the endowment deed of Rustem Pasha in the following words: "[. . .] shops whose revenues yield a surplus after covering the expenses of that Friday mosque."[8] Furthermore, the second half of the *vakfiye* document notes that the surplus funds would finance the construction of public fountains and paved roads.[9] Sinan cleverly juxtaposed the Rustem Pasha Mosque with the Süleymaniye Mosque situated above it on the hilltop.

Despite the architectural dominance of the Süleymaniye, the Rustem Pasha Mosque makes its own statement to the ordinary people working around it. With its 15.2-metre dome, it dominates the domes of the buildings surrounding it, the covered bazaar and the spice bazaar to name a few. This reflects the pasha's dominant role in the Ottoman social hierarchy and reinforces his involvement in the Bursa silk industry where merchants would have traded at the bazaars below his mosque.[10] After Sinan drew up the plans for the mosque, the building supervisor, Mehmet Bey, received instructions from Princess Mihrimah (the pasha's widow and Süleyman's daughter). According to Necipoğlu, the final product of the Rustem Pasha Mosque was made possible through the combined deliberations of the trio.[11] Rustem Pasha initiated the building of the mosque before his death in c. 1561. The project was then taken over by his wife Mihrimah Sultan. Although it is not certain who made the final decision to decorate the interior of the mosque with tiles, including both sides of the galleries, contemporary sources indicate the involvement of Mihrimah Sultan, who became the sole patron and financier for the mosque after her husband's death. Although the stated aim of the mosque is to glorify Rustem Pasha and Süleyman, it also indirectly glorified Mihrimah who is the patron, main contact, and provider of funds.

Due to the limited sources available regarding the involvement of Mihrimah Sultan in the decoration of the mosque, the few that survive hold singular importance. This view has been supported by historians from the period, such as Ramazanzade Mehmed (c. 1562–65) and Hasanbeyzade (1595–1635), who praised Mihrimah Sultan's patronage for building such a mosque for her husband's soul. According to Ramazanzade:

> [. . .] the Sultana's religious endeavor on behalf of the late Rustem Pasha's soul: the Sultana built such a resplendent Friday mosque, ... resembling Garden of Eden. Ever since the sapphire dome of the moon and the sun [a reference to Mihrimah's name] no such ornate and beautiful building has ever been built, designed, or established on the surface of the earth and under the heavens.[12]

Hasanbeyzade concurs with Ramazanzade, attributing the building of the "elegant Friday mosque" to the pasha's wife.[13] As the executor of her husband's will, Mihrimah Sultan did not spare any expense in providing her husband's soul with a beautiful mosque. Similarly, Rustem Pasha's own *vakfiye* (endowment) document praises his wife for her contributions.[14] Such documents confirm both that the project was initially a husband-wife venture and that through the patron-client relationship Sinan had to accommodate the patron's desires in his planning and decoration of the mosque. For example, in the interior aesthetics of the Selimiye Mosque (1575) the architect and the sultan exchanged correspondence in which Sinan sought advice from his patron about the interior design. Selim II leaves the interior design to Sinan, writing, "I order you to have all of them built according to the manner you have reported."[15] This suggests that the final product—the layout, design, motifs, colour, and the insertion of the tile panels to create a visual narrative—rested solely with

Sinan. Just as Sinan had "private conversations" with the sultan during the construction of the Süleymaniye, the correspondence similarly suggests that he had a fair amount of artistic licence.

Although it still needed sultanic approval, it is likely that the same relationship would have operated with Mihrimah Sultan. She became the most powerful woman in the empire after the death of her mother (Hürrem Sultan) in 1558. She was the only female Süleyman turned to for advice in his old age.[16] With two imperial mosques built in her name at Üsküdar (1548) and Edirnekapı (c. 1562), her involvement in the posthumous mosque of her husband, as well as her continuing dialogue with Sinan on the interior decoration, resulted in a building that is celebrated as Sinan's masterpiece.

Technical mastery of Iznik *Çini*

The production of tiles demonstrates the technical mastery of the Iznik artisans. After Iznik potters had placed the formed clay and quartz compound into a frame and left it to dry for twenty days, the dried product was ground to a perfectly smooth surface. It was then sized and each tile individually cut. In most ceramic arts the next step would typically involve painting and decorating the tiles, applying a protective glaze and then firing in a kiln. However, as Işil Akbaygil reveals, the Iznik process was unique. After grinding and smoothing the surface of the tiles, potters poured a thin liquefied quartz glaze over each tile, and then fired them in a kiln, which gave the Iznik tiles the vibrancy that became synonymous with them.[17] The vibrancy achieved at Iznik and used in the mosque through Mihrimah Sultan's patronage reflects her name—bright as the sun and moon. It can therefore be stated that there are deeper meanings reflecting the identity of the mosque's main patron.

Another aspect of this technical process that was unique to Iznik tiles is that they were baked twice at 900 degrees Celsius and with a double glaze.[18] Between pulverising, moulding, drying, and baking the tiles, the Iznik Foundation calculated that it took six weeks to produce a batch of tiles, not including any time needed for decorating, which was considered to be the most painstaking part. The Iznik Foundation has found that including the design process a total of ten weeks was needed to produce a completed Iznik tile.[19]

After the tiles had been baked, the decorating process consisted of applying black ink contour lines that would later contain the coloured pigments. As Julian Raby states, a "stencil is laid over the tile or vessel and charcoal dust sprinkled over the pricking, so that the design is pounced on to the pottery."[20] There is some debate over whether Iznik artists also used stencils for their designs. However, according to Raby, evidence to support this is found in *firmans* (Ottoman edicts), which refer to the sultan's court sending stencil *numūne* (samples) to Iznik in 1595.[21]

Colour

Perhaps one of most innovative and striking aspects of the tiles that set them apart them from the Timurid-inspired Bursa tradition is their vibrant and innovative use of colours. Işil Akbaygil has shown that, to achieve this, 85 percent of the material in Iznik tiles was made of ground quartz, a substance unlike any other. This was a groundbreaking innovation at the time that gave the tiles their lasting lustre and would allow them to retain colour for many centuries. As Kerim Akbaygil states, "[t] hat's what makes the colors so good and bright as well as durable."[22] The Iznik Foundation has described how the quartz was mixed with earth or sand and clay into a mouldable compound. John Covel, the chaplain to the Levant Company who visited Iznik in 1677, noted the sand mixture used by Ottoman artisans at the kilns. [23] However, Raby believes that even during the decline of Iznik in the mid-seventeenth century, potters would have used quartz-silica instead of sand, as indicated by a chemical analysis of pottery fragments. His findings indicate a composition of 85 percent quartz, 10 percent white clay, and 10 percent glass frit.[24]

The colouring techniques of the tiles required technological innovation. For the potters, the "most important Iznik color was blue."[25] They produced this "from cobalt oxide" and then "combined cobalt oxide and copper oxide in the glaze."[26] Such processes are what make Iznik colours so unique. However, between the painting process and turning out the final product, the artists and potters sometimes found that the final colour was not as expected. The kiln workers faced a challenge in getting the tiles the right colour. For example, the colour red used during the decorating process might turn into turquoise blue during the baking process, while light pink might become red. The colouring techniques attained at the Iznik kilns saw the abandonment of the yellow that was introduced to Bursa by the "Masters of Tabriz" in the previous century. Iznik tiles used blue, cobalt blue, turquoise, green, and red, but rarely used brown, aubergine purple, or black.

By the second half of the sixteenth century, the Ottoman use of the *cuerda seca* technique introduced by the Masters of Tabriz had shifted to underglaze. This occurred first in the Süleymaniye Mosque. Sinan's sparse use of tiling in the Süleymaniye signifies the changing nature of the court's taste, and demonstrates that Süleyman's aesthetic vision was breaking from the Bursa and Edirne traditions once and for all. This self-fashioning of the sultan was associated with new and innovative ways of representing the magnificence of his court.

The production of Iznik tiles during the first half of the sixteenth century also saw the abandonment of the hexagonal shape of tiles from the Bursa tradition. One of the main reasons for this was that hexagonal tiles had been associated with dadoes which constricted the design. With the square format, the edges of the tiles became more emphasised. Like the *cuerda seca*, this format was more suitable for the design of multi-unit compositions. From the 1550s onwards this gave the artists the potential to develop pictorial and calligraphic tile panels. In this way, the visual representation of the Qur'an together with the calligraphic inscriptions could become, according to Geir Hellemo, "an expression of the utmost possibility earthly man has to see God face to face."[27] This was important because the *mihrab*, as the central attraction of the mosque's interior, needed to present this metaphoric meeting with God. This was to be achieved through a repetition of forms in a continuous pattern that gave a unified effect. Furthermore, the calligraphic roundels above the *mihrab* and window lunettes by Ahmet Karahısarı needed to form a unified elaborate knot to create visual appeal that was missing from the Yeşil Camii in Bursa. The calligraphic roundels of Karahısarı, fused with the pictorial aesthetics of floral naturalism and *saz* arabesques (serrated leaves) on underglaze tiles, provided the impetus needed to move beyond the Timurid-inspired Bursa tradition, leading to the enriched vibrancy, sheer brilliance, and effect of the tiles.

Vibrancy and materiality of the tiles

The tiles of the Rustem Pasha Mosque are characterised by their stark white background, against which the vibrant colours are brilliantly offset. From 1550 onward, underglaze tile work played a prominent role in mosque interior decoration. This accentuated the *mihrab* and the *qibla* walls through the expansion of the colour palette of the court. The Timurid *cuerda seca* was limited to certain dominant colours: white, blue, green, and yellow. Although purple was introduced during the last century along with turquoise, their poor visibility was not suited to *cuerda seca* tilework (figs. 6.1 and 6.2). Matte opaque tones were not suitable for architectural decoration because they needed to have a visual impact on the observer and more importantly, signifying the patron's power and prestige through the vibrancy of the colours. Ottoman artists therefore sought new decorative media that employed brilliant glazes and sharp clear colours over such a background. As Raby explains, "[t]he brilliance of these colours was not, of course, visible to the [tiler . . .] as he painted. It was the heat of the furnace which transmuted them from a sludge to grey to a brilliant hue. The [tiler . . .] had, therefore, to imagine the polychrome effect as he painted."[28] W. D. Kingery and P. B. Vandiver have also shown that red is perhaps the most difficult of underglaze colours to attain during the baking process, and would therefore have become the most highly sought after.[29] Around the 1550s Iznik potters were able to achieve the colour red by using Armenian bole, which they called *kil-i ermeni*. The coral colour effect this created was unmatched by any other ceramic tradition.[30] This colour innovation from the Bursa tradition replaced the dominant Timurid yellow with a more distinctly Ottoman flavour.

The introduction of red was a decisive factor in the new Iznik aesthetic. To maintain its vibrancy it had to be applied "slip, thick and upstanding," according to Raby.[31] This technique contributed to Iznik's texture and enhanced its tactile quality through its thick application. The colour red had been attempted during the thirteenth century in Syria and Cairo. It was also attempted at Bursa and Edirne in the Yeşil Türbe and Muradiye Mosque, and most likely became a challenge for the Ottoman artists to produce in the sixteenth century. But its application was matte, lacking the shine of an enamel or underglaze colour. It took time for artists to master its production and achieve the visual effect desired. To achieve the vibrancy and consistency of the red the slip had to be applied liberally so that, according to Raby, "it lay in thick relief like sealing-wax."[32] This was not achieved until 1595 in the mausoleum of Süleyman's grandson, Sultan Murad III. While Sinan introduced red to the Rustem Pasha Mosque in 1561–62, it was still in its experimental stage. Nonetheless, attaining it was a technical triumph for visual and aesthetic purposes. For this reason, Denny calls the tiles of the Rustem Pasha Mosque a "debut" triumph of tile innovation.[33] This innovative approach of the interior wall decorations represents, according to Denny, "the first time an elaborate program of decoration in which there was a massive attempt in many places to coordinate the actual manufacture of the tile revetments very meticulously with the wall surfaces of the building itself."[34] This technical innovation during the middle of the sixteenth century was matched by stylistic change.

Stylistic change and progress

Many artists made their mark on the Iznik tiles. Although Sinan was chief artistic director and architect, prominent artists of the day made their mark on the Iznik tile decorations and indeed on Islamic aesthetics more generally at the Ottoman court. Some artists who left their signatures on their works included Şah Kulu, Kara Memi, Ahmet Karahısarı, and Ibrahim. As noted in Chapter Three, the birth of the Ottoman court style is seen in the Timurid-inspired chinoiserie floral decoration in the Yeşil Camii and Yeşil Türbe in Bursa. However, the sixteenth-century tile repertoire expanded and became more refined than in the previous exemplars. The progress of the tiles from the Bursa to the Iznik tradition witnessed Ottoman artists developing their own variant of the Timurid style. Ottoman artists brought changes to the Timurid chinoiserie forms: they tightened the broad leaves into compact roundels by twisting the ends of the leaves and turning them in on themselves to create movement and animation. A close inspection of the tiles demonstrates the artists also made the buds on stems appear to be clasping at the rinceaux scrolls, and the motifs were evened out in size.[35] All this contributed to a greater sense of three-dimensionality and a more intense appearance.

Two main Iznik designs are seen in the first half of the sixteenth century: *rumi* and *hatayi* or *saz*. Şah Kulu from Tabriz, who in 1526 coordinated forty-one *nakkashane* (ateliers) artists at the court of Süleyman, is primarily recognised for introducing the distinctive style known as the *saz* or the *hatayi* style to the Ottoman court. In Ottoman art, this style is composed of thin-stemmed plants with long feather-like leaves, interspersed with complex floral palmettes. These are derived mainly from elements of Chinese art such as the lotus to convey the visual representation of the arabesque nature of Qur'anic calligraphy. The *saz* style came to be used around the borders of the *mihrab* panels to accentuate the *qibla* wall and the *mihrab*, and was supplemented with calligraphic inscriptions on top of the *mihrab*. The term *hatayi* literally means "Chinese" or "Cathayan" style, an arabesque of complex lotus palmettes, curving vines, and feathery leaves. This Chinese-inspired style was introduced from Iran and developed by the Ottomans in the early sixteenth century. The *rumi* style is inspired by animals and dates back to the tiles from the Seljuks of Rum, hence the term *rumi*. *Rumis*, which are highly stylised, became an integral part of the Iznik design. This continuation of past traditions in the Istanbul court was a way of legitimising the Ottomans' connections to their inherited Seljuk legacy. While retaining past stylistic motifs from the previous century, the Ottoman Iznik style of the sixteenth century adapted and broadened the floral designs and colours to create something original. This reflected the self-awareness and confidence of the Süleymanic court, asserted its cultural greatness and celebrated the magnificence of the patron-sultan.

Şah Kulu's pupil Kara Memi introduced a distinctly Ottoman floral repertoire in the Rustem Pasha Mosque. He moved away from the chinoiserie decorations seen in the Yeşil Camii and Yeşil Türbe in Bursa that had included mainly *hatayis* and *rumis*. In the Rustem Pasha Mosque, Kara Memi introduced a more naturalistic floral style, which Denny refers to as "quatre fleurs."[36] The four principal flowers were the tulip, carnation, rose, and hyacinth. Other flowers included pomegranates, scarlet pimpernels, and stylised rows of reeds. Kara Memi's flowers fit well into single tiles and were supplemented with *saz* leaf decorations. This became known as the "Kara Memi style" and was widely used during the Süleymanic century in tile decorations, illuminations of Qur'ans, the sultan's insignia the *tughra*, and illustrated manuscripts.[37] It was a move towards greater realism in floral depiction, compared with the *saz* style introduced from Iran. In this way Kara Memi's style was distinctly Ottoman.

The Kara Memi style, like the introduction of the square underglaze tiles, marked a shift from the Timurid–Persian aesthetics of the previous century and reflected the historical consciousness of a dynasty whose universal ambitions were being cemented on three continents. The new style also echoed the new self-awareness of the dynasty's cultural greatness over its inherited legacies of the East. The contributions of artists who aided Sinan, like Ahmet Karahısarı's calligraphic inscriptions on the portico, *qibla* wall, and the *mihrab*, augment the visual splendour of the interior and enhance the overall Iznik narrative Sinan wished to convey. Sinan achieved this by integrating the naturalism of the tiles with the textual inscriptions. Similarly, the windows by stained glass artist Ibrahim complement the array of colours reflected from the Iznik tiles, further accentuating the soft, harmonious and secure feeling the observer experiences from the warm yellows, greens, and light blues.[38] The illusion of the paradisiacal garden acting as a symbol of the world to come reinforces Ibn Arabi's words, where "[. . .] knowledge . . . is . . . effected by a penetration of the sense impressions of the outside world into the interior of the soul."[39]

Iznik *Çini* of the Rustem Pasha Mosque (1561–62): anagogical and eschatological readings

The Iznik çini that Sinan carefully orchestrated on the walls of the Rustem Pasha Mosque convey an anagogical and eschatological narrative through both classical and Sufi ideals. The aesthetic of the mosque confronts its human subjects with a spiritual decision of whether or not to enter the mosque and seek salvation. Within Sufism, Rumi says that to do this one must be able to look within and acknowledge mistakes. That is, one must look through the "ego of the *nafs*" (the ego of the self). In addition, Necipoğlu notes that the "eschatological inscription programme" attributed to Sinan's mosques requires attention.[40] In this rare mosque Sinan sought to express God's artistic creativity of the natural world. Within the Renaissance mindset, the Iznik narrative enunciates and alludes to the Divine, paradise, and salvation, all of which the viewer may seek in this sacred space. Sinan articulated a psychological and spiritual narrative, using the abstraction of Iznik styles to convey the individual's desire for salvation beyond earthly materialism and for a relationship with God.

In the Rustem Pasha Mosque's aesthetics, God awakens the visitor's search for Him by revealing the beauty of this world and by giving glimpses of the world to come. Because that beauty exists in the world, it manifests itself as derived from Divine Beauty. The sixteenth-century Ottoman intellectual and spiritual rebirth exemplified in the Iznik narrative of the mosque's tiles is fused with Platonic and Sufi ideals. Artistic and intellectual maturity are thematised within this frame. The convergent point between God and the seeker is therefore the aesthetic of the Iznik çini, where the experience of the tiles' beauty is understood as the place where God can be experienced.

Vasari, Ali, and Sinan understood artistic achievements in cosmological and eschatological terms. Both cultures perceived their accomplishments as imperfect signposts of God's greater plan for the salvation of humanity. Just as Vasari's narrative was imbued with a Sufi humanist impulse, so too was the Ottoman experience imbued with the Sufi humanist compulsion. Like the Italian Renaissance, the Ottomans sought a broader understanding of their world through past intellectual developments such as classical Greece (neo-platonism) and their own particular humanist tradition: Sufi.

Like the Platonist perception of God as the craftsman, both Christianity and Islam perceive God as the Maker, the Great Artist. Sinan saw himself as "the blessed architect, I who am the spiritual master *pir* of the dervish convent of the world."[41] The historical consciousness for both Vasari and Sinan, then, was to interpret artistic creations as inspirations from God who reveals snippets of the hereafter to humanity. For Sinan, the Mosque of Rustem Pasha was one of these signposts.[42] By imitating the perfection of God the Maker, the artists' imitations of nature provided a glimpse of the unity of the One. As an artist, Sinan, like his Tuscan counterparts, saw himself as "a wise architect . . . a master engineer, pious and without defect" who "with God's help . . . find[s] divine guidance for the immortality of his work. And in this there is no doubt."[43] This creativity resonates with Vasari's description of Leonardo da Vinci: "And truly the heavens occasionally send us some who represent not only humanity, but divinity itself, so that from this, as from a model, by imitating it, we can approach the highest parts of heaven with our mind and with the excellence of the intellect."[44] Sinan's artistic achievement in this unique mosque reflects his humanity, and as with Leonardo da Vinci, his divinity, and the brilliance of his intellect. Like Vasari's praise of the Tuscan artists attaining perfection in art, Sinan's self-aggrandisement exemplifies his belief that his works were divinely inspired to reveal God's perfection through his earthly "perfections." However, before this critical reading of the Iznik in the mosque interior, it is important to understand the significance of the Islamic garden and spirituality.

The symbolism of the Islamic garden

The Islamic garden serves as a reminder of both the world to come and immanence of God. Symbolically, the garden reinforces the Socratic idea of *elenchus* or self-examination. It allows for contemplation and self-reflection of one's worthiness in such a place. Additionally, it underlines Rumi's idea of achieving salvation and God's mercy. This is mentioned in the Qur'an about the world to come: "The parable of the Garden which the righteous are promised! beneath it flows rivers: perpetual is the enjoyment thereof and the shade therein: such is the end of the Righteous; and the end of Unbelievers in the Fire."[45] For Rumi, like Plato, the beauty of the garden is derived from God's beauty because, as Rumi writes, "In the garden are hundreds of charming beloveds and roses and tulips dancing around and limpid water running in the brook. All this is a pretext—it is He alone!"[46] Like Plato, for Rumi too everything created is a "pretext"—a glimpse of His power, majesty, and beauty. This allusion to the Garden of Eden as the world to come becomes the focal point for the worshipper. As Emma Clark explains, the garden "[. . .] is a love born of the deep belief that the beauty of nature was a reflection of transcendent truth; these plants and flowers are shadows of their heavenly archetypes, their beauty radiation of God's glory on earth."[47] This Platonic ideal manifests itself in the Islamic fine arts, none more so than the decorative Iznik tiles in the Rustem Pasha Mosque. In the Qur'an there are over one hundred and twenty references to "gardens": *jannat* (garden) al *firdaws* (paradise).[48] These references to paradise as a garden are epithets indicating:

> [. . .] not only blissful and eternal, but also a refuge, a sheltered and secure retreat (*khalwa*). The term "Gardens of Eden" suggests the spiritual peace and harmony of man's primordial state. Gardens of Eternity, Delight Bliss, Refuge, as well as Eden all recur several times, but the phrase most often used (over thirty times) is *Jannat tajri min tahtiha al-anhar*, "Gardens underneath which rivers flow."[49]

From this, one can sense the literal image of the flowing water to irrigate the flowers, but on a more reflective level it intimates the "nurturing" of the "garden within" the individual "by the ever-flowing waters of the spirit which purify" and renew the "soul."[50] The garden and water imagery, through the use of floral arrangements against the turquoise background, evokes a sense of the Islamic-Ottoman garden as paradise on earth.

At the centre of this garden is the water imagery conveyed by the colour blue. Just as the physical garden would, this representation of paradise creates a similar "cooling, cleansing and purifying" effect for the visitor.[51] This acts as a reminder that man is at once "body, soul and spirit, and that the outward habits by which we live cannot be disassociated from the inward."[52] For this rebirth to take effect, according to Sayyed Hossein Nasr,

> There is present something of both the lucidity and perfection of the snowflake and the beauty of a geometrically formed flower in the Islamic paradise which when manifest in Islamic art and architecture re-captures an echo of that paradise and prepares the soul for the experience of that *firdaws* promised in the Quran to the faithful.[53]

The manifestation of the natural garden in Islamic art allows architects and artists to understand the materials they use to create the illusion of the Garden of Eden as symbols of the world to come. In doing so, as Nasr states, they "[. . .] unravel the structure of the cosmos before the eye of the beholder."[54] In both the Platonic and Sufi philosophies, "[. . .] they are the result of the vision of the archetypal world by seers and contemplatives who then taught craftsmen to draw them upon the surfaces of tiles or alabaster."[55] Nasr points out that for the pious individual, the combination of the symbolisms associated with the art aesthetics activating the sensory perceptions and "[. . .] the continuous references in the Qur'anic phrases which remould the soul of the Muslim into a mosaic of spiritual attitudes, the emphasis upon the grandeur of God" can be achieved.[56] The scarcity of the Qur'anic inscriptions in the sacred space of the Rustem Pasha Mosque, however, is replaced with the floral and colourful Iznik tiles placing more emphasis on the Creative Imagination as noted by Ibn Arabi above. The sacred space of the mosque and its decorative aesthetics come to represent the world to come described in the Qur'an:

> They shall dwell in the gardens of Eden, with rivers rolling at their feet ... they shall be decked with bracelets of gold and arrayed in garments of fine silk and rich brocade . . . They will be among thorn-less lote trees . . . in long-extended shade, by constantly flowing water, and fruit in plenty.[57]

For Ibn Arabi, "[. . .] this theophanic function of Beauty will present the most perfect image of Divinity" and provide comfort and hope for the seeker.[58] It is thus the art of Iznik that acts as a reminder of the world to come and allows the individual to "remould" his soul in order to recognise *tawhid* and perhaps attain *ittihad* through this theophanic experience. At another level, the theophanic experience, according to Frithjof Schuon, also allows one to "look for the garden within" oneself and one's "[. . .] indestructible divine Substance; then this will give you a new and imperishable garden."[59]

Flower symbolism

As the trend toward naturalism became more refined and sophisticated in early modern Ottoman art, flowers became dominant motifs. Sinan's use of blossoms, brilliant red tulips, and carnations make their appearance at the Mosque of Rustem Pasha and are placed on the walls of the mosque in recurring patterns. Together, the floral motifs signify the Islamic concept of *zikr*—the remembrance of God through prayer and contemplation, which often incorporates the use of prayer beads (figs. 6.3, 6.4, and 6.5). In fact, the sheer number of flowers in the floral depictions symbolise the Qur'anic verse in 17:110, "His are the most beautiful names," as well as the beauty and wonder of His creation on earth, reinforcing the contemporary historian Ramazanzade's words for the description of the mosque—a "noble sanctuary" resembling the "fourth heaven."[60]

The floral motifs demonstrate a specific visual language that is tied to Iznik design. The tulip motif is primarily depicted as sitting flaccid, symbolising the submission of the believer to Allah, whilst the rose is shown in full bloom to indicate praise for His creation in a display of the Almighty's glory. During the sixteenth century the Turkish word *lale* (tulip) became an anagram of the Muslim term for Allah, as the letters in *lale* are also contained in the word for Al-lah, meaning The One.[61]

Like the tulip, the rose or *gül* had mystical overtones. The ancient Europeans believed the rose to have come from the blood of the goddess Venus. Similarly, Busbecq (1555), the Austrian ambassador to the court of Süleyman the Magnificent, discussed the Ottomans' belief that the rose had been born form the sweat of the Prophet.[62] This mystical association is also referenced by the thirteenth-century dervish poet Yunus Emre's (1240–1320): "the flower is he, that dervish rose is Muhammad's sweat."[63] Thus, in Sufi symbolism the rose came to represent Divine beauty and the face of the "beloved," His Prophet. It also entered Islamic mystical literature as the "flower of blood" and the "flower of suffering" to highlight the torment that the Prophet endured to deliver the Divine message to his people. It also came to symbolise the soul in search of the Divine just as the pasha's soul would do in his journey to the Hereafter. The endowment deed of Sultan Süleyman for the mosque and the accounts of contemporary historians Ramazanzade and Hasanbeyzade reflect this idea further.[64] The personified rose in Sufi poetry calls out to God, as the poet Yunus Emre writes, "and in the garden scent of roses is wafting, declaring God's name."[65]

When combined in floral arrangements, the two types of flowers—tulips and roses—evoke the first pillar of Islam: "there is no God but God, and Muhammad is the Messenger of God." As J. M. Rogers and R. M. Ward claim, Iznik floral imagery was imbued with religious significance, and was a visual complement to court poetry as well as to Qur'anic and *hadith* narrations.[66] Furthermore, the floral imagery of Iznik also served as a representation of Sufi mysticism.

More than forty variations of tulip motifs can be found within the mosque. Like the prayer beads in which every bead is a reminder of God's attributes during prayer time, so too in this sacred space every tulip represents God and acts as a reminder of Him. The dispersal of tulips throughout the mosque also symbolises the omnipresence of God, and reminds the individual that "He is with you wherever you are."[67] Aside from the floral symbolism, the Iznik also employed a wide variety of abstract decorative schemes such as cloud imagery inspired by Chinese tradition. Iznik also used çintemani, a more eclectic style made up of two undulating lines, three spheres (one at the top and two at the bottom), and tree motifs representing the creative force of "The Life Tree." Clouds bring forth rain and abundance and so are important in their symbolic life-giving. Such a life-giving force reflects the intentions of Mihrimah Sultan: "[. . .] for the expansive soul of her illustrious husband," as the endowment deed noted that his soul would find salvation in the afterlife.[68] According to Raby, these lines represent the pelt of the striped tiger and spotted leopard, signifying power and strength.[69] The "Life Tree" motif, on the other hand, demonstrates the power and artistry of God's creation as well as the efflorescence of cultural greatness. In the sixteenth-century Ottoman context it alluded to the magnificence and triumph of the aesthetics of the court of Sultan Süleyman, from its monumental architecture of imperial mosques to the fine arts of Iznik.

Another symbolic design is associated with the arabesques of Şah Kulu's *saz*. The combination of these visuals—the tulips, roses, hyacinths, and carnations, among many other flowers, *saz* arabesques, and the eclectic çintemani—became dominant motifs used to enhance the Iznik narrative for the visitor. In this way, Sinan was able to achieve a balance between tension and clarity. The style conveyed the hope of a better world to come represented by the paradisiacal imagery of the Iznik tiles. Sinan recites this narrative to the viewer through the mosque's decoration and thereby activates his visual sensory perception and engages him at the philosophical, physical, cerebral, and anagogical levels. This begins from the moment one sets foot on the portico and comes face to face with the tile panels at the entrance.

Entry panels

There are two panels situated to the left and right of the entrance door (fig. 6.6). Only the left panel remains intact as the right one has been looted over the centuries. At close viewing of the panels, the artists who have tried to restore it in subsequent times have left it in a dismal state (fig. 6.6a). The left panel shows a spring tree coming to life. It depicts a unified-field niche on a cobalt-blue ground. Forty-five 9 x 5 square tiles cover the space from floor up to the portico ceiling. The whole panel looks like a painting in the naturalistic style stuck to the wall of the portico signifying the rebirth of creation in the spring. The spring tree blooms with flowers of all sorts, representing the rebirth of life and reinforcing Mihrmah Sultan's intention for the mosque to help her husband find salvation in the Hereafter.

The left tile panel at the entrance is decorated with an array of floral ensembles. The tomato red on the left panel of the Rustem Pasha Mosque is applied to the tulip. On the bottom left and right tiles, one can see two tulips enveloped in "a swirling *saz* leaf, which bears a hyacinth spray."[70] To the upper right, the tile is decorated with "a bulbous round floral motif, seemingly a lotus or peony bud."[71] As part of this combination there is a single white blossom—the profile of a fan-like carnation shown among spring tree buds.[72] Additionally, the panel's petals are enhanced with çintemani. Like the pelt of the striped tiger and spotted leopard, the çintemani motif's location at the bottom of the panel, where it accompanies the tulips and is enveloped by the *saz* scrolls, alludes to the power that is holding this creation together.

The positioning of this floral work suggests that if such beauty exists within the Ottoman "Paradise" of the Rustem Pasha Mosque, then surely such inner splendour is worthy striving for. In fact, the multitude of floral arrangements at the entrance panel complement and symbolise the artistic creativity of God. For Ibn Arabi, God's "[. . .] creation is an act of the divine imaginative power: this divine creative imagination is essentially a theophanic Imagination" where the observer through the flower symbolism begins to gain knowledge about the visible manifestations or signs of God to humanity.[73] Although it is difficult to ascertain which flower is ascribed to which attribute of God, some, such as the carnation symbolising yearning, stand out from the panels and evoke spiritual contemplation during prayer.[74] Thus, the entrance creates a sense of excitement and suspense for the devout waiting to enter God's house, and assures the visitor that what is found within will not disappoint. From the entryway, the viewer's sensory perceptions are awakened to receive and make meaning of the interior aesthetics.[75] The fact that the new Ottoman style is immersed in a rich and time-tested past legitimises Kara Memi's new floral repertoire and reinforces Ali's and Sinan's ideas of refining past *sūret* or üsl'ub (style) to attain *nezāket* (elegance, refinement), *cemile* (beauty), and *zuhūrat* (perfection).[76]

On the remaining surface of the panel a plethora of different flowers calls out to the visitor. The large leaves at the bottom of the panel envelope a pair of tulips, and the same flower appears elsewhere on the panel, but with different petals. Flanking the trees at the bottom are sprays of tiny spring flowers, and between the trees are a rosebud and a rose with a swirling red centre, with white hyacinths gathered on the left side. In Fatih Cimok's description of the panel, we see "blossoming spring trees of manganese-purple springing from cluster of large leaves with sawtooth-like edges," with leaves "shown in a wind-blown movement and decorated with thin hyacinth sprays."[77] Unlike the static Bursa–Timurid floral representations in the Yeşil Camii and Yeşil Türbe *mihrabs,* the awakening of new life through Kara Memi's innovation in the Rustem Pasha Mosque celebrates both the stylistic and technical progress of Ottoman artists. The animated flowers of the panels in the mosque echo the patron's intentions for the salvation of the pasha's soul. Rumi, similarly, shouts to the seeker to:

> Awake, the time hath arrived, awake, awake! Without union with Him, Detest thyself, detest thyself!
> . . . In an inexplicable way He shall purify Thee, and make thee rosy-faced, He shall remove the thorn from thy Hand; become a garden of roses, become a garden of roses![78]

Like the flowers on the tree of the Iznik panel, Rumi too is calling out to the seeker to awaken and be purified and become a garden of roses (i.e. to become one with Him). This understanding about making one's life a rose garden is further reflected in the poetry of Ahmedi (d. 1413), who writes, "May thy life's rose-garden never fade away! May thy glory's orchard never see decay!"[79] These words were written in the fifteenth century to describe the life and legacy of Alexander the Great and compare him to the then sultan Mehmed II. As Ali notes, the words resonate equally well with Süleyman's reign. This idea is further reinforced by the court poet Baqi (1526–1600), who describes the sultan as the "Iskender of his day!"[80]

The sultan's reign is thus perceived as a "rose garden" that will never decay. As God's representative on earth, Süleyman established an earthly paradise that is reflected in the mosque's çini aesthetics. The fashioning of the sultan in this context unites the paradise in the world to come with the paradise that he created on earth through the beauty of Iznik çini. For Ahmedi, this paradise will never decay or fade away. His words echo Süleyman's words quoted early that the mosque serves as a reminder of the continuation of his reign. Similarly, in his poetry Süleyman's references to the rose garden reflect the cultural greatness of the Süleymanic Age he ushered in: "In the world's rose garden, we . . . pure of soul . . . are the Süleymanis."[81] With divine guidance, souls can be purified in the rose garden of the world (i.e. in the mosque) that Süleyman created. Süleyman thus expresses the triumph of Ottoman "paradise on earth" under the "Süleymanis."

Like the flowers in bloom celebrating life, Kara Memi's distinctive *quatre fleurs* style makes its appearance in the mosque. The *quatre fleurs* augment and differentiate the identity of court culture in the Süleymanic Age from that of previous Ottoman rulers. Having refined the past chinoiserie style of the Bursa and Edirne traditions to suit the tastes of the Süleymanic court, Kara Memi's distinct floral style is fused with that of Şah Kulu's *saz* scrolls and the Chinese-inspired floral decorations of the past. Under the patronage of Mihrimah Sultan, Şah Kulu's *saz* style provided the impetus for innovation and progress in the fine arts. The combination of Şah Kulu's *saz* scrollwork and Kara Memi's symphony of floral arrangements on the panels reflect the mature phase of the fine arts, which are now more refined with greater *nezāket* (elegance) than in the previous century. This aesthetic innovation moves forward through the representation of the floral ensemble, making it distinctly more Ottoman in style than the Timurid-inspired Bursa tradition. The ensemble of flowers with their sheer brilliance and vibrant colours not only signify the triumph of Süleyman's achievements, but also reflect the illuminating effect of the sun and moon brightening the interior– like Mihrimah

Sultan. In this way the self-fashioning of both father and daughter are expressed in the mosque aesthetics. This innovation thus reflects the Ottomans' new self-awareness that shaped their historical consciousness and sense of identity in the sixteenth century.

Sunni Ottoman religious identity challenged the Shi'a Safavids of Iran, who claimed to be the true representatives of Islam and the Muslim world. The state recognised the Sufi order in the Ottoman Empire in the sixteenth century. However, for the Sufis of Safavid Iran, tensions existed between the ruling household and the dervish order. As Rula Jurdi Abisaab states, the Safavid Shi'a clerics "strove to expunge heterodoxy and Sufism from Twelve Shi'ite practices."[82] The Ottomans therefore sought to produce representations of "true" Islam to legitimise their larger role within the Muslim world. One of the ways to express this "true" form of Islam was through Sufi humanism. Süleyman states in one of his poems that the soul becomes purified when the seeker "withdraw[s] from cares of earth."[83] In other words, the mosque's representation of earthly paradise is closely connected to the piety and purification of oneself from worldly desires. The mosque's visitor may feel drawn to reflect on his past sins, which he must "detest" according to Rumi. He must distance himself from worldly materialism. Only through detesting one's past sins can one become purified and attain salvation. By becoming "a garden of roses," the seeker in search of the Divine becomes beautiful like the rose because its beauty is God's own. Thus, the garden as represented in the Iznik panel and Rumi's verse is available for the seeker to relate to when he experiences the desire to communicate with the Divine.

Chinese cloud bands can be seen at the top and bottom of the panel. resemble the form of the dragon, which represents the fire from the beak of the mythical bird the *simurg*—similar to the phoenix in the Western tradition—depicted widely in Ottoman miniature paintings (fig. 6.7).[84] The *simurg* is also referenced in court literature and is described as resurrecting itself after death, or *ihya*, to begin life anew, like the Iznik çini. It denotes, according to Zulfi Güler, "maturity in mystical sense and intimacy with God," suggesting that the narrative of the Iznik tiles is intertwined with the transcendental message it is conveying.[85] The symbolism of the *simurg* also reflects the rebirth of the Ottoman Empire after Timur's invasion in the fifteenth century and, here, in the Rustem Pasha Mosque, it echoes the triumph over past Ottoman accomplishments. The tiles' aesthetics provide the observer with the hope of finding the Paradise that is described in the Qur'an.

This aesthetic development reflects the Ottoman Renaissance experience at Süleyman's court. In addition to the motifs already discussed, there is an undulating red band at the top of the panel with rectangular knots derived from metalwork. Large *rumis* decorate the spandrels outside the lobed arch and include split-leaves and *palmettes* with a multitude of white blossoms that are executed with meticulous detail. These symbolise both life and death and act as reminders for transience of life. This further echoes Mustafa Sa'i's words in Sinan's autobiographies quoted earlier about the impermanence of life.

The exterior panel inspires a feeling of exhilaration, invoking the image of spring that is synonymous with rebirth and life. This suggests that all of this growth and budding meets at an end point towards the source of that spring. Like the Qur'anic verses informing the faithful of a Garden with flowing water, this rebirth of life is an underlying power expressed by Rumi in one of his verses:

> Again, the violet bows to the lily. Again, the rose is tearing off her gown! The green ones have come from the other world, tipsy like the breeze up to some new foolishness . . . Again, the season of Spring has come and a spring-source rises under everything, a moon sliding from the shadows.[86]

However, the source of that power still remains hidden from the viewer but He does yearn to be known, because, as noted by Ibn Arabi, it is the intention of the divine to be known.[87] One of God's attributes in the Qur'an is Al-Baatin (to be The Hidden). Despite all the visible colours—violets, reds, greens—the "spring-source" (God) remains in the shadows like a mystery. Green is synonymous with the Garden of Eden. For Rumi, the colour green is a visitor from "the other world"—a world the individual is seeking in this space. From Rumi's perspective, however, this transcendence is not accessible to everyone because not everything is visible.

From neo-platonic and Sufi perspectives, then, the mosque can be understood as symbolically indicative of the world to come. It is not Paradise, but it reminds the viewer of the paradise that has been promised in the Qur'an. When one takes a closer look at the white spring flowers against the blue background, one finds that they reveal a velvet-like texture with feather-like leaves. This texture looks as if it had been painted free-hand by following the outlines of the floral forms. It is these brush strokes—in translucent blue pigment—that produce the subtle yet evocative mystical effects. This imagery acts as a reminder of Paradise but it also reflects Ottoman perceptions of cultural greatness in having created their own "paradise" on earth under Süleyman, the ideal Muslim ruler. This self-fashioning of the dynasty is closely connected to its justification of itself as the true rulers of the Muslim world.

This garden theme and the hope of paradise are further reinforced by the pasha's *vakfiye* (endowment). The document affirms that the sultan's daughter Mihrimah Sultan had a mosque built for her husband that "in beauty . . . is . . . the envy of the awe-inspiring Garden of Eden, as if it were a sign of the pavilions of heaven."[88] This hope is echoed in the contemporary historian Ramazanzade Mehmed's description of the mosque as a "noble sanctuary resembling paradise."[89] Although these descriptions avoid identifying the mosque with the gardens of paradise, they establish a symbolic relationship between paradise and the Iznik tiles. Ramazanzade's reference to the paradise-resembling mosque also indirectly alludes to Mihrimah Sultan's name and patronage. In this way, the mosque also reflects the beauty and self-fashioning of its patron. Furthermore, as Hellemo notes, the *vakfiye* document and historians' descriptions "emphasise" that the beauty of the decoration creates a dynamic, psychologically coloured desire for the sublime garden of paradise."[90] Thus the floral arrangements of the tiles in the mosque are able to trigger religious and spiritual experiences that are "transgressive in the sense that brings this world into contact with the world to come."[91] Through the theophanic experience, the world to come promises a garden with blooming trees, such as those depicted in the tile panel and the Qur'an.

The repetition of the Iznik floral motifs reinforces the idea of the Qur'anic message of paradise and the attainment of salvation. In his autobiography Sinan repeatedly reinforces this message about his mosques. For example, he writes, "[t]he mosque became a meeting place of the lovers of purity, *ehl-i safa* (i.e. spiritual seekers and the Sufis). A joy-giving abode like Paradise . . . With their images (i.e. reference to the interior aesthetics) confounding the artists of China."[92] Sa'i's reference to Sinan's aesthetics suggests that the Ottomans have surpassed the Chinese masters from whom they derived inspiration. This reliance on naturalism through experimenting with colours to replicate the imagery of paradise in the Qur'an challenged tile makers to advance the use of colour to make the Iznik style even more aesthetically appealing and meaningful. At times, however, certain colours had to be abandoned. Unfortunately, Iznik tile workers eventually stopped using the manganese-purple applied in the branches of the panel due to its poor visibility from a distance (fig. 6.8).[93]

The Rustem Pasha Mosque confronts its human subjects with a spiritual decision: whether to enter the mosque and seek salvation. Within Sufism, Rumi says that to do this one must be able to look within and acknowledge mistakes. That is, one must look through the "ego of the *nafs*" (the ego of the self). As Rumi states, "[s]ometimes angels envy our cleanliness and sometimes the devils run away from our evil . . . What a mysterious creature is man that different habits, virtues, goodness and evil come together in him."[94] The interior's dominant colours of cobalt and turquoise blue suggest safety, protection, and security from worldly desires.[95] The red tulips and roses are reminders of the beauty of God and His Prophet, and the rest of the floral arrangements represent paradise, reinforcing the words of the endowment deed for the mosque to become the ". . . envy of the sublime garden of paradise."[96] Before entering the mosque, the seeker encounters Ahmet Karahısarı's Qur'anic inscriptions on the portico panels. Taken together, these visual elements provide the observer with a larger view of the Qur'anic paradise.

Portico inscription

The art of calligraphy and Iznik çini in order to represent the Word and Beauty of the Divine also serves as a reminder that salvation is only achieved through God and the message of the Qur'an. The mosque's religious inscriptions on the wall of the portico include white cursive *thuluth* script on Iznik tiles, work of the gifted court calligrapher Ahmet Karahısarı.[97] These inscriptions adorn the window tops along the portico enclosure. These Qur'anic inscriptions set the thematic tone of the mosque's message. They read: "He is Allah, the Creator, the Shaper out of naught, the Fashioner. His are the most beautiful names. All that is in the heavens and the earth glorifieth Him, and He is the Mighty, the Wise."[98] The theme of the portico inscriptions thus affirm Ibn Arabi's words above for the Hidden One to be known and that "[. . .] creation is essentially a theophany (*tajalli*)."[99]

The absence of inscriptions on the panels complements the message of the verse through the visual representation of God's creative beauty reflected in the natural world. The blossoming tree shows carnations in full bloom and budding tulips growing out from the branches, with other flowers and serrated green leaves of Şah Kulu at its base enveloping a pair of tulips. Sinan's use of the Qur'anic message has a powerful emotional impact on the viewer, yet the precise meaning remains subject to interpretation.[100] Because it relies on subjective interpretation, the artwork makes meaning through the viewer's self-reflection. The combination of the Qur'anic inscriptions and the floral representations of God's creativity enhance the theophanic experience for the visitor. In this way Sinan seeks to impact the seeker's sensory perceptions and lead him to the experience of self-transformation.

The imagery of the paradisiacal garden also gives the visitor hope. Sufism asserts that those who believe in Paradise will be blessed by His Light and worshiped by angels because God has chosen the believers to be viceroys on earth.[101] In the Rustem Pasha Mosque, it appears that the road to salvation begins at the entry to the mosque, where the floral arrangements and blossoming tree provide hope by mimicking the beauty of the kingdom of heaven. This hope offers temporary relief from worldly desires. Like Platonic philosophy and humanist thought, Sufi humanism seeks to make sense of one's relationship with God and his existence on earth. With this relationship re-established through hope in a blissful eternal life—represented by the entrance panel—worldly desires begin to dissipate. At this point believers are encouraged to examine their actions and see through the ego of the self. The profusion of flowers on the surface of the panels interspersed with leaves and enhanced with myriad colours invite the observer to the Garden of Eden, asking him to reflect on whether he is worthy of that blissful Garden. This self-reflection begins with the ego. Sinan expresses this letting go of the ego in the following words: "I could not find the key to the lock of the treasure of contentment. Until from my heart and soul I many times shouted, 'O, Revealer!'"[102] The use of the words "shouting" and "many times" in the verse are reinforced in the vibrancy of the floral imagery of God's flowers in bloom on the entrance panel. From a close viewing the flowers seem to shout to the observer about what is waiting beyond this existence. The multitude of flowers swirl about on the blooming tree as if dancing, and invite the seeker to embrace his destiny just as Plato and Rumi ask individuals to do.

At the entrance portico Sinan enunciates the Socratic method of *elenchus* (self-examination and reflection) through the questioning of one's actions. Sinan achieves this through the two external *mihrab* niches, with one on either side of the portico's entrance panels (fig. 6.9). Beside each *mihrab* there is a single Iznik tile panel that represents the Ka'ba, which is centrally placed and signifies the presence of God on earth. As Avinoam Shalem notes, "the Ka'ba image is permanently present in the mind of the Muslim faithful"[103] (fig. 6.10). These external *mihrabs* and the Ka'ba tiles allow for contemplation and reflection before the uncertainty of this existence comes to an end. Indicating the direction to Mecca both architecturally (with the *mihrabs*) and visually (with the Ka'ba images) heightens the viewer's awareness of his religious responsibilities, such as daily prayers and God consciousness even before he enters the mosque. These pointers act as reminders to prepare for the "real judgement" once he enters the mosque and faces the central *mihrab* panels in the centre of the *qibla* wall.

At the same time, however, the intricate floral motifs lead the faithful to contemplate not so much the world but the promise of paradise to come. The blossoming tree with large leaves, white hyacinths, peony buds, carnations, rose buds, and tulips are paradisiacal imagery in grand form on the walls of the mosque, which becomes even grander as one walks through the entry door into the main mosque. Through their use, Sinan creates a sense of apprehension and hope. Observers reflect first on their own shortcomings on earth and their need for self-examination, and second, on the hope that they are worthy of entering Paradise. Even if one has "broken his vows a thousand times," per Rumi, one cannot lose hope of salvation and God's forgiveness. This angst is also felt in the Süleyman's self-fashioning. Süleyman's poems composed during the construction of the mosque reflects his own spiritually self-reflective tone:

> If you aspire to God's compassion, kindness should come from you too; be sure to offer your benevolence and mercy to people of virtue. If you hope to reach the gardens of Paradise to find love and grace. Instead of terrifying destruction when the end comes to you, Humble yourself like a skirt[104], bow at the sage's feet and rub your face.[105]

Just as Sinan's Iznik aesthetic offers the visitor a moment to reflect, Süleyman, too, in his poem conveys a similar message. To "reach the gardens of Paradise," the visitor can find salvation, love, grace, kindness, and mercy in this sacred space. This emphasises the words of the *vakfiye* of Sultan Süleyman above and the hope that the sacred space of the mosque and "prayers for the pasha's soul" will enable him to find peace and mercy.[106]

After detesting oneself for past mistakes as Rumi suggests, Süleyman urges the visitor on a journey of transformation to humble himself before the One. By encouraging a reflective state of mind through the imagery of the flowers on the panels, the visual depiction of the Ka'ba and the *mihrabs* resonate with Süleyman's identity formation. Even though he is a world ruler, he recognises the need to humble himself before the One. This humility through self-reflection, however, must ultimately result in one deciding to change. As Sinan writes in his autobiographies, "If one does good in this world, he endures."[107] This belief is linked to the Qur'anic verses 13:11, 21:47, 59:18, and 91:9: "Verily never will Allah (S) change the condition of a people until they change what is in their hearts . . . Indeed he succeeds who purifies his own self."[108] As the observer takes steps towards its interior, the release of tension through the use of the two floral panels on either side of the entrance provides the observer with comfort. As gateways to "paradise", the two entrance panels ease the visitor's anxiety and suggest that there may be hope and salvation ahead once the he / she steps inside. Sinan's Iznik floral images and the deliberate visual representation of the Ka'ba, as well as the employment of inscriptions, play on the psychology of the visitor before entering the mosque and arguably assist in the progression of the self-transformation process.

The mosque's interior and the *qibla* wall

Sinan indirectly subverts the act of judgement in the interior of his mosque. When entering the mosque, the visitor is struck by the sheer brilliance of the tiles which appear as one large painting and allude to God's artistry in the natural world. The vibrancy of the tiles, mesmerising to the eyes, is also a reflection of God's artistry with light (fig. 6.11). The sheer brilliance immediately distances the mind from comprehending the One and instead alludes to His attribute as The Hidden. Staring at the *qibla* wall from a distance, the observer is unable to see the intricacies of each Iznik tile design, just as he is unable to see The Hidden.

In aesthetic terms Denny has criticised this decision, arguing that the tile decorations are lost in the huge interior of the mosque.[109] However, from an Islamic perspective of *tanzih* (God cannot be comprehended nor represented), the Iznik design signifies the transcendence of God and the fact that He cannot be represented in images or comprehended by the human mind. One of His attributes in the Qur'an is the Al-Badi (the Incomparable, 2:117, 6:101). In this sacred space, Sinan found a powerful medium through which to communicate notions of earthly experience being subsumed by the infinite artistry of the Almighty. This creativity of the mosque is echoed in Rustem Pasha's endowment deed and by the contemporary historian Ramazanzade: "elegant," "sublime garden of paradise," "unequalled and hitherto unseen," "rarity of the age," "heart attracting," "pleasant-looking," "made of light," "azure dome," and "encompassing all kinds of artistry."[110] Symbolic of God's creative artistry, the esoteric narrative articulated by Sinan through the aesthetics of Iznik naturalism allows for visitors to reflect on the inner self in a way that resonates in both the Qur'an and mystical Sufi teachings.[111]

Upon entering the Rustem Pasha Mosque, one comes face-to-face with an enormous façade carrying inscriptions. This runs along the corridor in dark blue calligraphic letters on a white background. Again the work of the imperial calligrapher Ahmet Karsahısarı, his first usage of large calligraphic roundels in tile decorations can be seen on the enormous *qibla* wall facing Mecca. These calligraphic decorations thematise the Divine Creator's glory and forgiving nature. The inscription above the *muqarnas* and the white marble *mihrab* resonate with the verse from the entrance (that salvation is possible through the worship of God).

The tiles, with their floral designs and patterns, shine brilliantly and are reflected in the light. Ramazanzade refers to this in his praise of the mosque's female patron Mihrimah Sultan in the following words: "She built such a luminous Friday mosque, / That those who saw it would think it was made of light."[112] The message conveyed here, however, is not so much about the power of God reflected in the symbolism of the dome, but about His other attributes mentioned in the Qur'an: Al-Khaaliq (The Creator) and Al-Nur (The Light). Eventually, when the observer reaches the centre of the mosque he is compelled to look upwards at the dome at the *thuluth* inscription. Here one is reminded of God's power that firmly holds the heavens and earth in place.[113]

The difference between this mosque and the Süleymaniye and Selimiye mosques discussed in the previous chapter is in part this emphasis on God's artistry in the natural world, powerfully evoked by the thousands of tiles enveloping the visitor. When looking at the dome, the viewer is surrounded by blue and white on blue tile work roundels. Using the traditional Chinese colour of blue[114], these tiles mark the eight pendentives of Allah, Muhammad, and his companions Abu Bakr, Omar, Othman, Ali, and the Prophet's grandsons Hassan and Hussein—considered to be Muslim saints—and who look down upon the congregation, as if to bless them.

The spiritual transformation induced by Sinan's artwork requires the observer's self-examination. In fact, from the moment one walks into this sacred space, one feels compelled to rotate a full 360 degrees to take in all the beauty. This "revolving" of the observer can be likened to the Sufi *sema* ceremony, where whirling dervishes become one with God, and to the pilgrimage (*hajj*) to Mecca and circumambulation of the Ka'ba. In a similar way, Richard Etlin writes that the "whirling" space becomes

> an integral constituent of the self . . . Our aesthetic response to scenes of nature and to works of art, to their qualities of line, from, and mass, is a composite sentiment that involves a bodily sense of self, which also has its spatial dimension. At the deepest end of the aesthetic scale, in situations to which we attach the notion of the sublime, it is the spatial sense of self that is most directly engaged in a pantheistic feeling of transport and transcendence.[115]

Thus, this sacred esoteric art form "[. . .] enables man to experience spiritual union [*ittihad*] and integration into the supreme Centre."[116] This sublime experience is in accordance with the writings of Sufi masters like Rumi and reinforces the early modern Ottoman cultural aesthetics of the thirteenth century whose *sema* ceremonies were reintroduced to the court during the reign of Süleyman the Magnificent. Experiencing a *sema*-like ceremony in the sacred space of the mosque, however, is not easily achieved.

Emotional intensity and the uncertainty of salvation are apparent in the work of Sinan. Sinan followed the abstract style, like his Renaissance contemporary Michelangelo. The architecture of his mosque and his reliance on the abstractness of Iznik design both affirms and challenges the religious ideology of the day.[117] Sinan's abstract style leaves the destiny of the individual's salvation in the aesthetics of the mosque and the hands of the Divine. Standing within the sacred space of his work, one feels compelled to reflect on one's actions and whether one is worthy of God's companionship in Paradise as one is in a state of ritual prayer in the presence of God.

Like the flowers dancing in the spring breeze on the Iznik panels on the portico, this rebirth can be transient when "hostile winds" change everything. Süleyman, like the visitor to the mosque, is reflecting on his life. While Süleyman's reign may be represented in the mosque's earthly paradisiacal imagery and in his hope of continuing his imperial reign, he still questions his actions and is not fooled by the illusion of immortality. This is exactly what is required of the visitor. In Sinan's work, the viewer is surrounded by a sea of blue, tulips, roses, hyacinths, and Qur'anic verses, among other visuals, as reminders of the world to come. As noted by Ramazanzade in his praise of Mihrimah Sultan, the mosque's "[. . .] spherical dome, composed of lofty strata and elevated tiers like the fourth heaven, has been designed in the same form as the soaring roof to the sky" serve to provide hope for the widow of the pasha that her husband finds salvation in paradise.[118]

The choice of turquoise throughout the mosque's decorative aesthetic is historically significant. The use of blue inscriptions interspersed with turquoise on a white background to represent God's pure Word and Light on the window lunette tiling alludes to ancient Turkic belief of protection.[119] The Ottomans' ability to produce the colour turquoise is significant. Its achievement connects the pagan nomadic heritage of the Turks to the court of Sultan Süleyman. Ali speaks of this in his *Essence of History*. The colour traces its origins to the fifth century Göktürk Empire (c. 439–c. 681) of Central Asia or the Empire of the T'u-chüeh (Turks mentioned in Chinese chronicles) who established the Turkic Khanate.[120] The word Göktürk means "Celestial Turks" or "Blue Turks." The seventh-century inscription of a Göktürk prince Kul-tegin at Kosho-Tsaidan reads, "Over all the land . . . the Blue Turks held sway as sovereigns."[121] Rene Grousset informs that their religion was a vague shamanism based on the cult of *Tängri* or Heaven. *Tanrı* is still used in modern Turkish today interchangeably with the word Allah.[122] The turquoise of the stone represented to the pagan Turks the protection and security provided by the sky deity *Tängri*.[123] Carrying or wearing a turquoise stone was believed to assure one of divine protection. The Blue Turks' descendants, the Oğuz, Seljuk and other Turkic tribes mentioned by Ali, took on these pagan practices in subsequent centuries. By connecting the fifth century pagan colour symbolism of protection with that of the seventh century Qur'anic verses, Süleyman's dynasty augments its claim to legitimacy over the Islamic and Turkic peoples of the East.

Therefore, the decorative aesthetics of the Rustem Pasha Mosque symbolically echo "historical memory in the form of orientation of the present" and propagate the self-fashioning of the dynasty.[124] David Lowenthal concurs with Rüsen that the past was interpreted as and fused with the contemporary urge to "justify present attitudes and actions, to underscore changes of faith."[125] The visitor, therefore, becomes an active participant in the historical consciousness of the Ottomans' inherited legacies and in its appropriated present by walking around, observing, stopping, admiring, sitting, and reflecting. This merging of past and present, and the physical and sensory experiences that they trigger, allows the observer to feel a stronger sense of being protected. This feeling of being protected reaches a climax when the observer faces the central niche, the *mihrab,* and is compelled to get closer to uncover the hidden intricacies of the çini. Aesthetically speaking, the multiple frames around the *mihrab* crescendo into the central attraction.

The *Mihrab*: a mirror to the Hereafter

The frame around the *mihrab* niche consists of tiles that use repeated designs. Some of these patterns were never repeated in later Iznik tilework, such as the "stippled" *saz* leaves that overlap and appear to move, dragon-like as if blown by a strong wind (fig. 6.12). The inner border is also composed of large *palmettes* with a pair of serrated leaves. These draw one's eyes to the *mihrab*. Thus, the *mihrab* and *qibla* signify that the worshipper is standing before the Almighty—in one-on-one dialogue with Him. Sinan achieves this effect by filling the *palmettes* with *rumis*. His use of red on white without any other colour gives the impression of a richer texture to the panels. This richer texture is further accentuated by the stippling technique of dark cobalt blue dots on the *hatayi* motifs. The colour red interspersed in the borders heightens the sense of yearning for God as the eye continues its motion towards the *mihrab* niche, further reinforcing Ibn Arabi's words above. This represents progress from the Bursa and Timurid traditions in which a limited colour range had been used, and reflects the mature and triumphant phase of the Süleymanic Renaissance. The effectiveness of the border accentuates the visual and symbolic intricacies of the *mihrab*.

What is most striking about the *mihrab* revetment inside the Rustem Pasha Mosque is that it consists of five identical panels that perfectly fit into the space reserved for them. Each panel includes a blossoming spring tree enclosed in a large blue ground cartouche, budding from a vase that faces the worshipper. Just as in Christian humanism, so for the Sufis, "[t]he one who allows the masterpieces to be produced, gives the artist that inspiration, that power, and that talent . . . Yet that great unique and peerless Artist conceals Himself."[126] For Rumi, only the true "Lovers" with "pure hearts" get glimpses of Him. With the *mihrab* Sinan provides that glimpse for the seeker. For Rumi, only the true "Lovers" with "pure hearts" get glimpses of Him. With the *mihrab* Sinan provides that glimpse for the seeker. According to Suhuwardi, the observer enters the Imaginal World (*mithal*) and "[. . .] rising from one degree to another discovers on each higher level a subtler state, a more entrancing beauty, a more intense spirituality, a more overflowing delight."[127] It is the decorative aesthetics of the *mihrab* stimulating the Creative Imagination of the observer and transmuting them into symbols, thus heightening the theophanic experience. In this way, the *mihrab* decoration alludes to God's promised Garden of Eden. The lobed niche at the top is repeated in the spandrels. The surface of each panel is decorated with a cartouche, inside which are cloud bands in white reserve on blue and *hatayi* blossoms with small leaves. The dark red used in the border is replaced for the first time by the vibrant tomato red that attracts the eye away from the blue. The introduction of the vibrant tomato red colour here for the first time is significant. For Rumi, red symbolises the emotions of the heart and the vulnerability of the created. The Sufi believes that the Divine gives new life and eternal beauty to all who love, suffer, and wait longingly to unite with Him. But no one can enter this Light or His presence because His glorious magnificence burns all, turning the seeker red. Applied liberally in the *mihrab* panels, the intensity of the colour becomes even more attractive to the viewer. This way the red allows the viewer to focus on his contemplation of salvation facing the *mihrab*. Facing the *mihrab* stirs the viewer's sense of longing to unite with the One.

Close viewing of the five panels symbolise the five daily prayers of Muslim worship where one is in continuous dialogue with God. The use of the repetitive design on white reserve and the tomato red in the *mihrab* create a mesmerising waterfall- and shade-like effect and represent the two indispensable elements of Islamic gardens, water and shade to cool the "burning" of the seeker, as alluded to by Rumi above in the parable of the garden. This allusion to the Garden of Eden as the world to come becomes the focal point for the worshipper. The classical mindset here renewed, reflects Sinan's Renaissance outlook. The dominant cobalt blue on all sides of the mosque's interior symbolises water—the life-giving force with the four rivers of Paradise flowing from its centre, the *mihrab*. This theme is mentioned in the Qur'an and in the *hadiths* of the Prophet's Night Journey in which the rivers run with water, milk, honey, or wine.[128] Therefore, the symbol of water as a life-giving force brings to life God's Beauty, as shown by the diverse blossoming flowers in the vases. In fact, they not only allude to His Beauty, but also to His Eden and His Creation.

At the entrances to the gardens' high walls were often large gateways. According to Clark, "[t]he gateway is associated with the *mihrab* … and provides the defining motif of the prayer carpet."[129] One of the fundamental meanings of both the gateway and the *mihrab* is that they represent, according to Clark, the entrance to the "celestial world, the heavenly gardens."[130] For this reason the *mihrab* acts like an örtü (a Turkish word meaning "shawl" or "veil"). This örtü or veil effect suggests that the *mihrab* resembles a small waterfall, the water falling over the Iznik floral arrangement in the vases. According to Clark's comparison of the veil and the waterfall: "[t]he … [v]eil is like a small waterfall, the water falling over carved stone, breaking up the image reflected in it and thereby reminding us of the transient nature of this world."[131] The waterfall effect created by the çini in the *mihrab* produces, like the veil, a subtle interplay between the intended movement of the water and the light that enters the mosque through the windows and duly reflected in the glazed tiles.[132] It is only here that the soft, flickering light of the afternoon sun can glow through the interior and create a serene mood.[133] In doing so, it ties the earthly paradise of the mosque to the echoing sounds of calls to prayer, making prayers come to life for the viewer. The light, in combination with the colours of the tiles at the *mihrab,* saturates the niche wall, enhancing the "illusion" of the three-dimensional effect of the tiles'. In this example, Sinan's art appeals to both the visual and aural senses. According to Nina Ergin, "[a]s in so many buildings with religious functions, the architecture did not exist merely as a medium for the contemplation of but for the sensory participation in the sacred."[134] At the same time, however, the repetition of the motifs creates a certain kind of fulfilment. At this moment, within the "garden space" and through prayer and contemplation, one can transcend the physical and reach the metaphysical. According to Phoebe Crisman, "[such] contemplation is induced through the juxtaposition of finite human life and nature as an infinite force, with its serene beauty and scale beyond human control."[135] In contrast, when sunlight hits the *mihrab,* it breaks up the repetitive images reflected in it, thereby reminding the faithful of the transient nature of this world. The *mihrab* as the object becomes the symbol through which the observer can make sense of the metaphysical and the world to come. As Ibn Arabi states, "And that is why a *ta'wil* is possible, because there is symbol and transparency" and "[i]t is through the Active Imagination that the manifested being becomes transparent."[136]

The reliance on natural light in this paradisiacal garden, with its constant changeability, enriches the interior of the mosque and creates an added dimension to the visitor's contemplation within the sacred space. By illuminating the interior in such a way, Sinan hid any view of the world outside and therefore allowed the observer to remain in the heavenly space for as long as possible. In this sense Sinan's work is a masterfully created sanctuary that supports Rose's idea of audiencing. Sinan's technique is to produce intense union with, and interplay between, the natural and man-made aspects of the mosque's inner garden.

The örtü effect of the *mihrab* is an example of what Lisa Golombek has called the "draped universe."[137] Just as Süleyman achieved his "draped universe" by covering the exterior of the Dome of the Rock with tile revetments in 1545, which symbolically beautified and prepared the "throne of God" for the Last Judgement of humanity, in Sinan's internal draped world of the mosque an individual must first prepare oneself before being called to account before His throne.[138] The *mihrab* or niche symbolises the spiritual compass of both the earthly direction of God and where one should turn to reflect on one's daily actions. However, there is no intense anguish in Sinan's work. Instead, he leaves the sins of humanity for God and God alone to pardon, while allowing the individual standing before the *mihrab* to reflect upon his last judgement, as death may come at any time.

Like the visitor reflecting on his mortality before the *mihrab*, Süleyman too in his poems reflected on the impermanence of his life:

> Though thy life-days were in number even as the desert sand,
> In the sphere's hour-glass they'd show not as a single hour, ah me![139]

Although the great sultan realises his mortality, the continuation of his imperial reign is symbolically represented by the timeless work of Sinan in the mosque's aesthetics. This transitory view of earthly life expressed by Süleyman is consistent with Rumi's philosophy that what we experience now is only a glimpse of the eternal life to come. The *mihrab* thus puts one's fleeting life into perspective. It represents one coming face to face with the Almighty. Therefore, it acts as a reminder of the Qur'anic verses above, that is, how one will be judged by God when standing before Him. It allows for spiritual reflection on one's intimate connection to God and the degree of his earthly righteousness. Similarly, this act of righteousness represented by the *mihrab* imagery as one of the keys to paradise is also reflected in Süleyman's writings:

> Lay aside this mirth and frolic, for the end thereof is death; If thou seekest love abiding, there is naught like piety.[140]

For the visitor, as for Süleyman, the keys to salvation are piety and righteousness, and the Iznik aesthetics help trigger these soul-searching qualities through the self-reflective process.

Other sacred spaces from the Renaissance era also attempt to induce a similar experience within the viewer. As Patricia Trutty-Coohill explains of her experience at the Sistine Chapel: "[w]hile the world was above me, it was not beyond me. I recognized the sense of that world because it was an extension of my own. It transcended the room, yet was also immanent."[141] Just as one can attain a transcendental state through the act of whirling, so one can also find God through the influence of art, like a moth that is drawn to the light. In such a spiritual state, even personal salvation becomes de-emphasised, as the only thing that matters in such a moment is union with the One. Rumi elaborates on this idea and the allusion of paradise:

> It was clapping hands because it escaped death and was dancing in the air like the branches and leaves of trees. When the branches and the leaves come out of the prison of soil they raise their heads above the ground and become friends with the wind and start to dance with it. When the leaves break out of the buds on the branches they climb up to the top of the tree. Each leaf and each fruit sings the graces of God . . . say[ing] "God who has a lot of graces and favours has nourished our root and from the root a strong tree grew, it grew wide, erect and high." . . . They dance to the tune of love and attain perfection as the moon . . . Their bodies move and dance. But in what state are their spirits? . . . There is no way to explain them.142

Rumi considered the dancing of the figures resurrected from their graves and saved from death as the first stage of salvation, just like the dead flowers brought back to life in the spring tree of the Iznik panel.[143] This rebirth of life is similarly echoed in the endowment deed describing the fountain (şadırvān) Mihrimah Sultan built near her deceased husband's mosque, "[. . .] whose sprouts flow with the water of life" to give hope that the pasha's soul finds peace and salvation in the next life.[144] In conjunction with the recitation of the Qur'an in the mosque for the soul of Rustem Pasha, as noted in Süleyman's endowment deed above, the structure appeals to all the senses. As Nina Ergin confirms, "[h]earing, seeing, feeling, smelling, and participating in all of these aspects would lead to an experience greater than the sum of the separate sensory perceptions; ideally it would lead to a multisensorial experience of the divine."[145] Sinan's abstraction of the floral images displayed on Iznik tiles, which become more intense in the *mihrab* panels, also resonates with Rumi's couplets (above). The architect facilitates the movement from the material world to the spiritual realm and frees the spirit from the constrictions of the physical body. Here observers, standing in front of the *mihrab* after entering the sacred space, may feel their spirit to be like leaves breaking out of the buds on branches as they climb up the metaphorical tree of Paradise. Like Süleyman, the piety and righteousness of the observer may be tested before attaining salvation. However, because these two media are earthly representations of salvation and Paradise, there still remain questions about what happens to the spirit. Even Rumi could not explain this. Like the *mihrab* in the Rustem Pasha Mosque reflecting the Divine and Hereafter, the highpoint of mysticism is similarly expressed in Gothic art of the twelfth century. During the renovations of St. Denis in Paris in 1122, Abbot Suger (1081-1151), through the use of stained glass windows in the abbey, comments on flooding the interior with light and attaining closeness with God. Reflecting on seeking to define God through Gothic art, and influenced by Neo-Platonic philosophers and Christian doctrine, Suger states: "Bright is that which is brightly coupled with the bright, and bright is the noble edifice which is pervaded by the new light [*lux nova*]."[146] Like Sinan's allusions to God, Suger similarly alludes to seeking to define God through his art. For Suger, like Sinan, God's Light becomes more pure as one gets closer to the pure light that is God.

Conclusion

In summary, this chapter has articulated an alternative reading of the Mosque of Rustem Pasha. It has looked beyond the grand-scale production of the work—which involved highly technical composition and innovation, aesthetics and styles to create beautiful, unique and spiritual art. The chapter examined the allegorical message the mosque conveyed through anagogical and didactic readings consistent with the Renaissance mentality. Such alternative perspectives exemplify the Renaissance expression of the human spirit based on the themes of "the Divine" and His artistic mastery in the natural world, "salvation," and "Paradise" as represented in Qur'anic scripture and Sufi humanism. Through Sinan's reliance on abstraction and floral naturalism, the Iznik tile art form brings to life the Qur'anic narrative. The metaphorical message conveyed through the use of Iznik naturalism provided Sinan with what Patricia Rubin, writing about Vasari's metaphorical construction in his *The Lives*, describes as "a model by which, through contemplation, the mind arrives at divinity."[147] The mosque's decorative aesthetic allows for individual self-examination and at the same time elevates the artist's greatness.

Such a reading of the mosque presents Sinan as a Renaissance artist of Ottoman art. According to architectural historian Phoebe Crisman, the works allow for "paying attention, and reflective states that are considered to contribute more to psychological, intellectual, and spiritual development, rather than the kind of calming contemplation which might be seeking to eliminate thought."[148] This transcendental notion is consistent with Sufi mysticism, with which Sinan was closely associated. I have described the Sufi *sema* (whirling) ceremony, during which the whirling dervish spiritually leaves the physical body and enters the spiritual realm. In one of his poems Süleyman writes, "Lover, if you want peace and quiet, leave all worldly care: The hermit's niche is the best place for one to meditate."[149] In his religious self-fashioning, Süleyman represents himself as the true Muslim ruler of the Islamic world and propagates the Sunni doctrine over the Safavid Shi'a belief. In doing this he acknowledges the mystical elements of Sufi philosophy and brings the focus onto the importance of self-awareness for individual growth. In the individual's journey in the sacred space of the mosque, Süleyman's personal "niche" becomes the *mihrab* of the mosque for the visitor. In this way, Süleyman informs the visitor that although one may seek God through man's aesthetic representations of Him, which give a glimpse of the Divine, the real *mihrab* is the *mihrab* of the self. In other words, one must also seek His Beauty within oneself because, according to Rumi, "We are God's Light; we are God's mirror."[150] To attain this esoteric level of spiritual and self-awareness, the Sufi humanist context of Sinan's tile work inspire spiritual growth and inward contemplation. In this way, the journey of the self begins to shift from the physical search for God to a more intimate dialogue with Him through self-awareness. The mosque's aesthetics thus become the catalyst for the visitor to discover God and the "rose-garden" within himself. As Rumi states,

> You are the One who puts up curtains before our eyes to prevent them from seeing the truth and who tears up those curtains.[151]

To achieve this metaphorical lifting of the veil from one's eyes, aesthetically speaking, Sinan uses the spatial organisation in the mosque and the heterogeneity of the tiles. His use of these techniques embodies the Ottoman Renaissance mindset of the period.[152] To reiterate Rose's words above, it becomes possible for the artist to awaken the visitor's senses from slumber. In this way, the aesthetics of the mosque's interior validates Sinan's claims in his autobiographies, when he writes that his works will not only be recorded on the "pages of time" but will also attract the "admiration of all humankind."

Sinan's creativity demonstrates the technical and aesthetic progression from the fifteenth-century Timurid-inspired *cuerda seca* to underglaze tile production. By reigniting the Iznik kilns of the sixteenth century, the aesthetic refinement of the Rustem Pasha Mosque expressed the intellectual and cultural sophistication of the age of Sultan Süleyman. His rule was the catalyst for the aesthetic maturity of the Ottoman fine art of tile making as it progressed through experimentation from the Timurid matte finish of the *cuerda seca* to the vibrancy and brilliance of the colours of Iznik production. This technical progression witnessed the rebirth of a more refined and sophisticated tile art form, one that also symbolically reflected the court culture of the time. Appropriating the Timurid chinoiserie style to a more distinctly Ottoman *quatre fleurs* expression of dynastic identity also reinforced the stylistic progression from the imitation of past examples to the creation of something new and original.

Moreover, from the "dawn" of the Ottoman state under Mehmed I in Bursa, to a world empire under the aegis of Süleyman, the intellectual sophistication embedded in the narrative of the mosque's tiles also reflects the dynasty's historical consciousness and its engagement with both the Platonic and Sufi ideals of Divine Beauty and of the world to come. By drawing the individual into a state of spiritual contemplation and self-reflection, Sinan's aesthetic was designed to prompt a consideration of one's relationship with the Divine. Süleyman's own poetry, composed at the same time, also reflected this search for a greater meaning of one's existence and a yearning for salvation and paradise.

Of course, such works of art would have been impossible without the patronage of wealthy individuals. Aside from its sheer beauty, metaphorically speaking, the artwork of Iznik represents the sense of "self" of the artist. Sinan's genius is that he was able to create an anagogical and didactic work full of symbolism through the technological innovation of Iznik. His creation both reinforced and made sense of his place in the faith system of the Ottoman world. The next chapter will elaborate on the notion of the triumph of Ottoman rebirth within the Renaissance self-fashioning of Sultan Süleyman the Magnificent, specifically through the art of calligraphy and illustrated history of the sultan.

CHAPTER SEVEN

FROM *TUGHRA* CALLIGRAPHY TO ILLUSTRATED HISTORIES: RENAISSANCE SELF-FASHIONING OF SÜLEYMAN THE MAGNIFICENT

Throughout his forty-six-year reign, Süleyman looked to the past to reshape and define the present. Süleyman's self-fashioning represented the triumph of the Ottoman Renaissance of the arts from monumental imperial architecture and fine art of Iznik tiles, to the stylistic progression of the art of calligraphy and illustrated manuscripts. Both the architectural and fine arts of early modern Ottoman art, therefore, act as constant reminders of Süleyman's universal power. These artistic achievements reflected the political and religious atmosphere at the time and further aided in augmenting and legitimising the universality of the image of the sultan. According to Ali, Süleyman equalled the legendary heroes of the past 'Alexander, Cengiz Khan and Timur'.[1] This world-conquering image and unifier of diverse cultures secured his legacy in the Muslim, Turkic and Latin Christian worlds. By invigorating the arts to reflect the image of the court, Sinan triumphed over the past achievements of the Ottoman rebirth that began in Bursa in 1413 with the Süleymanic Age.[2] As noted in chapter two, the *Epic Deeds of Artists* by Mustafa Ali and the architectural treatise of Sinan echo this triumph of the Süleymanic Renaissance and of Ottoman cultural greatness of the sixteenth century. As chapters four and five have shown, the distinctive nature of the Ottoman rebirth experience was achieved predominantly through Süleyman's and his daughter Mihrimah Sultan's patronage of monumental architectural structures and refinement in the interior decorative aesthetics using tiles.

The aim of the current and final chapter of the study is to focus on the rebirth of the art of *tughra* calligraphy and miniature paintings of the illustrated history of Süleyman in the *Süleymanname* manuscript through Ottoman artists' engagement with past exemplars. The art of the *tughra* stylistically progressed from the *kufic* calligraphic style in the seventh century to the sophisticated and intricate form in the sixteenth century representing the power, authority and legitimacy of Süleyman. Its symbolic representation of the past, present and future additionally reflects the historical consciousness of the sultan in his Renaissance self-fashioning that exemplified the rulers of the age.

The Ottoman artists made use of the mythical, heroic and historical criteria established by the eleventh-century Iranian poet Firdausi Tusi (c.940–1020). Firdausi's chronological history of pre-Islamic history of Iran's legendary war heroes in the *Shahnama* (Book of Kings) entered the consciousness of Muslim writers, historians, artists and most significantly rulers in subsequent centuries—including the Ottomans in their attempt to legitimise their political and religious power in the Muslim world. Firdausi sets his structure according to the criteria of three ages: the mythical, heroic and the historical. By establishing historical continuity between the past and present, and by showing how the past helped improve the present to better shape the future, Firdausi helped form not only national and cultural identities but also those of the early modern 'eastern' rulers.

Arifi appropriates Firdausi's work into the Ottoman context. His 1558 *Şahname-i Al-i 'Osman* (The Royal Book of the House of Osman), of which the *Süleymanname* manuscript is fifth and last volume, not only rejuvenates the miniature painting genre at the court, but by looking back to the past, he is able to tap into Süleyman's Turco-Mongol lineage and shared heritage to construct the history of the sultan depicting him as having surpassed the legendary figures of the past. Arifi does this by intertwining Süleyman's mythical past, heroic deeds, and historical feats to promote the sultan's universal religious and political status in the image of the Biblical Solomon, Alexander, Cengiz Khan and Timur. This strategy of looking to the past to construct the present will be demonstrated through selected illustrations that depict the rebirth of the sultan as a universal and ideal ruler just like the predecessors he sought to emulate. By reviving the artistic language of the past, Süleyman's connection to Alexander, Cengiz Khan and Timur was solidified. Ultimately, such an approach served a strategic political purpose: to legitimise the sultan's rule over the Muslim world and Latin Christendom and to propagate it through powerful artistic projects.

The art of the Ottoman *tughra* in the Süleymanic age

The *tughra* was created to represent the authority and identity of the sultan. It originated during the time of Orhan Ghazi (1284–1359), the second ruler of the nascent empire, who first used the *tughra* in 1324. The *tughra* affixed to the documents translates as:

> Süleyman, son of Selim Khan, ever victorious. This is the noble, exalted monogram, the world-illuminating and adoring cipher of the Khakan, may Lord and the protection of the Eternal, be given force and effect. His order is that ...[3]

The edict will then follow underneath the affixed *tughra.*

The sultan's insignia was first used on documents called *fermans* or edicts, the earliest examples of which are from the fourteenth century. Its use was then extended to coins, seals, entrances to mosques and palaces.[4] The use of the *tughra* on coins, *akçes,* seen in the numismatic evidence from the reigns of Bajezid I (1389–1402), Mehmed I (1413–1421), Murad II (1421–1444), Mehmed II (1451–1481) and Sultan Süleyman (1520–1566), demonstrate a stylistic progression from the *kufic* to a more sophisticated and refined Ottoman *thuluth* style during Süleyman's rule (*figures 7.1a-b*). The easy circulation of coins transported these representations of unity and sovereignty from one end of the empire to the other. As the embodiment of law and justice, the sultan's seal ring ensured he represented these attributes as the lawgiver or *kanuni,* a sobriquet attributed to him by his subjects (*figure 7.1c*).

The *tughra* of Süleyman the Magnificent reflects both his grandeur and the imperial zenith of the empire (*figures 7.2 and 7.3).* As seen in Figure 7.2, the crude amalgamation of the *kufic* and *thuluth* styles of Orhan's *tughra* reflects the progression of this artform from past exemplars and signifies the birth of the early Ottoman state in the fourteenth century in Bursa. The *tughra* of Süleyman at the entrance to the imperial *divan* (council) in the Topkapı Palace signifies his role as the political and juristic leader of his subjects and as the representative of the ideal Muslim ruler. The depiction of the *tughra* at the entrance to palaces suggested both his political and private role (*figure 7.3a*). As a visual medium for dynastic propaganda the *tughra* carried the message to the masses from Istanbul to Mecca, from Cairo to Budapest, and from Crimea to foreign heads of state. Like a signature or as recognisable as a portrait, the *tughra* allowed the reader to understand the importance of the identity of the ruler. Its symbolic import reflected the effectiveness of the sultan's self-fashioning.

In the sixteenth century, the creation of the *tughra* was the task of a High Chancellor or *nişancı* of the *divan*. From the time of Süleyman the Magnificent, the *tughras* came to be illuminated, further evidence of the importance given to the fine arts during his reign. Since the sultans did not personally sign their decrees, the *tughra* served as the ultimate authentication. The continuation of this art form in subsequent centuries following Süleyman's reign represented the historical endurance of the dynasty's self-fashioning image as the culture transitioned from the medieval era to the Renaissance and beyond. The *tughra* aesthetic was thus continually adapted and modified to suit the context of the historical period. Thus, the *tughra* as a symbol of sultanic authority represents the perception of Ottomans' self-awareness of the historical continuity that connects the past, present, future and the hereafter. This is expressed in *The Encyclopedia of Islam*:

> Tuğra *[sic]* is a very significant, historical and difficult art. ... there are three vertical and two horizontal lines. ... [The three vertical] lines are the symbols of: Today – Tomorrow – Yesterday. The horizontal [ones] [are] the symbols of Here and Hereafter ... The S-shaped lines crossing the *tuğ* [i.e. the vertical lines on top of the tughra]... together with the tops of the *tuğ* that also look to the right, signify that the winds blow from east to west, the traditional movement of the Ottomans.[5]

This definition of the *tughra* exemplifies the early modern mindset of the Ottoman court. Representations of Süleyman in art and architecture not only served to augment his image in the sixteenth century context, but also to signify the continuity of his and the dynasty's imperial reign. In this way the *tughra* was a symbol of 'Today – Tomorrow – Yesterday' as in the above description. This evokes historical consciousness by highlighting the present ('Today') with 'Süleyman'; 'Tomorrow' with 'the protection of the Eternal' to ensure the longevity of the sultanate; and 'Yesterday' with references to his ancestry 'son of Selim Khan' and 'Khakan', alluding to his inherited Turco–Mongol heritage.

In the calligraphic insignia, Süleyman and previous sultans only referred to themselves as sons of Khans (i.e. the ruler), after the Mongol ruler Cengiz Khan. Süleyman's father Selim I added the 'Şah' to his titles and this continued until the eighteenth century. As with other forms of visual representation of political authority, its scriptoral nature meant that it could be adapted and modified, signalling the stylistic progression of the imperial *tughras* by the addition of titles. This reflected the fluctuating political and ideological circumstances of the ever-changing nature of the self-fashioning of the ruling sultan. This Renaissance self-fashioning was significant politically and ideologically to visually represents the dynasty and the individual ruler by tapping into the shared legacies of the past. These adaptations to suit the contemporary historical context reflect the level of sophistication attained in the art of calligraphy under Süleyman. For example:

> [d]uring the reign of Bayezid I the word '*Han*' (Khan: the ruler) appeared after the father's first name and his signature became '*Beyazid bin Murad Han*'. In the reign of Sultan Murad II the word '*muzaffer*' which means victorious was added and his signature became '*Murad bin Mehmed Han muzaffer*'. After Mehmed II the motto became '*el-Muzaffer daima*' (the ever victorious) and his signature became '*Mehmed bin Murad Han muzaffer daima*'. Starting with Sultan Selim I, the word '*Şah*' was inserted after '*Han*'.[6]

As the Ottoman state grew and became a universal empire after the capture of Constantinople in 1453, so too did the art of *tughra* of the ruling sultans grow to reflect their military and political achievements. Each carefully selected title added after the particular sultan's victories revealed the embellishments made to the ever-growing empire. For example, Mehmed II added 'the ever victorious' to his *tughra* to celebrate his many victories and as a reminder of his famous historic conquest of Constantinople in 1453. For Selim I (1512–1520), the title Şah (in Turkish) reflects his success against Shah Ismail of Iran in the Battle of Chaldiran and the sultan's triumphant entry into Tabriz (the capital of the Safavid Empire) in 1514. One common title shared by the sultans since the time of Bajezid I (1389–1402), however, had been the inclusion of the Mongol label 'Khan'. The inclusion of 'Khan' during this time is significant because of Timur's expansion westward into Ottoman territories in 1400. This addition to the *tughra* symbolically challenged the authority of the Central Asian conqueror by directly linking the sultanate to its nomadic steppe Turco–Mongol heritage.

Therefore, through the *tughra* the self-fashioning of the dynasty in the early years of the fifteenth century came to reflect their concerns for legitimacy as universal sovereigns. In *Essence of History* Mustafa Ali reminds the reader of the significance of this looking back to the Mongol heritage as a way of justifying the political legitimacy of the Ottoman Empire. If the Ottomans needed to justify universal sovereignty, they needed to go directly to their roots in Mongolia, by-passing Timur, where Cengiz Khan ruled an area of the earth larger than any ruler had done before or since, with a conglomeration of Mongol and Turkic tribes. The many other titles the sultans inherited through their conquests over the centuries culminated in a long list of entitlements which they saw as appropriate to endorse their universal legitimacy. This ideological progression and historical consciousness reflected the stylistic progression of the art of the *tughra* from the fourteenth to the sixteenth century. Like the conglomeration of titles and lands duly recorded on the *tughra*, the stylistic development of the calligraphy also attests to a renaissance of form: that is, taking the *kufic* style of the past and rebirthing it as *thuluth* script (fancier, more intricate and uniquely Ottoman); a script that symbolises the Ottoman domination of Persian, Turkic and Arabic.

Ottoman political and ideological expressions in the *tughra* are exemplified in the letters Süleyman sent to heads of state. One such example is a letter Süleyman sent to Francis I of France, where his *tughra* is affixed at the top. Süleyman the Magnificent, like his great-grandfather Mehmed II, sought to fashion himself as a wise and universal sovereign by engaging with both the classical antiquity of the West and with Islamic and Turco–Mongol–Timurid traditions. In his letter to King Francis I of France in 1536 Süleyman boasted of his image as a universal ruler in the words that followed his *tughra*:

> I who am the Sultan of the Sultans of East and West, Lord born under a fortunate conjunction, of the kingdoms of the Roman and Persians and Arabs, hero of all that is, pride of the arena of earth time; Sultan and Padishah of the Mediterranean and the Black Sea, and the glorified Ka'ba and the illumined Medina, the noble Jeru-

> salem and the throne of Egypt, the rarity of the age, and the province of Yemen, and Aden and Sana, and Baghdad the abode of rectitude, and Basra and al-Hasa and the Cities of Nushiravan, and the lands of Algiers and Azerbaijan, the steppes of the Kipchak and the land of the Tatars, and Kurdistan and Luristan, and of the countries of Rumelia and Anatolia and Karaman and Wallachia and Moldavia and Hungary all together, and many more kingdoms and lands mighty of esteem: Sultan and Padishah, ... Süleyman Khan, ... Majestic Caesar ... Refuge of all the People in the whole World, the Shadow of the Almighty dispensing Quiet in the Earth.[7]

Süleyman's long list of the provinces under his rule encapsulates both in writing and in visual aesthetics the image of a universal sovereign. This message further complemented the message of his *tughra* affixed at the top of the letter. According to Gillian Rose, 'the viewer creates meaning of a product by making links between the signs.'[8] The key geographical places listed, the references to God, and the final affirmation of the sultan's many titles that are also reinforced in his colourfully illustrated *tughra,* all reinforce the image of Süleyman's power and augment the universalist message of Süleyman. Like a 'saviour' or 'messianic' figure of humanity, Süleyman saw himself as the unifying figure of both the East and West (*figure 7.3b*). Süleyman saw himself as remaining true to his ancestral heritage of the steppes by bringing the lands of the Turkic Kipchaks, Tartars and Azerbaijan under his control. His empire also included the holy sites of Islam: Mecca and Medina, the capital of the classical Islamic history and the once capital of the Abbasid caliphate, Baghdad, and the lands of the Christian Hungary, Wallachia and Moldavia. He controlled all the territories that once were ruled by his ancestors as they continued in their movement from East to West leaving their mark. Encompassing the lands of the past civilisations of medieval Islam, the Timurid–Persian and Turkic, Süleyman's *tughra* reminds the reader that the glories of 'Yesterday' are reborn under his rule (i.e. 'Today'), and ensured that the 'Tomorrow' will continue to speak of his legacy. In his words he united the Roman, Persian and Arab peoples under the banner of the Ottomans, just as Alexander the Great had done by bringing together the classical Greece of the West and the imperial Persia of the East. This idea of emulating Alexander's achievements is reinforced through his frequent discussions of the classics with his closest confidant and later Grand Vizier, Ibrahim Pasha. One book in particular was the *Iskendername* by Ahmedi (d. 1413), the story Alexander the Great. Like his great-grandfather Mehmed II, Süleyman saw himself as the neo-Alexander of the age.[9]

In another letter, this time sent to Shah Tahmasp I of the Safavid Empire during the treaty negotiations of 1555, Süleyman accuses his religious rival of heresy. Ottoman historian and chancellor, Celalzade Mustafa Çelebi (d. 1567) includes the letter in his history of Süleyman:

> You should be informed that those who obey you are lost, deceived and gone astray. You have [to] stand up to change ... and accept customs and prohibitions. And it is clear that you have abandoned all shame and gone astray ... I believe that you can wake up from this delusional [heresy], and come back to the [true] religion of Islam.[10]

The letter begins with the *tughra* that listed all of Süleyman's accolades and triumphs, as in the letter to Francis I. These accentuate his status as a universal ruler of East and West. The letter then asks Tahmasp to accept the 'true' Islam exemplified by the Ottoman sultanate and caliphate because Süleyman alone represents the 'true' form of Islam as the 'Shadow of the Almighty'. Furthermore, according to Ali's interpretation of Ottoman history from a late sixteenth century perspective, by Süleyman's time:

> [t]he universal caliphate was indeed a dead letter by the fifteenth–sixteenth centuries; although the title 'caliph' was used in diplomatic correspondence throughout this period, it signified nothing more than 'Muslim sovereign.'[11]

During Süleyman's time, however, the title 'caliph' was still important politically when it came to Safavid claims of supremacy in the Muslim world. The ideological propagation expressed by Süleyman's *tughra* represents him as the ideal and 'true' leader of the Islamic world. Letters like this sent to many foreign leaders only served to augment the image and prestige of his sultanate, emphasising the preferred symbolic meaning to concretise the political message they contained.

From the framework of visual semiology, the calligraphic image of the *tughra* reflects the Ottoman mindset of the early modern period. The identity and authority of the sultan takes on a religious tone through the calligraphic nature of the *tughra.* Its association with the artistry of the Word represented in the Iznik çini also connects the sultan to his caliph and religious role in the empire and the Muslim world. As seen in the two letters above, the *tughra* produces '[p]referred meanings or ideologies [that] become preferred readings when they are interpreted by audiences in ways that retain 'the institutional / political / ideological order imprinted on them.'[12] The compositional intricacy of the *tughra* expresses the court's absolutist nature through Süleyman's self-aggrandising tone. The three vertical and two horizontal lines also reflect the continuity of the empire and celebrate the triumph of the rebirth of the 'Süleymanis' as having surpassed the previous civilisations it inherited as part of its unique legacy.

The notion of Süleyman as the ruler of both East and West is seen in contemporary accounts of 1559. The Ottoman admiral Seydi Ali, on his visit to the Mughal Emperor Humayun, assures him that even in China, the Muslims are living under the rule of the 'The Great Khan' and that the sermons or *hutbe* in the mosques are read in the name of Sultan Süleyman, with echoes of the *tughra's* message above:

> [T]he seven regions over which the Great Alexander had dominion were identical with the present Empire of the Padishah of Rum … [and even] … the *hutbe* [i.e. Friday sermon] read in the name of the Padishah of Mecca and Medina … during the holy festivals of Eid ... in the lands of China.[13]

The reading of the *hutbe* in Süleyman's name signifies and affirms Süleyman's image as a universal sovereign in the image of Alexander the Great. In Seydi Ali's view, the Ottoman ruler was recognised as a de-facto suzerain of Chinese Muslims of the East. This justifies the sultan's use of the ancient Turco–Mongol title 'Khan', bolstering his image as the supreme ruler of the Turkic, Tartar, and Mongol peoples of the East. It was very important for the Ottomans to make this connection to the Mongol heritage and the use of the title 'Khan' because, as Mustafa Ali reminds us, the title 'represented the most enduring and powerful legacy of the steppe to the Ottoman Empire'.[14]

The tops of the *tuğ* of Süleyman's tughra point to the right, signifying the winds blowing from east to west. Although the direction of writing is much more determinant of the shape, its symbolic significance as noted in the *Encyclopedia of Islam* cannot be discounted. In a similar way, the Friday sermon read in his name in China as the 'Khakan' and in Istanbul in the west in his imperial mosque in the Süleymaniye as the 'Padişah of Rum' (Rome) solidify the celebration of his name and rule from one end of the world to the other, like Alexander and Darius. Just as Mehmed I expressed 'the rise of the dawn of the Ottoman State' signalling its rebirth to the Timurid ruler in the fifteenth century, Süleyman's *tughra* now boasted the triumph of this rebirthing under his 'world-illuminating' rule.[15] This signals the triumph of the rebirth of the Turkic peoples embodied in the achievements of the Ottomans in the Süleymanic Age by fusing all the features of their inherited legacies in a unique early modern Ottoman context.

The *tughra,* therefore, is symbolically the artistic and literary representation of that east–west synthesis of the Turks' migratory path throughout their history. This unbroken bond of their inherited legacies continued to be expressed and represented throughout the Ottoman Renaissance. In other words, the *tughra's* symbolic significance expresses both visually and literally the historical continuity of the Ottoman rebirth experiences from the fifteenth century Bursa to the sixteenth century Istanbul of Süleyman. From a simple monogram in Orhan's time, the *tughra* became an elaborate and intricately decorative political and ideological expression of the ruler of the Ottoman dynasty.

The *tughra* spoke to the populace of the ever-present sultan and served, firstly, as a unifying symbol. Secondly, when sent to foreign heads of state in Europe and Iran, as a letter, the dragoman or translator would begin reading it out loud, echoing the triumphs, deeds, and titles of Süleyman and reinforcing his universal claim to both the East and West, as the Khan, Sultan, Şah, Caliph and Caesar. Through letters, documents, edicts and others forms that all shared the *tughra* the early modern Ottoman worldview had a mobility that travelled across multi-cultural and multi-religious contexts.[16] In other words, the centrifugal spread of the message behind the *tughra* is its propagandist message focusing on the person of the sultan. The significance of the *tughra* is therefore illustrated through both the visual expression of its message and as well as the spoken word. They propagate Süleyman's image to both the East and West, echoing a powerful symbolic message of the early modern cultural greatness. Applied to the *tughra,* Gillian Rose's term 'preferred meaning' becomes highly significant and symbolic for two reasons. First, the *tughra* accentuates the self-fashioning of the sultan and his universal legitimacy as the ideology by the dynasty; and secondly, the visual expression of the *tughra* promotes Ottoman artistic flair beyond the palace signalling its artistic and aesthetic triumph over past exemplars.

The *tughra* as an art form and its stylistic evolution throughout the centuries highlights only one area of the self-fashioning of the dynasty. In the genre of illustrated histories, Süleyman also played a role in ensuring his legacy in the area of fine arts would leave its mark on the pages of history. The next section of the chapter provides, first, a brief history of rebirth of illustrated manuscripts at the Ottoman court in the *Shahname* (Book of Kings) genre of the eleventh century Iranian poet Firdausi. It then looks at the composition of the *Süleymanname* (The History of Sultan Süleyman) manuscript and its reliance on the Turkmen–Safavid and Timurid court traditions to further bolster the image of the sultan.

Illustrated histories and Ottoman historical consciousness

Firdausi Tusi's epic work *Shahnama* greatly influenced Ottoman historiography and illustrated histories. Firdausi Tusi, the Iranian poet composed the original epic poem *Shahnama* (Book of Kings, c. 970–1010) under the patronage of the Turkic Ghaznavid dynasty.[17] Firdausi's *Shahnama* had a significant historical influence on the identity formation of the Timurids and Safavids as well as the Ottomans.

The original work is divided into mythical, heroic and historical ages.[18] The epic tells the story of the ancient mythical kings of Iran with Turkic and Iranian ancestry. Firdausi explores the mythical age from the creation of the world and of man, before moving to the heroic age. Here, he devotes his epic story to the age of heroes like Alexander the Great and Jamshid (Cemşid in Turkish), the mythical Iranian king. He ends his poem with the historical age by further romanticising the history of Alexander to the fall of the Sassanids (224 CE–651 CE) and the conquest of the Arabs of Iran in 651 CE. Firdausi's eleventh century epic became a catalyst for Ottoman history writing. Within the court, it was appropriated and then developed to the mature phase with the illustrated history of the Şahname Al-i 'Osman (Royal Book of the House of Osman). The *Süleymanname* is the final volume of this series. Firdausi's work, including the existing *shahnama* from Tabriz and Herat at the Topkapı Palace, encouraged the production of illustrated manuscripts at the Ottoman court by adapting the old examplars into the Ottoman historical context.

Ottoman historiography dates from the founding of the empire, with a work entitled *Tarih-i Al-i Osman* (History of the House of Osman). This work was written by a number of historians from the fourteenth and fifteenth centuries including Ahmedi (d. 1413) and Aşıkpaşazade (d. 1484) who followed Firdausi's model.[19] However, attempts to illustrate the imperial history of the empire did not appear until the beginning of the sixteenth century. By the middle to the latter quarter of the century these illustrated histories were flourishing as the empire reached its political, military, economic and cultural zenith under Süleyman and his successors.

Süleyman's concerns with glory resulted in ongoing attempts to refine and perfect the historiographical representations of the monarch through different mediums. As Necipoğlu notes, 'This mid-sixteenth century transformation was a process of state formation and self-imaging by the ruling elite of an Empire at the crossroads of the East and West that had come to perceive its identity as different from its neighbours'.[20] For Ottoman artists the use of Firdausi's illustrated histories as a model was not accidental but nurtured the growing cultural self-awareness and political assertiveness experienced under Süleyman. Emulating and appropriating this genre to suit Süleyman's historical consciousness was paramount, for it meant using the past to recreate the present by legitimising one's rule over the entire region and thus challenging the authority of any rivals. Firdausi's construction of identity therefore suited the Ottoman sultans' desire to bolster his imperial image from the capital, the former Constantinople that served as the 'New Rome'.[21] As Casale states:

> This new political ideology portrayed the Ottomans' struggles with the Habsburgs and the Safavids in a messianic vein, as a prelude to the eventual establishment of a universal empire under the aegis of the Ottoman dynasty.[22]

Within this context, the identity of Süleyman as the religio-political monarch, leader of Sunni Islam as well as Latin West, creates the context for the construction of the *Süleymanname*.

The importance of Fridausi's work in the Ottoman Renaissance mindset dates from the early decades of the fifteenth century. Firdausi's epic poem was not only illustrated at the Iranian court but also translated during the reigns of Mehmed II (1451–1481) and Bajezid II (1481–1512) by Ilyas Firdevs-i Çelebi (b. 1453) under the pseudonym Firdevs-i Rumi. The Ottoman manuscript was later illustrated during the reign of Selim I (1512–1520) at the Topkapı Palace by *nakkashane* artists. Their styles blended with those of the artists who were arriving from Tabriz and Herat with Selim, bringing with them numerous illustrated manuscripts.[23] This suggests, that together with the artists from Herat and Tabriz, the *nakkashane* artists began to utilise this genre. More illustrated *shahname* appeared at the palace, leading to the creation of the first illustrated Ottoman manuscript in 1515, *Mantık at-Tayr*, which appropriated the Timurid model.[24]

Timurid–Persian and Turkic influences from Tabriz and Herat respectively are evident in the stylistic development of illustrated manuscripts at the Ottoman court. The style of Tabriz is seen in a number of literary manuscripts illustrated at the court, including the *Shahname* of Firdausi (c. 940–1020) and the *Hamse* of Nizami (1141–1209), while that of Herat appears in such works as the *Divans* of Jami (1414–1492) and Turkish copies of Nizami composed by Ali Sir Nevai (1441–1501) and Fuzuli (1494–1556) to name a few. They had the strongest impact on the illustrated manuscripts produced at the court between the 1520s and 1540s prior to Arifi's monumental Ottoman Şahname-i *Al-i 'Osman* (Royal Book of the House of Osman). In a number of manuscripts these influences are amalgamated with the styles of *nakkashane* artists, who use Ottoman apparels and headdresses on the figures and attempt to create local settings. The 1530–31 works of Pir Ahmed Iskender, who illustrated Ali Sir Nevai's *Hamse* and the *Tercüme-i Şahname*, are among some of these initial works.[25]

The illustrated history's imitation of past examples is particularly perceptible in Şukri Bitlisi's first Ottoman şahname, the *Selimname* (History of Selim I). This work, commissioned by Süleyman in his father's honour, was composed in c. 1520/25 in Turkish verse and illustrated with twenty-four paintings revealing stylistic influences from Timurid Herat. Süleyman commissioned this work to capitalise on his father's military conquests of the Safavid capital Tabriz in 1514 and the holy lands of Mecca, Medina and Jerusalem with the transferring of the caliphate to the Ottomans sultanate in 1517 from the Mamluk Sultan Mutevekkil III. Süleyman's patronage of this work served as a precursor to Arifi's Şahname-i Al-i Osman and the *Süleymanname*. This progression from calligraphic medium to the first illustrated Ottoman şahname thus served a political purpose: that of competing with their Safavid rivals in propagating their ever-burgeoning imperial and religious image in the illustrated history genre.

Parallel rebirths of the *Shahnama* genre are, thus, unmistakeable in the Timurid, Safavid and Ottoman courts. The first three illustrated *Shahnama* manuscripts of Firdausi's work in the Timurid court that ruled Iran from the capital Herat (Afghanistan) were commissioned by the sons of Shahrukh (i.e. Timur's grandsons) in 1430 and 1435.[26] Following this, in the sixteenth century on the order of Shah Ismail I (1487–1524) in Tabriz, the Safavid *Shahnama* was commissioned in the 1520s.[27] The Safavid *shahnama* intertwined Firdausi's myths and legends into the illustrated narrative to create a distinct Iranian national identity. Following Ismail's death in 1524, his son Tahmasp I had the work completed by the middle of the 1530s. A copy exists in the Topkapı Palace. According to Piotrovsky and Rogers, Shah Ismail intended the manuscript as a gift to Sultan Süleyman.[28] This is significant as Ismail and later Tahmasp intended to promote their own politico-religious legitimacy in the Muslim East by challenging the Sunni power of Süleyman. Sheila Canby describes these parallel rebirths of the *Shahnama* genre at the Safavid and Ottoman courts by appropriating Firdausi respectively:

> Essentially, Tahmasp's *Shahanama* served as incubator and proving ground for two generations of Safavid artists and is the locus for the synthesis of the two painting styles that coexisted in Iran at the start of the sixteenth century, those of Turkmen Tabriz and Timurid Herat.[29]

This suggests that the tradition of Herat had been absorbed into that of Tabriz. According to Esin Atıl 'it is often difficult to determine which school had the strongest direct impact on the *nakkashane*'.[30]

The artists, thus, used older illustrated versions of Firdausi's *Shahnama*, which they appropriated into Ottoman landscape, architectural and historical settings. With the copying, illustrating and adapting of past works a distinct Ottoman style began to evolve at the *nakkashane* during this time. For example, Bitlisi produced a highly ornamental work with a limited selection of scenes depicting hunting, enthronements and palace sceneries with formulaic landscapes or architectural settings. The figures are depicted with long, drooping moustaches and wearing voluminous turbans wrapped around tall batons. This style, which shows the influence of Timurid Herat, dominated Ottoman painting between 1520 and 1560 (*figures 7.4*).

Figure 7.4 from Herat (1430) shows the Timurid courtiers playing chess while observed by Shahrukh's son, Prince Bayasanghori, who is sitting on the throne surrounded by his turbaned ministers in colourful kaftans. On either side of the prince and the adjacent walls are rectangular windows looking out into the garden with blossoming trees. The scene takes place in the palace. The three-dimensional perspective is suggested by the angled sidewalls moving into the back wall behind the throne. The blue and white tiling on the walls is rendered in typical Timurid style. Along with the hexagonal patterned carpet, the tiling accentuates the square patterns of the chessboard in the foreground, drawing to it not only our attention but also that of the observers in the painting. Similarly, in Bitlisi's c. 1520/25 *Selimname*, the geometric patterns of rectangles, squares and hexagons from windows, carpets and tiles appear in the miniature painting, 'Selim I in His Library'. Selim is seen in a larger pose in contrast to his students to his right. Sitting in the Timurid manner like the prince in Figure 7.4, the backdrop is highly geometric. Two smaller windows showing similar images flank the large rectangular central window behind Selim. This window looks into a garden with a blossoming tree. The Timurid tile aesthetic is clearly seen in the hexagonal tiling of Selim's library. This work was created just before the onset of the Iznik revolution under Süleyman. The figure seen at the bottom right at the entrance gives the illusion of stairs leading the upper level of the library. However, a distinct Ottoman aesthetic begins to take shape in this painting with the *saz*-serrated leaves of Şah Kulu seen in the ornamental double border. These leaves use the colours dark blue and gold to a fuller extent than in its Timurid precursor. Therefore, the divergent illustrated histories signify that the Ottomans were engaged in a competitive dialogue with the Timurid rulers of the East. By incorporating known and powerful Timurid references into a newly-burgeoning Ottoman expression, the visual narrative assisted the Ottomans in professing their legitimacy and asserting their primacy over the entire Muslim world, including the Timurids and the Safavids. .

The stylistic influence under which the *Süleymanname* manuscript was created is closely associated with the circulation of many copies of the *shahnama* in the region. A dialogue took place between Arifi's *Süleymanname* and Timurid–Turkmen works from Herat and Shiraz, and Safavid manuscripts created under the first Safavid Shah Ismail I (1501–1524), and Shah Tahmasp (1524--1576). This cultural interconnectedness between the Timurid–Turkmen and Iranian tribes after the waning power of the Timurids by the 1490s reveals a mixture of traditions employed at the Ottoman court.[31]

The Ottomans were influenced by this Eastern tradition because of the significance of the symbolism of the epic work of Firdausi. This looking back to Firdausi's work of the eleventh century was politically and culturally significant because it was reference back to the mythological beginnings of both the Turks and Iranians. Annemarie Schimmel sums up the shared mythological connection between the Turks and Iranians as follows:

> … as much as early rulers felt themselves to be Turks, they connected their Turkish origin not with Turkish tribal history but rather with the Turan[32] of *Shahnameh*: in the second generation their children bear the name of Firdosi's heroes, and their Turkish lineage is invariably traced back to Afrasiyab [the legendary founder of the Iranian dynasty].[33]

In order to dominate this shared past, it was very important for Süleyman to represent himself in the *shahnama* illustrated genre. Like his past and present Timurid and Safavid contemporaries, Shahrukh, Ismail, and Tahmasp, Süleyman needed to historically justify his legitimacy as a universal ruler by connecting his lineage to the mythical and heroic past of the Mongols, Timurid–Turkic–Perso, and Islamic heritage. As Fatma Eryılmaz notes:

> Adapting an epic that chronicles the mythic past of a rivaling eastern neighbor in order to glorify Ottoman lineage and its contemporaneous descendants could have been considered downright haughty.[34]

Indeed, Süleyman intended to challenge his Safavid rival and to promote the idea that there was only one universal ruler. The *shahnama* was intricately associated with Muslim kings and princes, and was a symbol of royal sovereignty at both the Ottoman and Safavid courts. By competing to connect the lineage of their royal households to past heritage, both the Ottomans and Safavids were vying to represent themselves as the legitimate rulers of the Muslim world. The *shahnama* of the Safavids, like their Ottoman equivalent, thus came to reflect their emerging identities and legitimacy. Moreover, the Ottomans began to tap into these mythological beginnings that 'postulate[d] a kind of knowledge, a past, a memory'. This new self-awareness culminated in the rebirth of the genre in the Şahname-i Al-i Osman.[35]

These manuscripts rejected perspectival realism in favour of a more abstract two-dimensional representation of the rulers. While Timurid, Iranian and Ottoman artists were aware of perspective and capable of critical observation, their rejection of three-dimensional representation dissociated the viewer from physical reality and directed the viewer to concentrate on the illustrations' spiritual and emotional aspects.[36] While the Renaissance art of Italy used the human body as a metaphor and medium for everything it wanted to convey about the universe, this distinctive style of Ottoman miniature painting concentrated on the depiction of human emotion as its principal metaphor and instrument. The *shahnama* focused on the use of colours and gestures, the relationships and situations represented, as well as the architecture and natural life in the background. All these features constituted pointers to emotional truths about the human condition and historical memories necessary in articulating a powerful imperial identity for Süleyman.

The *Süleymanname*: the illustrated history of Süleyman the Magnificent and the self-fashioning of a Renaissance Sultan

Arifi's 1558 Ottoman *şahname-i*, including the *Süleymanname*, encapsulates a deliberate strategy to connect the past, present and future of the Ottoman dynasty in visual associations with meaningful legacies, including Alexander the Great and the Ottoman dynasty's Turco–Mongol ancestry. In doing so, the *Süleymanname* successfully negotiates a contested politico-religious primacy by visually representing the sultan's triumph and legitimacy.

Arifi, who arrived at Süleyman's court from Shiraz in 1547, headed the project commissioned by the sultan. He coordinated the *nakkashane* artists of the palace in the creation of the official illustrated history of the Ottoman dynasty at the Topkapı Palace. The five-volume work comprises the history of the prophets, the life of the Prophet Muhammad and the history of the Ottoman dynasty from its founding father Osman to 1402 before the interregnum period. The final volume is the *Süleymanname* which encapsulates the overarching message of the entire şahname, representing Süleyman as an ideal Muslim ruler in accordance with prophetic tradition, divinely selected and favoured to lead and guide humanity, just as the prophets and Alexander had done.[37] Arifi presents five epochs in history from the time of creation, ending with the Süleymanic Age. To do this he elevates the history of Süleyman espoused by Firdausi's model by amalgamating the mythical, heroic and historical characteristics of the sultan to suit the sixteenth century context through carefully selected scenes from Süleyman life. Süleyman, reborn as the new Solomon, Alexander the Great, Cengiz Khan and Timur in Arifi's illustrated narrative are cleverly integrated into the sultan's deeds: the wise sultan dispensing justice like Solomon; the Mongol descendant Crimean Khan kneeling before him demonstrating Süleyman surpassing his ancient predecessor; exploiting Süleyman's heroic qualities like the newly reborn Alexander of the age at the Battle of Mohacs; receiving the Holy Crown of Hungary; and the legendary cup of Alexander from the Safavid Şah. In this way, Arifi presents to the intended audience a monarch worthy to rule the world.

Süleyman: links to the mythical past

In Volume IV, before Süleyman is introduced in the *Süleymanname,* Arifi introduces the sultan for the first time by augmenting his image as the prophet-king figure. This painting links the sultan directly to the lineage of the prophets to demonstrate the new reborn Solomon of the age: the wise and just ruler. Volumes II and III are missing and volume IV is undated. A single painting from an unknown painter, on display at the Los

Angeles County Museum of Art titled 'Sultan Süleyman in the Guise of King Solomon' presents the sultan as the Biblical/Qur'anic prophet-king of Israel The painting is divided into two halves. The top half depicts an elderly bearded figure with a burning halo above his head signifying the sultan's prophet-like status. He is sitting at the pulpit delivering a sermon or teaching three figures that are seated in a respectful manner with heads bowed before the wise teacher.

The bottom half portrays six scholarly or religious figures in discussion. Süleyman, in the guise of Solomon, stands with his left hand outstretched, giving counsel to his viziers or disciples. He is protected and divinely guided by five winged angles hovering above him. Their presence reinforces his 'holiness' as noted by Çelebi. This is complemented by the burning halo behind his head and echoed in the following words of the sultan's chancellor from 1534 and 1555, Celalzade Mustafa Çelebi (d. 1567):

> The rays of light that are marks (of holiness) were manifest and visible, evident and clear like lights in his noble character, on his face that resembles the shining sun.[38]

The wise king Solomon dispensing wisdom is personified in Süleyman in the painting. Süleyman's demeanour, his regal facial expressions with his eyes wide open and raised eyebrows, demonstrate that he is the one who is leading the conversation while his three ministers/viziers listen respectfully with their eyes closed. Symbolically the figures may also represent the past rulers like Timur where Süleyman is seen discussing or giving advice on *kanuns*. Six figures are also depicted in the lower half of the painting in various poses— reading, conversing face to face, and listening. They are seen debating and perhaps discussing Süleyman's *kanuns* (laws). This is further reinforced by Çelebi:

> Especially necessary and important are the attributes of the earlier kings who were adornment of the rank of world-rulers and personification of the imperial position such as subjects-nourishing endeavors and justice- spreading affairs.[39]

Comparing the sultan to past kings, Çelebi elevates the sultan to the 'rank of world-rulers'. The painting confirms Çelebi's perceptions of the sultan as the living embodiment of righteousness, wisdom and justice, three qualities dispensed by God to His prophets. In the *Süleymanname* volume Arifi endorses this prophet-king image of the sultan in the Qur'anic verse he includes at the introduction of his manuscript. Arifi's intention in choosing this particular verse referring to Solomon is related directly to the person of the sultan.

> It is from Solomon and is: In the name of God, the Merciful, the Compassionate ... God commands justice, the doings of good, and liberality to kith and ... God loveth those who do good.[40]

The inclusion of the Qur'anic verse with Solomon's name, Arifi is The Ottoman setting of the painting further highlights this aspect of the sultan. The blue and white Iznik tile decorations in the shape of Solomon's Star further reinforce the claim that the reign of Süleyman was the manifestation of paradise and its reflection on earth, and suggests a link to wisdom and justice as per Solomon. The mythical past is reborn in the person of Süleyman, who is the next 'messiah', descended from a line of prophets since the beginning of creation. This of course solidifies his claim to a divinely sanctioned right to rule the world.

The *Şahname-i Al-i Osman* appropriately concludes with Arifi's *Süleymanname*. This volume, the fourth in the narrative history of the Ottoman sultans, echoes the triumph of Ottoman rebirth. The volume traces Süleyman's lineage from Bursa in 1413 and signals a new Ottoman age with the 'Prince of the Epoch! Sultan Suleiman! Triumphant Aye!'[41] Arifi exploits Süleyman's narrative in the final volume to propagate not only the mythical but also the heroic and historical feats of the sultan, following Firdausi's model.

Arifi begins his introduction to the manuscript with a dedication and title. The dedication and title are illustrated with scrolls with blue stencil like *hatayis* and blossoms with petals. The concentric formations of the scrolls are reminiscent of the sultan's *tughra,* allowing Arifi to introduce the intended purpose of the illustrated history by connecting the 'Yesterday', 'Today' and 'Tomorrow' through the life of the sultan. After the title he dedicates it to his patron-sultan with the Renaissance sobriquet: '*muhteşem* [magnificent] sultan, son of the sultan, hakan, son of the hakan, Sultan Süleyman Han, son of Selim Şah Han, son of Bayezid Han, son of Sultan Mehmed.'[42] With references to Turco-Mongol titles 'Hakan' and 'Han', Arifi places him as heir to his Eastern ancestral forebears.

Süleyman: links to the ancestral past

Arifi cleverly exploits the connection between the House of Osman and the Crimean Khanate of the Giray Khans. As the successors to the Golden Horde, the Crimean Khanate, established in 1449, is the longest surviving Turkic dynasty with historical links to the Mongols. In the manuscript the mythical beginnings of the Turks are intertwined with the legacy of the Mongols and climax in the birth of the Turkic dynasties. In the triumph of the final epoch of history in Arifi's Şahname-i Al-i Osman the story culminates in an episode in which the Crimean Khan submits to Süleyman. Here, the ruling Giray family become vassals of the Ottomans, an event which took place during the rule of Mehmed II in 1478. The Şahname-i Al-i Osman clearly shows the Ottomans inheriting that tradition. In one of the miniature paintings, folio 519a, titled 'Reception of Devlet Giray Han', Arifi depicts the visit of the recently crowned Han of the Crimea in 1551 paying a visit to Süleyman at the Topkapı Palace to convey his allegiance to the sultan (*figure 7.5*). Like Timur's connection to the Turco-Mongol lineage, Süleyman is also related to Giray Han through his mother, Hafsa Sultan, who was the daughter of Mengili Giray, Devlet's grandfather. This illustration connecting the two houses justifies the direct lineage of the Ottomans to the steppes of Central Asia and depicts the historical continuity of the successes of the Turkic peoples from a nomadic to a sedentary high culture. In the setting of the Arz Odası (Reception Room) at the Topkapı Palace, Arifi portrays Süleyman sitting on a gold hexagonal throne, extending his hand to be kissed by Devlet Giray Han, his maternal cousin. Giray Han is shown kneeling before Süleyman to demonstrate his humility and submission to the sultan. The seated position of the sultan alludes to the ancient Turkic palace etiquette of Central Asia when the original Turks had come under Buddhist influence.[43] In an eleventh century text written by Yusuf Khass Hajib for a Karakhanid ruler, *Knowledge that Brings Happiness*, the kneeling pose is recommended as a sign of humility, 'Kneel on both knees, be humble.'[44] Süleyman's seated position alludes to his ancestral past of the steppes. His guest, Giray Han, is shown wearing the traditional Crimean headdress, a tall cap with a fur brim, and the *hil'at* or the Ottoman kaftan decorated with a çintemani pattern consisting of a series of double wavy lines and triple balls. These popular patterns at the

Ottoman court are based on an ancient Turkic talisman and symbolise the might and power of tigers and leopards. Wearing the Ottoman *hil'at* signifies Han's submission to the sultan as he bends to kiss the monarch's hand. By subjugating the descendants of the Mongols to his rule, Süleyman is reborn as the new leader of the Turco–Mongol world of the East. He is the neo-Cengiz Khan, who united the warring Mongols and Turks, and went on to establish one of the largest empires the world had even known. Similarly, having established his Turco–Mongol lineage, Süleyman is also reborn as the new Timur who ruled over the Turkic, Iranian and Islamic realms. With the sultan's mythical past and his eastern heritage established, Arifi next develops the narrative of the sultan's heroic qualities by recognising him as the ruler of Latin and Byzantine Christendom. Here, Süleyman emerges as the new Alexander of the Age.

Süleyman: links to the heroic past

Representing the sultan as the heroic figure of the Age, Arifi depicts the historic triumph of Süleyman at the 1526 Battle of Mohacs (*figure 7.6*). The double folio 219b and 220a commemorates the triumph of Süleyman against the Hungarian forces, aided by the regiments from Spain, Germany and Austria. The sultan's troops were outnumbered two to one by enemy forces, like Alexander in the Battle of Gaugamela in 331BCE, so the Battle of Mohacs scene expresses the heroic attributes of the sultan. Folio 219b illustrates the battle scene, while 220a represents the sultan's camp with his entourage and weapons facing the enemy. The paintings depict the excitement of the battle. The two folios are united by the depiction of the plains of Mohacs. The setting spreads horizontally across both folios. In this way the painter utilises the extended picture frame. The colourful landscape of rolling hills with trees across the foreground depicts the condition of the battlefield. In folio 220a Süleyman is seen in the centre. He is mounted on a black horse with jewelled trappings and saddle. He is surrounded by his *solaks* (janissary bowman belonging to the sultan's personal guard). Other riders behind the sultan include the Has Oda aghas, flag-bearers, and *mehter* (military band) beating their drums and playing horns to augment the battle's urgency. In front of the sultan are seen the janissaries and canons facing the enemy.

At this battle Süleyman's orderly and disciplined army inflicted a heavy blow on the enemy, losing only 150 men compared to the 25,000 Hungarians who drowned in the swamp after continuous rainfall. In the two-hour battle King Louis II also lost his life. The left folio 219b is animated and full of action, showing fighting between the two sides. It is divided into two sections. The top section portrays the Ottomans at the top of the painting maintaining a highly disciplined and regimented formation. The foreground shows men charging on horseback with their spears stretched out as well as hand-to-hand combat. The illustration shows the enemy line in disarray and retreating. This illustration sharply juxtaposes the disciplined nature of the sultan's troops in folio 220a. The centre of the folio depicts two Ottoman commanders challenging the enemy. The central figure wears a turban and is using a bow and arrow; the other is seen directly below him wearing a helmet and holding a metal-like weapon. At the Battle of Mohacs, Süleyman is wounded by the attack of thirty Hungarian knights who break through the front ranks and pierce the central flank. They succeed advancing as far as the sultan and wounding him with an arrow. He is saved from death by his armour and continues fighting off his attackers by slaying them with his sword. This is suggested by the dead Hungarian troops in the bottom left and right corner of folio 220a. The sultan's heroic stance at Mohacs against an overwhelming enemy was like the confrontation between Alexander against Darius, which had entered the collective consciousness of the Ottomans by 1558 at the time of the creation of the *Süleymanname*. The court poet Baqi (1526–1600) draws the analogy: 'The Hero of the battlefield … Darius of the fight … Iskender [Alexander] of his day!'[45]

By not explicitly depicting the wounded sultan, Arifi leaves space for the viewer to imagine and embellish Süleyman's heroic deeds, further propagating this gallant image through the ages. Arifi instead depicted the sultan in a triumphant and victorious pose with his assailants at his feet. Just as Alexander vanquished the ancient Persians from Europe and took Hellenism to the East, so Süleyman vanquished Christendom from Hungary and turned it into an Ottoman vassal state, bringing the civilisation of Islam there. In this way the painting symbolically legitimises Süleyman's role as the next Alexander of the age.

Süleyman: links to the classical past

Arifi continues the narrative in the next scene. He interweaves myth, legend and history into the narrative by representing the sultan receiving the Crown of Hungary in 1529 in folio 309a (*figure 7.7*). After giving the crown to Zapolya following his victory at Mohacs three years earlier, Süleyman once again turned his attention to Hungary when Charles V and Ferdinand reoccupied Buda. Before the Hungarians withdrew from Buda, Ferdinand's men stole the Holy Crown. The sultan asked his Grand Vizier Ibrahim Pasha to recapture the crown and return it to him for he understood the significance of the crown. In September 1529 Süleyman came to the aid of his vassal Zapolya. The crown was presented to the sultan by October of the same year. Three years later, with the commissioning of a crown from the Venetian craftsmen to surpass the Papal tiara Süleyman symbolically achieved his superiority over both Latin and Eastern Christendom.[46]

The symbolism of the crown is highly significant for Süleyman. It is merged with classical and Christian history. The crown symbolises a halo and one who wears it rules by Divine Right. Numerous interpretations surround the origins of the crown. One is that it was made for King Stephen I, later cononised as saint, for his coronation in the year 1000, marking the beginning of the birth of Hungary. Another is that it was given by the then Pope Sylvester II (946–1003) to King Stephen I.[47] In 1163 one of Stephen's successors, Bela III, was sent to Constantinople for his education and training. He was given the title *Despotes* by the Byzantine emperor before taking the Crown of Hungary in 1172. The Byzantine embellishments on the crown date from Bela's period. Just as the Ottomans in the sixteenth century crowned their Hungarian vassal kings, the Byzantine emperors had similarly used this practice in the past. This continuation of the Eastern Roman heritage embedded into the crown's symbolism from Byzantine to Hungarian monarchs justified Süleyman's desire to retrieve it. Possession of it meant further legitimising his connection to the classical Roman-Byzantine past of the caesars.

The crown consists of two parts: the corona *graeca* (Greek crown) and the corona *latina* (Latin crown). The Byzantine influence on the crown is prominent. It has a cross on the top and four *pendilia* dangling from chains on each side of the diadem and the back. The bottom half of the crown is the *corona graeca.* The Byzantine Emperor Michael VII Doukas (1071–1078) is depicted on the back of the diadem. To his right is the Hungarian King Geza (1074–1077) with a Greek inscription. The top half of the crown symbolises the *corona latina.* It is made up of four gold strips. It has pictures of saints with Latin letters under each image. The *corona latina* has twelve pearls on the central panel symbolising the twelve apostles of Christ. In this way the symbolic meaning of the entire crown unifies and reinforces the historical continuity of the Roman/Byzantine heritage with Christian iconography. For Süleyman, possession of the crown meant propagating and legitimising his rule over Christendom, in both the Orthodox East and the Roman Catholic West. The crown bolsters his image as the legitimate sovereign of all the Roman territories. Its reference to Latin inscriptions and Christian iconography symbolically gives his claim validation to rule Latin Christendom as 'The Majestic Caesar'.[48]

In Arifi's painting the Crown of Hungary is the central focus. The scene takes place in a tent. Arifi places Süleyman slightly off centre as he is receiving the crown from the commander of Izvornik in Bosnia, Bali Bey. Seated at the edge of the central scene and much smaller in comparison to the sultan is Zapolya, observing and waiting to receive the crown from Süleyman. He is depicted wearing Ottoman attire, including a gold-banded translucent coat over a robe with split seams on its sleeves. He is seen holding a handkerchief, as in the Timurid style, signifying his *Ottomanised* royal status. Janissaries and other officers witness the event from either side of the tent. Figures behind the hill at the top of the painting stand separated by a large tree at the apex. Combined with the river in the foreground these figures draw our attention to the central scene. With Hungary under his firm control Süleyman takes possession of the Crown of Hungary and challenges the legitimacy of Emperor Charles V as the ruler of Christendom. By providing asylum to Protestants in his domain from Catholic persecution, Süleyman championed the cause of 'true' Christians against the Roman Catholic West. As noted by Hajji Ahmed in 1559, Süleyman from 'this noble progeny' and 'the greatest rulers of the ages' is the sole ruler of 'Hungary, and has extended its borders as far as Germany'.[49] In his own words Süleyman describes himself as:

> The majestic Caesar ... The Sultan of sultans, King of kings, giver of crowns to the kings of the world, the shadow of God on earth, the ever victorious [...][50]

Thus, Arifi's appropriation of Firdausi's model to narrate the history of Süleyman demonstrates the new epoch, in which the sultan revives the lost glory of Greco-Roman civilisation. The sultan is reborn as the new Holy Roman Emperor of Europe – a direct challenge to Charles V. Like the pope crowning the emperors of Europe, Süleyman crowns Zapolya, showing his augmented politico-religio role: he is the only world monarch who crowns kings with his hands. Moreover, in Süleyman's crowning of Zapolya, Hungary is reborn as a state once again, now under Süleyman's protection.

After demonstrating his triumph over the Christendom in Eastern Europe, Arifi completes the illustrated history of Süleyman with allusions to the classical figure Alexander the Great. In both classical Western and Islamic traditions Alexander holds a prominent place, not only as a world conqueror who was never defeated in battle, but also as someone who unified cultures and civilisations. Placing Süleyman in a long line of prophets and rulers from the past, Arifi establishes the religio-political role of the sultan in the sixteenth century. In *Essence of History*, Mustafa Ali informs the reader that after Alexander, Cengiz Khan, Timur, Mehmed the Conqueror, Selim I, Süleyman is the next ruler who can be categorised with the two epithets of: '*müeyyed min ınd Allah*, (succoured by God), and *sahib-kıran,* (master of an auspicious conjunction), signifying the ushering in of a new epoch in human history.[51] To represent this in the *Süleymanname*, Arifi adapts the legendary ruby cup once believed to have belonged to Alexander himself and passed on to the legendary Iranian King Jamshid, returning to the mythical origins of the Turks and Iranians.

Süleyman: back to the future—fusing the mythical and classical past

Using the ruby cup as a symbol Arifi explores the shared cultural heritage between the Iranians and Ottomans. The Iranian dynasty was founded by the legendary king Afrasiyab. According to Firdausi's *Shahnama,* King Jamshid (in Turkish - Cemşid), the fourth mythical king, plays a role in the narrative of the cup. Firdausi claims that Jamshid belongs to the pre-Islamic Sassanid period of Iran (c. 600BCE–650BCE) during which Zoroastrianism flourished. He is said to have received a revelation from Ahura Mazda to dispense law to his people. In Iranian folklore he became the prophet–king, popularised by Firdausi. Ahura Mazda endowed him with *khvarena,* the royal *farr,* shining radiance. He ruled for three hundred years from the *Takht-i Jamshid* (Throne of Jamshid) from a place near the ancient city of Persepolis that was burned to the ground by Alexander in the fourth century BCE. Although Jamshid does not belong to the period of Alexander, the existence of sculptured tombs of Sassanid kings near the ancient city suggest the area had once been occupied by the Sassanids. During his rule peace and prosperity reigned, and longevity increased.[52] The legend of the ruby cup grew out of the cup-scrying (i.e. foretelling the future using a reflective object) folktales. In the *Iskendername* of Nizami (1141–1209):

> the royal hero is represented as possessing no fewer than three magic specula of different properties: a mirror of the stars; a mirror of the seasons: and the Sikandariya [Alexander] mirror.[53]

By possessing the cup of Alexander, Iranian kings could see into the future. Firdausi explains the legend of King Hüsrev (Khusrau) as he stares at the cup:

> Then I will call for the cup that mirroreth the world, And stand before God's presence. In that cup I shall behold the seven climes of earth ... The cup will show me all.[54]

King Hüsrev takes the cup in his hands and gazes therein:

> He saw the seven climes reflected there, And every act and presage of high heaven, Their fashion, cast, and scope made manifest From Aries to Pisces he beheld All mirrored in it Saturn, Jupiter, Mars, Loe, Sol and Luna, Mercury, And Venus. In that cup the wizard-king, Was wont to see [the] future.[55]

From the medieval Abbasid consciousness of Firdausi right through the Ottoman centuries, the legendary cup of Alexander continued to influence the sultan's court in Istanbul, serving as a classical symbol that justified universal sovereignty. By the fifteenth century the legend of the cup passed into Ottoman consciousness and can be seen in Mehmed II's poems [c. 1460]: 'Take out the cam-i Cemşid from the treasury, if you seek knowledge of the world.'[56] The following century the Ottoman Bosnian writer Sûdi (d. 1596) in *Hafız Şerhi* states, 'Whenever Cemşid desired to gain knowledge of a country he would simply look into the cup.'[57] Zülfi Güler has shown that according to Şehy Galib's (1757–1799) philosophy, for whoever desires this cup, it symbolises the mirror of Alexander showing him the far distant lands of the East.[58] In this way, the ownership of the cup, in particular during Süleyman's reign, symbolised and justified his status as *sahib kıran* (master of an auspicious conjunction). As Ali notes, it was during Süleyman's rule that the empire expanded from the gates of Vienna to the southern tip of Yemen, in the Arabian Peninsula.[59]

The cup's legend spread far and wide. According to Indian mythology, Cem arrived in Azerbaijan from India one sunny day. He rested on a golden throne on a mountaintop. The sun's rays gleaming on his throne led him to be called the Cam-ı Cemşid (one who illuminates) and that day came to be known as *nawruz* (new day). To this day *nawruz* is celebrated in the Middle East and Central Asia. It marks the beginning of spring, symbolising rebirth, renewal, rejuvenation and hope.[60] From the eleventh century, Cemşid became synonymous with the biblical Solomon or Prophet Süleyman in the Qur'anic tradition who was also the Sultan's namesake, and had miraculous powers over nature, spirits or jinns, and birds.[61]

Whatever the cup represented, its possession meant symbolic triumph and ownership over the past. Using its symbolic power reflected the early modern mindset of Ottoman rulers like Süleyman, who, at the pinnacle of Ottoman political, military and cultural greatness ensured the longevity of 'this noble progeny', echoing the words of Celalzade Mustafa Çelebi. Thus, the significance of the cup enshrined in myth, legend and history enters Ottoman historical consciousness and serves to highlight the triumph of Ottoman rebirth of a new epoch under the aegis of Süleyman.

There are two possible explanations for Süleyman's desire to possess this cup. The first explanation is the symbol of Ottoman power over the Safavids. According to Giancarlo Casale:

> by accentuating Alexander's credentials as the vanquisher of the ancient Persians … in age, such as the 1550s, in which the empire's greatest rivals were no longer the Habsburgs of the Christian West but the Safavid Shi'ites to the east.[62]

The second explanation is that the possession of Alexander's mythical cup represents Süleyman's universal majesty. The literal meaning of the term for the cup in the text of the illustration—*cam-ı cihannüma*—is 'a glass cup of the world'. Whoever has possession of the cup, like Alexander, rules the world and, like the transparent glass, his gaze encompasses all. In this way, according to Casale, the myth came to define Süleyman's empire as the 'New Rome' destined to revive the lost legacy of Greco-Roman antiquity, and another that defined it as quintessentially Islamic.'[63] Possessing it would legitimise Süleyman's many attributes and titles: 'prophet-king', 'ruler of all the ages', 'Prince of the Epoch', 'Shadow of God on earth', 'Refuge of all the People in the whole World', 'Caesar', 'Padişah', and 'Sultans of East and West, Lord born under a fortunate conjunction, of the kingdoms of the Roman and Persians and Arabs' to list just some.

Allusions to the cup of Alexander are displayed in two paintings from the *Süleymanname*. The first is 'Tahmasp Receiving the Ottoman Ambassador' in folio 550a; the second is folio 557a showing 'Süleyman Presented with the Ruby Cup' (*figures 7.7 and 7.8*) The former painting is set at a time when the Safavid ruler Tahmasp and his son Ismail Mirza took advantage of Ottoman preoccupations in Hungary to invade the Ottoman eastern territories in 1552. This prompted a war that would conclude with the Treaty of Amasya in 1555. The Safavids captured the fortress of Ahlat and besieged Erzurum. The scene in folio 550a continues the narrative. It shows how the Ottomans, under the command of Iskender Pasha who incidentally shares the legendary figure's name, repel the Şah's forces defending these areas. As the victor, the pasha insists that the Iranians surrender all booty gained and he sends a letter to the Şah's court with his request. He then captures the Georgian fortress, locates the famous cup and sends it to Sultan Süleyman. Esin Atıl notes:

> In the ensuing battle Iskender Pasha surrounded the fortress of Ardanuc in Georgia, where a treasured ruby cup called *cam-ı Cemşid*

> was hidden. This cup (called *cam-ı cihannüma* in this text) was thought to have belonged to the legendary founder of the Iranian empire, Cemşid, and was associated with Alexander the Great. Cherished throughout the centuries, it had passed from one king of Iran to another as a symbol of power and legitimacy of rule.[64]

Possession of this cup symbolised Süleyman's success as a universal ruler.Because of its universal application as well as its earthly and heavenly power, the cup was appealing to a monarch like Süleyman as a means of cementing his universal image. Figure 7.8 depicts Shah Tahmasp receiving a letter from the Ottoman envoy to relinquish all claims to the cup. Having lost the battle, the Shah is in no position to negotiate. The imperial tents are set up in front of a hill with a number of figures surrounding the central protagonist, the Shah himself. The Shah's riders appear in the background. His sword bearers surround Tahmasp and he is seen sitting in a kneeling position on a rug instead of a throne keeping to the Timurid–Persian tradition. Shah Tahmasp and his courtiers seen to his left are either sitting cross-legged manner on the ground or standing around the royal tent. The Shah and his courtiers are differentiated from their Ottoman counterparts by their elongated Safavid turbans with jewelled daggers in their belts, an alien tradition to the Ottomans. The Ottoman envoy sent by Iskender Pasha respectfully bends his head before Shah Tahmasp as he hands the letter to him asking to forfeit the rights to the *cam-ı Cemşid* depicted in the painting. For Tahmasp, giving up his claims to the cup meant forfeiting the rights to universal rule. Aside from the military victory, this symbolic act represents Süleyman's superiority over his Safavid rival. It also represents a victory over Shi'a 'heresy' and the triumph of Sunni orthodoxy.

In folio 557a Arifi continues the narrative in the painting 'Süleyman Presented with the Ruby Cup'. This painting explores the majesty of *muhteşem* (magnificent) Süleyman and his court. Süleyman is seen receiving the cup in a formal ceremony at the Topkapı Palace. The painting is divided into three vertical sections. These sections are then subdivided by architectural components depicting gates, entranceways, courtyards, gardens, arcades, terraces, balconies, windows and domes. These architectural elements of the palace are elaborately decorated.

Decoration ranges from abstract styles to stained-glass windows, Iznik tiles on the walls, marble columns in classical Doric style seen in the upper left chamber, and pavements signifying the highly structured and disciplined society. The compartmentalising of the narrative in rectangular boxes is reflected in figure 7.10 from Shah Tahmasp's album c. 1490–1530 available at the palace (H.2154) (*figure 7.10*).

The similarities between Arifi's composition and that of the Safavid example are very close. In the Safavid example various artists compose the painting. Artists include Şah Kulu before his arrival at Süleyman's court and Bihzad from Herat. The painting shows the miniature painting in progress. The page is divided into segments like the one seen in folio 557a, Süleyman receiving the ruby cup. Like Arifi's painting, these segments are shown through vertical and horizontal lines that separate the sub-narratives. These sub-stories merge with the theme of the main storyline depicted in the centre of the page. This focuses on the figure seated on a throne. The viewer is led to read the painting moving out from the centre. According to Rogers, rather than showing the influence of Tabriz and Herat, the illustrations in the *Süleymanname* resonate more with Shah Tahmasp's Safavid portrait album and pages from *Kalila wa Dimna* manuscript. This latter was available at the Topkapı Palace Library H.2154 compiled in 1544 for the Iranian prince Bahram Mirza (1517–1549) by Dost Muhammad (*figure 7.11*). The imagery of the paradise depicted behind Süleyman's golden throne mirrors Timurid and Chinoiserie painting, and as Rogers claims, this 'kept the great tradition of Muslim painting before Süleyman's eyes.'[65]

Like *Cam-ı Cemşid* who illuminates the world, Süleyman sits majestically on his elaborate golden throne and dominates the centre of the painting. Süleyman's throne is shown rising above a marble-inlaid courtyard with a central fountain. Behind his golden throne an archway opens onto gardens in the background that represent the paradise he created. Above the garden is a stained-glass window with a central cypress tree. The garden above Süleyman acts like a large crown: the peak of his throne directly merges with it. Two cypress trees flank the blooming pink flowers. In Islamic gardens, the cypress tree symbolises death and mourning, while blooming flowers represent life.[66] Through his possession of the ruby cup, the metaphorical Ottoman paradise Süleyman's rule created demonstrates that in his hands the sultan holds the key to life, death and everlasting happiness, in the past, present and future. Thus the painting echoes the symbolisms of his *tughra*, except that now these are amplified through Süleyman's possession of the Alexander cup. By juxtaposing these two floral arrangements above Süleyman's golden throne the painter fully manipulates the narrative of the cup in the context of the Renaissance self-fashioning of the sultan.

Süleyman is painted resting on bright golden coloured cushions that glow like a halo behind him, further reinforcing his prophet-king like image. The cushions are patterned with çintemani motifs. Çintemani are made up of two undulating lines and three spheres (one at the top and two at the bottom). This pattern represents the pelt of the striped tiger and spotted leopard. These motifs symbolise the power, strength and sovereignty of the monarch.[67] Süleyman is depicted holding the ruby cup in his raised right hand as he displays the cup to the four viziers to his lower right. The other figures include the *kapıcılar* (doorkeepers), Has Oda *aghas* (sultan's personal servants) and attendants. They guard the entrances to the throne room and the gardens. The two figures in the upper left chamber are shown pointing to and discussing the arrival of the cup. Here in this painting the painter captures the magnificence of Süleyman who, as ruler of three continents, is now the inheritor of the realm of Cemşid. He is possessor of the ruby cup 'that mirroreth the world' which will allow him to 'behold the seven climes of the world' over most of which he rules.[68] Furthermore, when Süleyman's Safavid adversary Shah Tahmasp admits defeat in 1555 and acknowledges Süleyman in a letter to the sultan, he pays him homage as a world-conquering hero. He likens him to Alexander the Great and the great Persian ruler Darius.[69] Echoing the symbolism represented by the ruby cup, this royal submission recognises Süleyman's symbolic triumph over the Safavid Empire, and that of Shi'a Islam. Süleyman is now the supreme ruler of the Muslim world and the representative of 'true' Islam. His name resonates from Buda in the West to China in the East. The court poet Baqi also captures these universal perceptions of Süleyman in the following lines:

> the monarch with the crown of Alexander, the army of Darius / the sphere bowed its head in the dust at his feet / the earth before his gate served as prayer mat for the world.[70]

Connecting the mythical, heroic and historical past to Süleyman's feats culminating in his possession of the ruby cup, Arifi's *Süleymanname* thus brought to life the dawn of the new Ottoman epoch during the sultan's reign. Possession of the cup meant Süleyman was now the rightful symbolic ruler of Iran. His symbolic triumph over Shi'a Safavids confirmed his caliph-sultan status and supremacy of Sunni orthodoxy over all the Muslim lands. His possession of St Stephen's Holy Crown of Hungary made him the symbolic ruler of Latin Christendom and the Byzantine Empire, reviving the glory of the Roman Empire from his capital, New Rome. From the East to the West, he united the peoples of the whole world under his rule and ushered in the era of the 'Süleymanis'.[71] He challenged the legitimacy of the Emperor of Latin Christendom as the ruler of Hungary and brought most of the Muslim world under his dominion. He created the Ottoman paradise on earth and ruled the world like the lord of the East and West, just as 'he of the two-horns' (a reference to Alexander in the Qur'an, 18:83–101) had done. Just as Alexander spread Hellenic culture and learning, building cities in the classical age, Süleyman is represented as dispensing wisdom, justice, *kanuns*. He adorned his empire with architectural works on three continents in the early modern period. Like Alexander giving crowns to rulers, Süleyman, too became the 'King, whom the kings of the earth obey' as Baqi writes.[72] He gave crowns to rulers like Zapolya. It is correct to state that Ottoman symbolism represented *Muhteşem* (Magnificent) Süleyman as the new Alexander of the age, 'Lord born under a fortunate conjunction'.[73]

A master at self-fashioning and propagating his universal image, Süleyman used art to reflect his religious and political motives through which he validated his power. He relied on the past to help him create new and innovative artistic expressions of his power in the present. He used the myths and legends of old and turned them into present reality in various genre. Süleyman propagated his universal image as the newly-reborn Solomon, Alexander, Cengiz Khan and Timur. Representing himself as the wise and just ruler, a world conquering hero and one who wears the Crown of Hungary challenges Catholic Christendom and also reinforces his identity as the new Caesar of the age. Through his patronage of art, he ensured the longevity of the magnificent century he helped forge in the early modern period.

CONCLUSION: A DISTINCTIVELY OTTOMAN RENAISSANCE

This study has re-evaluated early modern Ottoman art in terms of its participation in and contribution to the Renaissance. It specifically contributes to current scholarship in the field, led by such historians as Gülru Necipoğlu, Jerry Brotton, Matteo Burioni, Lisa Jardine, and Giancarlo Casale, to name but a few. Looking beyond the European purview, such studies highlight the shared cultural heritage of the Mediterranean basin. In this vein, the main objective of this study is to place Ottoman art from the fourteenth to the sixteenth centuries definitively within a more globalised Renaissance narrative.

As this book has demonstrated, with specific regard to the court of the sultans, the Ottoman Renaissance blossomed in 1413 and ended with the Süleymanic Age in 1575. By the end of the Süleymanic century the interactions between artistic and architectural productions, and the cultural identity that they produced, created an Ottoman canon of visual arts. Within this canon, the disciplines of architecture, ceramics, painting, and scriptorial works were sophisticated, demonstrating the vibrancy, dynamism, and individualism of the Ottoman artistic repertoire.

This work uniquely interrogates both Western, or Vasarian, and Eastern, or Ottoman, notions of rebirth. To this end Giorgio Vasari's *The Lives of the Painters, Sculptors, and Architects* (1550/1568), Mustafa Ali's *The Essence of History* (1591–99) and *Epic Deeds of Artists* (1587), and Mimar Sinan's *Treatise on Architecture* (c. 1587–88) have been mined for convergences and divergences on the theme. Not surprisingly, given their divergent cultural and religious traditions, their understandings of the hierarchy of the arts and their sources of inspiration were different. For the West, painting, sculpture, and architecture were considered the most excellent of the arts and were inspired largely by the grand tradition of classical Greece and Rome. The Ottomans, on the other hand, placed greater value on the fine arts of calligraphy, ceramics, illumination, miniature paintings, and architecture. Here, the stimuli were much more complex with origins in Eastern, Islamic, and Roman/Byzantine models.

Notwithstanding these disparities, this study noted forceful connections between the writers and notion of rebirth, the main attribute underpinning the idea of the Renaissance. Vasari, Ali, and Sinan considered artistic rebirth—*rinascita* or *ihya*—to involve looking to the past to create something new. All three perceived art, like history, as a cumulative process. For Vasari that process included *imitazione* (imitation), *adeguazione* (adaptation), and *perfezione* (perfection). Similarly, for Ali and Sinan, artistic development had to go through a series of phases: first, using *nūmūne* (a sample model), then *tecdid* (restoring, making anew), after that creating *ihtira* works (original) with *nezaket* (elegance), before attaining *zuhūrat* (perfection) in order to *a'zam* (surpass) the past. By giving voice to Ottoman Renaissance contemporaries, this study intervenes in current scholarship to provide historians with a clearer picture of the period's complexities and interconnections.

The existence of an Ottoman Renaissance has been largely overlooked or has been placed within the Western narrative of Renaissance that highlights the significance of Europe, and its roots in classical Greece and Rome. Careful not to prioritise European experiences of rebirth, this book has sought to tease out specifically Ottoman features which characterise the cultural rebirth at the other end of the Mediterranean. Because the centre of the empire was Istanbul, not Rome or Florence, this study thus seeks to place the Ottoman Renaissance experience within its own context. This means looking at both the Eastern and Western influences on Ottoman notions of rebirth. Whilst acknowledging that the Ottoman rebirth saw a classicising trend, I argued that this was only one aspect of the Ottoman Renaissance. The novel argument I put forward here is that the most significant element of the Ottomans' rebirth was tied to its Eastern and Islamic heritage. By honing in on its Turkic–Mongol–Timurid and Islamic past, a separate and distinct cultural rebirth occurred at the Ottoman court. This new reading has shown that the Renaissance was not an exclusively Italian or even European phenomenon but that many cultures in the Mediterranean and beyond developed a similar historical self-consciousness and, through it, sought to proclaim a new identity with which to engage in an increasingly globalised world.

After establishing the rebirth paradigm from the Ottomans' perspective and the impact of Sufi Humanism on Islamic art, this book presented extensive examples to demonstrate the emergence and complexity of Ottoman rebirth. In line with Jörn Rüsen's argument about historical consciousness, this study has revealed that a culture using quotations from the past as exemplars expresses "itself narratively [via] structured representations of the past" through "concrete images that represent histories, e.g., monuments or historical symbols," thereby forging its rebirth.[1] By firmly connecting to its Eastern Turkic heritage and its meaningful Islamic legacy, in both real and imagined ways, the Ottoman dynasty signalled both the political and artistic rebirth of the empire. This rebirth occurred after the interregnum period that saw Timur ousted from the lands of Rum. It was led by the patronage of Sultan Mehmed I and announced by the commissioning of the Yeşil Camii (Green Mosque) and Yeşil Türbe (Green Tomb) from the ashes of Timur's annihilation in 1413. In this initial phase of its *rinascita*, taking place in a politically fragile empire, the Ottomans looked to the aesthetics of the Turkic–Timurid–Persian East to establish and construct dynastic legitimacy and identity. The introduction of the Timurid *cuerda seca* technique (monochrome glazed hexagonal green tiles) and underglazed painted Chinese-inspired blue and white tiles occurred first in the Yeşil Camii and Tomb of Mehmed I. These stylistic appropriations served not just to link the Ottomans visually to an authoritative past but also acted as a catalyst for the Renaissance of tile making in the Ottoman world. Indeed, the distinctive nature and quality of Iznik tiles places Ottoman fine arts at both the aesthetic and technological forefront of the early modern era. In addition, the masters of Tabriz also introduced Timurid embellishments: large circular rosettes decorated with elegant *rumi* motifs in white, arabesque yellow, and blue. The incorporation of contemporary Timurid influences demonstrates the Eastern flavour of the Ottoman Renaissance—and signals the Ottomans' ascendency over their Timurid cousins.

Mehmed II's capture of Constantinople in 1453 marked a psychological shift in the Ottoman dynasty's imperial vision. Adding to his existing titles, the sultan became the new caesar of the Romans. He took up residence in the newly constructed Topkapı Palace overlooking the Golden Horn on the site of the former residence of the Byzantine/Roman emperors. Aside from his conquering zeal, Mehmed II was a Renaissance patron of the arts who used the city he captured as a symbol of geo-cultural polity to represent his universal mission. Situated between

East and West, Ottoman Istanbul or the "New Rome" allowed Mehmed II to mediate between these two contrasting worlds.

Mehmed II's invitation to both Italian and Persian artists gave him the opportunity to commission works that saw the fusion of diverse international styles created for and in an Ottoman context. Mehmed II commissioned bronze medallions (c. 1480) by Costanzo de Ferrara, for example. These depicted him in an equestrian style imitating Roman emperors of antiquity. The Venetian Gentile Bellini's famous oil painting (c. 1479) of the sultan in typical Renaissance style shows him flanked by three golden crowns, a nod to his rule over three continents. Sinan Bey and Ahmed of Bursa were also trained in the Western tradition by Bellini and produced Eastern and Western styles. Such intercultural Renaissance experiences are shown in this work as evidence of an exciting cross-cultural exchange of local artists. This hybridity reveals that the Renaissance was not a mono-cultural phenomenon but rather one that was broader, more complex, and culturally inclusive.

This fusion of West and East is also seen in the architectural endeavors of Mehmed II, who became the first sultan in Istanbul to build an imperial mosque following the Roman/Byzantine Hagia Sophia model. Although the collapse of the mosque's dome meant that this attempt at appropriating the Roman/Byzantine model into the Ottoman architectural idiom was not fully successful, it did serve as a reminder of the Ottomans' competitive spirit—their attempt to embrace contemporary technological and engineering challenges in their attempt to surpass the past. The appropriation of the Hagia Sophia into a distinctly Ottoman art form during the Renaissance signifies not only Ottoman continuity with the Roman/Byzantine past but also the creation of something new in its place; ultimately, such an appropriation announces the symbolic victory of Islam over Christianity.

The aesthetics of the East continued to attract the Ottomans as a way to further legitimise their dynastic rule over their Timurid–Turkic brothers. Mehmed II demonstrated this by commissioning the building of the Tiled Pavilion in 1473 in the Timurid–Persian style decorated with blue and white tiles and *kufic* Qur'anic calligraphy. The pavilion emulated the Samarkand mosque of Bibi Hatun (1399–1404), wife of Timur, with its large seventh-century *kufic* tiled inscriptions showing underglaze blue and white painted tiles as well as *cuerda seca* tiles. These various creations confirm the positive influence of the cultural exchanges that were taking place at the time. In the latter quarter of the fifteenth century Mehmed II realigned Ottoman cultural rebirth to accommodate a more pluralistic aesthetic. The result of this is distinctly Ottoman in nature. This highlights the Ottomans' engagement in the creative artistic discourse of the period through their fusion of the Eastern and classical mediums. Rather than rejecting cultural differences, the Ottoman sultans instead accommodated the many, often conflicting, influences of their forebears, adopting and adapting them, as custodians of their lands and customs into a new and meaningful contemporary identity. So important was this imperial self-fashioning that it propelled the Ottomans onto a triumphant trajectory into the sixteenth century.

Diverse cultural aesthetics continued to develop and reach maturity in the art and architecture of the Süleymanic Age in the sixteenth century, particularly with the work of the imperial architect of the court, Sinan, and the palace artists. Sinan's appropriation of Byzantine/Roman architectural aesthetics became a catalyst for progress towards "cultural production," refinement, and greatness.[2] Sinan took Ottoman art to its "complete realisation" in his mosque aesthetics.[3] Both the Süleymaniye (1550–57/8) and Selimiye (1569–75) complexes signify the Renaissance competitive spirit and the Ottomans' aim to surpass the ancients in magnificence or *azim*. The Süleymaniye Mosque was built on the orders of Sultan Süleyman in the style of the Hagia Sophia. This mosque achieved a more open interior space suitable for Muslim worship, surpassing the Byzantine/Roman structure. Claiming to have created a more *nezāket* (elegant) form in the Süleymaniye Mosque, Sinan refined his art aesthetics and originality. Furthermore, he pushed the boundaries of art in the Selimiye Mosque by achieving an uninterrupted space over a single dome of 45 metres, higher than that of the Hagia Sophia, bringing the engineering challenge of the Byzantine/Roman structure to its completion. Like his Italian Renaissance counterparts, Sinan's contributions to the making of the Renaissance through his competitive spirit and creative genius underpin this study and signify the distinctive nature of the Ottoman Renaissance.

Aside from monumental architectural, the Iznik aesthetic also played a crucial role in the development and refinement of Ottoman fine arts during the sixteenth century. The technical mastery and artistic sophistication attained by the palace and kiln ateliers both in Istanbul and Iznik exemplified the taste of the Ottoman court. Artists experimented with new (*ihtira*) vibrant colours like tomato red or *kil-i ermeni*, turquoise and deep blue, manganese, and green to represent the paradise depicted in the Qur'an. This dynamic tiling became Ottoman art *par excellence*. This was combined with Qur'anic calligraphy, Şah Kulu's *saz* scrolls, arrays of floral motifs carnations, hyacinths, roses, and the crown of flowers, the tulip. This exquisite arrangement was first attempted on a massive scale by Sinan at the Rustem Pasha Mosque. It demonstrated both artistic sophistication and the master artist's construction of an existentialist narrative for the viewer. The anagogical and eschatological reading of the tiles of the Rustem Pasha Mosque in Chapter Six showed how Sinan's art was bolstered by the Sufi humanist approach to the Divine. A philosophical reading of Ottoman Iznik art and the naturalist aesthetic of the Word demonstrated the ways in which the mosque designers realised the Renaissance humanist experience which characterised the period.

The Ottoman intellectual Mustafa Ali, a contemporary of Giorgio Vasari, writes that the Ottomans believed that calligraphy was the most important expression of art. For the Ottomans this art surpassed illumination, miniature painting, limning, gilding, and even gold illumination. Just as Vasari saw painting, architecture and sculpture as the epitomes of art, the Ottomans held a similar belief about the written "Word" due to its decorative, scriptorial nature and its association with the "Word of God." Chapter Seven explained how Ottoman calligraphers contributed to the self-fashioning of Süleyman the Magnificent by exploiting the *tughra* genre to represent his power, identity, and piety. The link to Islamic calligraphic origins in the seventh century and the continuous refinement of the calligraphic aesthetic throughout the centuries contributed to new stylistic sophistication under Ottoman patronage. In Chapter Seven examples showed the continuous striving by the court artists to perfect the art of the *tughra*. The sultan's *tughra* was a symbol of authority, for example, in imperial edicts and foreign correspondence. It both propagated the sultan's royal message and reinforced his self-professed image. Chapter Seven also demonstrated the ways in which the illustrated manuscript of the *Süleymanname* (The Illustrated History of Süleyman) presented Süleyman's achievements. Arifi, the creator of the

Şahname-i Al-i Osman (The Royal Book of the House of Osman), was conscious of the usefulness of propagating the sultan's universal sovereignty in both the East and West. In the last volume of the *Süleymanname*, Arifi appropriated past examples and adapted them to suit the sixteenth-century Ottoman context. He used the eleventh-century Iranian poet Firdausi's *Shahnama* criteria to present his targeted audience with a history that connected the mythical past and heroic deeds with Süleyman's historical achievements. In this way the historical consciousness of the past was reflected in the present.

By explicating a broad range of examples, this research has revisited the concept of the Renaissance from an Ottoman viewpoint. While drawing on European notions of rebirth as a point of departure, this research has gone well beyond this, offering a more global framework for the discipline of Renaissance studies. This framework definitively includes non-European cultures in the dominant Renaissance discourse. This research has therefore shifted the Renaissance narrative away from the West to recognise the East's contributions to early modern Ottoman art. By demonstrating the impact of the fusion of East and West on early modern Ottoman art, the study has shown that the traditionalist understanding of the Renaissance is no longer tenable. Like their European contemporaries, Ottoman artists turned to history: they relied on past exemplars to redefine and shape the present. However, the Ottomans drew on a different history—their unique Eastern heritage—as well as that of the Western tradition.

The limitations of this research can be overcome through future research on early modern Ottoman art. Such research needs to consider the Ottoman Renaissance legacy and its centrifugal influence on the neighbouring regions of the Ottoman Empire. Throughout the book, it has been established that early modern Ottoman art reflected the greatness of the Empire's rulers and the magnificence of the sultans' court. Ottoman material culture was positively received in fifteenth- and sixteenth-century Europe, from Moscow, Warsaw, Budapest, and Venice to London. These Ottoman objects of material culture represent more than just objects appropriated by local artists. They are not of interest simply as supplements to help shed light on influences on the Western Renaissance of Italy and other European courts. These objects celebrate the global nature of the Renaissance. They are a product of a vibrant culture and demonstrate that its creative, aesthetic, and stylistic progress influenced visual tastes beyond its borders. The evidence used to support this comes from the many Ottoman objects, both original and imitative, which found their way into the courts and palaces of the time. These objects include ceremonial helmets, maces, armor, and carpets in Anatolian Uşak styles. There are also Ottoman-inspired thrones, where uncut gemstones have been independently mounted in flower-shaped gold mounts, made possible by techniques that had been copied from Ottoman craftsmen; textiles with distinct Ottoman embroidery depicting tulip and carnation motifs; and ceramics that were inspired by Iznik ware. The Ottoman styles and techniques that are embedded in such objects leave little doubt about the positive influence that Ottoman visual culture had in Europe. Furthermore, the *Ottomanising* of the Renaissance can be seen in the influence of Ottoman visual aesthetics on European ceremonials. The intertwining of Ottoman and European visual motifs in such public ceremonials reflected the close inter-cultural exchanges in the Mediterranean basin.

To insist on an exclusively Florentine, Italian, or European *rinascita* or cultural rebirth would fail to appreciate the cultural interconnectedness of the early modern period. In contrast, by recognising Ottoman arts as part of a larger Renaissance narrative this book celebrates the globalisation that took place in that period, and presents a more objective version of the historical and cultural contexts of the sixteenth-century Mediterranean. This study hopes to inspire future scholarship to recognise the significance of seemingly peripheral cultures in established narratives. By reorienting the purview, a greater understanding of the value of less dominant centres can be achieved, ultimately broadening our understanding of human history.

NOTES

INTRODUCTION

1 Ayesha Ramachandran, *The Worldmakers: Global Imagining in Early Modern Europe* (Chicago: The University of Chicago Press, 2015), 7.

2 Gülru Necipoğlu, *The Age of Sinan: Architectural Culture in the Ottoman Empire* (London: Reaktion Books, 2005).

3 Necipoğlu, *The Age of Sinan,* 13, 15.

4 This literature will be reviewed mostly in Chapter Two but is also addressed throughout the thesis.

5 See Marina Belozerskaya, *Rethinking the Renaissance: Burgundian Arts Across Europe* (Cambridge: Cambridge University Press, 2002).

6 Necipoğlu, *The Age of Sinan*, 13, 15.

7 Some of the main works which globalise the Renaissance include David Abulafia, *The Great Sea: A Human History of the Mediterranean* (Oxford: Oxford University Press, 2011); Anna Contadini and Claire Norton, eds., *The Renaissance and the Ottoman World* (Farnham: Ashgate Publishing Limited, 2013); Rosamond E. Mack, *Bazaar to Piazza: Islamic Trade and Italian Art, 1300-1600* (Berkeley: University of California Press, 2002); Nancy Bisaha, *Creating East West: Renaissance Humanists and the Ottoman Turks* (Philadelphia: University of Pennsylvania Press, 2006); Jerry Brotton, *The Renaissance: A Very Short Introduction* (New York: Oxford University Press, 2006); Jerry Brotton, *The Renaissance Bazaar: From the Silk Road to Michelangelo* (New York: Oxford University Press, 2002), Kindle; Deborah Howard, "Venice between East and West: Marc'antonio Barbaro and Palladio's Church of the Redentore," *The Journal of the Society of Architectural Historians* 62, no. 3 (2003): 306-25; Lisa Jardine, *Worldly Goods: A New History of the Renaissance* (New York: W. W. Norton & Company, Inc., 1996); Gülru Necipoğlu and Alina Payne, eds., *Histories of Ornament: From Global to Local* (Princeton: Princeton University Press, 2016); and Ramachandran, *The Worldmakers.*

8 See Stephen Greenblatt, *Renaissance Self-Fashioning: From More to Shakespeare* (Chicago: University of Chicago Press, 1980).

9 For more on the question of temporality, see Andrew Glencross, "Historical Consciousness in International Relations Theory: A Hidden Disciplinary Dialogue" (Paper prepared for Millennium Conference, Aberdeen, Scotland, October 16-17, 2010).

10 Jörn Rüsen, "What is Historical Consciousness? A Theoretical Approach to Empirical Evidence," trans. Wolfgang Gebhard (Paper presented at Canadian Historical Consciousness in an International Context: Theoretical Frameworks, Vancouver, BC, 2001), 5.

11 See Belozerskaya, *Rethinking the Renaissance*; Peter Burke, *The Italian Renaissance: Culture and Society in Italy* (Princeton: Princeton University Press, 2014); Paul Strathem, *The Medici: Godfathers of the Renaissance* (Pimlico: Florence, 2005); Lisa Golombek and Donald Wilber, *The Timurid Architecture of Iran and Turan* (Princeton: Princeton University Press, 1988).

12 Such a broad thematic focus which examines so-called major and minor arts amidst complex global interactions has gained currency in the recent past with impressive results, including Necipoğlu and Payne, *Histories of Ornament.*

13 See Jerry Brotton, *The Renaissance: A Very Short Introduction* (New York: Oxford University

Press, 2006), 8; see also Matteo Burioni, 'Vasari's Rinascita: History, Anthropology or Art

Criticism,' in *Renaissance Perceptions of Continuity and Discontinuity in Europe, ca. 1300-1550*, ed.

Schnitker H., Péporte P., and A.C. Lee (Leiden: Brill, 2008), 117.

14 Gerald MacClean, ed., *Re-Orienting the Renaissance: Cultural Exchanges with the East* (New York: Palgrave Macmillan, 2005), 1.

15 Heather E. Grossman and Alicia Walker, eds., *Mechanisms of Exchange: Transmission in Medieval Art and Architecture of the Mediterranean, ca. 1000-1500* (Leiden: Brill, 2013), 303.

16 Grossman and Walker, *Mechanisms of Exchange*, 303.

17 Jack Goody, *Renaissances: The One or the Many?* (New York: Cambridge University Press, 2010), 1-6.

18 Karl R. Popper, *The Open Society and its Enemies* (Princeton: Princeton University Press, 2013), 473.

CHAPTER 1

1 See Fleischer, *Bureaucrat and Intellectual in the Ottoman Empire,* 235-310.

2 Cornell H. Fleischer, *Bureaucrat and Intellectual in the Ottoman Empire: The Historian Mustafa Ali, 1541-1600* (Princeton: Princeton University Press, 1986), 101, 226–27, 280.

3 Fleischer, *Bureaucrat and Intellectual in the Ottoman Empire*, 280.

4 Aydın Sayılı, Lamaan Ball, and Salim Ayduz, "Turkish Contributions to Scientific Work in Islam," *Foundation for Science, Technology and Civilisation* 5 (2004): 1-18. http://www.muslimheritage.com/uploads/TurkishScience.pdf.

5 Marshall Broomhall, "II: China and the Arabs from the Rise of the Abbasid Caliphate," in *Islam in China: A Neglected Problem* (London: Morgan & Scott Ltd., 1910), 25-26.

6 See David Talbot Rice, *Islamic Art* (London: Thames and Hudson, 1991), 77–96.

7 See Rene Grousset, *The Empire of the Steppes: A History of Central Asia* (New Brunswick, NJ: Rutgers University Press, 1970).

8 FFleischer, *Bureaucrat and Intellectual in the Ottoman Empire*, 170.

9 Fleischer, *Bureaucrat and Intellectual in the Ottoman Empire*, 141; see also Mustafa Ali, *Epic Deeds of Artists*, ed. and trans. Esra Akın-Kıvanç (Leiden, The Netherlands: Brill: 2011), 109, 191, 217.

10 Mustafa Ali, cited in Fleischer, *Bureaucrat and Intellectual in the Ottoman Empire*, 278.

11 On the Timurid Renaissance see Linda Darling, "The Renaissance and the Middle East," in *A Companion to the Worlds of the Renaissance*, ed. G. Ruggiero (Malden, MA: Blackwell Publishing, 2007), 59. See also Ilber Ortaylı, *Türklerin Altın Çağı* (The Golden Age of the Turks) (Istanbul: Kronik Kitap, 2017), 78.

12 Darling, "The Renaissance and the Middle East," 59. See also Ortaylı, *Türklerin Altın Çağı*, 78.

13 Fleischer, *Bureaucrat and Intellectual in the Ottoman Empire*, 277.

14 Fleischer, *Bureaucrat and Intellectual in the Ottoman Empire*, 276.

15 Mehmed I, cited in Dimitris Kastritsis, *Sons of Bajezid: Empire Building and Representation in the Ottoman Civil War of 1402-13* (Leiden: Brill, 2007), 204-5.

16 Mustafa Ali, cited in Fleischer, *Bureaucrat and Intellectual in the Ottoman Empire*, 178.

17 Fleischer, *Bureaucrat and Intellectual in the Ottoman Empire*, 141.

18 John Monfasani, *George of Trebizond: A Biography and a Study of His Rhetoric and Logic* (Leiden: Brill, 1976), 192.

19 Franz Babinger, *Mehmed the Conqueror and His Time*, 2nd ed., ed.W. C. Hickman, translated by R. Manheim (Princeton: Princeton University Press, 1992), 500.

20 See I. E. Petrosyan, "An Illustrated Turkish Manuscript of 'Iskender-nāme' by Ahmedi," http://www.islamicmanuscripts.info/reference/articles/Petrosyan-1995-MO-1-2-Iskenderna. PDF, 47-48.

21 See Fleischer, *Bureaucrat and Intellectual in the Ottoman Empire*, 109, 191, 217.

22 For folio 519a see See Esin Atıl, *Süleymanname: The Illustrated History of Süleyman the Magnificent* (Washington: National Gallery of Art, 1986). See also Fleischer, *Bureaucrat and Intellectual in the Ottoman Empire,* 277. Huma Hatun was the mother of Mehmed II and Hafsa Hatun was the mother of Süleyman.

23 Fleischer, *Bureaucrat and Intellectual in the Ottoman Empire,* 274–75.

24 See Fleischer, *Bureaucrat and Intellectual in the Ottoman Empire*, 280–88.

25 Sultan Süleyman had Mimar Sinan design plans that included widening the courtyard and building porticoes. Mimar Mehmed Ağa carried out the plan in 1590 during the reign of Murad III. In 1571, Sultan Selim II ordered Mimar Sinan to renovate the mosque and replace the prayer hall's roof with domes and reinforce it with new columns. For more, see Necipoğlu, *The Age of Sinan*, 167–69.

26 Rüsen, "What is Historical Consciousness?," 8.

27 David Lowenthal, *The Past is a Foreign Country* (Cambridge: Cambridge University Press, 1985), 336.

28 Rüsen, "What is Historical Consciousness?," 4.

29 Necipoğlu, *The Age of Sinan*, 13, 15.

CHAPTER 2

1 The book will refer to both electronic and hard copies of Vasari's *Lives*. Giorgio Vasari, *The Lives of the Painters, Sculptors and Architects*, trans. Gaston Du C. de Vere, 10 vols. (London: Macmillan & Co. Ld. & The Medici Society, LD, 1912-14) http://members.efn.org/~acd/vite/VasariLives.html; Giorgio Vasari, *The Lives of the Painters, Sculptors and Architects*, trans. Jonathan Foster (New York: Dover Publications, 2005), Kindle; for book publication, Giorgio Vasari, *The Lives of the Painters, Sculptors and Architects*, ed. William Gaunt, 4 vols. (New York: Dent, 1963).

2 For more see E. H. Gombrich, "The Renaissance Conception of Artistic Progress and its Consequences," in *Norm and Form: Studies in the Art of the Renaissance* (London: Phaidon Press, 1966), 1-10.

3 "…della loro perfezione e rovina e restaurazione e per dir meglio rinascita…," Giorgio Vasari, *Le vite de' piu eccellenti pittori, scultori ed architetti* (Torino: Letteratura italiana Einaudi, 1986), 125, http://www.letteraturaitaliana.net/pdf/Volume_5/t129.pdf. For English translation see Vasari, Preface to Part I, *The Lives*, accessed May 5, 2016, http://members.efn.org/~acd/vite/VasariPreface.html

4 Vasari, Preface to Part II, *The Lives*, accessed May 5, 2016, http://members.efn.org/~acd/vite/VasariPreface2.html

5 Vasari, Part III of *The Lives*

6 For more see Hans Baron, *The Crisis of the Early Italian Renaissance* (Princeton: Princeton University Press, 1966).

7 Vasari, Preface to *The Lives.*

8 "…lavorata di mano d'Andrea Taffi con la medesima maniera greca, ma invero molto piú bella …" Giorgio Vasari, *Le vite de' piu eccellenti architetti pittori, et scultori italiani da Cimabue insino a'tempi nostri* (Firenze: Torentino, 1550), http://bepi1949.altervista.org/vasari/vasari10.htm

9 Vasari, Part I of The Lives, accessed May 5, 2016, http://members.efn.org/~acd/vite/VasariGioPisano.htm1

10 Vasari, Part I of *The Lives*, accessed May 5, 2016, http://members.efn.org/~acd/vite/VasariGioPisano.htm1

11 Vasari, Part III of *The Lives*, accessed May 5, 2016, http://members.efn.

org/~acd/vite/VasariMichelangelo7.html

12 Lee Sanstead, "The Meaning of Michelangelo's David" (5 September 2004), accessed February 19, 2017, http://www.sandstead.com/essays/david.html

13 Vasari, Part III of *The Lives*, http://members.efn.org/~acd/vite/VasariMichelangelo3.html

14 Vasari, Part III of *The Lives*, http://members.efn.org/~acd/vite/VasariMichelangelo3.html

15 Vasari, Preface to *The Lives.*

16 See Ulrich Libbrecht, "Comparative Philosophy: A Methodological Approach," in *Worldviews and Cultures: Philosophical Reflections from an Intercultural Perspective*, ed. Nicole Note et al. (Brussels: Springer, 2009).

17 Libbrecht, "Comparative Philosophy," 34.

18 Vasari, Preface to *The Lives.*

19 Vasari, Preface to *The Lives.*

20 Also see Alexander Nagel and Christopher Wood, "Towards a New Model of Renaissance Anachronism," *Art Bulletin* 87 (2005): 408.

21 Fleischer, *Bureaucrat and Intellectual in the Ottoman Empire*, 274.

22 Giorgio Vasari, *Vasari's Lives of the Artists*, translated by Jonathan Foster (New York: Dover Publications, 2005), Kindle, Loc. 29.

23 Vasari, *Vasari's Lives of the Artists*, Kindle, Loc. 28.

24 Fleischer, Bureaucrat and Intellectual in the Ottoman Empire, 123.

25 Akın's commentary in Mustafa Ali, *The Epic Deeds of Artists: A Critical Edition of the Earliest Ottoman Text about the Calligraphers and Painters of the Islamic World*, ed. and trans. by Esra Akın-Kıvanç (Leiden: Brill, 2011), 118, 378. Translation of "silsile-i celileye ihtisasla": reaching state of specialization in one's craft from one era to the next.

26 Esin Atıl, *Süleymanname: The Illustrated History of Süleyman the Magnificent* (Washington, DC: National Gallery of Art, 1986), 32-49.

27 See Ali, *Epic Deeds of Artists*, 273.

28 Ali, cited in Fleischer, Bureaucrat and Intellectual in the Ottoman Empire, 278.

29 Ali, *Epic Deeds of Artists*, 147.

30 Ali, *Epic Deeds of Artists*, 273.

31 Ali, *Epic Deeds of Artists*, 198.

32 Ali, *Epic Deeds of Artists*, 410, 417. For Ottoman-Turkish definitions see Ottoman-Turkish Dictionary, *Yeni Cep Lügat* (Istanbul: Envar Neşriyat, 2000).

33 Ali, *Epic Deeds of Artists,* 174.

34 Ali, *Epic Deeds of Artists,* 319.

35 Ali, *Epic Deeds of Artists,* 313.

36 Ali, *Epic Deeds of Artists,* 196.

37 Ali, *Epic Deeds of Artists,* 196.

38 Ali, *Epic Deeds of Artists*, 294, 330, 334, 384.

39 J. M. Rogers and R. M. Ward, *Süleyman the Magnificent* (London: British Museum Publications, 1990), 55.

40 Ali mentions the original "six styles" of Arabic as *thuluth, naskh, tafiliq, rayhani, muhaqqaq,* and *riqa.*

41 Ali, *Epic Deeds of Artists,* 147.

42 Ali, *Epic Deeds of Artists,* 202.

43 Mustafa Sa'i, *Sinan's Autobiographies: Five Sixteenth Century Texts, Introductory Notes, Critical Editions, and Translations by Howard Crane and Esra Akın*, ed. Gülru Necipoğlu (Leiden: Brill, 2006), 124.

44 Ali, *Epic Deeds of Artists*, 454.

45 Ali, *Epic Deeds of Artists*, 273.

46 Ali, *Epic Deeds of Artists*, 273. According to Maria Pia Pedani, Paoli might be the Maestro Paolo of Ragusa, Sicily. The author shows that in 1480 Sinan Bey was sent to Venice as an envoy. Esin Atıl includes a list of other Italian painters who worked at Topkapı Palace: Bartholomeo di San Marco, Gentile Bellini, Costanzo da Ferrara, Matteo de Pasti, Paolo da Pistoja, Paolo da Ragusa, Paolo Uccello, and Pinturicchio. See Esin Atıl, "Ottoman Miniature Painting Under Sultan Mehmed II," *Ars Oreintalis* 5, no. 9, (1973): 103-20.

47 Also known as Ahmed of Bursa, another Ottoman artist who painted Sultan Mehmed II, in his portrait Mehmed II "Smelling a Rose." See Gülru Necipoğlu, "From Byzantine Constantinople to Ottoman Konstantiniyye: Creation of a Cosmopolitan Capital and Visual Culture Under Sultan Mehmed II," in *From Byzantium to Istanbul: 8000 Years of Capital*, ed. Nazan Ölçer (Istanbul: Sabanci University, Sakip Sabanci Museum, 2010), 265-76.

48 Necipoğlu, "From Byzantine Constantinople to Ottoman Konstantini-

yye,"274.

49 See Hans Georg Majer, "New Approaches in Portraiture," in *The Sultan's Portrait: Picturing the House of Osman*, ed. Selmin Kangal and trans. Priscilla Mary Işın (Istanbul: İşBank, 2000), 336–75, 344; see also Gülru Necipoğlu, "The Serial Portraits of Ottoman Sultans in Comparative Perspective," in *The Sultan's Portrait: Picturing the House of Osman*, ed. Selmin Kangal and trans. Priscilla Mary Işın (Istanbul: İşBank, 2000), 37; Robin Beuchat, "**Échange interculturel et transfert de representations** Sur les portraits turcs de Paolo Giovio" ("Intercultural exchange and transfer of representations of Turkish portraits of Paolo Giovio"), Université de Genève,' Arborescences: revue d'études françaises, n° 2, 2012, 6-7, accessed August 23, 2014, http://www.erudit.org/apropos/utilisation.html

50 Rüsen, "What is Historical Consciousness?," 4.

51 D. Soyini Madison, *Critical Ethnography: Method, Ethics, and Performance* (Los Angeles: Sage Publications, 2012), 58.

52 Madison, *Critical Ethnography*, 58.

53 Sa'i, *Sinan's Autobiographies*, 130.

54 " "…bu şerh ü tafsili sahayıf-ı rüzgârda nümüne ü yādgār kalmak içün." See Sa'i, *Sinan's Autobiographies*, 62, 59.

55 "her küngüre-'i eyvāndan bir gūşe ve her zāviye-'i virāndan bir tūşe peydā eyleyūp ..." See Sa'i, *Sinan's Autobiographies*, 115, 142.

56 Sa'i, *Sinan's Autobiographies*, 74, 85, 156.

57 Sa'i, *Sinan's Autobiographies*, 65, 75, 85. For definitions of Ottoman-Turkish words see *Yeni Cep Lügat*.

58 "günden güne envā'-i 'imaretler ihtira' olınup nezāket izdiyād bulmışdur ..." See Sa'i, *Sinan's Autobiographies*, 65, 78, 131.

59 Sa'i, *Sinan's Autobiographies*, 74-5.

60 a'i, *Sinan's Autobiographies*, 74.

61 Sa'i, *Sinan's Autobiographies*, 123.

62 See Giorgio Vasari, Preface to Part I, *The Lives*.

63 Sa'i, *Sinan's Autobiographies*, 123, 131.

64 Selen B. Morkoç, "Reading Architecture from the Text: The Ottoman Story of the Four Marble Columns," accessed February 9, 2018. https://www.aca-

demia.edu/27608699/Reading_Architecture_from_Text_The_Story_of_the_Four_Marble_Columns, 34.

65 Sa'i, *Sinan's Autobiographies*, 122.

66 Lowenthal, The Past is a Foreign Country, 339.

67 Gülru Necipoğlu-Kafadar, *Muqarnas* 3 (1985): 92-117. 2018http://www.jstor.org/stable/1523086?origin=JSTOR-pdf, 92.

68 Rüsen, "What is Historical Consciousness?," 4.

69 Vasari, Preface to Part I, *The Lives*.

70 See Vasari, Part III of *The Lives*, http://members.efn.org/~acd/vite/VasariMichelangelo8.html; and Sa'i, *Sinan's Autobiographies*, 74-75.

71 Aristotle, '"Nicomachean Ethics," Book IV, http://www.sacred-texts.com/cla/ari/nico/nico036.htm

72 "Ayasōfya gibi qubbe aslā yapılmaz diyu bahs eyledi dünyā / Bu 'ālī qubbe andan oldı a'zam ... bir cami' binâsına emr-i hūmāyūnları oldı ki rüzgârda misāl olmaya." See Sa'i, *Sinan's Autobiographies*, 130, 150.

73 Sa'i, *Sinan's Autobiographies*, 66.

74 Sa'i, *Sinan's Autobiographies*, 66.

75 Sinan makes references to "tecdid" and "zuhūrat" in his autobiographies to describe his works. See pp. 71, 78, 79, 85; *Tecdid* literally means to "restore, give rebirth, renovate, renew"; *zuhur* / *zuhūrat* means "bring to life, to create anew, perfection." See Ottoman-Turkish Dictionary, *Yeni Cep Lügat*, 325, 327.

76 ee *Yeni Cep Lügat*, 128. *Ihya*: diriltme, canlandırma, şenlendirme, (literal translation: rebirth, resurrect, renovate, restore).

77 See Mustafa Selaniki Efendi, *Tarih-i Selaniki*, ed. Mehmet Ipsirli, 2 vols (Istanbul: Türk Tarih Kurum Basımevi, 1989), I: 95-96.

78 "Murādım caāmi-i şerifi ihyā idüb eşer-i haāşş idinmekdür." See Mustafa Selaniki Efendi, *Tarih-i Selaniki*, 120-21.

79 See Vasari, Preface to Part I, *The Lives*, and Part III, http://members.efn.org/~acd/vite/VasariMichelangelo8.html

80 Baş Başbakanlık Arşivi, Istanbul, Muhimme Defteri 22, no. 171, 82.

81 See also Ahmed Refik, "On Altıncı," 18 (1935): 22-24 and partial translation in William Emerson and Robert L. Van Nice, "Hagia Sophia and the First Minaret Erected After the Conquest of Constantinople," *American Journal of*

Archaeology 54, no. 1 (1950): 33-34.

82 Atıl, *Süleymanname*, 206.

83 Oleg Grabar, *The Formation of Islamic Art* (New Haven and London: Yale University Press, 1987), 49, 51, 63, 68.

84 Grabar, *The Formation of Islamic Art*, 49, 51, 63, 68.

85 Grabar, *The Formation of Islamic Art*, 49, 51, 63, 68.

86 Sa'i, *Sinan's Autobiographies,* 66, 79.

87 Başbakanlık Arşivi, Muhimme Defteri 10, no. 391, 253, dated 19B, 979, Istanbul.

88 A c. 1581 miniature painting by Lokman depicts Ottoman architects and craftsmen working at the Holy Precinct.

89 Necipoğlu, *The Age of Sinan*, 168.

90 Vasari, Preface to Part II, *The Lives,* http://members.efn.org/~acd/vite/VasariPreface2.html

91 Sa'i, *Sinan's Autobiographies,* 150.

CHAPTER 3

1 Seyyed Hossein Nasr, *Islamic Art and Spirituality* (Albany, NY: State University of New York Press, 1987), ix.

2 See David P. Brewster, "The Study of Sufism: Towards a Methodology," 31, http://doi.org/10.1016/0048-721X(76)90047-6.

3 Brewster, "The Study of Sufism: Towards a Methodology," 31.

4 Seyyed Hossein Nasr, *Islamic Art and Spirituality* (New York: State University of New York Press, 1987), 7.

5 Nasr, *Islamic Art and Spirituality*, 7.

6 Nasr, *Islamic Art and Spirituality*, 11.

7 Nasr, *Islamic Art and Spirituality*, 4.

8 Nasr, *Islamic Art and Spirituality*, 8.

9 Şefik Can, *Fundamentals of Rumi's Thought, A Mevlevi Sufi Perspective* (Clifton, NJ: Tughra Books, 2009), 136.

10 Can, *Fundamentals of Rumi's Thought,* 137..

11 Ayla Esen Algar, *Architecture, Art and Sufism in Ottoman Turkey* (Berkeley:

University of California Press, 1992), 20.

12 Can, *Fundamentals of Rumi's Thought*, 137.

13 Reynold A. Nicholson, *The Mesnevi of Jalalu'ddin Rumi*, Vols. I and II (Lahore: Islamic Book Service, 1989), vol. I, no. 2842.

14 Rumi, *Divan-i Kabir*, trans. Bediuzzaman Furuzanfar (Tehran: Darneshgah-e, Tehran, 1957), 3: 1414.

15 Rumi quoted in Faridun B. Ahmed, *Risale-i Sipehsalar*, trans., Mithat Bahari Beytur (Istanbul: Eles, 2006).

16 Rumi, *The Essential Rumi*, trans. Coleman Barks and John Moyne (New York: Harper One, 2004), 32.

17 Nasr, *Islamic Art and Spirituality*, 13.

18 Emma Clark, "The Symbolism of the Islamic Garden," Islamic Arts & Architecture (October 2, 2011), http://islamic-arts.org/2011/the-symbolism-of-the-islamic-garden/

19 On Sufi influence on art see Mehmet Önder, *Mevlāna and the Mevlāna Museum*, ed. Zümrüt Akşit (Istanbul: Akşit Culture and Tourism Publication, 1985), 66-85. See also Algar, *Architecture, Art and Sufism in Ottoman Turkey*, 62.

20 Jurgen W. Frembgen, "Calligraphy from Ottoman Dervish Lodges," *Islamic Art and Architecture*, September 5, 2013, http://islamic-arts.org/2013/calligraphy-from-ottoman-dervish-lodges/

21 For more see Osman Horata, "Mevlāna ve Divan Şairleri," *Hacettepe Üniversitesi Edebiyat Fakültesi Dergisi* (2008): 47-48, http://akademik.semazen.net/article_detail.php?id=417

22 Önder, *Mevlāna and the Mevlāna Museum*, 68.

23 Önder, *Mevlāna and the Mevlāna Museum*, 42.

24 See Qur'an: 20:82, 38:66, 39:5, 40:42, 71:10

25 Can, *Fundamentals of Rumi's Thought*, 271.

26 Can, *Fundamentals of Rumi's Thought*, 273.

27 Celaleddin Rumi, cited in Talat S. Halman, *Rapture and Revolution: Essays on Turkish Literature* (Syracuse, NY: Syracuse University Press, 2007), 297.

28 Henry Corbin, *Alone with the Alone: Creative Imagination in the Sufism of Ibn Arabi*, trans. Ralph Manheim (Princeton, NJ: Princeton University Press, 1998), 193.

29 Nasr, *Islamic Art and Spirituality*, 182.

30 Nasr, *Islamic Art and Spirituality*, 107.

31 Suhrawardi, cited in Henry Corbin, *Spiritual Body and Celestial Earth: From Mazdean Iran to Shi'ite Iran*, trans. Nancy Pearson (Princeton, NJ: Princeton University Press, 1977), 131.

32 See Corbin, *Alone with the Alone,* 80-81, 145, 182-83.

33 Ibn Arabi, cited in Corbin, *Alone with the Alone*, xvii-xviii.

34 Ibn Arabi, cited in Corbin, *Alone with the Alone*, xvii-xviii.

35 Ibn Arabi, cited in Corbin, *Alone with the Alone,* xvii-xviii.

36 Ibn Arabi, cited in Corbin, *Alone with the Alone,* xvii-xviii.

37 Ibn Arabi, cited in Corbin, *Alone with the Alone*, 80-81.

38 Nasr, Islamic Art and Spirituality, 129, 186.

39 Ibn Arabi, cited in Corbin, *Alone with the Alone,* 80.

40 Ibid., 185, 200-201

41 Henry Corbin, *The Man of Light in Iranian Sufism*, trans. Nancy Pearson (New York: Omega Publications, 1994), 141.

42 Goethe, cited in Corbin, *The Man of light in Iranian Sufism*, 152.

43 Although there is no explicit Hell imagery depicted in mosques, the many references to 'Hell-Fire' in the supplications adorning the walls of the Rustem Pasha Mosque reflect this view: 'O God! Remove us from the Fire and make us enter Paradise together with the righteous ones by forgiving us with your mercy. For Thou art the most merciful of all.' Translation of the invocation on the window lunette.

44 Nicholson, *The Mesnevi of Jalalu'ddin Rumi*, vol. V, no. 3278.

45 Toby Mayer, 'Theology and Sufism,' in *The Cambridge companion to Classical Islamic Theology*, edited by Tim Winter (Cambridge: Cambridge University Press, 2008), 265.

46 Sa'i, *Sinan's Autobiographies*, 58.

47 Sa'i, *Sinan's Autobiographies*, 64.

48 Sa'i, *Sinan's Autobiographies*, 131.

49 Sa'i, *Sinan's Autobiographies*, 132. Kevser in the Qur'an is one the rivers of Paradise.

50 Sa'i, *Sinan's Autobiographies*, 132.

CHAPTER 4

1 Suna Çağaptay, "Prousa/Bursa, a city within the city: chorography, conversion and choreography," accessed February 9, 2018, https://cambridge.academia.edu/SunaCagaptay, 51; see also Suna Çağaptay, "Frontierscape: Reconsidering Bithynian Structures and their builders on the Byzantine Ottoman cusp," https://cambridge.academia.edu/SunaCagaptay.

2 Çağaptay, "Prousa/Bursa, a city within the city: chorography, conversion and choreography," 52.

3 Çağaptay, "Prousa/Bursa, a city within the city: chorography, conversion and choreography," 51.

4 Robert Ousterhout, "The East, the West, and the Appropriation of the Past in Early Ottoman Architecture," *Gesta* 43, no. 2 (2004): 165-76.

http://www.jstor.org/stable/25067103.

5 Linda Darling, 'The Renaissance and the Middle East,' 59. See also Maria Eva Subtelny, 'Socioeconomic Bases of Cultural Patronage under the Later Timurids,' *International Journal of Middle East Studies*, 20/04 (1988): 479-505; and Guido Ruggiero, ed., *A Companion to the Worlds of the Renaissance* (Malden, MA: Blackwell Publishing, 2007), 58-60.

6 See Lisa Golombek and Maria Subtelny, eds.,Timurid Art and Culture: Iran and Central Asia in the Fifteenth Century (Leiden: Brill, 1992).

7 See Kevin Krisciunas, "The Legacy of Ulugh Beg," *Bulletin of the Association for the Advancement of Central Asian Research* 5 (1992): 3-6. http://vlib.iue.it/carrie/texts/carrie_books/paksoy-2/cam6.html.

8 Scott Redford, "The Seljuks of Rum and the Antique," https://www.academia.edu/4245845/The_Seljuks_of_Rum_and_the_Antique

9 See Golombek and Wilber, *The Timurid Architecture of Iran and Turan* (Princeton: Princeton University Press, 1988). For more on Timurid influence in Anatolia see Mustafa Çağhan Keskin, "Timurid Tile Style in Anatolia and Footprints of Masters of Tabriz" (Paper presented at the International Conference on Architecture & Urban Design, April 19-21, 2012), http://

archnet.org/system/publications/contents/10066/original/DTP102451.pdf?1427898487.

10 Kastritsis, *Sons of Bajezid*, 204-5.

11 Gönül Öney, *Islâm Mimarîsinde Çini* (Istanbul: 1987), 60-1.

12 Godfrey Goodwin, *A History of Ottoman Architecture* (London: Thames and Hudson, 1971), 62; and Stefanos Yerasimos, *Constantinople: Istanbul's Historical Heritage* (Paris: H. F. Ullmann Publishing, 2012), 168.

13 Translation of the inscription of the entrance portal of the mosque.

14 See Rüsen, "What is Historical Consciousness?"

15 Rüsen, "What is Historical Consciousness?," 12.

16 Patricia Blessing, "Seljuk Past and Timurid Present: Tile Decoration of the Yeşil Külliye in Bursa," *Gesta* 56, no. 2 (2017): 225, https://doi.org/10.1086/692804.

17 Goodwin, *A History of Ottoman Architecture,* 61.

18 Gillian Rose, *Visual Methodologies: An Introduction to Researching with Visual Materials* (London: Sage Publications Ltd., 2016), 38-9.

19 Doğan Kuban, *Ottoman Architecture* (Suffolk: Antique Collectors Club Distributors, 2010), 98.

20 Blessing, "Seljuk Past and Timurid Present," 225.

21 Rose, *Visual Methodologies,* 39.

22 Differentiating it from the commonly used pointed arch with a high crown of the Timurids

23 Rüsen, "What is Historical Consciousness?," 13.

24 Goodwin, *A History of Ottoman Architecture*, 62.

25 Rose, Visual Methodologies, 64.

26 Rose, *Visual Methodologies,* 64.

27 For more on this see Goodwin, *A History of Ottoman Architecture*, 58-91.

28 Yerasimos, *Constantinople: Istanbul's Historical Heritage*, 168.

29 Yerasimos, *Constantinople: Istanbul's Historical Heritage*, 168.

30 Taşköprülüzade, *Es-Sekaiku n-Nu'maniye fi Ulema'i d-Devletil-Osmaniye* (Crimson Peonies of the Ottoman State's Ulema), ed. A. S. Furat (Istanbul: 1985), 437.

31 Translation of the inscription of the sultan's loge.

32 Translation of the inscription from the Sultan's loge.

33 See Yerasimos, *Constantinople: Istanbul's Historical Heritage*, p. #?

34 See Kuban, *Ottoman Architecture*, 98-108.

35 Goodwin, *A History of Ottoman Architecture*, 66.

36 Rüsen, "What is Historical Consciousness?," 13.

37 R. Mantran, "Les inscriptions arabes de Brousse," *Bulletin d'Etudes Orientales* 14 (1952-4): 106.

38 Ananda Coomaraswamy, "Notes on the Philosophy of Persian art," *Ars Islamica* 14/15 (1951): 127.

39 See Yerasimos, *Constantinople: Istanbul's Historical Heritage*, 182-86.

40 Gülru Necipoğlu, "From International Timurid to Ottoman: A Change of Taste in Sixteenth-Century Ceramic Tiles," *Muqarnas* 7 (1991): 137, http://isites.harvard.edu/fs/docs/icb.topic570061.files//articles/Necipoglu.%20From%20International%20Timurid%20to%20Ottoman%20A%20Change%20of%20Taste%20in%20Sixteenth-Century%20Ceramic%20Tiles.pdf.

41 Necipoğlu, "From International Timurid to Ottoman," 137.

42 See Goodwin, *A History of Ottoman Architecture*, 92-141; Kuban, *Ottoman Architecture*, 123-30.

43 Yerasimos, *Constantinople: Istanbul's Historical Heritage*, 196.

44 Y Yerasimos, *Constantinople: Istanbul's Historical Heritage*, 196.

45 See Goodwin, *A History of Ottoman Architecture*, 100; and Kuban, *Ottoman Architecture*, 148.

46 Spiro Kostof, *A History of Architecture: Settings and Rituals* (New York: Oxford University Press, 1985), 459..

47 See Harry J. Magoulias, ed., *Decline and Fall of Byzantium to the Ottoman Turks by Doukas: An Annotated Translation of 'Historia Turco-Byzantina* (Detroit: Wayne State University Press, 1975), 106.

48 For Jacques de Helly, see Jean Froissart, *Collection des chroniques nationales françaises: Chroniques de Froissart*, 14 vols., ed. J. A. Buchon (Paris: Verdiere, 1824–26), 13: 401, 408, 412, 417.

49 See Tahsin Öz, *Topkapı Sarayı Müzesi Arşivi Kılavuzu II* (Istanbul: Devlet Basımevi, 1938), document 21, 8. See also Ahmed Ibn Arabshah, *Tamerlane or Timur the Great Amir* (Gujarat, India: Isha Books, 2013), 216-17. For more

on the tapestries see Jardine and Brotton, *Global Interests,* 76.

50 The inscription is found on the Imperial Gate of the fortified outer walls of the Topkapı Palace (1478).

51 Kritovoulos, *History of Mehmed the Conqueror*, trans. Charles T. Brigg (Westport, CT: Greenwood Press, 1970), 3.

52 Kritovoulos, *History of Mehmed the Conqueror*, 3.

53 Fatih Mehmet II Vakfiyeleri, "Türkçe Vakıf Vesikası" (Ankara: Vakiflar Umum Müdürlügü, 1938), facs. 31-32 and 63-65. This document is a sixteenth-century translation of the original fifteenth-century Arabic endowment deed. See also Kayoko Hayashi, "Fatih Vakfiyeleri'nin Tanzim Süreci Üzerine," *Belleten* 72, no. 263 (2008): 1-15.

54 Qur'an: 18:83. For more on Alexander the Great in Islamic history see Z. David Zuwiyya, *Islamic Legends Concerning Alexander the Great* (Albany, NY: State University of New York Press, 2001). See also Abolqasem Ferdowsi, *Shahnameh: The Persian Book of Kings*, trans. Dick Davis (New York: Mage Publishers, 2006).

55 Tursun Beg, *Târîh-i Ebü'l-Feth* (Istanbul: Istanbul Fetih Cemiyeti, 1977), 3, 123–25, 142, 150–51.

56 For the scriptorium of Mehmed II see Julian Raby, "Mehmed the Conqueror's Greek Scriptorium," *Dumbarton Oaks Papers* 37 (1983): 15-34, http://www.jstor.org/stable/1291474.

57 Lauro Quirini quoted in Gülru Necipoğlu, "Visual Cosmopolitanism and Creative Translation: Artistic Conversations with Renaissance Italy in Mehmed II's Constantinople," *Muqarnas* 29 (2012): 8. For more on Mehmed II's interest in the classics see Babinger, *Mehmed the Conqueror and His Time,* 488-508; also see John Freely, *The Grand Turk: Sultan Mehmed II – Conqueror of Constantinople and Master of an Empire* (New York: The Overlook Press, 2009), 95-107.

58 Necipoğlu, "Visual Cosmopolitanism and Creative Translation," 9.

59 Kritovoulos, *History of Mehmed the Conqueror*, 136.

60 Gülru Necipoğlu, "From Byzantine Constantinople to Ottoman Konstantiniyye," 262.

61 Rüsen, "What is Historical Consciousness?," 6.

62 M. M. Bakhtin, *The Dialogic Imagination: Four Essays* (Austin: University of

Texas Press, 1982), 1: 359.

63 Marwan Kraidy, *Hybridity, Or the Cultural Logic of Globalization* (Philadelphia: Temple University Press, 2005), 152.

64 Gülru Necipoğlu, "Visual Cosmopolitanism and Creative Translation: Artistic Conversations with Renaissance Italy in Mehmed II's Constantinople," *Muqarnas* 29 (2012): 4, http://isites.harvard.edu/fs/docs/icb.topic570061.files//articles/M29%20Necipoglu.pdf.

65 For more see Babinger, *Mehmed the Conqueror and His Time*, 488-508.

66 Rose, *Visual Methodologies*, 35.

67 Necipoğlu and Payne, *Histories of Ornament*, 132.

68 For more see Julian Raby, "Pride and Prejudice: Mehmed the Conqueror and the Italian Portrait Medal," *Studies in the History of Art* 21 (1987): 171-194.

69 Gülru Necipoğlu, "The serial portraits of Ottoman sultans in comparative perspective," in *The Sultan's Portrait: Picturing the House of Osman*, ed. Selmin Kangal (Istanbul: IşBank, 2000), 25, http://isites.harvard.edu/fs/docs/icb.topic572595.files//chapters_and_prefaces/Word%20and%20Image%20in%20Portraits%20of%20the%20Ottoman%20Sultans.pdf.

70 An aigrette is a headdress consisting of a white egret's feather or other decoration such as a spray of gems.

71 For more on Bellini's and Costanzo da Ferrara's bronze medallions of Mehmed II see Catalogues 307 and 309, Oxford Ashmolean Museum.

72 Rose, *Visual Methodologies*, 40.

73 Monique O'Connell and Eric R. Dursteler, *The Mediterranean World: From the Fall of Rome to the Rise of Napoleon* (Baltimore: Johns Hopkins University Press, 2016), 132.

74 Gülru Necipoğlu, *Architecture, Ceremonial, and Power: The Topkapi Palace in the Fifteenth and Sixteenth Centuries* (Architectural History Foundation Book) (Cambridge, MA: MIT Press, 1991), 91, 126.

75 Çiğdem Kafesçioğlu, "Representing the City: Constantinople and its Images," in *Constantinopolis/Istanbul: Cultural Encounter, Imperial Vision, and the Construction of the Ottoman Capital* (University Park, PA: The Pennsylvania State University Press, 2009), 150.

76 Kafesçioğlu, "Representing the City," 150.

77 Kafesçioğlu, "Representing the City," 143.

78 Kafesçioğlu, "Representing the City," 150.

79 Tursun Beg, *The History of Mehmed the Conqueror*, ed. H. Inalcık and R. Murphey (Minneapolis-Chicago: Bibliotheca Islamica, 1978), fols. 56a, 59a-59b

80 Necipoğlu, "Challenging the Past," 171.

81 Giorgio Vasari, *The Lives of Painters, Sculptors and Architects,* 4 vols., ed. William Gaunt (New York: Dent, 1963), 2: 183.

82 Yerasimos, *Constantinople: Istanbul's Historical Heritage,* 214.

83 Kafesçioğlu, "Representing the City," 14.

84 KKafesçioğlu, "Representing the City," 14.

85 Glencross, "Historical Consciousness in International Relations Theory," 3.

86 For more on this see Julian Raby, "A Sultan of Paradox: Mehmed the Conqueror as a Patron of the Arts," *Oxford Art Journal* 5, no. 1 (1982): 3-8, http://www.jstor.org/stable/1360098.

87 E. H. Ayverdi, *Fatih Devri Mimari Eserleri* (Istanbul: Istanbul Fethi Derneği Neşriyatı, 1953), 129.

88 Cornelius Gurlitt, *Istanbul'un Mimari Sanatı, Architecture of Constantinople, Die Baukunst Konstantinopels,* trans. Rezan Kæzæltan (Ankara: Enformasyon ve Dokumantasyon Hizmetleri Vakfı, 1999), 57-58. The work has been translated from Cornelius Gurlitt, *Die Baukunst Konstantinopels*, 2 vols (Berlin: E. Wasmuth, 1907).

89 Gülru Necipoğlu, "Creation of a National Genius: Sinan and the Historiography of 'Classical' Ottoman Architecture," *Muqarnas* 24 (2006): 171, http://isites.harvard.edu/fs/docs/icb.topic570061.files//articles/Creation_Genius.pdf.

90 Yerasimos, *Constantinople: Istanbul's Historical Heritage,* 238. Necipoğlu mentions an Italian pavilion on the Topkapı Palace grounds, which complimented the Tiled Kiosk. Mehmed II's claims of being a universal ruler with mastery of many different cultural idioms is also reflected in the palace gates: the second portal is in the shape of a European castle en miniature, while the third gate (Babüssaade) is in the form of a tent-like dome and hints at the Ottomans' Turkic Central Asian legacy. For more, see Necipoğlu, *Architecture, Ceremonial, and Power*, 32-57.

91 Yerasimos, *Constantinople: Istanbul's Historical Heritage,* 238.

92 See Kritovoulos, *History of Mehmed the Conqueror,* 104-5.

93 Warwick Ball, *Sultans of Rome: The Turkish World Expansion* (Northampton,

MA: Olive Branch Press, 2013), 116.

94 Translation of the inscriptions above the entrance door of the Çinili Köşk. For more on the English translation of the inscriptions of the Çinili Köşk see T. M. P. Duggan, "The Çinili Köşk," accessed November 13, 2015, http://www.hurriyetdailynews.com/the-cinili-kosk-or-ampquotkasr-i-kashiampquot----the-tiled-topkapi-royal-palace-pavilion.aspx?pageID=438&n=the-cinili-kosk-or-quotkasr-i-kashiquot----the-tiled-topkapi-royal-palace-pavilion-2003-02-23

95 Duggan, "The Çinili Köşk."

96 For more see Halil Inalcık, "The place of Ottoman-Turkish Empire in History," *Cultura Turcica* (1964): 57.

97 Titus Burckhardt, *Art of Islam: Language and Meaning* (Indiana: World Wisdom Inc., 2009), 73.

98 See W. R. Lethaby, *Architecture, Nature, and agic* (New York: Cosimo Classics, 2005), 21-56.

99 Lowenthal, *The Past is a Foreign Country*, 348.

100 Rüsen, "What is Historical Consciousness?," 13.

101 For more see Babinger, *Mehmed the Conqueror and His Time*. See also Halil Inalcık, *The Ottoman Empire: The Classical Age 1300–1600* (Princeton: Princeton University Press, second edition, 1992).

102 Madison, *Critical Ethnography*, 58.

CHAPTER 5

1 Sa'i, *Sinan's Autobiographies,* xi.

2 Sa'i, *Sinan's Autobiographies,* 122-32.

3 Sa'i, *Sinan's Autobiographies*, 122-32. See also Gülru Necipoğlu, "Preface: Sources, Themes, and Cultural Implications of Sinan's Autobiographies," in Sa'i, *Sinan's Autobiographies*, 12: 125. On the completion of the dome of the Süleymaniye, Sinan states, "I replied to his Majesty the padishah that it [i.e. dome] would be completed in two months and he bore witness [to my statement]," 125.

4 "her küngüre-'i eyvāndan bir gūşe ve her zāviye-'i virāndan bir tūşe peydā eyleyūp ..." See Sa'i, *Sinan's Autobiographies*, 115, 142.

5 Giorgio Vasari, Preface to Part III, *The Lives of the Painters, Sculptors and Architects*, 4 vols., ed. William Gaunt (New York: Dent, 1963), 154. For more on Sinan's competitive spirit see Necipoğlu, "Challenging the Past," 169–80.

6 See Charles Texier, *Description de l'Asie Mineure, faite par ordre du gouvernement francais de 1833 a 1837* (Paris: Ministere de l'instruction,1862); James Fergusson, *The Illustrated History of Architecture*, 2 vols. (London: John Murray, 1855); Banister Fletcher, *A History of Architecture on the Comparative Method* (London: B. T. Batsford, 1924); see also John Hale, *The Civilization of Europe in the Renaissance* (London: Harper Collins Publishers, 1993).

7 See Heinrich Glück, *Türkische Kunst* (Budapest and Istanbul: 1917); Celal Esad Arseven, *Türk Sanatı* (Istanbul: Türk Ocaklari Merkez Nesriyati, 1928); Suut Kemal Yetkin, *L'architecture turque en turquie* (Paris: Maisonneuve & Larose, 1962); B. Sewell, 'Sinan: The Architect of a Forgotten Renaissance,' *Cornucopia* 1992/93; also see Henry Matthews, 'Rethinking Ottoman Architecture.' Paper presented at the ACSA International Conference, 2001.

8 Stanford Encyclopedia of Philosophy, https://plato.stanford.edu/entries/eternity/

9 For more see Şefik Can, *Fundamentals of Rumi's Thought, A Mevlevi Sufi Perspective* (Clifton, NJ: Tughra Books, 2009); and Nasr, *The Pilgrimage of Life and the Wisdom of Rumi.*

10 For Rumi, see Seyyed Hossein Nasr, *The Pilgrimage of Life and the Wisdom of Rumi* (Charlottesville, VA: Foundation for Traditional Studies, 2007).

11 Richard Tarnas, *The Passion of the Western Mind: Understanding the Ideas That Have Shaped Our World View* (New York: Ballantine Books, 1991), 41.

12 Tarnas, *The Passion of the Western Mind*, 41.

13 Sa'i, *Sinan's Autobiographies*, 125.

14 Sa'i, *Sinan's Autobiographies*, 115, 129.

15 Sa'i, *Sinan's Autobiographies*, 125.

16 Sa'i, *Sinan's Autobiographies*, 122.

17 See Gürlu Necipoğlu, "The Süleymaniye Complex in Istanbul: An Interpretation," *Muqarnas* 3 (1985): 92–117.

18 Kuban, *Ottoman Architecture*, 280-81.

19 Kuban, *Ottoman Architecture*, 74-75.

20 Sa'i, *Sinan's Autobiographies*, 74.

21 Sa'i, *Sinan's Autobiographies*, 124.

22 Leon Batista Alberti, *On the Art of Building in Ten Books*, trans. Joseph Rykwert, Neil Leach, and Robert Tavernor (Cambridge, MA: The MIT Press, 1988), 24.

23 See Angel K. Nickerson, *A Journey into Michelangelo's Rome* (Berkeley: Roaring Forties Press, 2008), 117.

24 Michael Rogers, "The Arts under Süleyman the Magnificent," in *Süleyman the Second and His Time*, ed. Halil Inalcık and Cemal Kafadar (Istanbul: The Isis Press, 2010), 258-60.

25 As a gesture of goodwill Sultan Abdulhamid II returned this copy to Hungary in 1877.

26 Oda Juten, "Toruko-Minzoku-to-Isuramu"-ni- Kansuru- Kyoudou-Kenkyu-Houkokusho (Report of joint research on "Turk and Islam") (Tokyo: Gaikokugo-University, 1974), 14–33.

27 Theresa Grupico, "The Dome in Christian and Islamic Sacred Architecture," *The Forum on Public Policy* 3, no. 14 (2011): 1-3 http://forumonpublicpolicy.com/vol2011no3/archive/grupico.pdf

28 Sa'i, *Sinan's Autobiographies,* 124.

29 Sa'i, *Sinan's Autobiographies,* 114.

30 See Doğan Kuban, "The Style of Sinan's Domed Structures," *Muqarnas* 4 (1987): 74. See also Sa'i, *Sinan's Autobiographies*, 124-26.

31 Kuban, "The Style of Sinan's Domed Structures," 124-26.

32 Gülru Necipoğlu, "Challenging the Past: Sinan and the Competitive Discourse of Early Modern Islamic Architecture," *Muqarnas* 10 (1993): 169–80.

33 Ihsan Mungan, "Hagia Sophia and Mimar Sinan: How to Strengthen the Roof," Proceeding of the IASS International, Symposium on Shell and Spacial Structures, 2005, PT.1–2, 924.

34 Mungan, "Hagia Sophia and Mimar Sinan," 924.

35 For the functions of the Süleymaniye madrasahs (colleges) see Kemal Edip Kürkçüoğlu, *Süleymaniye Vakfiyesi* (Ankara: Vakıflar Umum Müdürlüğü, 1962). See also Lokman's 1582 miniature painting from *Sürname-i Hümayun*, folio.286r, TSK H.1344.

36 Goodwin, *History of Ottoman Architecture,* 216.

37 Darling, "The Renaissance and the Middle East," 62-63.

38 Evliya Çelebi, *An Ottoman Traveller: Selections from the Book of Travels by Evliya* Çelebi, trans. Robert Dankoff and Sooyong Kim (London: Eland Publishing, 2011), 14.

39 Necipoğlu, *The Age of Sinan,* 213.

40 Kuban, *Ottoman Architecture,* 289.

41 Kuban, *Ottoman Architecture,* 228.

42 Goodwin, *A History of Ottoman Architecture,* 232-35.

43 Sa'i, *Sinan's Autobiographies,* 124.

44 Sa'i, *Sinan's Autobiographies,* 74..

45 Sa'i, *Sinan's Autobiographies,* 129.

46 Sa'i, *Sinan's Autobiographies,* 122.

47 For more on the original mosque of Muhammad see K. A. C. Creswell, *Early Muslim Architecture* (New York: Hacker Art Books, 1979).

48 See Can, *Fundamentals of Rumi's Thought*, 134. See also Parviz Morewedge, ed., *Neoplatonism and Islamic Thought* (Albany, NY: State University of New York Press, 1992), 158; and Tarnas, *The Passion of the Western Mind*, 41-43.

49 Seyyid Huseyin Lokman, *Hünername*, 2 Vols, Topkapı Palace Library, H.1524, fol. 285v.

50 Mio Takikawa, "Hagia Sophia and Sinan's Mosques: Structure and Decoration in Süleymaniye Mosque and Selimiye Mosque," https://seijo.repo.nii.ac.jp/?action=repository_uri&item_id=3340&file_id=22&file_no=1, 106.

51 Tarnas, *The Passion of the Western Mind*, 42.

52 Charles A. Martin, "Hagia Sophia and the Great Imperial Mosques," *Art Bulletin*, 12 (1930): 321–44.

53 Qur'an, 24:35.

54 Oleg Grabar, *The Formation of Islamic Art* (New Haven, CT: Yale University Press, 1973), 69.

55 See the Qur'an, 24:35. On the number of candles used in the Süleymaniye Mosque see Rabah Saoud, "Sinan: A Great Ottoman Architect and Urban Designer," Foundation for Science Technology and Civilisation, Manchester: 2007, 12, http://www.muslimheritage.com/uploads/Mimar_Sinan_Great_Ottoman_Architect.pdf

56 Necipoğlu, "Preface," *Sources, Themes, and Cultural Implications of Sinan's Autobiographies*, xiii.

57 Çelebi, *An Ottoman Traveller*, 16.

58 Çelebi, *An Ottoman Traveller*, 17.

59 Çelebi, *An Ottoman Traveller*, 17.

60 John Sanderson, *The Travels of John Sanderson in the Levant, 1584-1602,* ed. Sir William Foster (London: Hakluyt Society, 1931), 70-71.

61 Necipoğlu, "Creation of a National Genius," 141–84.

62 Gülru Necipoğlu, "Challenging the Past: Sinan and the Competitive Discourse of Early Modern Islamic Architecture," *Muqarnas*, Essays in Honor of Oleg Grabar 10 (1993): 169-80, http://www.jstor.org/stable/1523183?seq=1#page_scan_tab_contents.

63 Robert Ousterhout, "Ethnic Identity and cultural appropriation in early Ottoman Architecture," ND, http://archnet.org/system/publications/contents/4470/original/DPC1020.PDF?1384785510, 49.

64 Sa'i, *Sinan's Autobiographies,* 74.

65 Sa'i, *Sinan's Autobiographies,* 126.

66 Necipoğlu, *The Age of Sinan*, 240.

67 See Necipoğlu, *The Age of Sinan,* 240-41.

68 Sanderson, *The Travels of John Sanderson in the Levant 1584-1602,* 71.

69 "Bu ʿali qubbelū cāmiʾde baş tācidur el-haqq / Edirne şehrinūn Tunca yūzi suyıydi […]." Sa'i, *Sinan's Autobiographies*, 132, 157.

70 Şehzade Mosque is the complex Sinan built for Süleyman and Hurrem's son Mehmed who died at a young age. Evliya Çelebi, *Seyahatname*, 10 vols. (Istanbul: Ikdam Matbaası, 1896-1930), 3: 443-44.

71 Sa'i, *Sinan's Autobiographies,* 131.

72 See Giorgio Vasari, *Vasari's Lives of the Artists,* Kindle, 55.

73 See Ali, *Epic Deeds of Artists,* 131-132, 135; and Sa'i, *Sinan's Autobiographies,* 131-32.

74 Le Corbusier, Journey to the East, ed. and trans. Ivan Zaknic (Cambridge, MA: MIT Press, 1989), 72.

75 Rüsen, *Western Historical Thinking*, 8.

76 "Sa'adetle çünki taht-ı develtde qarār eylediler şehr-i Edirneye kemāl mertebe-

de nazari ve şefqatleri olmağin bir cāmi bināsına emr-i hümāyūnlari oldı ki rūzgārda misal olmaya. Bu faqīr dahı bir resm-i cām-i ʿalī eyledümki Edirne içinde manzūr-i halq-ı ʿālem olmağa lāyıqdur." Sa'i, *Sinan's Autobiographies,* 130, 155.

77 "Dört minãresi qubbenün dört cānibinde vāqiʾ olmışdur. Ve hep üçer şerefelüdūr ve üçer yollu ve ikisinün yolları başqa başqa vāqiʾ olmışdur. Ol eskiden binā olınan Üç Şerefelü bir qulle gibidür. Gayet qalındur [...]." Sa'i, *Sinan's Autobiographies,* 130, 155.

78 Sa'i, *Sinan's Autobiographies,* 131.

79 Sa'i, *Sinan's Autobiographies,* 131.

80 Battisto Ferraro, cited in Necipoğlu, *The Age of Sinan,* 239.

81 Marcantonio Barbaro, cited in Necipoğlu, *The Age of Sinan,* 240.

82 Sa'i, *Sinan's Autobiographies,* 130.

83 Yerasimos, *Constantinople: Istanbul's Historical Heritage,* 270.

84 Sa'i, *Sinan's Autobiographies,* 133.

85 Takikawa, "Hagia Sophia and Sinan's Mosques," 108.

86 Nina Ergin, "The Soundscape of Sixteenth-Century Istanbul Mosques: Architecture and Qur'an Recital," *Journal of the Society of Architectural Historians* 67, no. 2 (2008): 217, doi: 10.1525/jsah.2008.67.2.204.

87 Geir Tryggve Hellemo, "Ottoman Sensoriness: Nature as a Source of Religious Cognition in Istanbul in the Mid-Sixteenth Century," in *Transcendence and Sensoriness: Perceptions, Revelation and the Arts* (Studies in Religion and the Arts), ed. Svein Aage Christoffersen et al. and trans. Frances E. Hopenwasser and Leif Stubbe Teglbjaerg (Leiden: Brill, 2015), 161.

88 "Aya Sōfya qubbesi gibi büyük qubbe devlet-i İslamiyyede binā olınmamışdur' diyü kefere-ʿi fecerenün miʾmār geçinenleri Müslümanlara galebemüz vardur dirler idi. Zu'm-ı fāsidlerince ʿOl qadar qubbe turgurmaq gāyet müşkildür. Nazīre mümkin olsa iderler idi' didükleri bu haqīrün qalbinde ʿuqde olup qalmış idi. Mezbūr cāmiʾ bināsında himmet idüu bi-ʿawni'llahi'l-Maliki'd-Dayyan devlet-i Sultān Selim Hānda izhār-ı qudret idūp bu qubbe-ʿi ʿālīnün andan altı zirāʾ qaddin ve dört zirāʾ devrin ziyāde eyledüm." Sa'i, *Sinan's Autobiographies,* 130, 155.

89 Sa'i, *Sinan's Autobiographies,* 130.

90 Sa'i, *Sinan's Autobiographies,* 130.

91 Necipoğlu, "Challenging the Past," 175.

92 Sa'i, *Sinan's Autobiographies*, 115.

93 Goodwin, *A History of Ottoman Architecture*, 261.

94 Goodwin, *A History of Ottoman Architecture*, 264.

95 Günkut Akın, "The Muezzin Mahfili and Pool of the Selimiye Mosque in Edirne," *Muqarnas* 12 (1995): 63-83, http://www.jstor.org/discover/10.2307/1523224?uid=2134&uid=369538981&uid=2&uid=70&uid=3&uid=369538971&uid=60&sid=21102548521367

96 Akın, "The Muezzin Mahfili and Pool of the Selimiye Mosque in Edirne," 63-83.

97 Goodwin, *A History of Ottoman Architecture*, 264.

98 Kuban, "The Style of Sinan's Domed Structures," *Muqarnas* 4 (1987): 74.

99 Tanju Cantay, "XVI. Yüzyil Türk mimarisinde bazi tasarim ve cizim esaslari," in *II. Uluslararasi Turk ve Islam Bilim ve Teknoloji Tarihi Kongresi Bildirileri* (Istanbul: Teknik Universitesi Yayını, 1986), 2: 55-56.

100 Thomas Barrie, *The Sacred In-Between: The Mediating Roles of Architecture* (New York: Routledge, 2010), 205-6.

101 J. G. Davies, *Temples, Churches and Mosques* (Oxford: Basil Blackwell, 1982), 127.

102 Barrie, *The Sacred In-Between*, 205.

103 Akın, "The Muezzin Mahfili and Pool of the Selimiye Mosque in Edirne," 63-83.

104 Qur'an, Surah, 108.

105 "Görenün ağzinun şuyı aqar bi't-tab' olur mā'il / Sanasın havż-ı Kevşerdür o şadırvān-ı bī-hemtā."'Sa'i, *Sinan's Autobiographies*, 132, 156.

106 Sa'i, *Sinan's Autobiographies*, 131.

107 Can, *Fundamentals of Rumi's Thought*, 191.

108 Can, *Fundamentals of Rumi's Thought*, 191.

109 "Kim oldur bānī-'i Beytü"l-Harām ü Mescid-i Aqsā ' Ser-i şāhān-ı a'zam a'ni zıllu'llahi fi'l-'alem […]." Sa'i, *Sinan's Autobiographies*, 131, 157.

110 See Qur'an, 7:40, 39:73.

111 For more see Oleg Grabar, *The Dome of the Rock* (Cambridge, MA: Harvard University Press, 2006).

112 Sa'i, *Sinan's Autobiographies*, 131-33.

113 Sa'i, *Sinan's Autobiographies*, 132.

114 Sa'i, *Sinan's Autobiographies*, 133.

115 Sa'i, *Sinan's Autobiographies,* 133.

116 Sa'i, *Sinan's Autobiographies*, 131.

117 Sa'i, *Sinan's Autobiographies*, 131.

118 Kuban, *Ottoman Architecture,* 312.

119 Necipoğlu, *The Age of Sinan,* 13.

120 Necipoğlu, *The Age of Sinan*, 13.

121 Goodwin, *A History of Ottoman Architecture,* 216-18, 224.

122 Muzaffer Özgüleş, "Fundamental Developments of 16th Century Ottoman Architecture: Innovations in the Art of Architect Sinan," Science and Technology Policy Studies, Ankara: Middle East Technical University, 2003, http://www.stps.metu.edu.tr/sites/stps.metu.edu.tr/files/0803.pdf, p.3.

123 See Brotton, *The Renaissance: A Very Short Introduction*, 8; Burioni, 'Vasari's Rinascita,' 117.

124 Sa'i, *Sinan's Autobiographies,* 74.

125 Vasari, *Vasari's Lives of the Artists,* Kindle, 131.

126 Sa'i, *Sinan's Autobiographies*, 114.

127 Rüsen, "Historical Consciousness," 7.

128 Rüsen, "Historical Consciousness," 4.

CHAPTER 6

1 Sa'i, *Sinan's Autobiographies,* 114.

2 See Sa'i, *Sinan's Autobiographies,* 126.

3 Ramachandran, The Worldmakers, 14.

4 Vakıflar Genel Müdürlüğü, Defter 648, 176 (Republic of Turkey, Prime Ministry, Directorate Generals of Foundations).

5 Walter B. Denny, *The Ceramics of the Mosque of Rustem Pasha and the Environment of Change* (New York: Garland, 1977).

6 Michael D. Willis, "Tiles from the Mosque of Rustem Pasa in Istanbul," *Artibus Asiae* 48 (1987): 278-84

http://www.jstor.org/stable/3249874; See also Fatih Cimok, *The Book of Rustem Pasha Tiles* (Istanbul: A Turizm Yayınları, 2001).

7 Vakıflar Genel Müdürlüğü, Defter 635/1, 7 (Republic of Turkey, Prime Ministry, Directorate Generals of Foundations).

8 Vakıflar Genel Müdürlüğü Arşivi (VGMA), Rüstem Paşa Vakfiyesi, D. 635/2, D. 648.

9 Vakıflar Genel Müdürlüğü Arşivi (VGMA), Rüstem Paşa Vakfiyesi, D. 635/2, D. 648.

10 For more on the wealth of Rustem Pasha see Veli Sırım, Financial Resources of Tekirdağ Rustem Pasha Kulliyah (Namık Kemal Universitesi, Iktsiat Bölümü, http://dergipark.gov.tr/download/article-file/256091. See also Vakıflar Genel Müdürlüğü Arşivi (VGMA), Rüstem Paşa Vakfiyesi, D. 635/2, D. 648; and Necipoğlu, *The Age of Sinan*, 314-17.

11 Necipoğlu, *The Age of Sinan*, 323-25.

12 Ramazanzade Mehmed, *Tarih-i Nişancı Mehmed Paşa* (Istanbul: Tabhane-yi Amire, 1862), 302-3.

13 Hasanbeyzade, cited in Nezihi Aykut, "Hasan-Beyzade Tarihi" (PhD diss., Istanbul University, 1980), 52.

14 See Vakıflar Genel Müdürlüğü, Defter 648, 176.

15 For more on this see Necipoğlu, *The Age of Sinan*, 242-43.

16 For more on this see Necipoğlu, *The Age of Sinan*, 242-43; see also Godfrey Goodwin, *The Private World of Ottoman Women* (London: Saqi Essentials, 2006).

17 Işıl Akbaygil appearing on "The Genuine Article with Gordon Elliot: IZNIK TILES: Art Renaissance after 300 hundred years," YouTube Video, Gordon Elliot, Producer, posted by Pablo Gandulfo for the Iznik Foundation, March 15, 2012, http://www.youtube.com/watch?v=CU6rvX3UHvY. For Iznik Foundation see "Iznik Vakıf Çinileri," http://www.iznik.com/about-the-iznik-foundation

18 See "The Genuine Article with Gordon Elliot," YouTube Video.

19 See "The Genuine Article with Gordon Elliot," YouTube Video.

20 Nurhan Atasoy and Julian Raby, *Iznik: The Pottery of Ottoman Turkey*, ed. Yanni Petsopoulos (London: Thames and Hudson, 1989), 59.

21 Atasoy and Raby, *Iznik*, 59.

22 "The Genuine Article with Gordon Elliot," YouTube Video.

23 John Covel, cited in Raby, "The Making of an Iznik Pot," in Iznik, Atasoy and Raby, 50.

24 For more on Iznik ware production see Raby, "The Making of an Iznik Pot," 50-64.

25 Atasoy and Raby, *Iznik*, 58-59.

26 Atasoy and Raby, *Iznik*, 58-59.

27 Hellemo, "Ottoman Sensoriness," 161.

28 Raby, "The Making of an Iznik Pot," 58.

29 W. D. Kingery and P. B. Vandiver, *Ceramic Masterpieces: Art, Structure and Technology* (New York: The Free Press, 1986), 132.

30 Raby, "The Making of an Iznik Pot," 58.

31 Julian Raby, "1560-1650: Maturity and Decline of Iznik Pottery," in *Iznik*, Atasoy and Raby, 221.

32 Raby, "1560-1650: Maturity and Decline of Iznik Pottery," 221.

33 Denny, *Iznik: The Artistry of Ottoman Ceramics,* 86.

34 Denny, *Iznik: The Artistry of Ottoman Ceramics*, 91.

35 For more on this development see Julian Raby, "Development and Growth of Iznik Pottery," in *Iznik,* Atasoy and Raby, 76-81.

36 For more see Raby, "1560-1650: Maturity and Decline of Iznik Pottery," 218-88.

37 For more on Kara Memi Style see Atasoy and Raby, *Iznik* and Denny, *Iznik: The Artistry of Ottoman Ceramics.*

38 For the glass artist Ibrahim see Necipoğlu, *The Age of Sinan*, 321-30.

39 Ibn Arabi, cited in Corbin, *Alone with the Alone,* 80.

40 Necipoğlu, *The Age of Sinan*, 327.

41 Sa'i, *Sinan's Autobiographies*, 126.

42 Sa'i, *Sinan's Autobiographies,* 126.

43 Sa'i, *Sinan's Autobiographies*, 59, 66.

44 Vasari, cited in Patricia Rubin, "What Men Saw: Vasari's Life of Leonardo da Vinci and the image of the Renaissance artist," *Art History* 13 (1990): 35.

45 Qur'an: 13:35.

46 Rumi, cited in A. Schimmel, *Rumi's World: The Life and Work of the Great Sufi Poet* (Boston: Shambala, 2001), 70.

47 Emma Clark, "The Symbolism of the Islamic Garden."

48 For some of these references to garden and paradise see Qur'an: 18:107, 47:15, 50:35, 76:13.

49 Clark, "The Symbolism of the Islamic Garden."

50 Emma Clark, *The Art of the Islamic Garden* (Wiltshire: Crowood Press, 2011), 26.

51 Clark, "The Symbolism of the Islamic Garden."

52 Clark, "The Symbolism of the Islamic Garden."

53 Seyyed Hossein Nasr, *Islamic Art and Spirituality* (Albany, NY: State University of New York Press, 1987), 48.

54 Nasr, *Islamic Art and Spirituality,* 48.

55 Nasr, *Islamic Art and Spirituality,* 48.

56 Nasr, *Islamic Art and Spirituality,* 10.

57 Qur'an, 56:10-38.

58 Ibn Arabi, cited in Corbin, *Alone with the Alone,* 145.

59 Frithjof Schuon, *The Essential Frithjof Schuon*, ed. Seyyed Hossein Nasr (Bloomington, IN: World Wisdom Inc., 2005), 530.

60 Ramazanzade, *Tarih-i Nişancı Mehmed Paşa,* 302-3.

61 For more on the tulip and its symbolic association with Allah see Mike Dash, T*ulipomania: The Story of the World's Most Coveted Flower and the Extraordinary Passions it Aroused* (London: Phoenix, 2011).

62 Ogier Ghiselinde Busbecq, *The Turkish Letters of Ogier Ghiselin de Busbecq*, trans. Edward Seymour Forster (Oxford: Clarendon Press, 1968), 28.

63 See Talat S. Halman, ed., *Yunus Emre and His Mystical Poetry* (Indianapolis: Indiana University Press, 1983).

64 See Ramazanzade, *Tarih-i Nişancı Mehmed Paşa*, 302-3; Hasanbeyzade in Aykut, "Hasan-Beyzade Tarihi," 52; and for the mystical meaning of the tulip see I. Melikoff, "La fleur de la souffrance. Recherche sur le sens symbolique de Lâle dans ka poésie mystique turco-iranienne,"'*Journal Asiatique* 205 (1967): 341-60. For more on Süleyman's poetry see Talat S. Halman, *Süleyman the Magnificent Poet* (Istanbul: Reyo Ofset, 1987).

65 Paul Smith, *Turkish Sufi Poets: Lives and Poems* (Victoria, Australia: New Humanity Books, 2014), 32.

66 Rogers and Ward, *Süleyman the Magnificent*, 85-89.

67 Qur'an: 57:4.

68 Vakıflar Genel Müdürlüğü Arşivi (VGMA), Rüstem Paşa Vakfiyesi, D. 635/2, D. 648.

69 Raby, "1560-1650: Maturity and Decline of Iznik Pottery," 260.

70 Fatih Cimok, *The Book of Rustem Pasa Tiles* (Istanbul: A Turizm Yayınları, 2001), 16.

71 Fatih Cimok, The Book of Rustem Pasa Tiles (Istanbul: A Turizm Yayınları, 2001), 19.

72 Fatih Cimok, *The Book of Rustem Pasa Tiles* (Istanbul: A Turizm Yayınları, 2001), 19. For a detailed account of this panel see Denny, *The Ceramics of the Mosque of Rustem Pasha*, 1977.

73 Ibn Arabi, cited in Corbin, *Alone with the Alone*, 182.

74 For more see Nurhan Atasoy, *A Garden for the Sultan – Gardens and Flowers in the Ottoman Culture* (Istanbul: Kitap Yayınevi, 2011); see also Marina Heilmeyer, *The Language of Flowers: Symbols and Myths* (Munich: Prestel Publishing, 2006).

75 Rose, *Visual Methodologies*, 34, 267.

76 Sa'i, *Sinan's Autobiographies*, 74, 85, 156.

77 Cimok, *The Book of Rustem Pasa Tiles*, 12.

78 Nasr, *Islamic Art and Spirituality*, 137.

79 Charles F. Horne, *Sacred Books and Early Literature of the East: Medieval Arabic, Moorish, and Turkish Vol. VI* (New York: Kessinger Publishing, LLC, 1997), 274.

80 Horne, *Sacred Books and Early Literature of the East*, 314.

81 Halman, *Süleyman the Magnificent Poet*, 53.

82 Rula Jurdi Abisaab, *Converting Persia: Religion and Power in the Safavid Empire* (New York: I. B. Tauris, 2004), 50.

83 Abisaab, *Converting Persia*, 86.

84 Folio 281a clearly depicts the simurg in the *Surname-i Humayun* of 1582 flying over the procession of the guilds before Murad III.

85 Zulfi Güler, "Symbols of Anka and Simurg in Sheikh Galib's Diwan," *International Journal of Language Academy* 2 (2014): 63, http://www.ijla.net/Makaleler/2069338573_6372%20Zülfi%20Güler%20(1)%20(2).pdf. It is also used to express some elements such as "beauty, dignity, modesty, disinterest-

edness, knowledge, talent, enlightenment, illumination and regeneration via metaphors and analogies."

86 Coleman Barks, ed., *Rumi: Selected Poems* (London: Penguin Books, 2004), 23.

87 Ibn Arabi, cited in Corbin, *Alone with the Alone*, 193.

88 Mehmed, *Tarih-i Nişanci Mehmed Paşa* (Istanbul: Tabhaney-yi Amire, 1862), 302-3.

89 Mehmed, *Tarih-i Nişanci Mehmed Paşa,* 302-3.

90 Hellemo, "Ottoman Sensoriness," 168.

91 Hellemo, "Ottoman Sensoriness," 168.

92 Sa'i, Sinan's Autobiographies, 124, 136.

93 See Atasoy and Raby, *Iznik*.

94 Reynold A. Nicholson, *The Mesnevi of Jalalu'ddin Rumi,* Vols. I and II (Lahore: Islamic Book Service, 1989), I: 316.

95 For more on the colour turquoise in ancient Turkic tradition see Hellemo, "Ottoman Sensoriness," 167. For more on ancient Turkic beliefs see George Frederick Kunz, *The Curious Lore of Precious Stones* (New York: Dover Publications, 1971), 109. See also Rene Grousset, *The Empire of the Steppes: A History of Central Asia* (New Jersey: Rutgers University Press, 1970), 80-87, 103-110.

96 See Vakıflar Genel Müdürlüğü Arşivi (VGMA), Rüstem Paşa Vakfiyesi, D. 635/2, D. 648.

97 Ali, *Epic Deeds of Artists*, 454.

98 Qur'an: 59:24.

99 Ibn Arabi, cited in Corbin, *Alone with the Alone*, 182.

100 Rose, *Visual Methodologies,* 151.

101 Nicholson, *The Mesnevi of Jalalu'ddin Rumi,* no. 311, 1353.

102 Sa'i, *Sinan's Autobiographies*, 126.

103 Avinoam Shalem, "The Four Faces of the Ka'ba in Mecca," in *Architecture and Pilgrimage, 1000-1500: Southern Europe and Beyond*, ed. Paul Davies et al. (Surrey, England: Ashgate Publishing Limited, 2013), 41.

104 Skirt, as a piece of cloth, can be laid flat on a surface imitating prostration and submission. Süleyman, as the slave of God, resembles himself to a piece of cloth like a skirt who humbles himself before Him.

105 Halman, *Süleyman the Magnificent Poet,* 37.

106 Vakıflar Genel Müdürlüğü, Defter 635/1, 7

107 Sa'i, *Sinan's Autobiographies,* 128.

108 See the Qur'an: 13:11, 21:47, 59:18, and 91:9.

109 Denny, *Iznik: The Artistry of Ottoman Ceramics,* 86.

110 See Vakıflar Genel Müdürlüğü Arşivi (VGMA), Rüstem Paşa Vakfiyesi, D. 635/2, D. 648; and Ramazanzade, *Tarih-i Nişancı Mehmed Paşa,* 302-3.

111 For more on this see Hellemo, "Ottoman Sensoriness," 161.

112 See Ramazanzade, *Tarih-i Nişancı Mehmed Paşa,* 302-3.

113 Qur'an: 35:41.

114 See Atasoy and Raby, *Iznik.*

115 Richard Etlin, "Aesthetic and the Spatial Sense of Self," *Journal of Aesthetics and Art Criticism* 56, no. 1 (1998): 1.

116 Nasr, *Islamic Art and Spirituality,* 80.

117 Ross Finocchio, "Mannerism: Bronzino (1503-1572) and his Contemporaries," Metropolitan Museum of Art, New York, http://www.metmuseum.org/toah/hd/zino/hd_zino.htm

118 See Ramazanzade, *Tarih-i Nişancı Mehmed Paşa,* 302-3.

119 See Hellemo, "Ottoman Sensoriness," 167; also see Kunz, *The Curious Lore of Precious Stones,* 109.

120 For more on this see Grousset, *The Empire of the Steppes,* 80-87, 103-10.

121 Grousset, *The Empire of the Steppes,* 86.

122 Grousset, *The Empire of the Steppes,* 23, 80-87, 103-10.

123 Grousset, *The Empire of the Steppes,* 23, 80-87, 103-10.

124 Rüsen, "What is Historical Consciousness?," 3.

125 Lowenthal, *The Past is a Foreign Country,* 325.

126 Can, *Fundamentals of Rumi's Thought,* 191.

127 Suhuwardi, cited in Corbin, *Spiritual Body and Celestial Earth,* 131.

128 See M. M. Khan, trans., *The Translation of the Meanings of Summarized Sahih Al-Bukhari* (Lahore: Kazi Publications Inc., 1995).

129 Clark, "The Symbolism of the Islamic Garden."

130 Clark, "The Symbolism of the Islamic Garden."

131 Clark, "The Symbolism of the Islamic Garden."

132 Clark, "The Symbolism of the Islamic Garden."

133 Clark, "The Symbolism of the Islamic Garden."

134 Ergin, "The Soundscape of Sixteenth-Century Istanbul Mosques: Architecture and Qur'an Recital," 214.

135 "Contemplation, Constructed Space, and Senses," YouTube Video, lecture by Phoebe Crisman with an introduction by Kim Tanzer, April 6, 2013, posted by University of Virginia Contemplative Sciences Center, August 19, 2013, http://www.youtube.com/watch?v=6FASJrighYE

136 Ibn Arabi, cited in, Corbin, *Alone with the Alone,* 193-94.

137 See Golombek, "The Draped Universe of Islam," in *Content and Context of Visual Art in Islam*, ed. P. Soucek (Pennsylvania: Pennsylvania State University Press, 1988), https://s3.amazonaws.com/files.digication.com/M05f7bff842e90d2d36e67917cdac3d50

138 For more see Grabar, *The Dome of the Rock*, 189-204. In particular, see pp. 196-99 regarding the Qur'anic verses chosen to represent this view.

139 Halman, *Süleyman the Magnificent Poet*, 86.

140 Halman, *Süleyman the Magnificent Poet,* 86.

141 Patricia Trutty-Coohill, "Agathos in Michelangelo's Sistine Ceiling," http://www.agathos-international-review.com/issue1/articles/01_AGATHOS_IN_MICHELANGELO_SISTINE_CEILING.pdf, 12.

142 Nicholson, *The Mesnevi of Jalalu'ddin Rumi*, vol. 1, no. 1341.

143 Nicholson, *The Mesnevi of Jalalu'ddin Rumi,* vol. 1, no. 1341.

144 Vakıflar Genel Müdürlüğü Arşivi (VGMA), Rüstem Paşa Vakfiyesi, D. 635/2, D. 648.

145 Ergin, "The Soundscapes of Sixteenth-Century Istanbul Mosques," 217.

146 Abbot Suger, cited in Lawrence S. Cunningham and John J. Reich, *Culture and Values: A Survey of the Humanities* (Boston: Clark Baxter, 2010), 216.

147 Patricia Rubin, "What Men Saw: Vasari's Life of Leonardo da Vinci and the image of the Renaissance artist," *Art History* 13 (1990): 35.

148 "Contemplation, Constructed Space, and Senses," University of Virginia Sciences Center.

149 Halman, *Süleyman the Magnificent Poet*, 79.

150 Can, *Fundamentals of Rumi's Thought*, 149.

151 Can, *Fundamentals of Rumi's Thought*, 129.

152 Rose, *Visual Methodologies*, 374.

CHAPTER 7

1 Ali, cited in Fleischer, *Bureaucrat and Intellectual in the Ottoman Empire*, 101, 226-227, 280.

2 Halman, *Süleyman the Magnificent Poet*, 53.

3 See Atıl, *The Age of Süleyman the Magnificent*, 26-30. Also see translation of Süleyman's tughra, Ercan Mensiz, 'Ottoman Sultan Tugras,' accessed November 14, 2016, http://www.tugra.org/en/hakkinda.asp

4 For more on this see Atom Damalı, *History of Ottoman coins = Osmanlı sikkeleri tarihi*, vol. 1 (Istanbul: Nilufer Damalı Eğitim, Kültür ve Çevre Vakfı, 2010); also see Şevket Pamuk, *A Monetary History of the Ottoman Empire* (New York: Cambridge University Press, 2000).

5 See C. E. Bosworth, J. Deny and M. J. Siddiq, 'Tughra', in *The Encyclopedia of Islam* vol. X (Leiden: Brill, 2000), 595-598; also see I. H. Uzunçarşılı, 'Tuğra ve pençeler ile ferman ve buyuruldulara dair,' in *Belleten*, Sayı: 17-18, (1941): 101-157.

6 See "TCF: Turkish Cultural Foundation," accessed November 15, 2016, http://www.turkishculture.org/traditional-arts/tugra-sultanic-cipher-116.htm

7 See Raphaela Lewis, *Everyday Life in Ottoman Turkey* (U.K: Dorset, 1988), 166; Katherine Leach, Documents and Debates: Sixteenth Century Europe (Hong Kong: MacMillan Education, 1980), 108; and Andre Clot, *Suleiman the Magnificent* (London: Saqi Books, 2005), 131.

8 Rose, *Visual Methodologies*, 133.

9 S. Z. Ahmed, *The Zenith of an Empire: The Glory of the Suleiman the Magnificent and Lawgiver* (Connecticut: A.E.R. Publications, 2001), 23.

10 Celâlzâde Mustafa Çelebi, *Tabakatü'l- Memâlik ve Derecâtü'l- Mesâlik (Kanunî'nin Tarihçisinden Muhteşem Çağ)*, Haz. Ayhan Yılmaz (İstanbul: Kariyer Yayınları, 2011), 317-318. (Translation by Metin Mustafa).

11 Fleischer, *Bureaucrat and Intellectual in the Ottoman Empire*, 286-287.

12 Fleischer, *Bureaucrat and Intellectual in the Ottoman Empire*, 133.

13 Seydi Ali, cited in Giancarlo Casale, *The Ottoman Age of Exploration (New York: Oxford University Press*, 2010), 122.

14 Fleischer, *Bureaucrat and Intellectual in the Ottoman Empire*, 286-287.

15 Kastritsis, *Sons of Bajezid*, 204-205.

16 Rose, *Visual Methodologies*, 279-280.

17 For the Turkic Ghaznavid dynasty, see Scott Cameron Levi and Ron Sela, eds., *Islamic Central Asia: an anthology of historical sources* (Indianapolis: Indiana University Press, 2010).

18 For more see Ferdowsi, *Shahnameh: The Persian Book of Kings.*

19 See Atıl, *Süleymanname.*

20 Gülrü Necipoğlu, 'A Kanun for the State, A Canon for the Arts: Conceptualizing the Classical Synthesis of Ottoman Art and Architecture,' in *Soliman le Magnifique et Son Temps, ed. Gilles Veinstein* (Paris: La Documentation Francaise, 1992), 195.

21 Giancarlo Casale, 'Seeing the Past: Maps and Ottoman Historical Consciousness,' in *Writing History at the Ottoman Court: Editing the Past, Fashioning the Future,* edited by Erdem H. Cipa and Emine Fetvaci (Indianapolis: Indiana University Press, 2013), Kindle Edition.

22 Casale, 'Seeing the Past: Maps and Ottoman Historical Consciousness,' Kindle Edition.

23 Atıl, *Süleymanname,* 42. Artists and intellectuals who arrived at the Topkapı Palace from Iran with Selim I are: Neyzen Seyh Murad; Imam Kuru; Imam Mehmed Kasım; Kanuni Şahmeran; Maksud Kemence; Şah Kulu. For more on Firdevs-i Rumi see Bekir Biçer, 'Firdevs-i Rumi ve Tarihciliği,' *Türkiyat Araştırmalar Dergisi,* 245-261. Also see Rogers, 'The Arts Under Süleyman the Magnificent,' 278.

24 For more see Atıl, *Süleymanname*, 42-49. Attar's illustrated Mantık at-Tayr is in the Topkapı Palace Museum, TSM, E.H. 1512.

25 For more on this see Atıl, *Süleymanname.*

26 Leslie Michelsen, *Ferozkoh: Tradition and Continuity in Afghan Art* (English Edition) (Qatar: A&C Black, 2013), 71.

27 For more on this see Canby, *The Shahnama of Shah Tahmasp.*

28 M. B. Piotrovsky and J. M. Rogers, *Heaven on Earth: Art from Islamic Lands* (Germany: Prestel, 2004), 112.

29 Sheila R. Canby, *The Shahnama of Shah Tahmasp: The Persian Book of Kings* (New York: The Metropolitan Museum of Art, 2014), 16.

30 Atıl, *Süleymanname,* 42.

31 For more on this see Canby, *The Shahnama of Shah Tahmasp*, 14.

32 A Persian word meaning 'land of Tur' that refers to the ancestral homeland of the Turks and Iranians.

33 See Annemarie Schimmel, 'Turk and Hindu: A Poetical Image and Its Application to Historical Fact,' in *Islam and Cultural Change in the Middle Ages,* edited by Speros Vryonis, Jr. (Undena Publications, 1975), 107–26.

34 Fatma Sinem Eryılmaz, 'From Adam to Süleyman: Visual Representations of Authority in Arifi's Shahnama-yi Al-i 'Osman,' in *Writing History at the Ottoman Court: Editing the Past, Fashioning the Future,* edited by H. Erdem and Emine Fetvaci (Indiana: Indiana University Press, 2013), 100.

35 Barthes, cited in Rose, *Visual Methodologies,* 131.

36 For more see Robert Hillenbrand, 'The Use of Space in Timurid Painting,' in *Timurid Art and Culture: Iran and Central Asia in the Fifteenth Century,* edited by Lisa Golombek and Maria Subtelny (Leiden: Brill, 1992), 92-95.

37 Similarly the *shahnama* could also serve as a statement of grief and powerlessness, as Sheila Blair has interpreted the Great Mongol *Shahnama.* See Sheila S. Blair and Jonathan M. Bloom, *The Art and Architecture of Islam, 1250–1800* (New Haven and London: Yale University Press, 1995).

38 Eryılmaz, 'From Adam to Süleyman', 120.

39 Eryılmaz, 'From Adam to Süleyman', 120.

40 See the Qur'an: 27:30; 16: 90; and 11:195.

41 Horne, *Sacred Books and Early Literature of the East*, 314

42 Atıl, *Süleymanname,* 86.

43 Necipoğlu, 'The Serial Portraits of Ottoman Sultans in Comparative Perspective,' 25.

44 Emel Esin, *Türklerde Maddi Kültürün Oluşumu* (Istanbul: Kabalcı Yayınları, 1971), 1-29.

45 Horne, *Sacred Books and Early Literature of the East*, 314.

46 For more on Süleyman's crown see Gülru Necipoğlu, 'Süleyman the Magnificent and the Representation of Power in the Context of Ottoman-Hapsburg-Papal Rivalry,' *The Art Bulletin*, Vol. 71, No. 3 (Sep., 1989): 401-427, http://www.jstor.org/stable/3051136?origin=JSTOR-pdf

47 For more see Patrick J. Kelleher, *The Holy Crown of Hungar*, (Rome: 1951). Also see László Péter, 'The Holy Crown of Hungary, Visible and Invisible', *The Slavonic and East European Review*, Vol. 81, No. 3 (July, 2003): 421–510.

48 Lewis, *Everyday Life on Ottoman Turkey*, 131.

49 For more see V. L. Menage, 'The Map of Hajji Ahmed and Its Makers,' *Bulletin of the School of Oriental and African Studies* 21 (1958): 291-314.

50 Lewis, *Everyday Life on Ottoman Turkey*, 131; and Clot, *Suleiman the Magnificent,* 131.

51 Fleischer, *Bureaucrat and Intellectual in the Ottoman Empire*, 279-280. Also see Eryılmaz, 'From Adam to Süleyman,' 100-125.

52 For more on Jamshid see Ferdowsi, *Shahnameh*, Kindle Edition.

53 W. A. Clouston, *On the Magical Elements in Chaucer's Squire's Tale* (London: Chaucer Society, 1888-90), 307.

54 A. G. Warner and E. Warner, trans., *The Shahnama of Firdausi* (London: 1905), 317- 318; also see Ferdowsi, *Shahnameh: The Persian Book of Kings*, Kindle Edition.

55 Warner and Warner, *The Shahnama of Firdausi*, 317- 318.

56 Ahmet Talay Onay, 'Eski Türk Edebiyatında Mazmunlar,' *Türkiye Diyanet Vakfı*, 77 (1993): 87-88.

57 Bosnavi Sûdi, *Hafiz Serhi,* Vol. 1, Matbaa-yı Amire 1288 (Istanbul, 1871), 359.

58 Zülfi Güler, 'Şehy Galib'in Divanı'nda Ayna Sembolü,' Firat Üniversitesi Sosyal Bilimler Dergisi, Cilt: 14, Sayı: 1, 115.

59 Fleischer, *Bureaucrat and Intellectual in the Ottoman Empire*, 279-280.

60 Ismail Avcı, 'Divan Şiirinde İskender-i Zülkarneyn' ('Alexander the Great in Divan Poetry'), *Uluslararası Sosyal Araştırmalar Dergisi* (*The Journal of International Social Research*) Vol.7, 29 (2014): 48-50, accessed March 23, 2017, www.sosyalarastirmalar.com

61 Öznur Üzgün-İbrahim Ekinci, 'Newroz Piroz Boe,' *Rengin Öğrenci Kültür Sanat ve Düşün Dergisi*, Mart-Nisan 5 (2001): 10.

62 Casale, 'Seeing the Past: Maps and Ottoman Historical Consciousness,' Kindle Edition.

63 Casale, 'Seeing the Past: Maps and Ottoman Historical Consciousness,' Kindle Edition.

64 Atıl, *Süleymanname*, 215.

65 Rogers, 'The Arts Under Suleyman the Magnificent,' 278.

66 See James Dickie, 'The Iconography of the Prayer Rug', *Oriental Art,* (Spring, 1972): 44, 46; and Julia S. Berrall, *The Garden* (London: Thames and Hudson, 1966), 57.

67 For more on this see Denny, *Iznik: The Artistry of Ottoman Ceramics*; and Emel Esin, 'Influences de l'art nomade et de l'architecture de Turkistan,' in 1st I.C.T.A., Ankara: 1961.

68 Ferdowsi, *Shahnameh*, Kindle Edition.

69 Christine Woodhead, ed., *The Ottoman World* (London: Routledge, 2012), 134-135.

70 Metin Kunt and Christine Woodhead, eds., *Süleyman the Magnificent and His Age: The Ottoman Empire in the Early Modern World* (London: Longman, 1995), 180.

71 Halman, *Süleyman the Magnificent Poet*, 53.

72 Horne, *Sacred Books and Early Literature of the East*, 314.

73 Lewis, Everyday Life on Ottoman Turkey, 108.

CONCLUSION

1 Rüsen, "What is Historical Consciousness?," 7, 13.

2 Rüsen, "What is Historical Consciousness?," 9.

3 Sa'i, *Sinan's Autobiographies*, 131.

LIST OF

ILLUSTRATIONS

CHAPTER 1

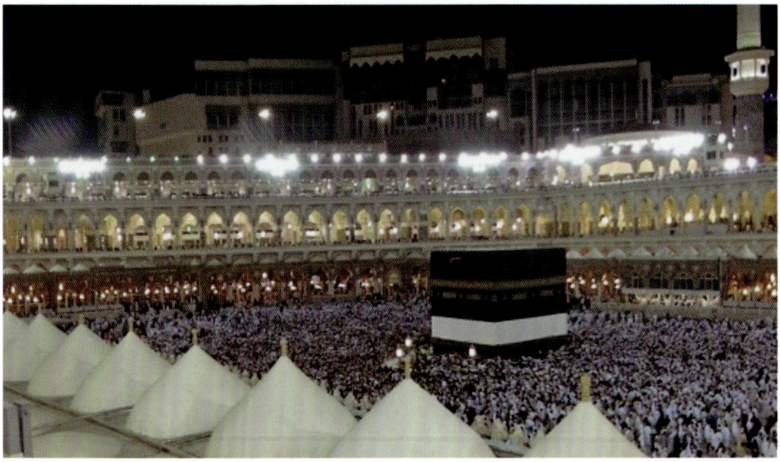

Figure 1.1: The semi-domical revamps at the Ka'ba by Sinan in 1571 showing the Ottomanising effect of the Holy Precinct with the distinctly Ottoman style semi-domes

Photograph by Metin Mustafa, October 13, 2011.

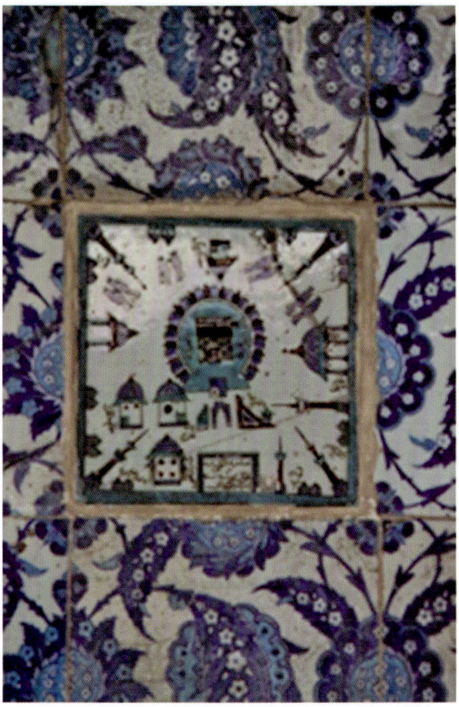

Figure 1.2: Iznik tile from the mosque of Rustem Pasha, Istanbul, c. 1560-61.

The tile shows the minbar of Süleyman at the Ka'ba precinct, depicted as a red triangle on the right of the arch in the centre tile of the panel. This indicates the attempt made by Süleyman to bolster his image as the caliph of the Islamic world and as the custodians of the Holy site.

Photograph by Metin Mustafa, December 4, 2014.

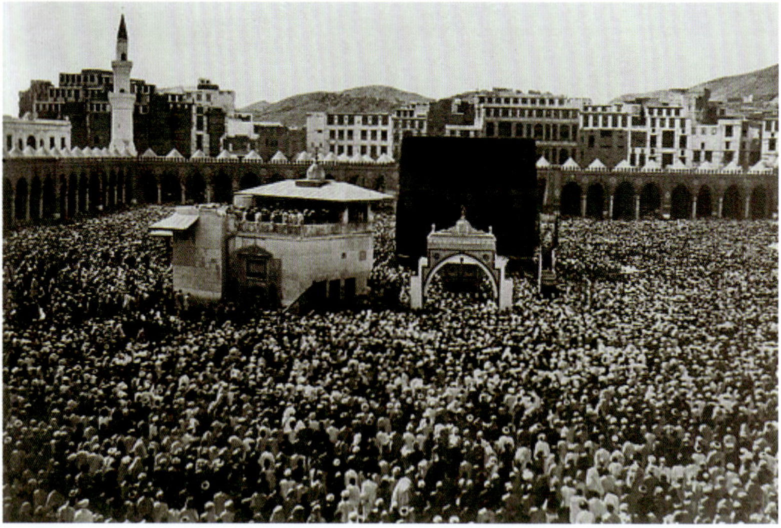

Figure 1.3: The Great Mosque of Mecca in 1910, showing the Ka'ba

Süleyman's minbar is seen on the right of the arch next to the Ka'ba, and the Ottoman minaret in the background. The Ottomanising of the Holy Precinct legitimises Ottoman claims to the caliphate and the rulers of the Islamic world. Source: 'Makkah: 1887 and Now,' photograph by Al Sayyid al Ghaffar, http://www.hajjsafe.com/blog/makkah-1887-and-now/

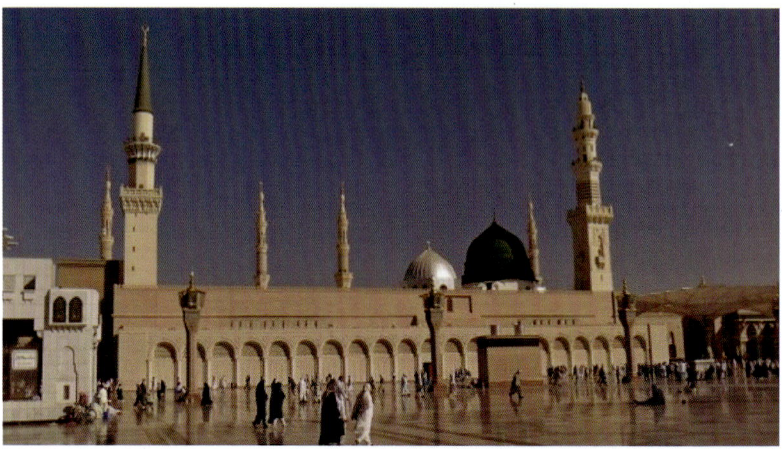

Figure 1.4: The minaret of Sultan Süleyman at the Prophet's Mosque in Medina seen on the front left in typical Ottoman style, 1589. It lays tenuous claim to Prophet Muhammad and also signifies that the sultan is the custodian of the Holy Site.

Photograph by Metin Mustafa, October 13, 2011.

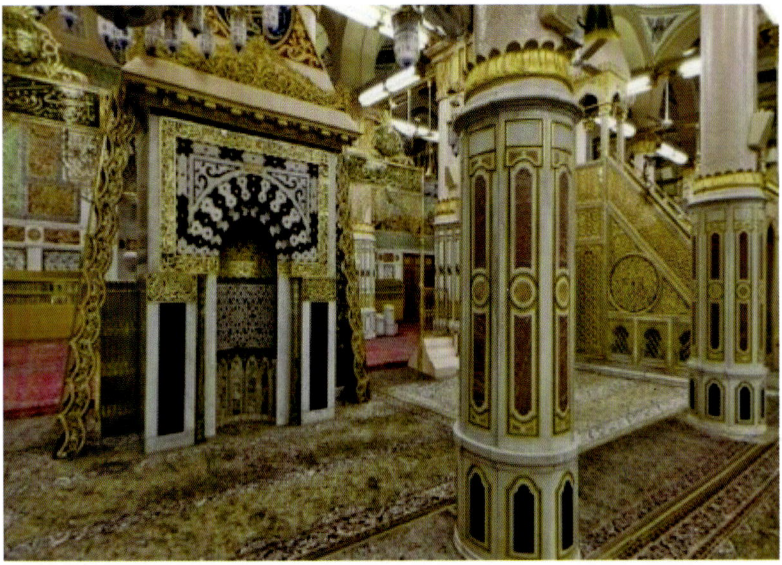

Figure 1.5: The mihrab of Süleyman at the Prophet's Mosque in Medina, 1589

Photograph by Metin Mustafa, October 13, 2011.

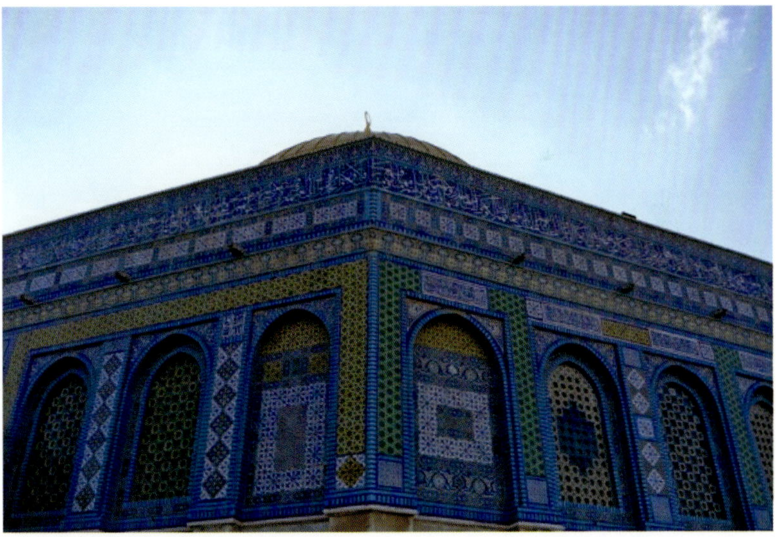

Figure 1.6: The Iznik tile embellishments of the Dome of the Rock in Jerusalem commissioned by Sultan Süleyman in 1545. The current tiles on the structure are recent replicas added during renovations.

Photograph by Metin Mustafa, January 5, 2015.

CHAPTER 2

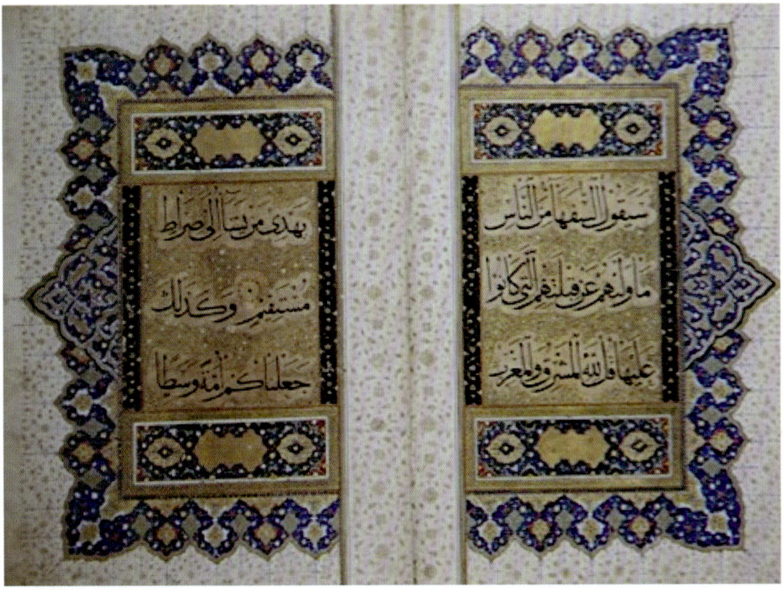

Figure 2.1: A Qur'an page from Yaqut al-Musta'simi (1282–1283)."

Source: Topkapı Sarayı Kütüphanesi, E.H. 227. Photograph by Metin Mustafa, January 20, 2015.

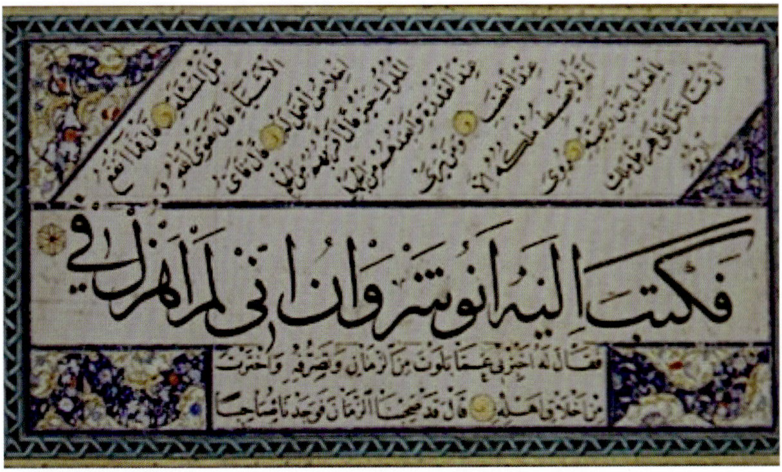

Figure 2.2: Pages from 15th century The Muraqqa Calligraphic Album of Sheyh Hamdullah

Source: The Museum of Turkish and Islamic Arts, Istanbul, Turkey. Photograph by Metin Mustafa, January 20, 2015.

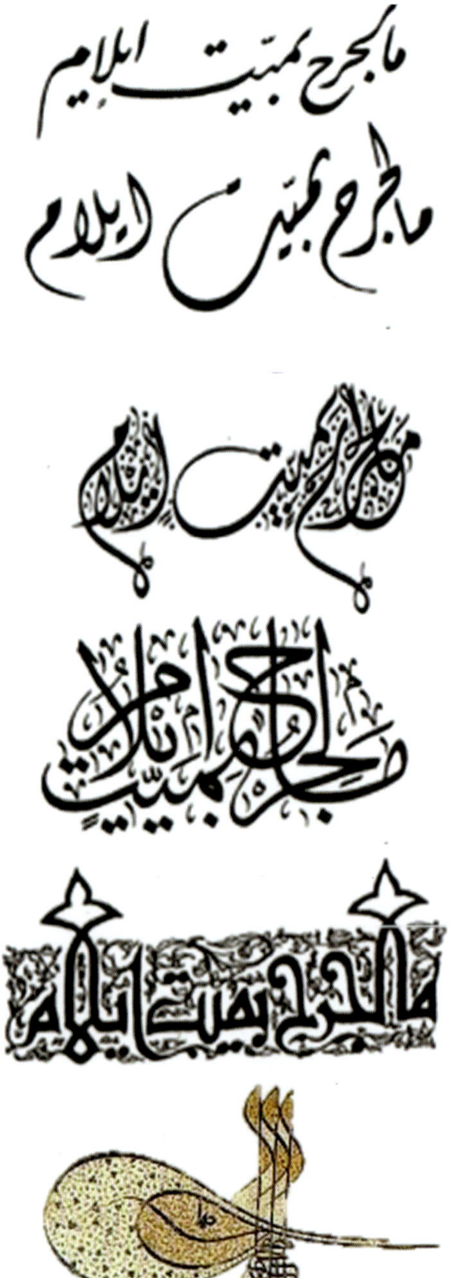

nasta'liq

divani

jele-divani

jele-thuluth kufi

tughra

Figure 2.3: Some Ottoman additions to the art of calligraphy

Source: Image posted on Wordpress March 12, 2005, https://29letters.files.wordpress.com/2007/05/arabic-styles.jpg

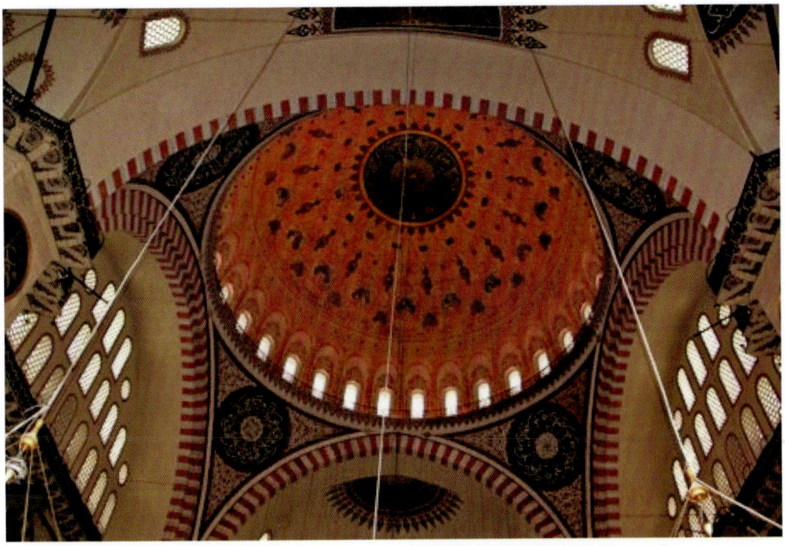

Figure 2.4: The central dome of the Süleymaniye Mosque 1557, Istanbul

Photograph by Metin Mustafa, December 4, 2014.

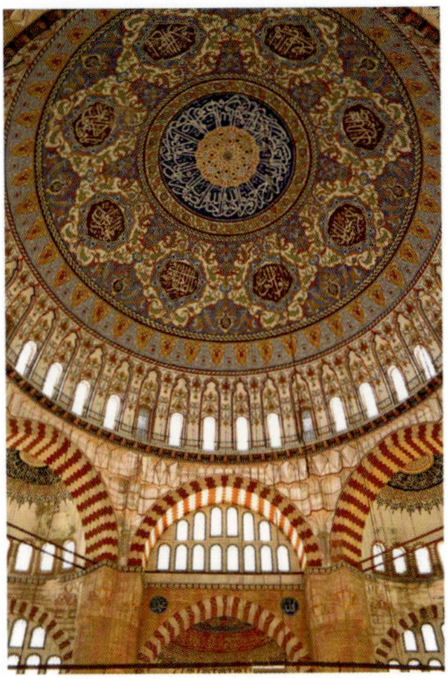

Figure 2.5: The central dome of the Selimiye Mosque 1575, Edirne, claimed by Sinan to have surpassed the dome of the Hagia Sophia.

Photograph by Metin Mustafa, December 12, 2014.

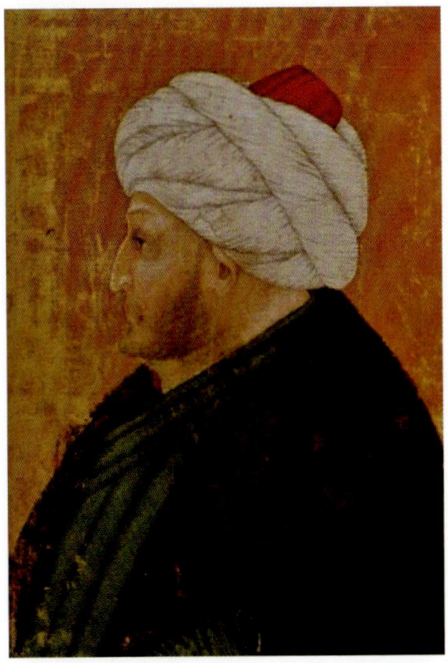

Figure 2.6: Three-quarter-profile portrait of Mehmed II, attributed to either Sinan Bey or Sibilzade Ahmed of Bursa, c.1480

Source: Topkapı Sarayı Kütüphanesi, Istanbul, H.2153, folio 145ba.

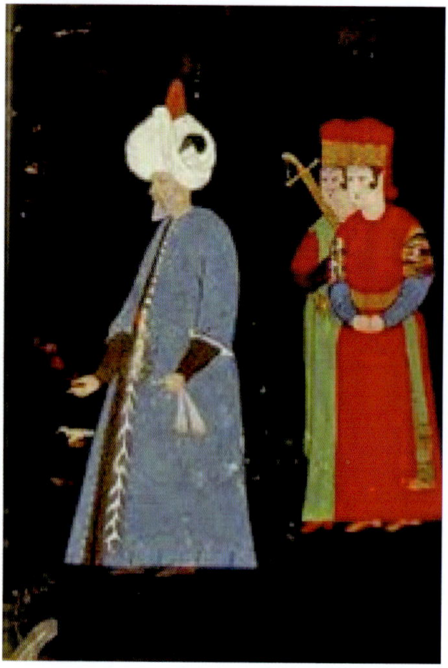

Figure 2.7: The ageing Sultan Süleyman with his attendants

Source: Topkapı Sarayı Kütüphanesi, Istanbul, H.2134, f.8a.

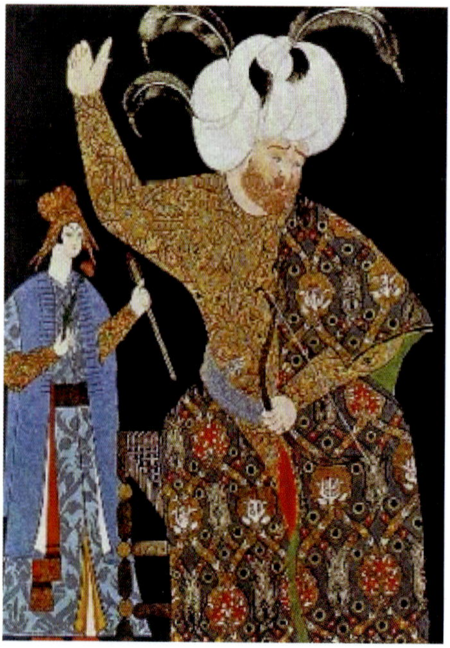

Figure 2.8: Selim II, by Nigari c.1560–65

Source: Topkapı Sarayı Kütüphanesi, Istanbul, H.2134, f.3.

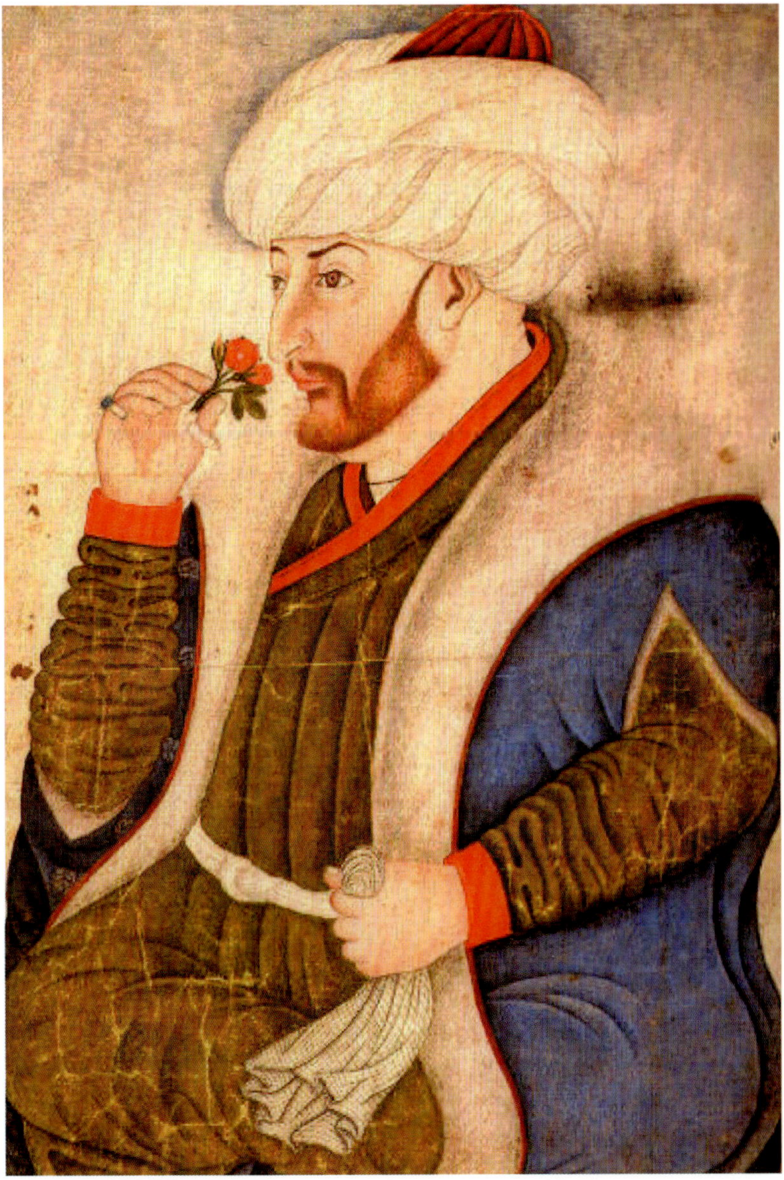

Figure 2.9: Mehmed II Smelling a Rose, attributed to Sinan Bey, trained by Gentile Bellini at the Topkapı Palace

Source: Topkapı Sarayı Kütüphanesi, Istanbul, H.2153, folio 10a.

CHAPTER 4

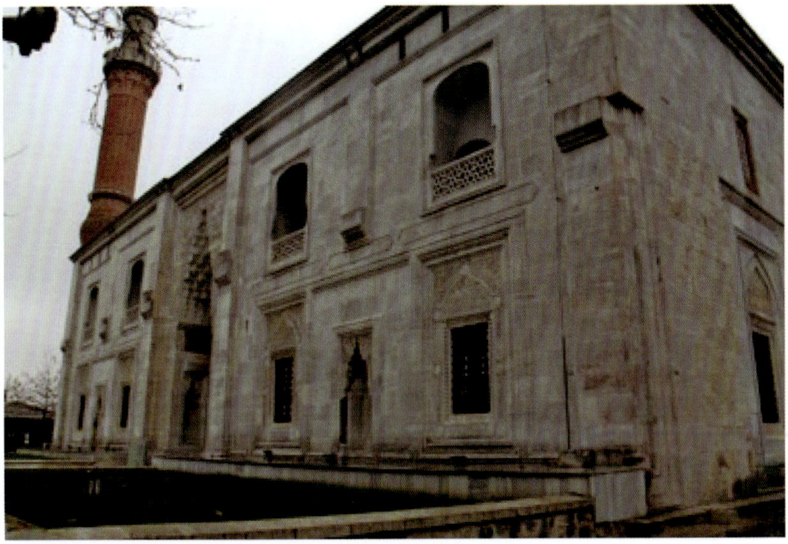

Figure 4.1: The Yeşil Camii (Green Mosque) of Sultan Mehmed I built 1414–1424 depicts Timurid aesthetics in the portal entrance.

Photograph by Metin Mustafa, December 16, 2014.

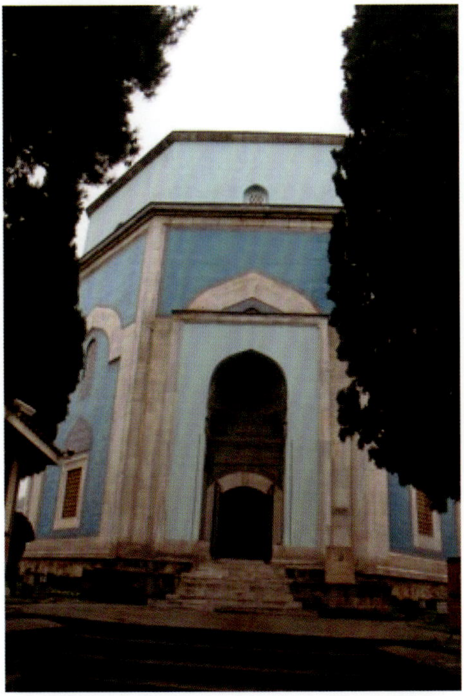

Figure 4.2: The Yeşil Türbe (Green Tomb) of Mehmed I built 1414 in the traditional Central Asian and Seljuk models.

Photograph by Metin Mustafa, December 16, 2014.

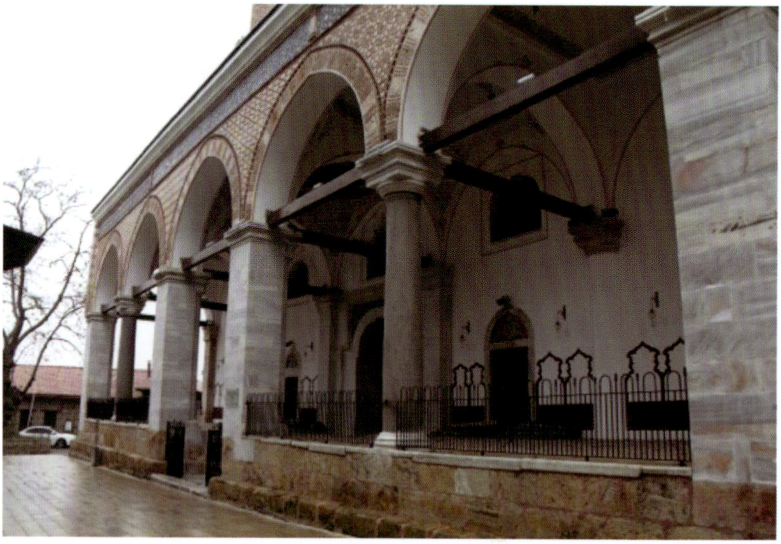

Figure 4.3: The portico of the Muradiye Mosque of Murad II in Bursa (1435) depicting the Greco-Roman inspired columns.

Photograph by Metin Mustafa, December 16, 2014.

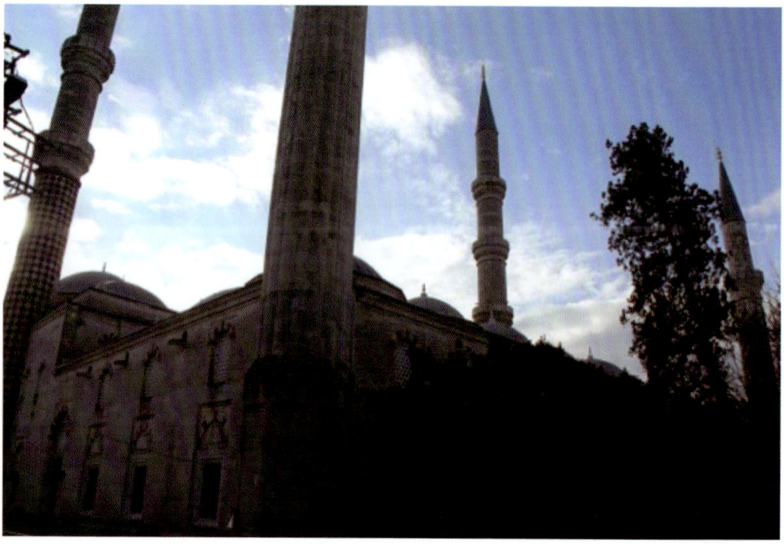

Figure 4.4: The Üç Şerefeli Mosque (1438-1447) built by Murad II in Edirne. Sinan criticised its minarets as being 'thick' ('Gāyet qalindur') compared to his more elegant minarets in the Süleymaniye and Selimiye mosques whivh he claims in his autobiographies.

Photograph by Metin Mustafa, December 12, 2014.

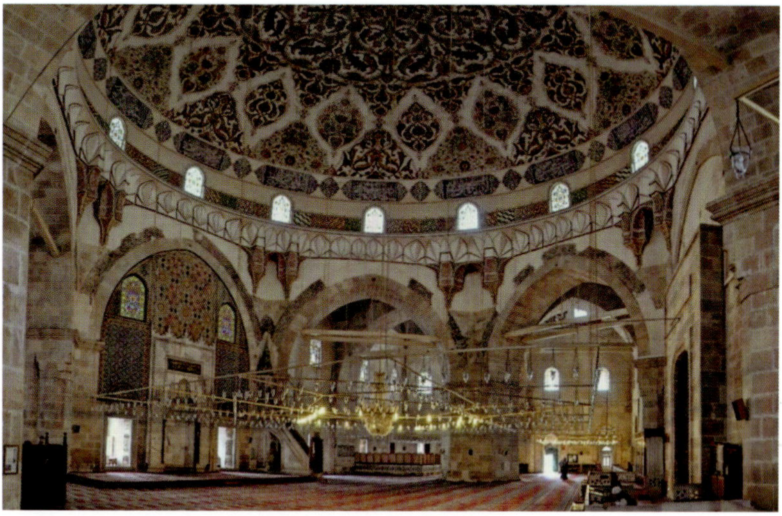

Figure 4.5: The interior of the Üç Şerefeli Mosque

This mosque is the Ottomans' first attempt to create an uninterrupted space under a single dome in the style of the Hagia Sophia

Photograph by Metin Mustafa, December 16, 2014.

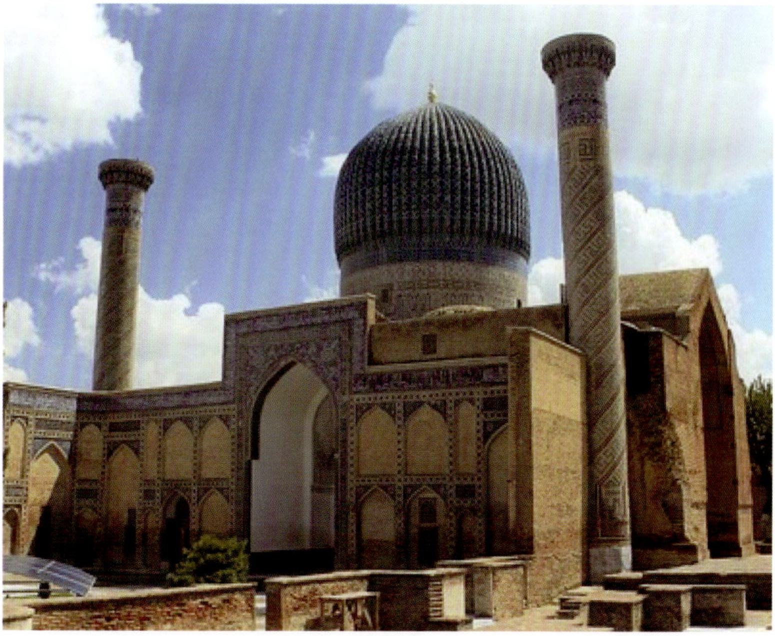

Figure 4.6: The mausoleum of Timur (1410), Samarkand, Uzbekistan

Photograph courtesy of M. Aksoy, August, 2011.

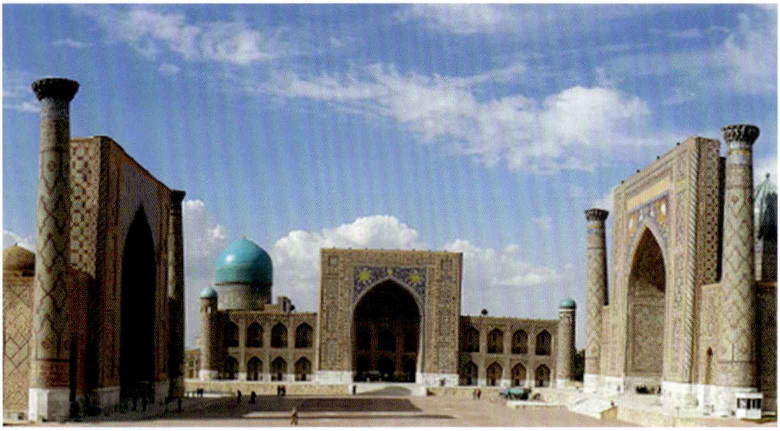

Figure 4.7: The Registan built by Timur's grandson Ulugh Bey between 1417-1421, Samarkand, Uzbekistan

Photograph courtesy of M. Aksoy, August, 2011.

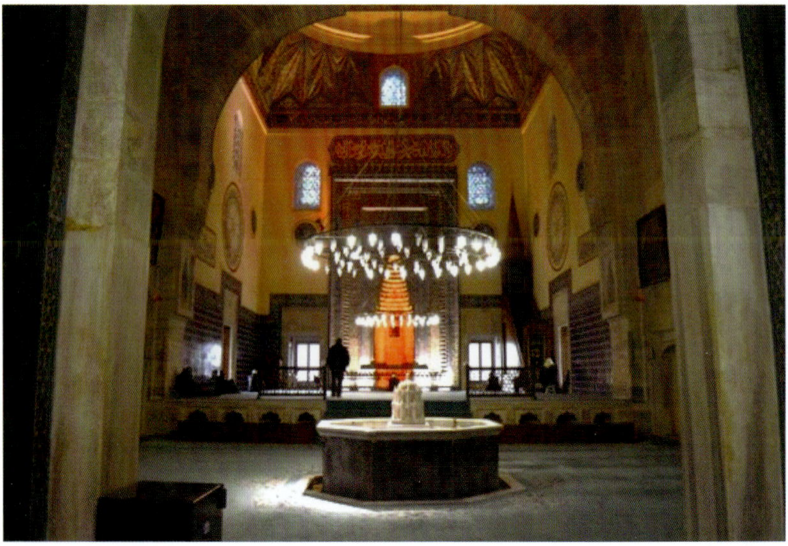

Figure 4.8: Interior of Yeşil Camii showing the T-Plan composition and Bursa arch facing the qibla wall

Photograph by Metin Mustafa, December 16, 2014.

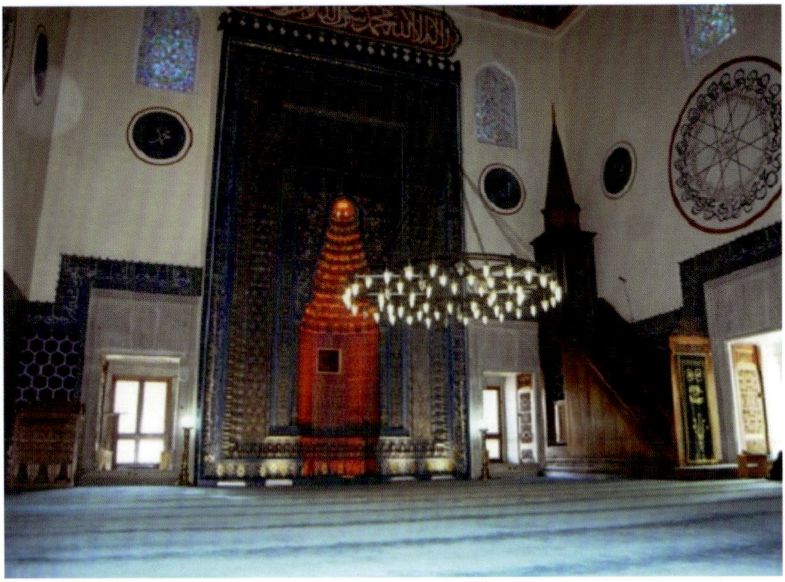

Figure 4.9: The qibla wall and the mihrab niche of the Yeşil Camii decorated in the Timurid style

Photograph by Metin Mustafa, December 16, 2014.

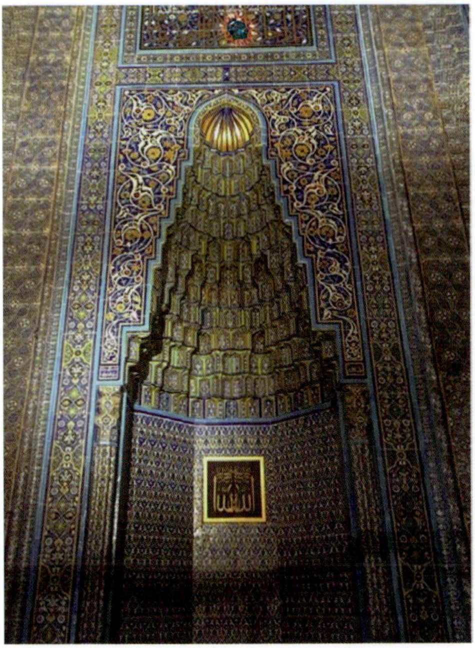

Figure 4.10: The muqarnas of the mihrab; calligraphic inscription bordering the mihrab in kufic style

Photograph by Metin Mustafa, December 16, 2014.

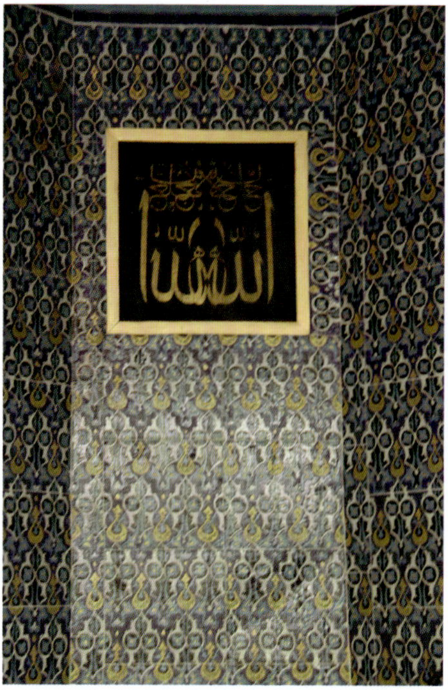

Figure 4.11: Calligraphic inscription bordering the mihrab in kufic style

Photograph by Metin Mustafa, December 16, 2014.

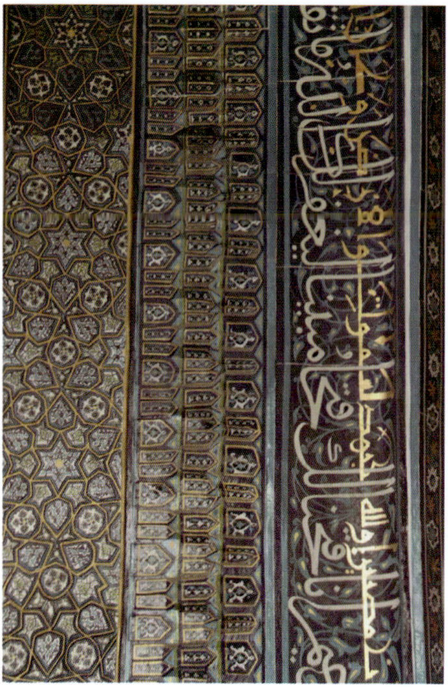

Figures 4.12: The mihrab inscription "God is Great" repeated in mirror image. Yeşil Camii.

Photograph by Metin Mustafa, December 16, 2014.

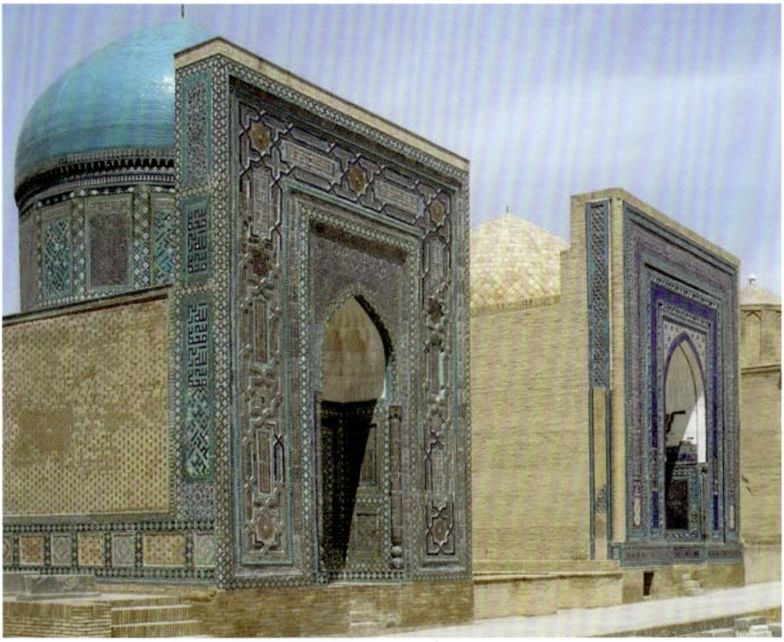

Figure 4.13: The Sha-i-Zinde cemetery in Samarkand, exterior view

Photograph courtesy of M. Aksoy, August, 2011.

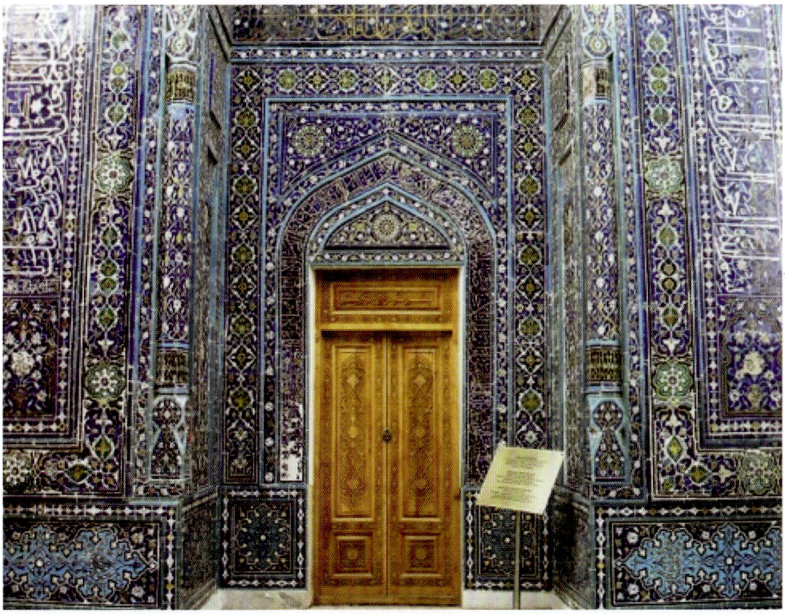

Figure 4.14: Entrance panel of the Sha-i-Zinde

Photograph courtesy of M. Aksoy, August, 2011.

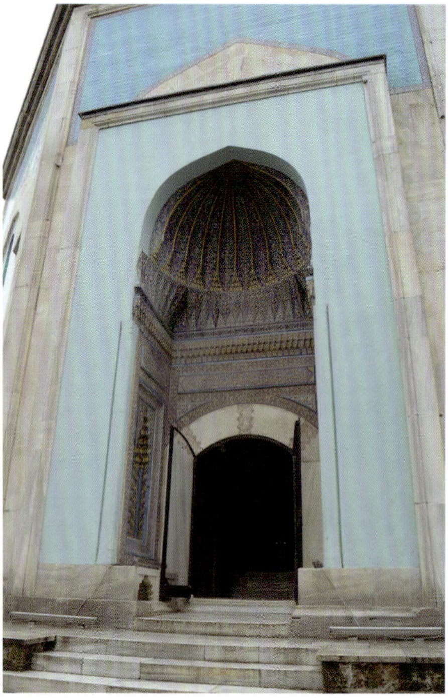

Figures 4.15: The portal of Yeşil Tomb, Bursa, Turkey

Photograph by Metin Mustafa, December 16, 2014.

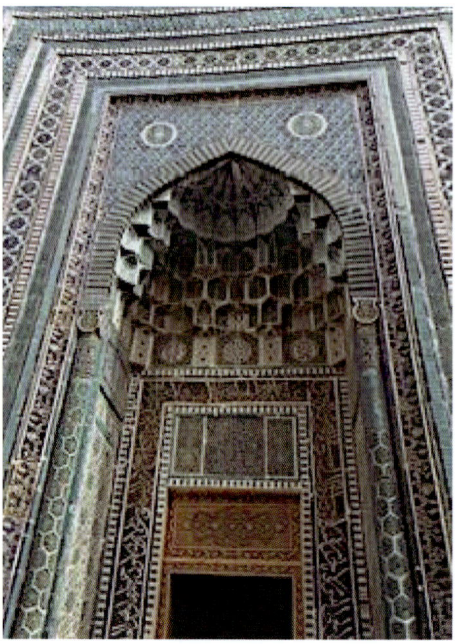

Figures 4.16: The portal of Yeşil Tomb of Shirin Bika Aka in Samrakand

Photograph courtesy of M. Aksoy, August, 2011.

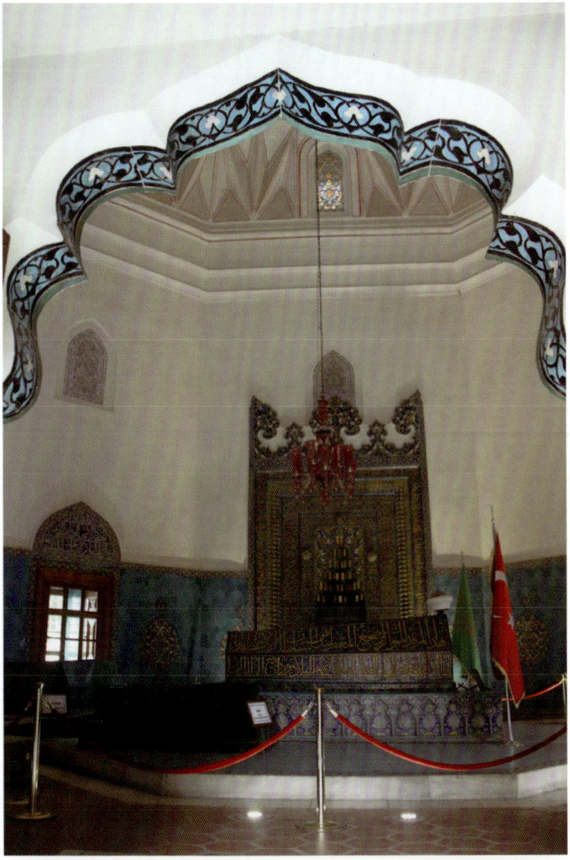

Figure 4.17: View of the interior of the Yeşil Tomb of Mehmed I in Bursa from the entrance portal showing tiled mahfils and multifoil arch

Photograph by Metin Mustafa, December 16, 2014.

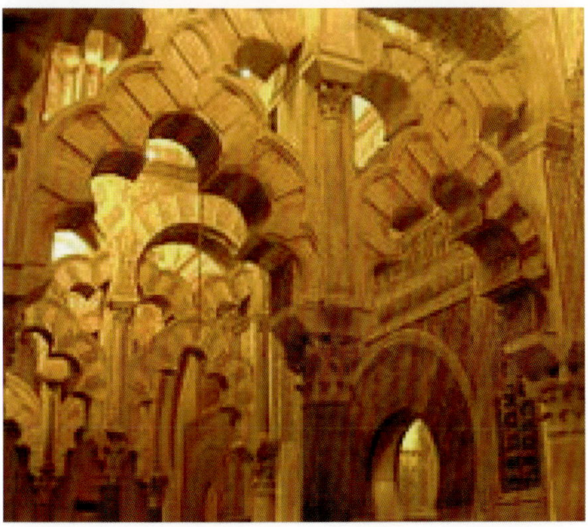

Figure 4.18: Mosque of Cordoba, Spain, from the Umayyad period-style

Photograph courtesy of O. Ibrahim, March, 2009.

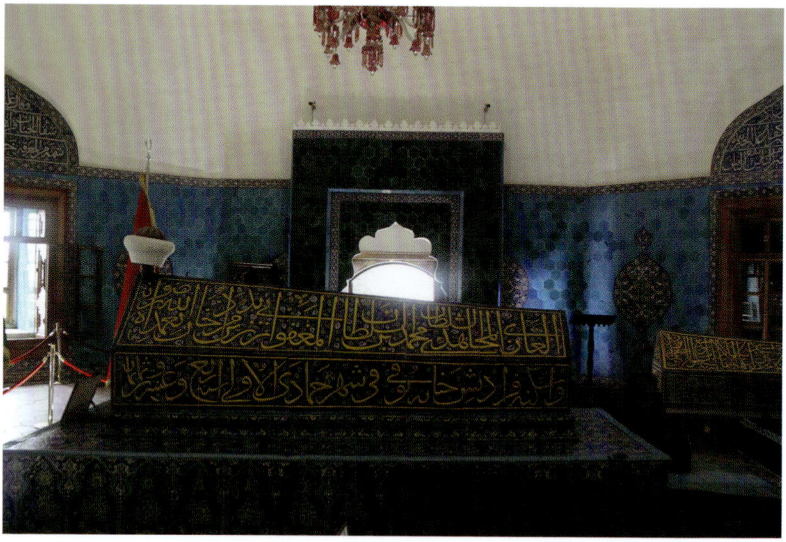

Figure 4.18a: Sarcophagus of Mehmed I, Bursa 1413-1421, Turkey

Photograph by Metin Mustafa, December 16, 2014.

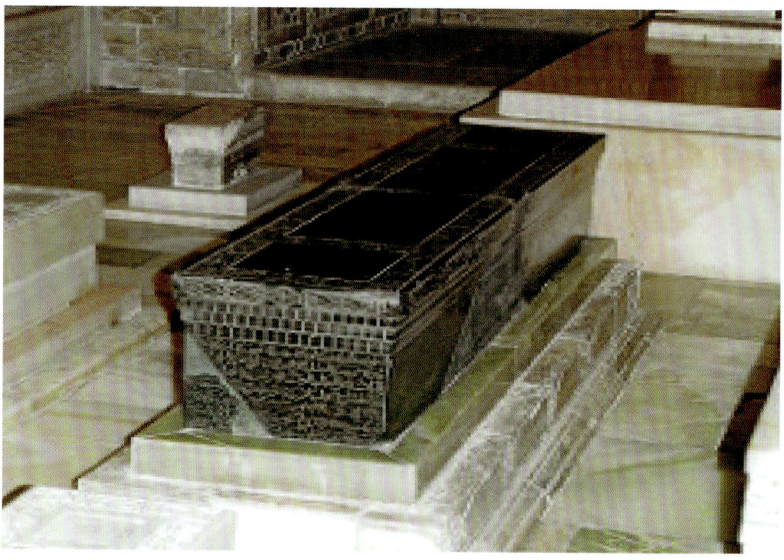

Figure 4.18b: Sarcophagus of Timur, Samarkand, Uzbekistan

Photograph courtesy of M. Aksoy, August, 2011.

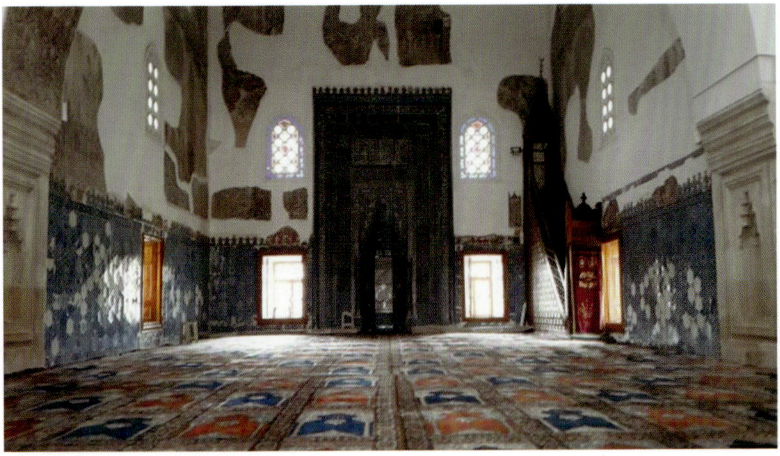

Figure 4.19: The qibla wall of the Muradiye Mosque (1435-1436) in Edirne with the mihrab in the similar style to that of Yeşil Camii in Bursa

Photograph by Metin Mustafa, December 12, 2014.

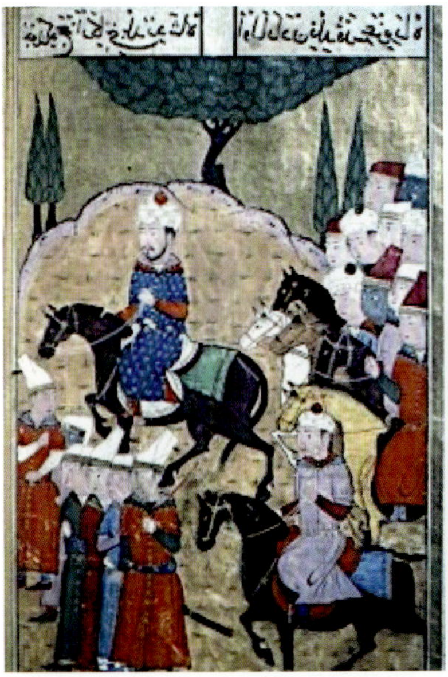

Figure 4.20a: Alexander Riding to Jerusalem, ca. 1460

Source: *The İskendernāme* of Ahmedi, Venice, Biblioteca Nazionale Marciana, Cod. Or. XC [=57], fol. 256r.

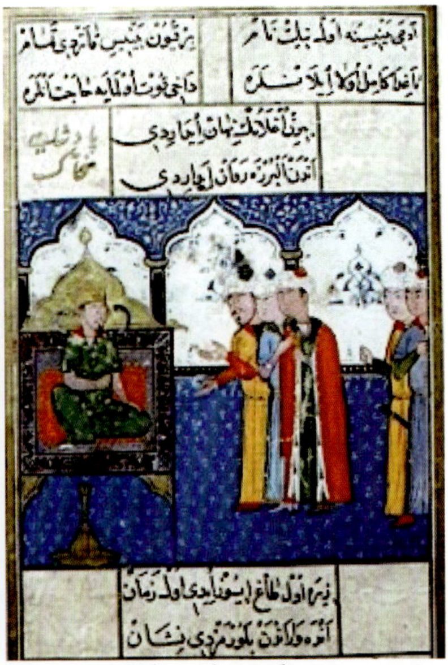

Figure 4.20b: Alexander conversing with his court philosophers, ca. 1460

Source: The *İskendernāme* of Ahmedi, Venice, Biblioteca Nazionale Marciana, fol. 158b. Photograph courtesy of A. Süleymanoğlu.

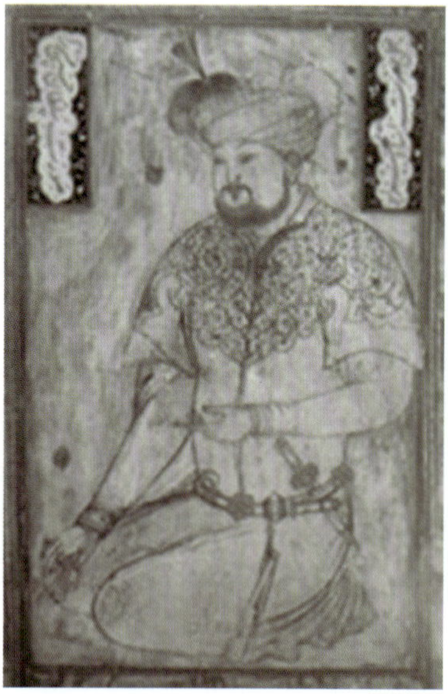

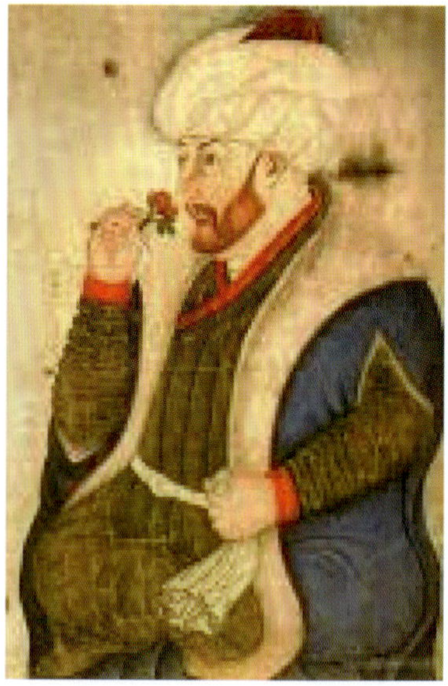

Figures 4.20c and 4.20d: Left, Sultan Husayn Bayqara, attributed to the artist Bihzad of Herat c.1470-80.

Source: Photographic reproduction of Bihzad's original. Harvard University Art Museum. https://commons.wikimedia.org/wiki/File:Behhzad_001.jpg

Right, Portrait of Mehmed II smelling a rose, attributed to Sinan Bey or Sibilzade Ahmed, c.1480.

Source: Topkapı Palace Museum, Istanbul, H.2153, fol. 10a

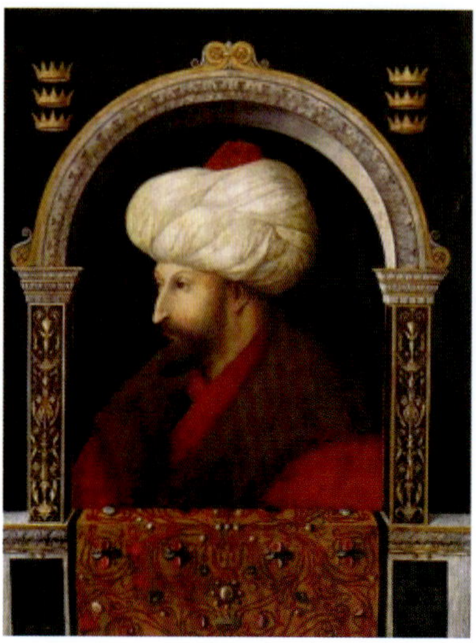

Figure 4.21: Gentile Bellini's portrait of Mehmed II made in Istanbul during the artist's stay c.1479

Source: National Gallery, London. Photograph courtesy of S. MacCallum.

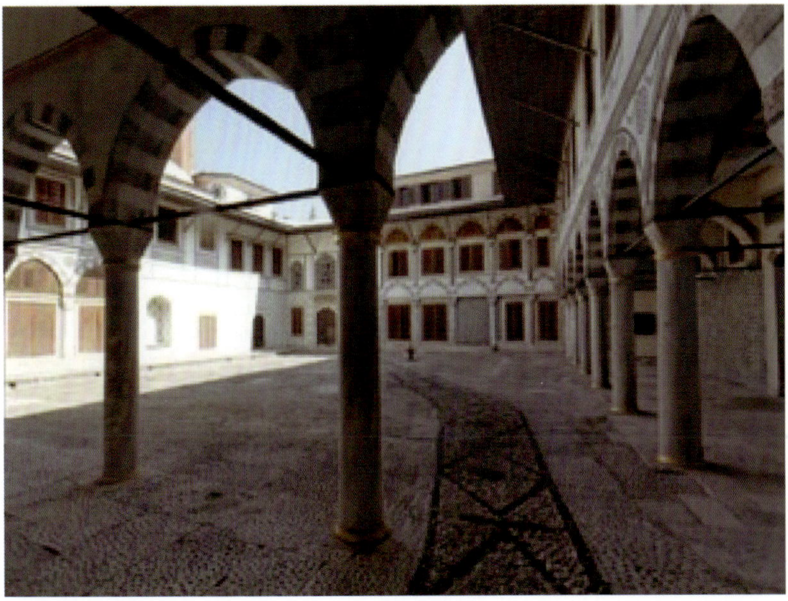

Figure 4.22a: Topkapı Palace courtyard, Istanbul

Photograph by Metin Mustafa, January 19, 2015.

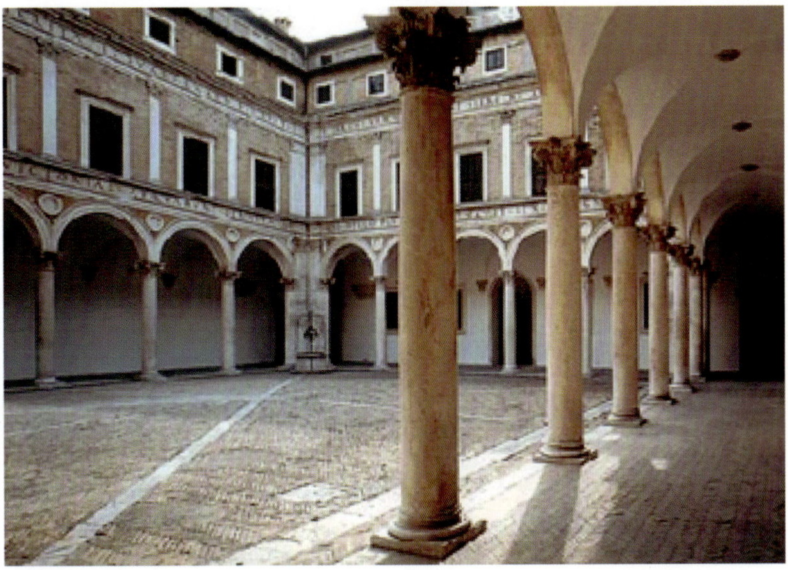

Figure 4.22b: Palazzo Ducale, Urbino, the arcaded courtyard 1454-1474 of Duke Federico

Photograph courtesy of G. Elgar, October, 1999.

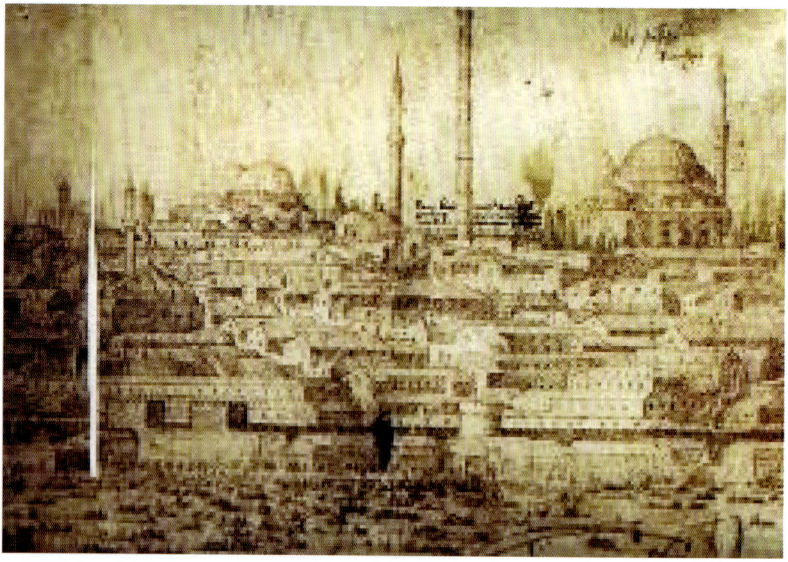

Figure 4.23: Engraving of Melchior Lorichs

The illustration shows the original fifteenth century Fatih Mosque in the top left corner

Source: Photograph courtesy of Faculty of Architecture, Middle East Technical University, Ankara, Turkey.

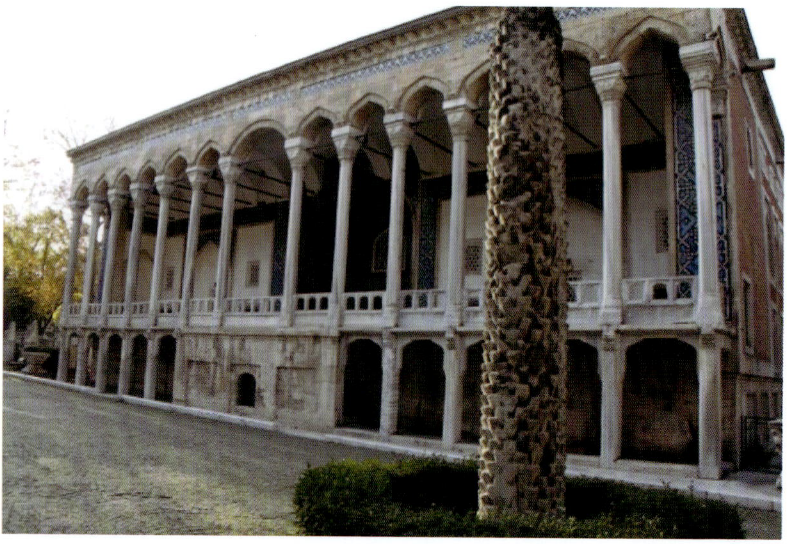

Figure 4.24a: The Çinili Köşk built by Sultan Mehmed II in Istanbul in 1473 in the Timurid style

Photograph by Metin Mustafa, January, 19, 2015.

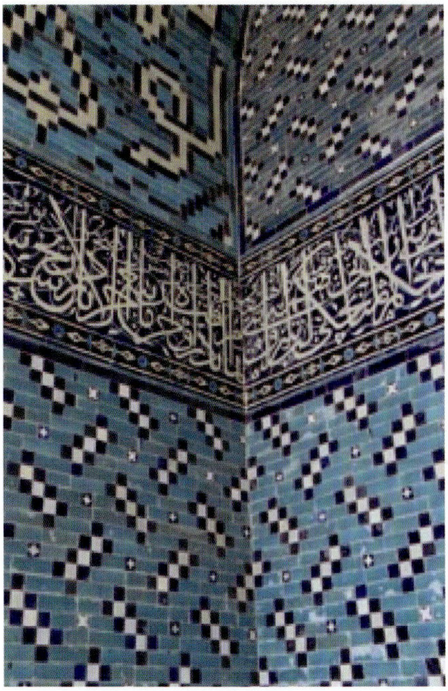

Figure 4.24b: Detail from entrance portal of Çinili Köşk, Rustem Pasha Mosque, c.1560-61.

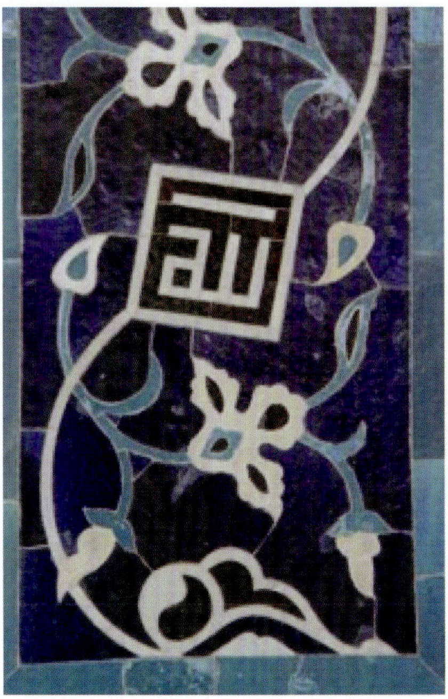

Figure 4.24c: Detail from entrance portal of Çinili Köşk, Rustem Pasha Mosque, c.1560-61

Photographs by Metin Mustafa, January 19, 2015.

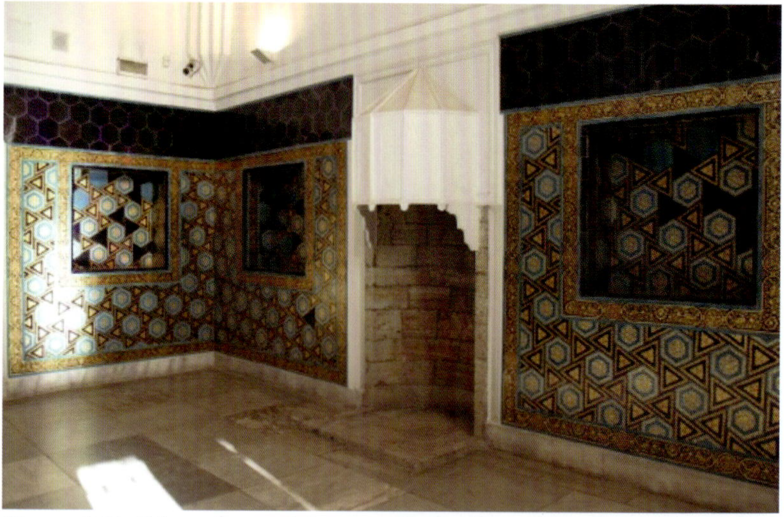

Figure 4.25: Triangular and hexagonal tiles from the interior of the Çinili Köşk, Istanbul

The tiles are stencilled with flowing gold patterns of interlacing leaves and blooming flowers, and clouds bordered by cartouche filled floral garden.

Photograph by Metin Mustafa, January 19, 2015.

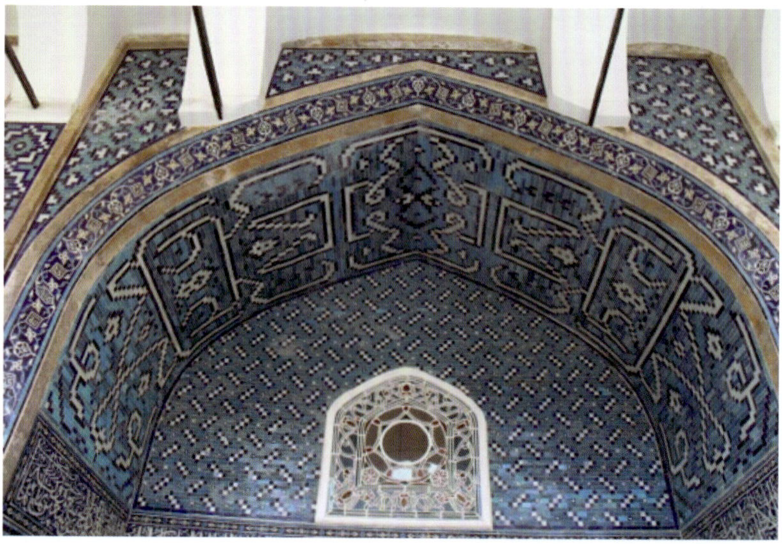

Figure 4.26a: Entrance portal of the Çinili Köşk, Istanbul, Turkey, 1473 depicting the calligraphers' engaging in the seventh century kufic style writing.

Photograph by Metin Mustafa, January 19, 2015.

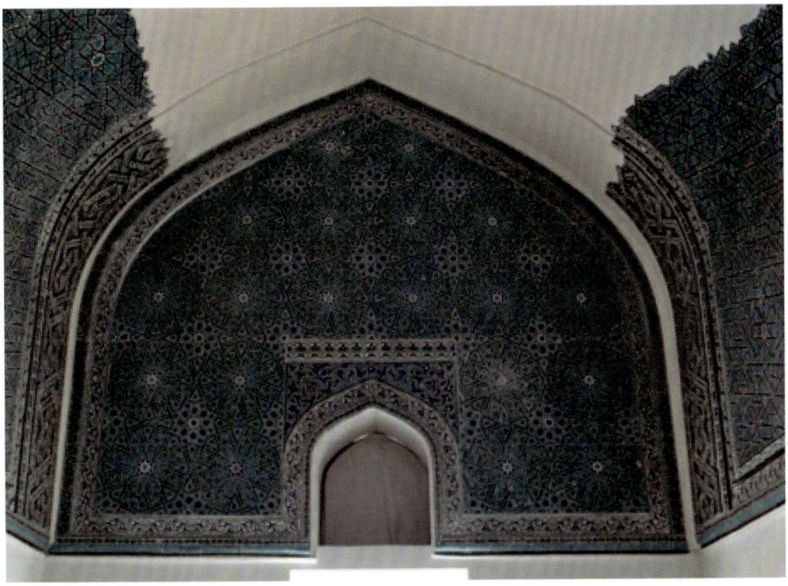

Figure 4.26b: Tiles from the Karatay Madrasah 1251, Konya, Turkey.
Photograph by Metin Mustafa, October 13, 1987.

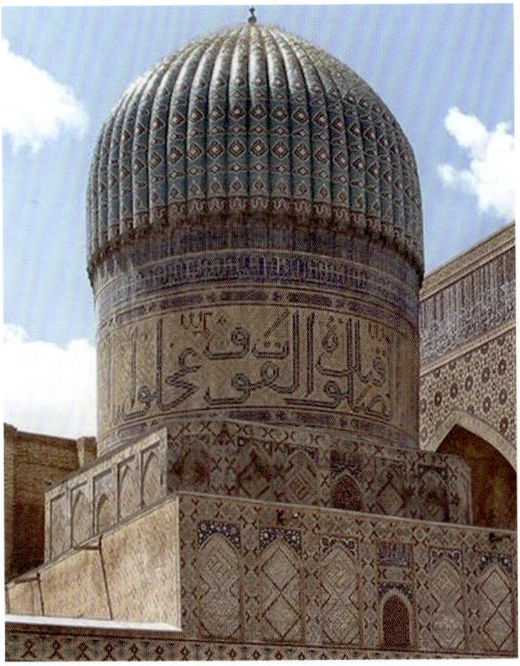

Figure 4.26c: The Mosque of Bibi Hatun, wife of Timur (1399–1404), Samarkand, Uzbekistan with its large kufic tiled inscriptions

Photograph courtesy of M. Aksoy, August 2011.

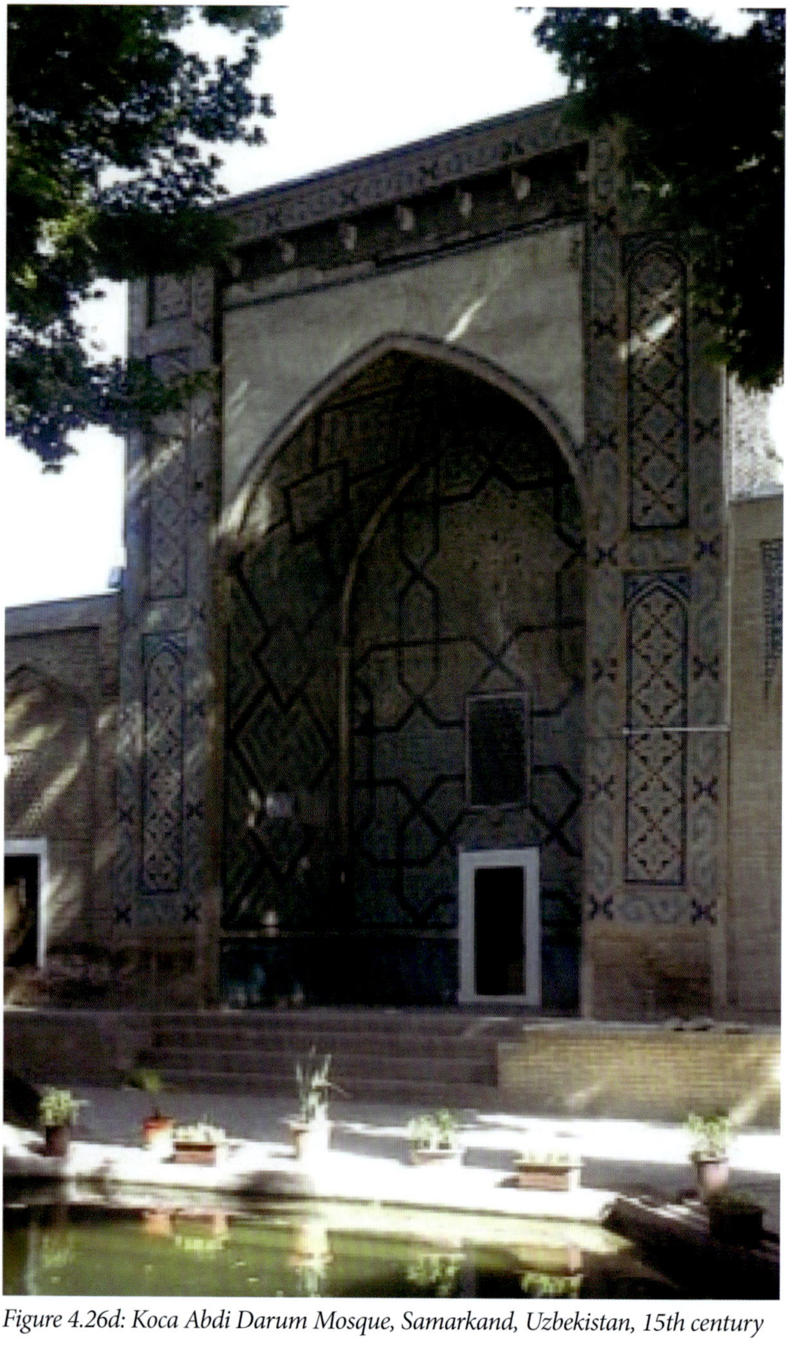

Figure 4.26d: Koca Abdi Darum Mosque, Samarkand, Uzbekistan, 15th century

Photograph courtesy of M. Aksoy, August, 2011.

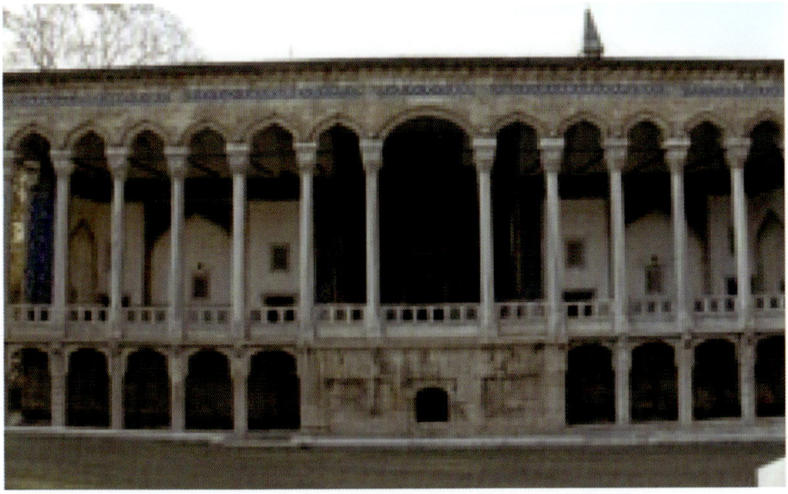

Figure 4.27a: Çinili Köşk, Istanbul, 1473

Photograph by Metin Mustafa, January 19, 2015.

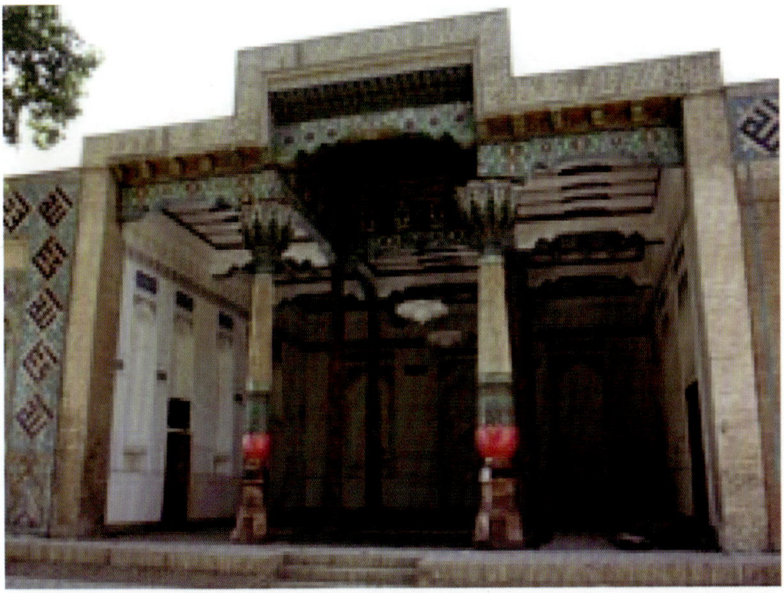

Figure 4.27b: Hoca Ahrar Mosque entrance, Samarkand, Uzbekistan c.1640 depicting similarities with the Çinili Köşk in the use of slender columns

Photograph courtesy of M. Aksoy, August, 2011.

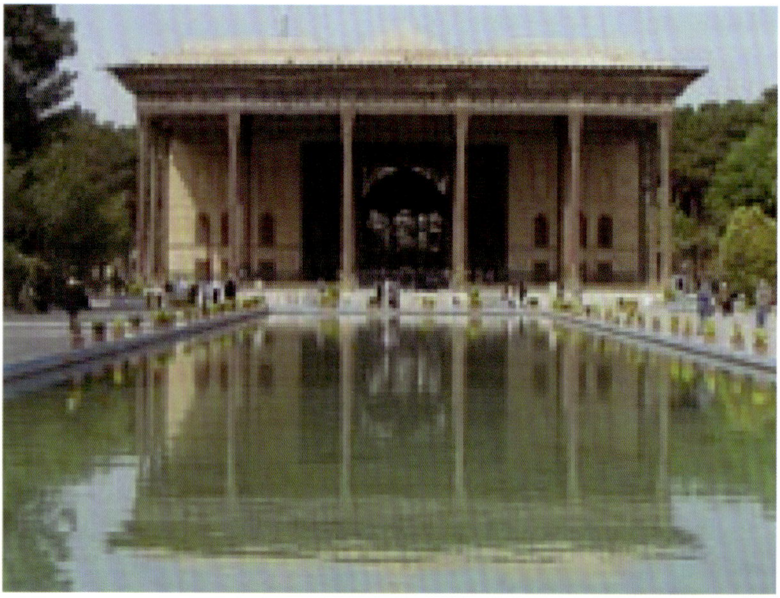

Figure 4.27c: Cilhil Sutun Mosque entrance, Isfahan, Iran, 1647 emphasising the recurring features like the loggia and diwan.

Photograph courtesy of T. Hosaran, May, 2009.

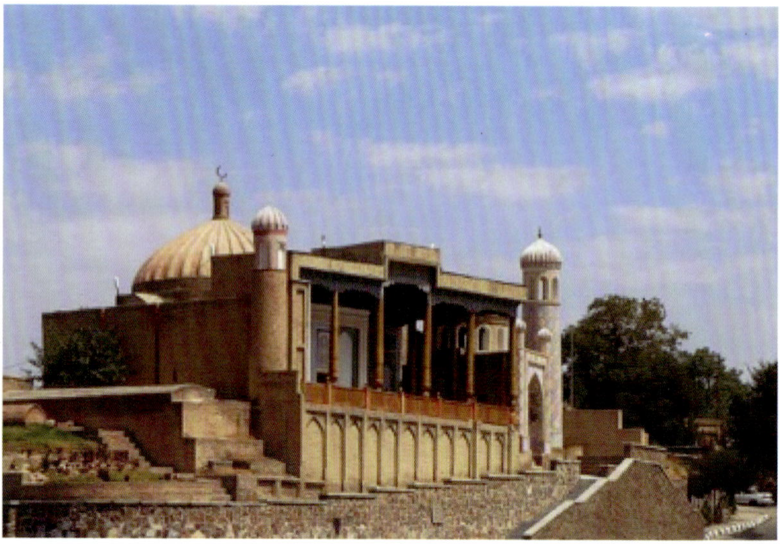

Figure 4.27d: The eighteenth-century Khidr Mosque in Samarkand in Uzbekistan showing similarities in the raised portico like the Çinili Köşk and the use of slender columns

Photograph courtesy of M. Aksoy, August, 2011.

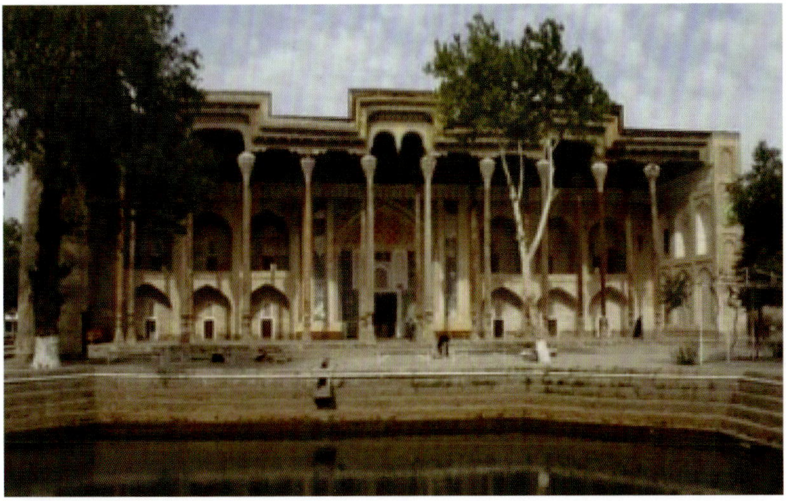

Figure 4.27e: The eighteenth-century Hoca Zayned-Din Mosque in Bukhara, Uzbekistan

Hoca Zayned-Din Mosque in Bukhara with its similar square central domed plan, ten slender columns, frontal iwans clearly resemble the Çinili Köşk inspired elements

Photograph courtesy of M. Aksoy, August, 2011.

CHAPTER 5

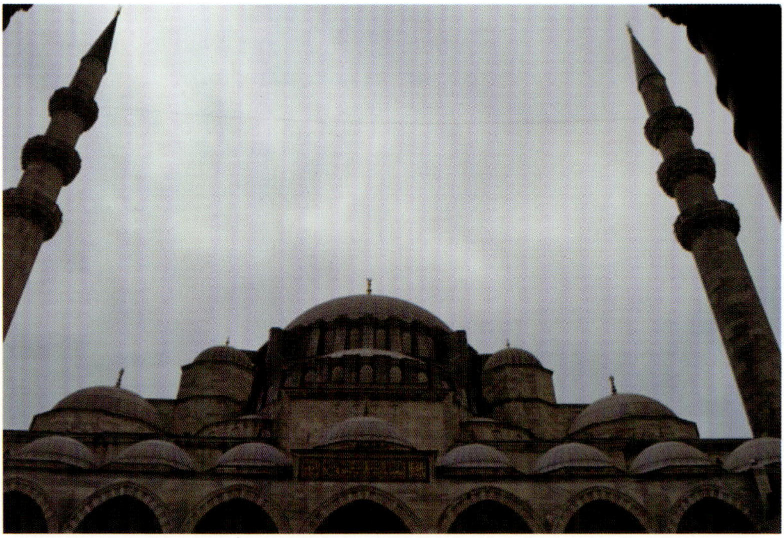

Figure 5.1: The pyramidal effect created by Sinan in the Süleymaniye Mosque, 1557

Photograph by Metin Mustafa, December 5, 2014.

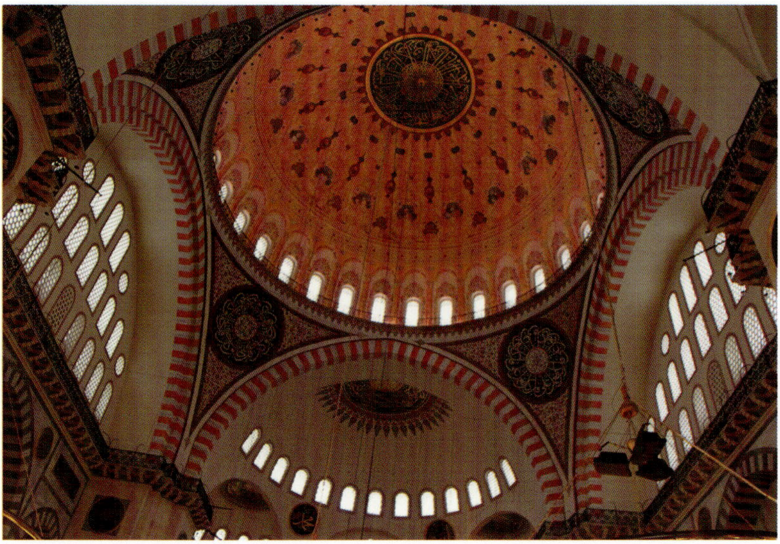

Figure 5.1a: The interior of the Süleymaniye, Istanbul, Turkey, 1557

Central dome with two half domes

Photograph by Metin Mustafa, December 5, 2014.

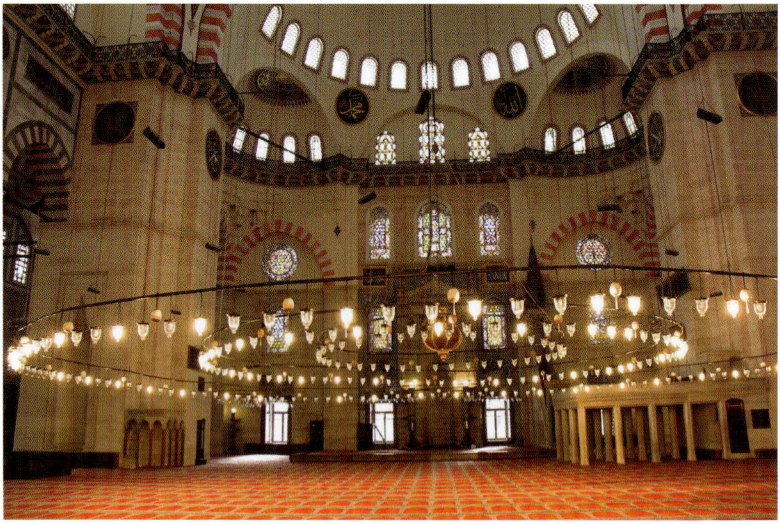

Figure 5.2: Interior of the Süleymaniye, Istanbul, Turkey, 1558

Sinan's attempt to opening up the central space by sitting the central dome on four large, rather heavy columns

Photograph by Metin Mustafa, December 5, 2014.

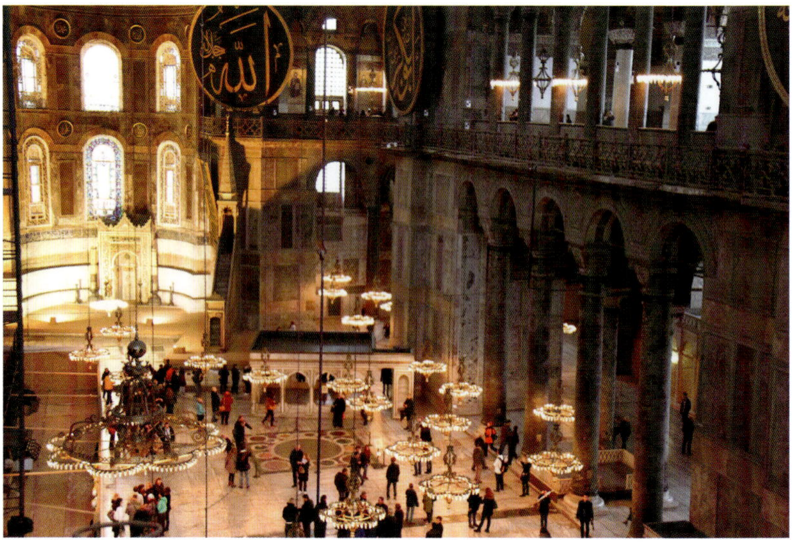

Figure 5.3: Interior of the Hagia Sophia, Istanbul, Turkey, c. 1557

The colonnaded wall seen on the right prevents a unified space needed for Muslim worship

Photographs by Metin Mustafa, January 20, 2015.

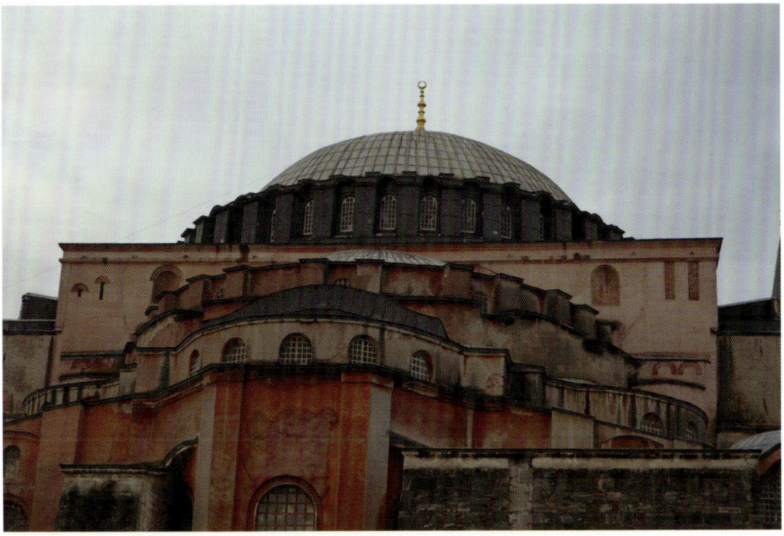

Figure 5.4: Exterior view of the Hagia Sophia, Istanbul, c.537

Photograph by Metin Mustafa, January 20, 2015.

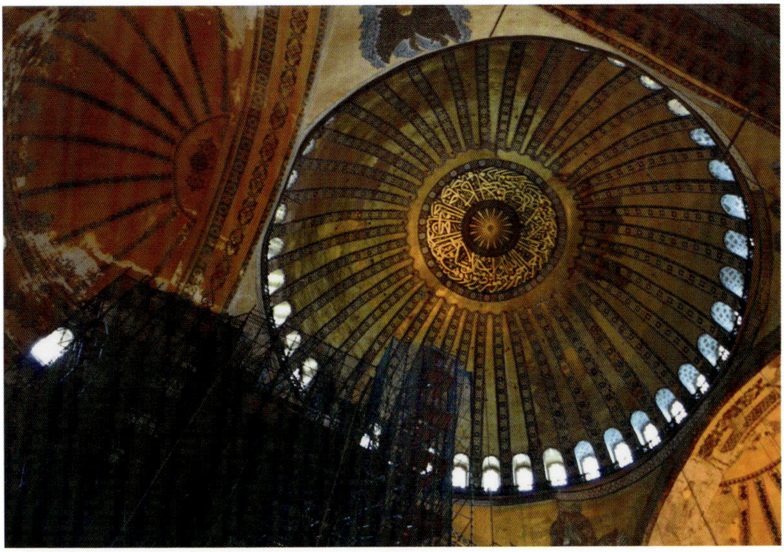

Figure 5.5: Interior, central dome with two half domes of the Hagia Sophia, c.537

The diameters of the half domes are almost equal to that of the central dome, i.e. almost 31 metres

Photograph by Metin Mustafa, January 20, 2015.

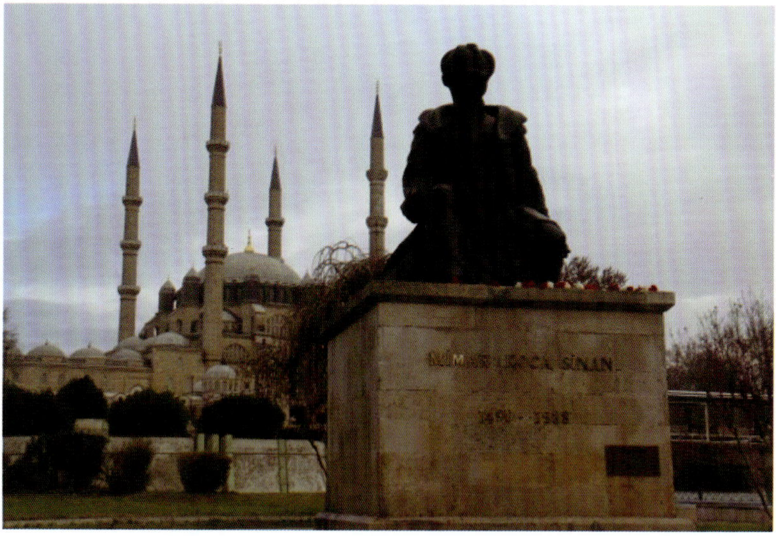

Figure 5.6: The Selimiye Mosque with its slender and 'nazik' (elegant) minarets, which Sinan refers to in his autobiographies.

Photograph by Metin Mustafa, December 12, 2014.

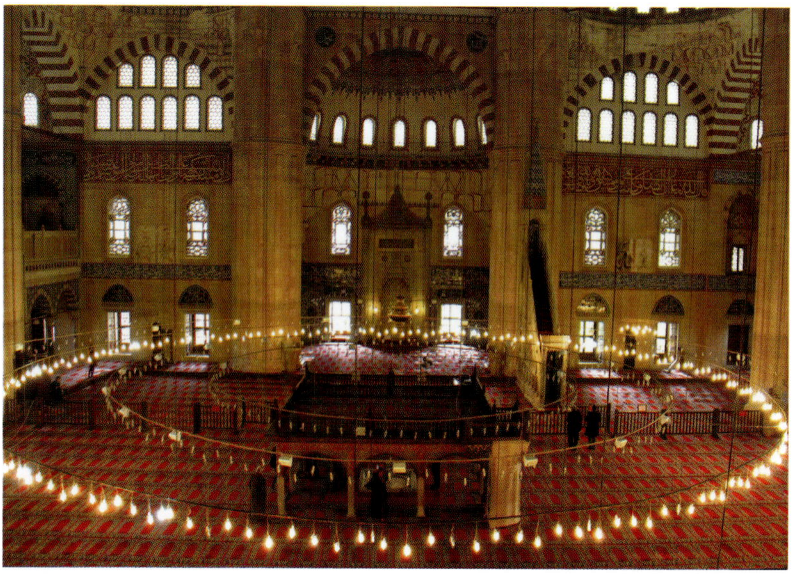

Figure 5.7: The unified space achieved by Sinan under a single dome, Selimiye Mosque, 1575

The central hall facing the qibla wall with the muezzin's tribune in the centre

Photograph by Metin Mustafa, December 12, 2014.

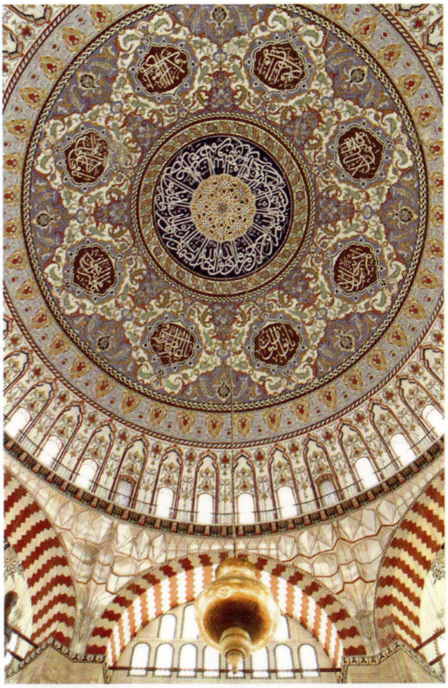

Figure 5.8: The dome of the Selimiye Mosque, 1575

Photograph by Metin Mustafa, December 12, 2014.

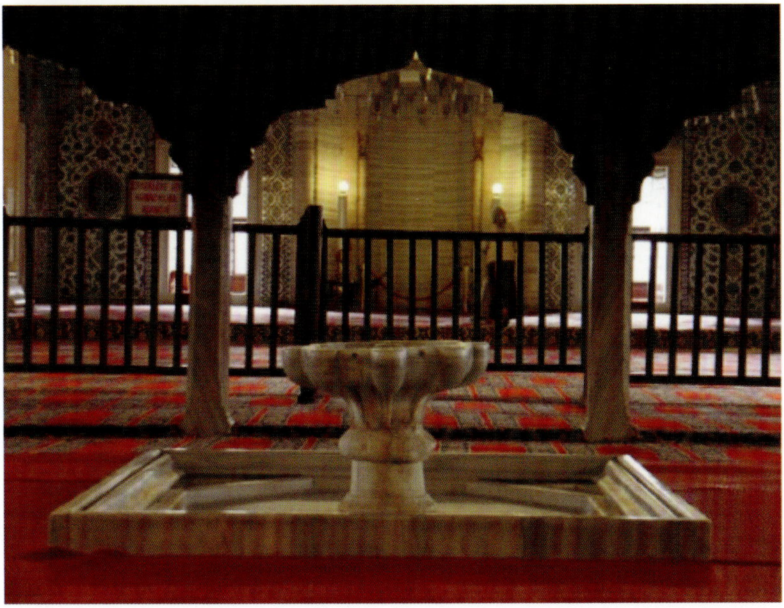

Figure 5.9: The pool under the muezzin's tribune facing the qibla wall, Selimiye Mosque, 1575

Photograph by Metin Mustafa, December 12, 2014.

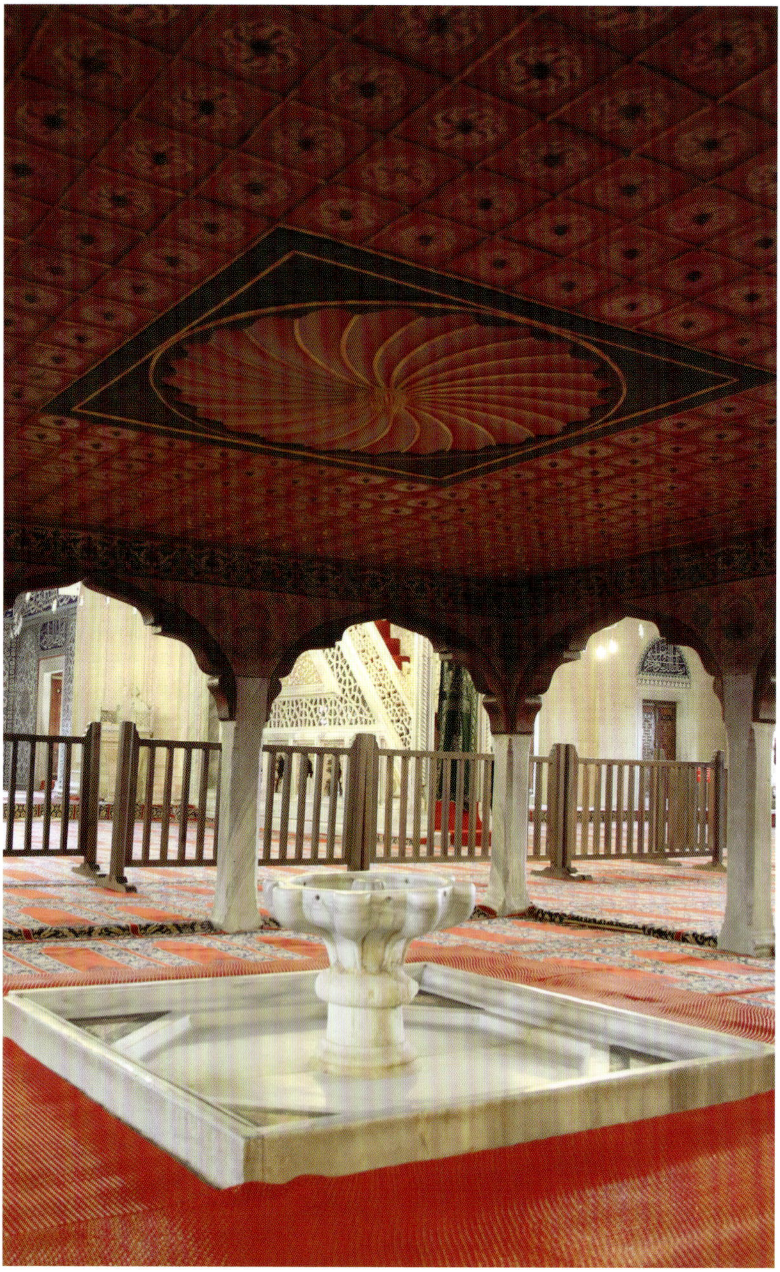

Figure 5.10: The wooden ceiling above the marble pool painted with a whirl motif, Selimiye Mosque, Edirne, 1575

Photograph by Metin Mustafa, December 12, 2014.

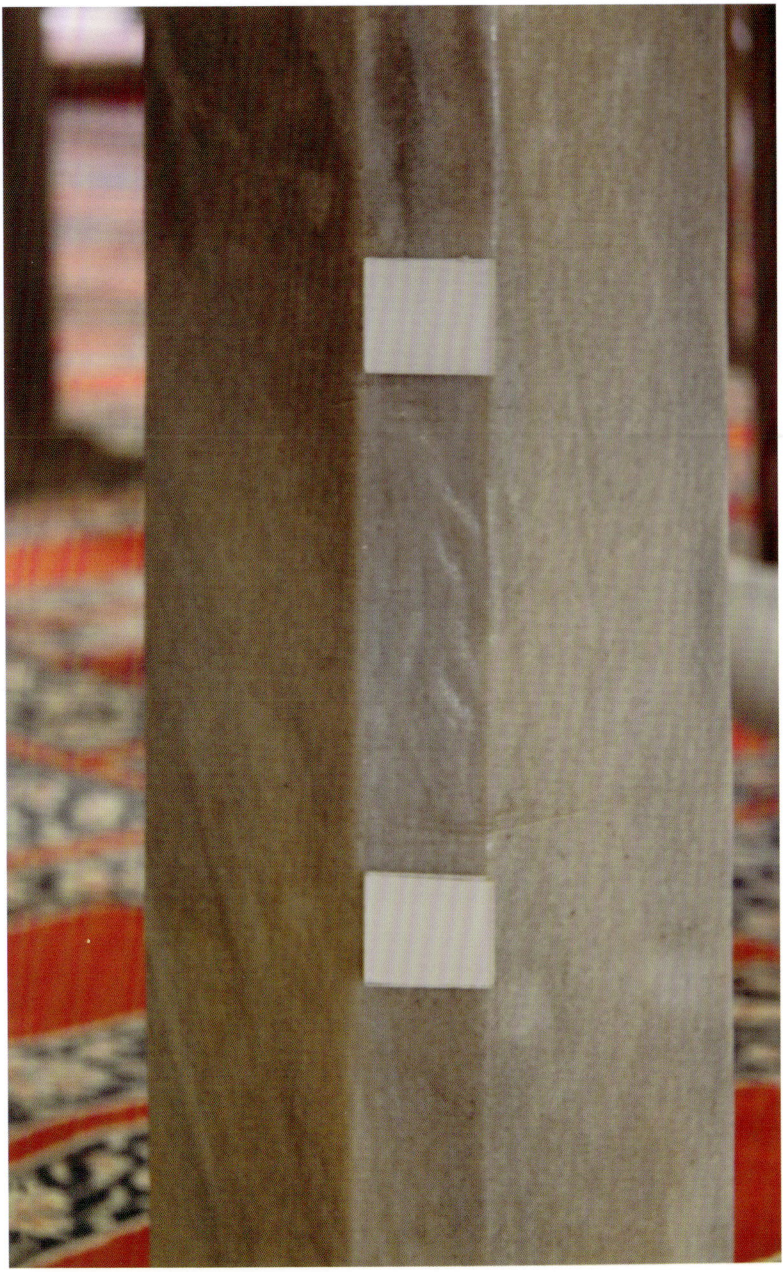

Figure 5.11: Detail of the northwest pillar of the muezzin's tribune showing Sinan's carving of an upside down tulip, Selimiye Mosque, 1575

Photograph by Metin Mustafa, December 12, 2014.

CHAPTER 6

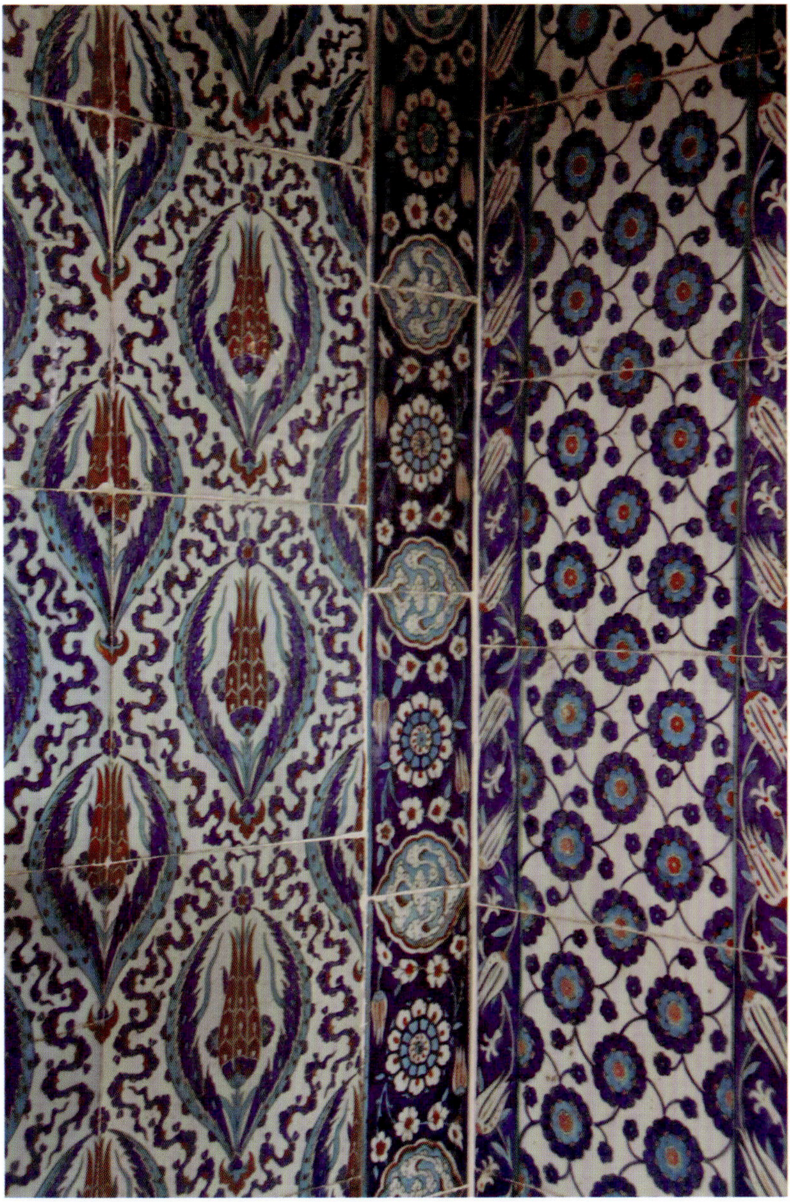

Figure 6.1: Detail of the stylised tulips and flowers, Rustem Pasha Mosque, Istanbul, c.1560-61

Photograph by Metin Mustafa, January 20, 2015.

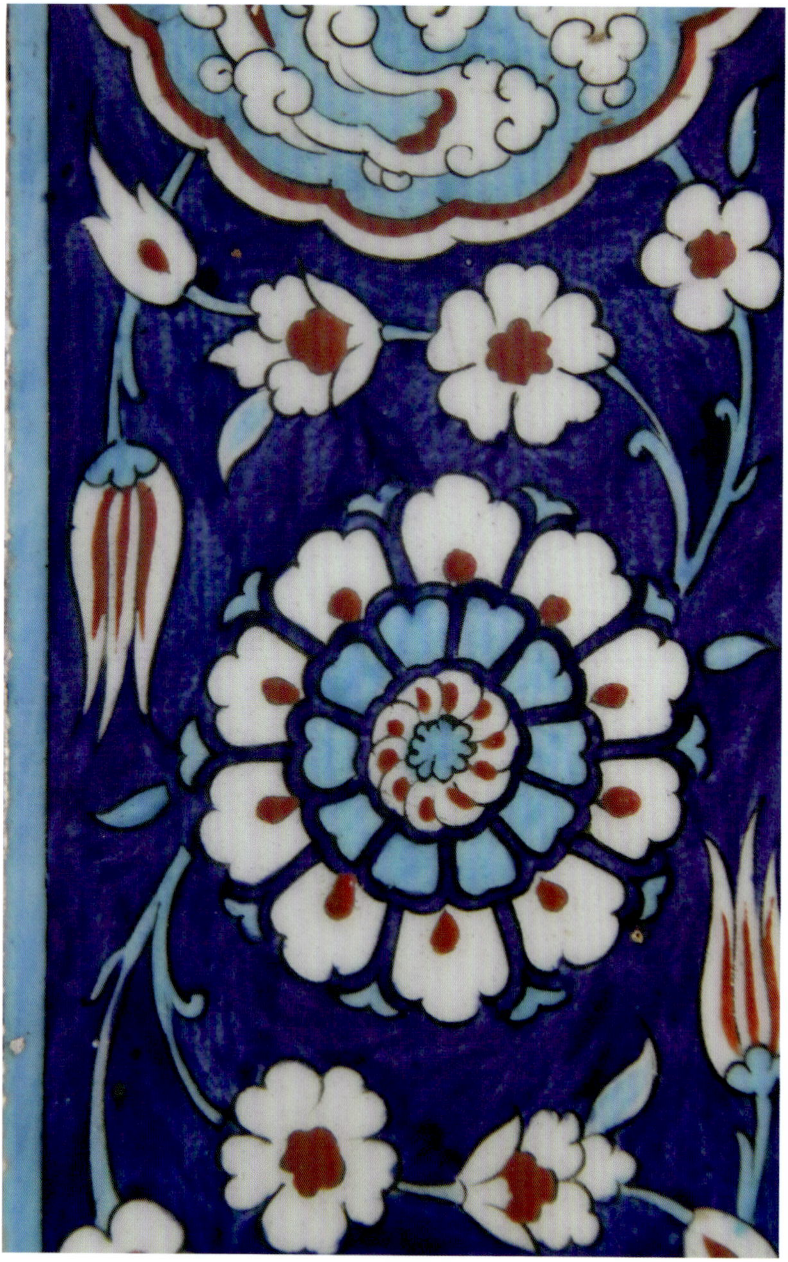

Figure 6.2: Detail of the stylised tulips and flowers, Rustem Pasha Mosque, Istanbul, c.1560-61

Photograph by Metin Mustafa, January 20, 2015.

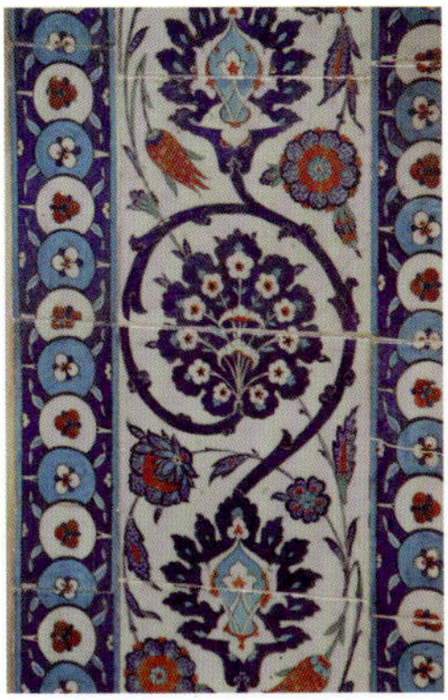

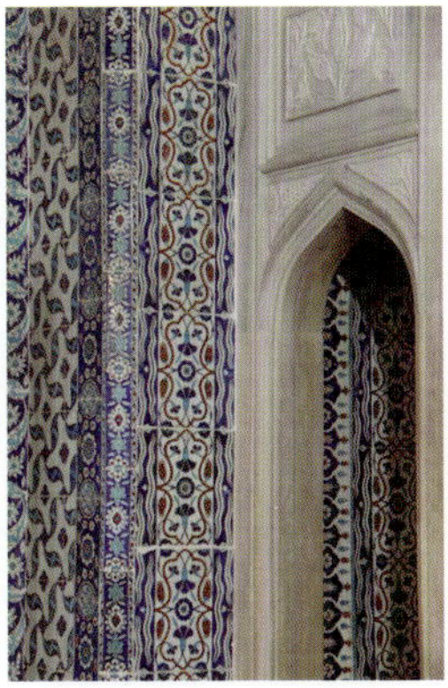

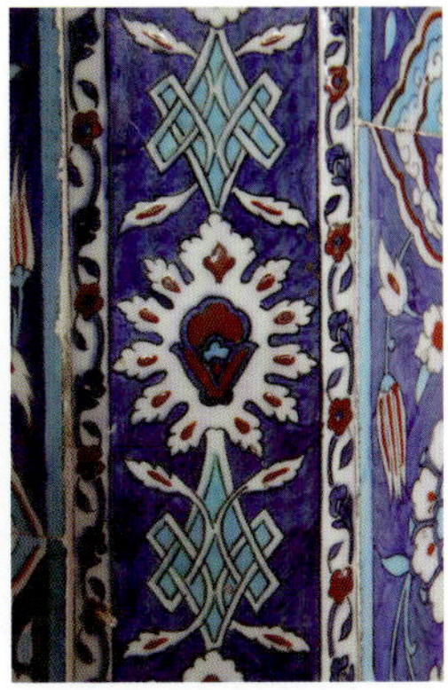

Figure 6.3, left: Tile details of the Rustem Pasha Mosque, Istanbul, c.1560-61. Together, the floral motifs signify the Islamic concept of zikr—the remembrance of God through prayer and contemplation, which often incorporates the use of prayer beads. In fact, the sheer number of flowers in the floral depictions symbolise the Qur'anic verse in 17:110, 'His are the most beautiful names', as well as the beauty and wonder of His creation on earth.'

Figure 6.4, centre: Tile details of the Rustem Pasha Mosque, Istanbul, c.1560-61

Figure 6.5, right: Tile details of the Rustem Pasha Mosque, Istanbul, c.1560-61

Photographs by Metin Mustafa, January 20, 2015.

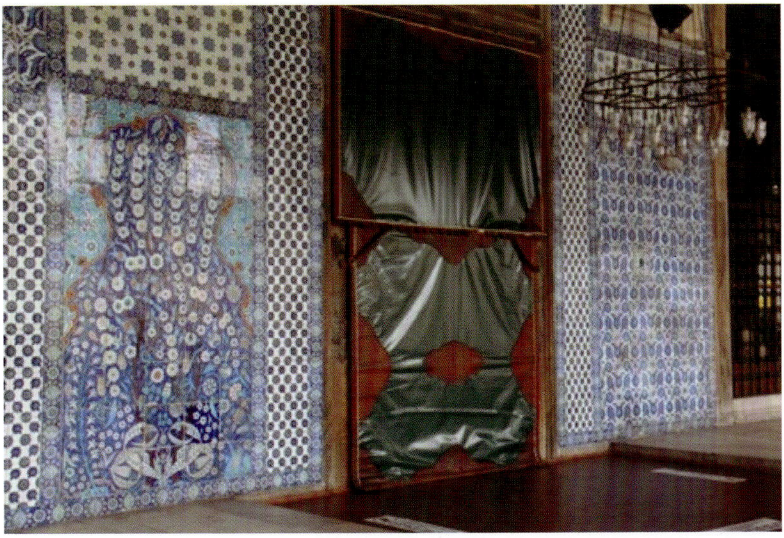

Figure 6.6: The tile panels on either side of the entrance of the Rustem Pasha Mosque, c.1560-61

Photograph by Metin Mustafa, January 20, 2015.

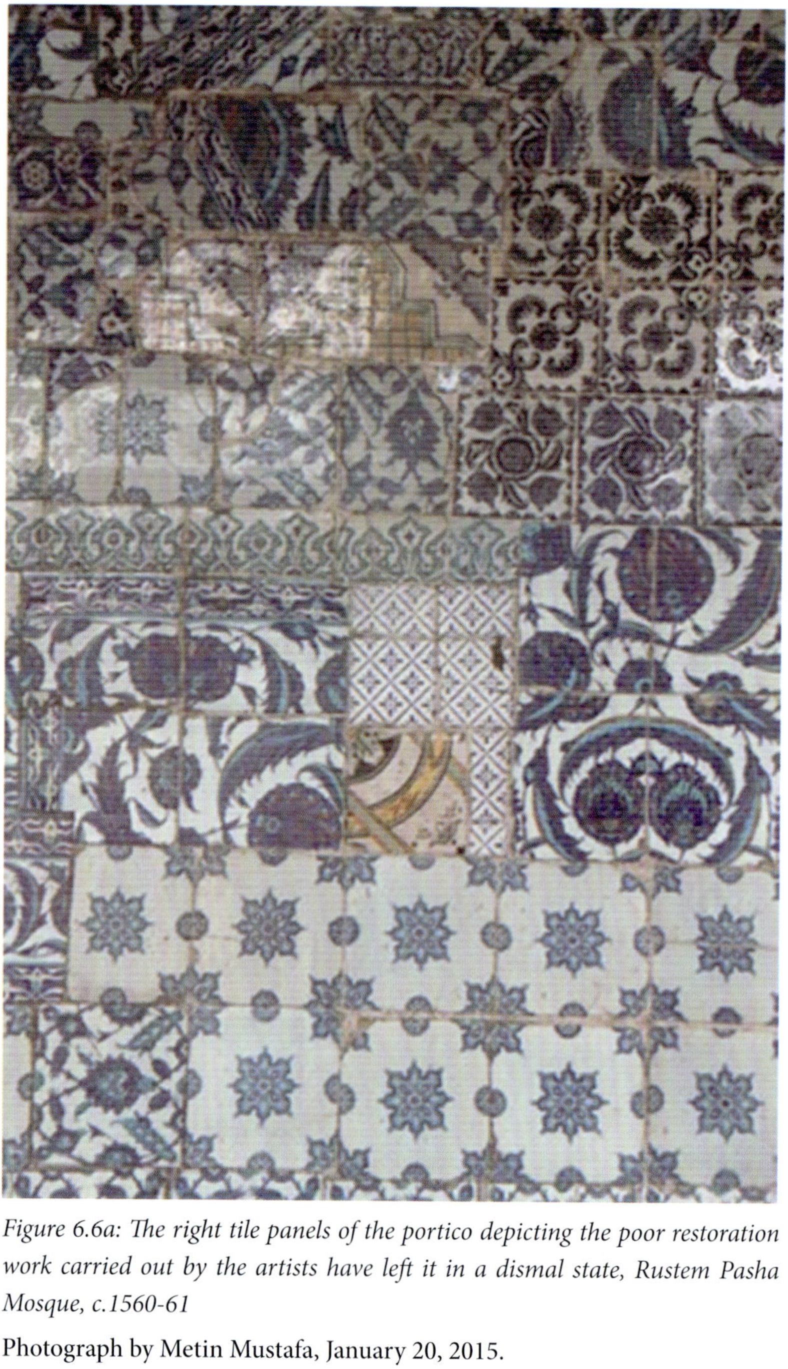

Figure 6.6a: The right tile panels of the portico depicting the poor restoration work carried out by the artists have left it in a dismal state, Rustem Pasha Mosque, c.1560-61

Photograph by Metin Mustafa, January 20, 2015.

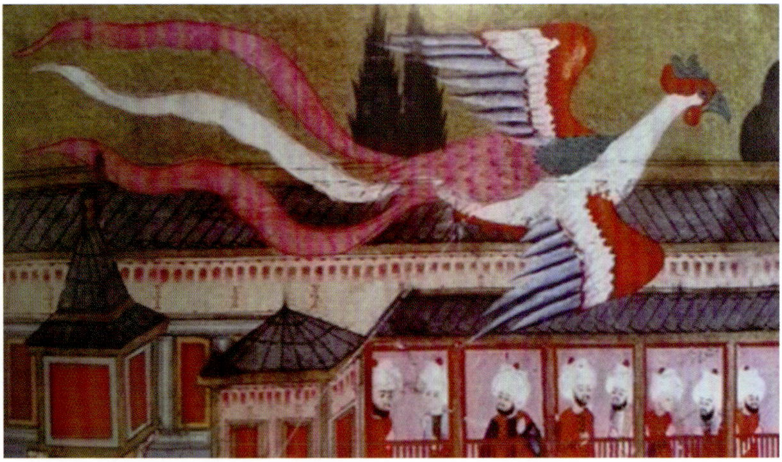

Figure 6.7: The simurg from Lokman's Surname-i Humayun 1582

Source: Seyyid Huseyin Lokman, "Sürname-i Hümayun," Topkapı Sarayı Kütüphanesi, H.1344, folio 281a.

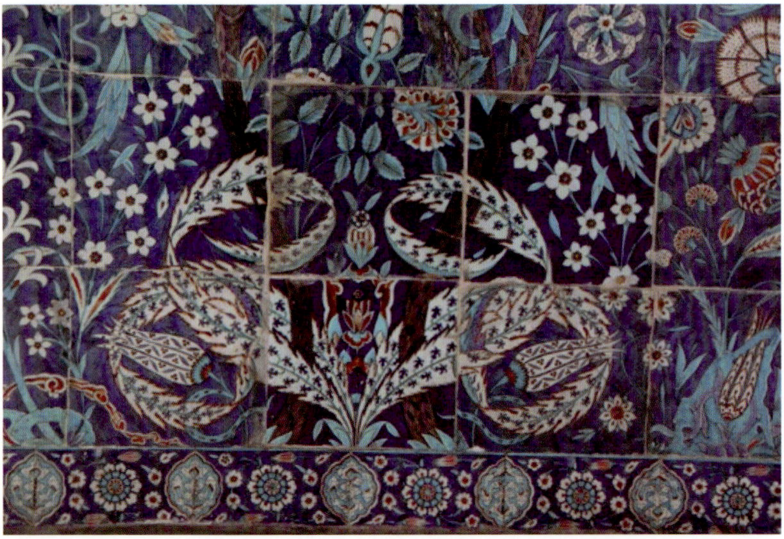

Figure 6.8: Detail of the left entrance panel of the Rustem Pasha Mosque, Istanbul, c.1560-61.

The manganese-purple can be seen in the bottom right panel surrounding the tulip. Due to its poor visibility from a distance the use of this colour was abandoned by the Iznik artists.

Photograph by Metin Mustafa, January 20, 2015.

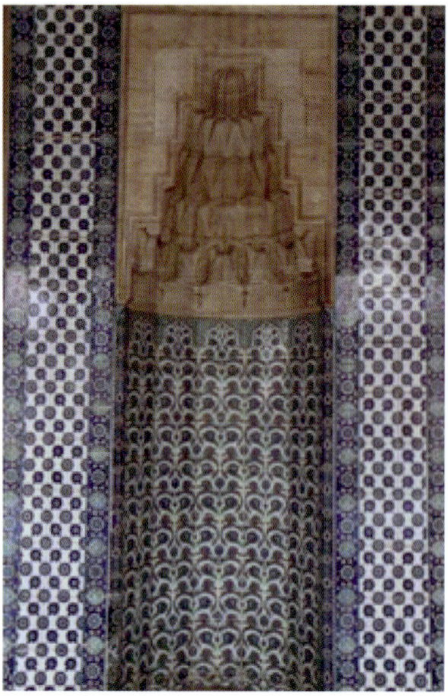

Figure 6.9, left: External mihrab, situated to the left floral panel of the entrance, Rustem Pasha Mosque, Istanbul, c.1560-61

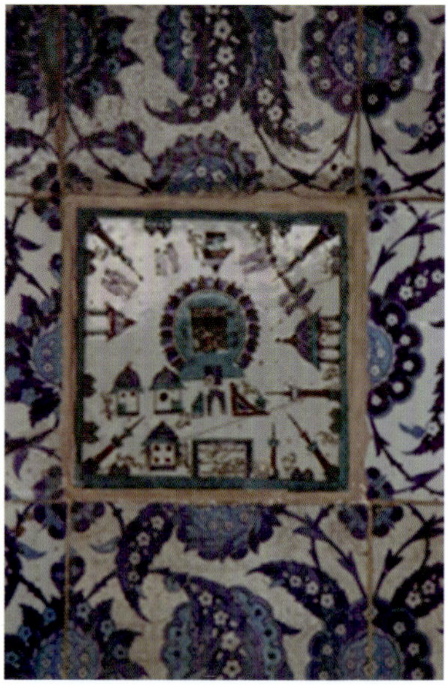

Figure 6.10, right: The Ka'ba tile inserted into a panel next to the mihrab niche, Rustem Pasha Mosque, Istanbul, c.1560-61

Photographs by Metin Mustafa, January 20, 2015.

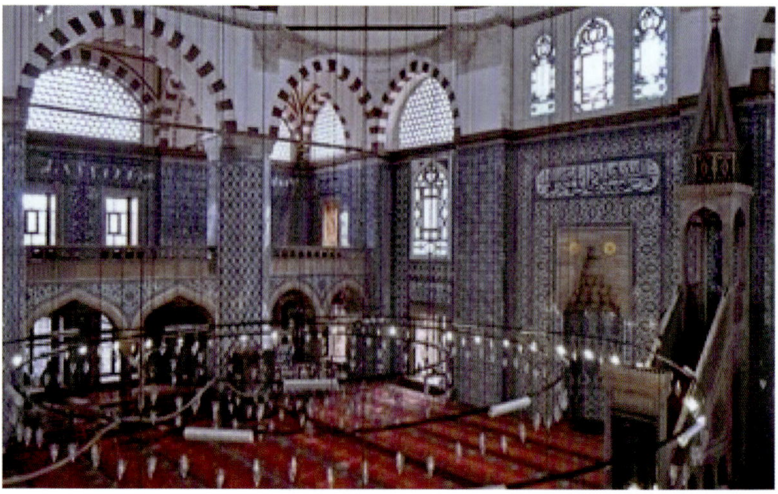

Figure 6.11: View of the qibla wall and the mihrab from the entrance of the Rustem Pasha Mosque, Istanbul, c.1560-61

Photograph by Metin Mustafa, January 20, 2015.

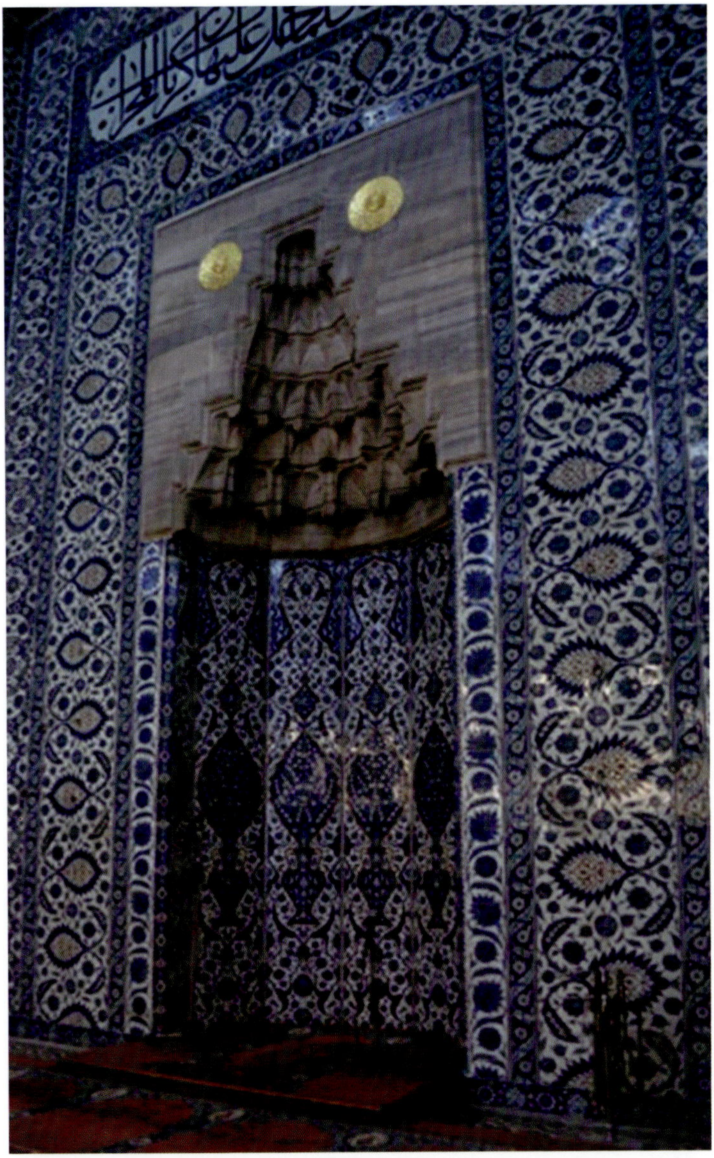

Figure 6.12: The mihrab on the qibla wall, interior of the Rustem Pasha Mosque, Istanbul, 1560-61.

The frame around the mihrab niche consists of tiles that use repeated designs. Some of these design patterns were never repeated in later Iznik tilework, such as the 'stippled' saz leaves that overlap and appear to move; dragon-like, as if blown by a strong wind.

Photograph by Metin Mustafa, January 20, 2015.

CHAPTER 7

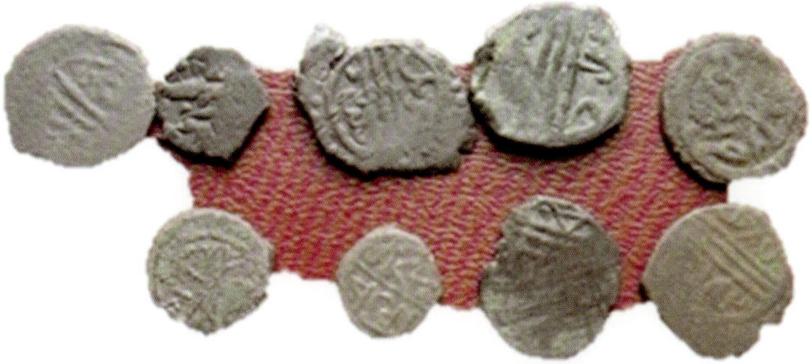

Figure 7.1a: Ottoman coins from Bajezid I to Mehmed II

Source: http://www.ancientresource.com/lots/islamic_arabic/ottoman_coins.html

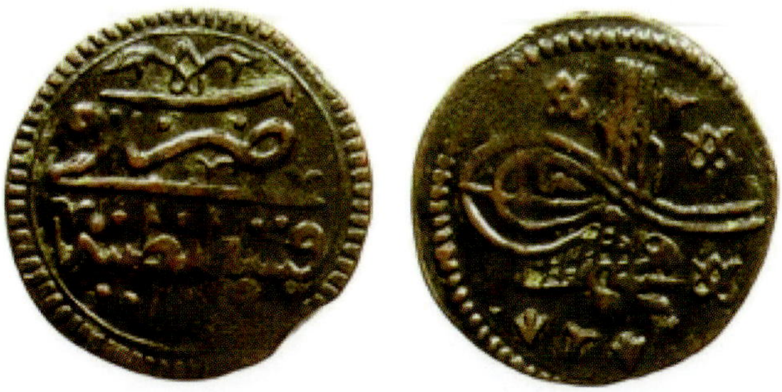

Figure 7.1b: Coins from the reign Sultan Süleyman with his tughra

Source: http://www.ancientresource.com/images/gold/islamic-gold/suleyman-gold-sultani-SA14370.jpg

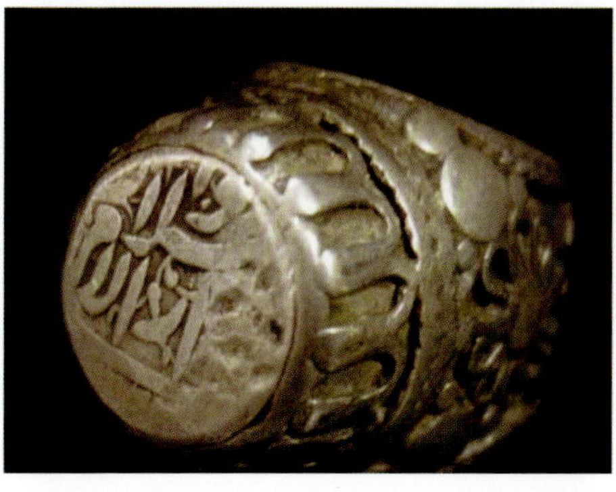

Figure 7.1c: Ottoman ring seal used between 14th to 17th centuries

Source: 'The Barakat Collection,' London. Photograph courtesy of H. Lower.

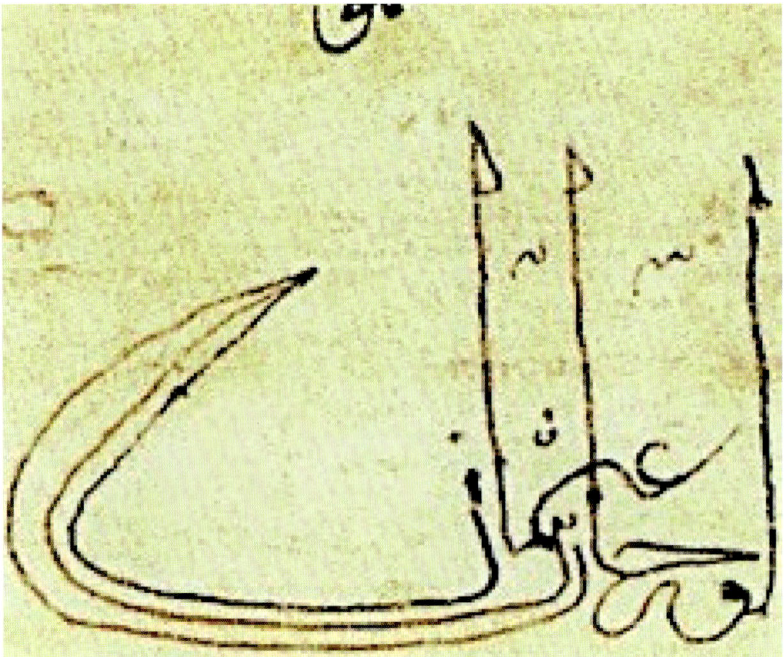

Figure 7.2: Tughra of Orhan Ghazi used in 1324, Orhan Ghazi Mosque, Bursa

Source: Photograph by Metin Mustafa.

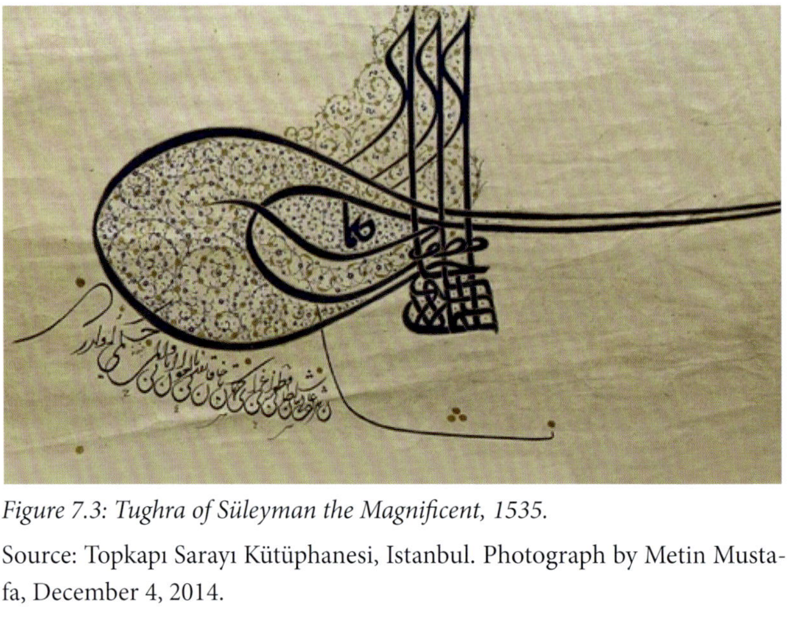

Figure 7.3: Tughra of Süleyman the Magnificent, 1535.

Source: Topkapı Sarayı Kütüphanesi, Istanbul. Photograph by Metin Mustafa, December 4, 2014.

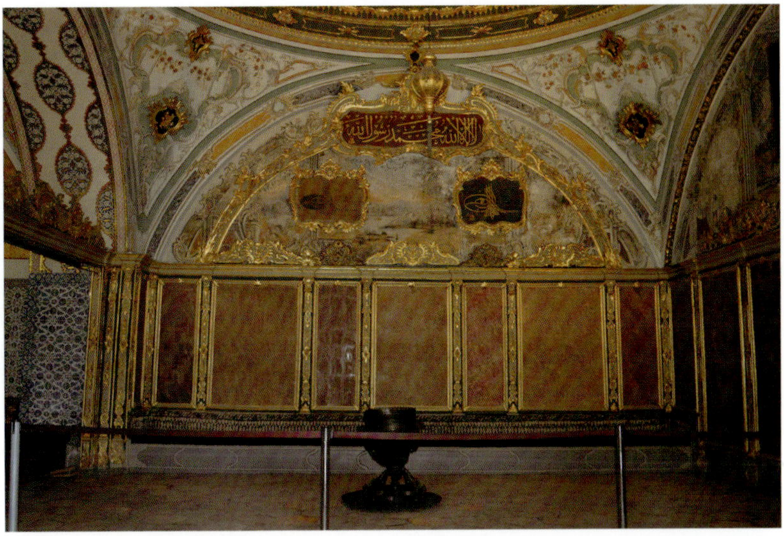

Figure 7.3a: At the entrance to the Divan Council room, Süleyman's tughra can be seen on the left, Topkapı Palace

Photograph by Metin Mustafa, December 4, 2014.

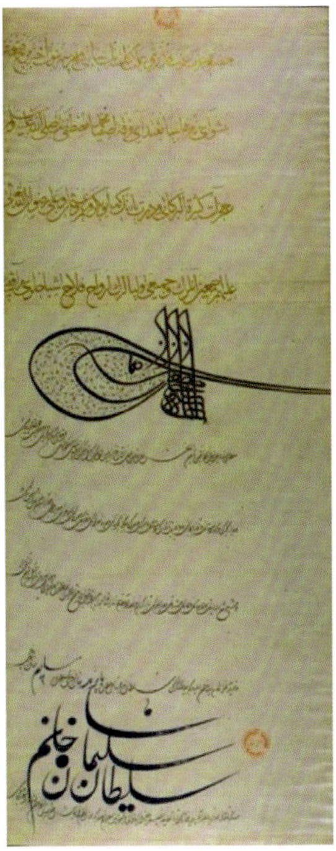

Figure 7.3b: A letter sent by Sultan Süleyman to King Francis I of France in 1536

Source: Photograph courtesy of N. Shield.

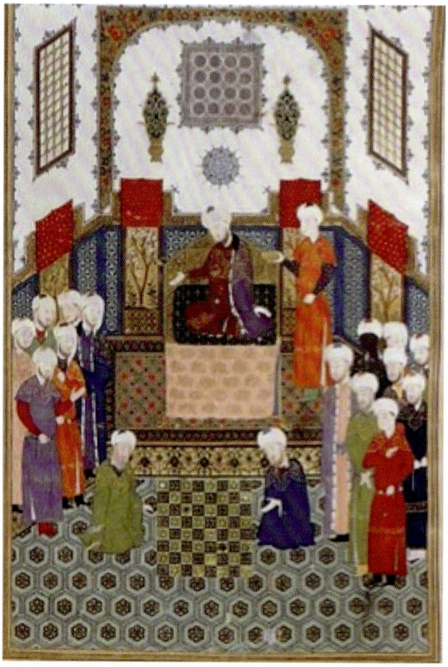

Figure 7.4: Courtiers of Bayasanghori playing chess

From the Bayasanghori Shahname — made in 1430 for Prince Bayasanghor (1399-1433), son of Shahrukh and the grandson of the legendary Central Asian leader Timur (1336-1405).

Source: Photograph reproduction of the miniature painting. http://portal.unesco.org/ci/photos/showgallery.php/cat/793

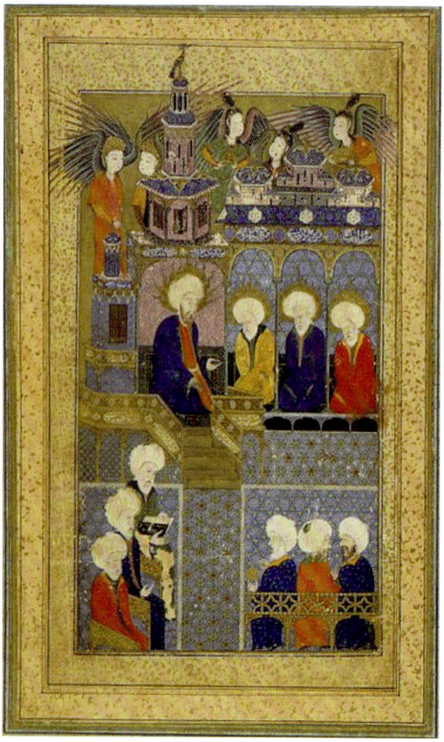

Figure 7.4a: 'Sultan Süleyman in the Guise of King Solomon.'

Page from a Manuscript of the Şahname-i al-i Osman (Royal Book of the House of Osman) of 'Arifi. Istanbul, Turkey, c.1558.

Source: The Nasli M. Heeramaneck Collection, gift of Joan Palevsky (M.73.5.446). Los Angeles County Museum. Photo © Museum Associates/ LACMA.

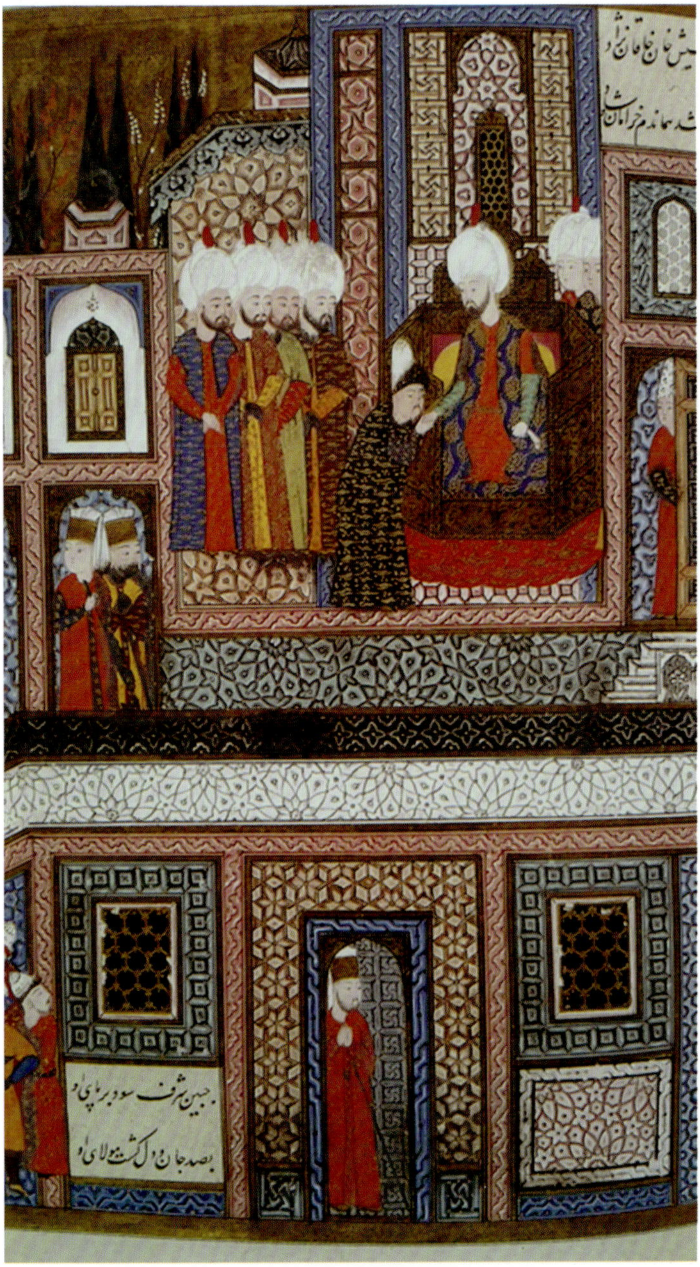

Figure 7.5: Reception of Devlet Giray Han

Source: *Süleymanname*, folio 519a, 1558, Topkapı Sarayı Kütüphanesi, H. 1517.

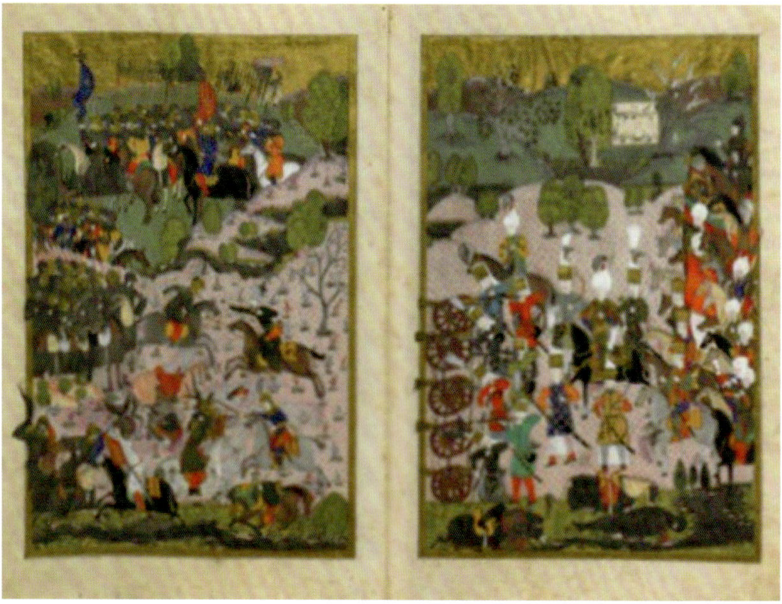

Figure 7.6: Battle of Mohacs

Right folio depicts the sultan's camp; left folio illustrates the battle scene.

Source: *Süleymanname*, Topkapı Sarayı Kütüphanesi, H. 517.

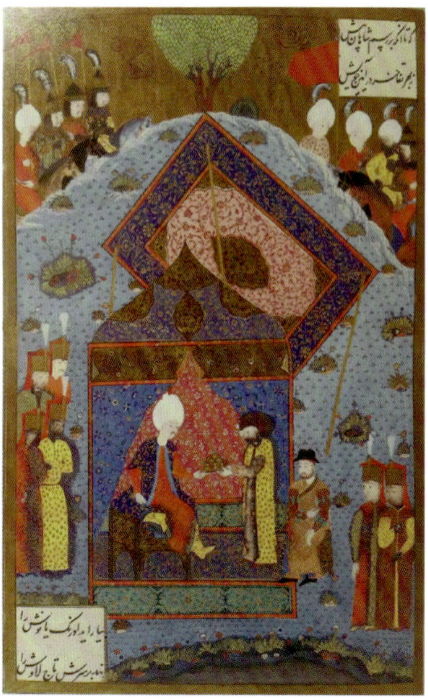

Figure 7.7: Süleyman receiving the Crown of Hungary

Zapolya is shown sitting on the right waiting to be re-crowned by Süleyman as the King of Hungary

Source: *Süleymanname*, folio 309a, 1558, Topkapı Sarayı Kütüphanesi, H. 1517.

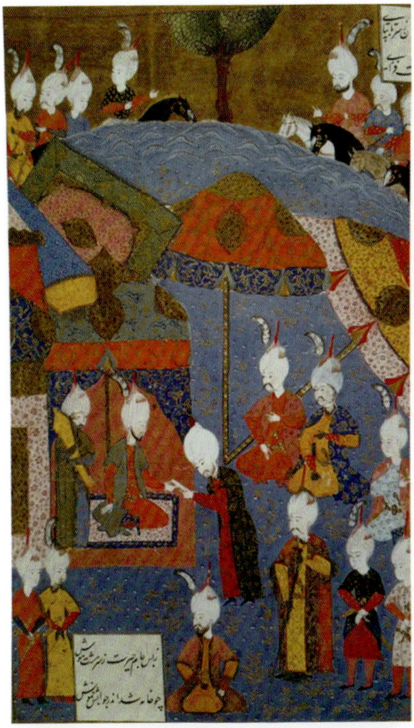

Figure 7.8: Shah Tahmasp of Iran receiving the Ottoman Ambassador

Source: *Süleymanname*, folio 550a, 1558, Topkapı Sarayı Kütüphanesi, H. 1517.

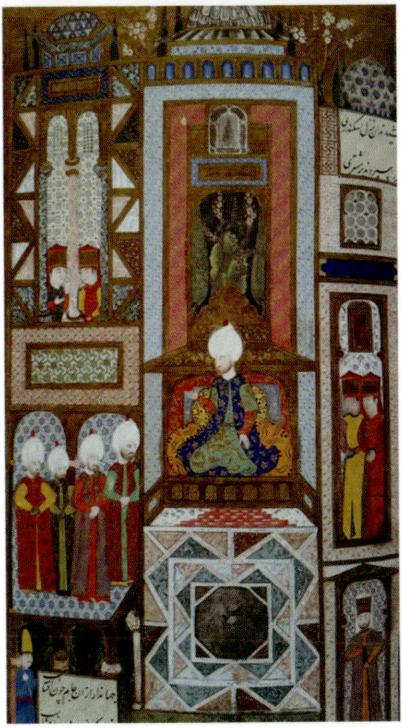

Figure 7.9: Süleyman Presented with the Ruby Cup

Source: *Süleymanname*, folio 557a, 1558, Topkapı Sarayı Kütüphanesi, H. 1517.

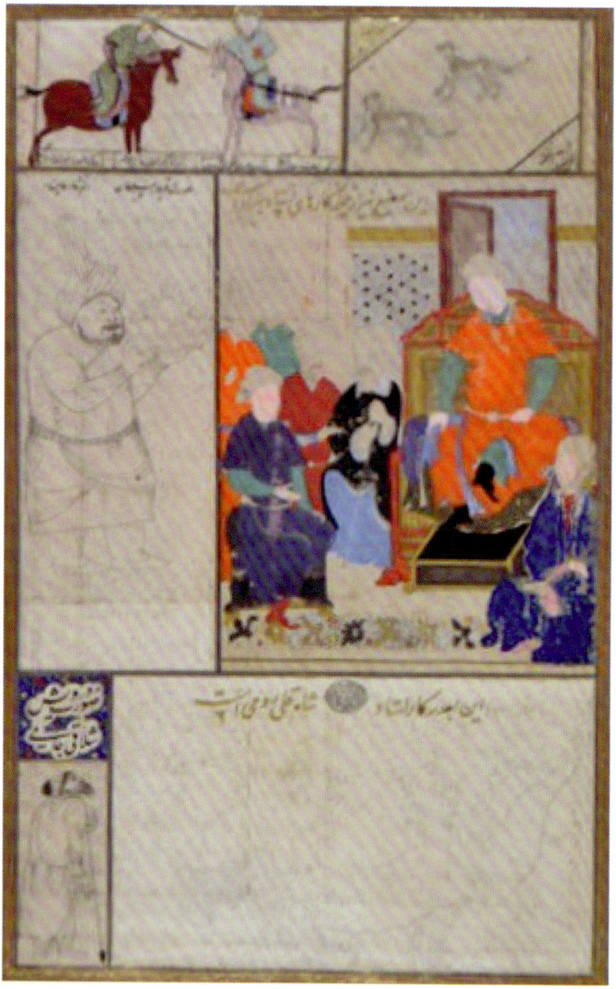

Figure 7.10: Composite page of paintings and drawings by various artists c.1490–1530

Figures in combat in top left; two cheetahs attributed to Shaykh Mahmud seen in top right; Qarpuz Sultan signed by Shah Tahmasp on the left; an enthronement attributed to Bihzad from Herat in the centre; the dervish Shallaqi Jami bottom left; and a dragon attributed to Şah Kulu Rumi seen in the faint drawing on the bottom carrying the artist's seal.

Source: Topkapı Sarayı Kütüphanesi, Istanbul, H.2154, fol.2a.

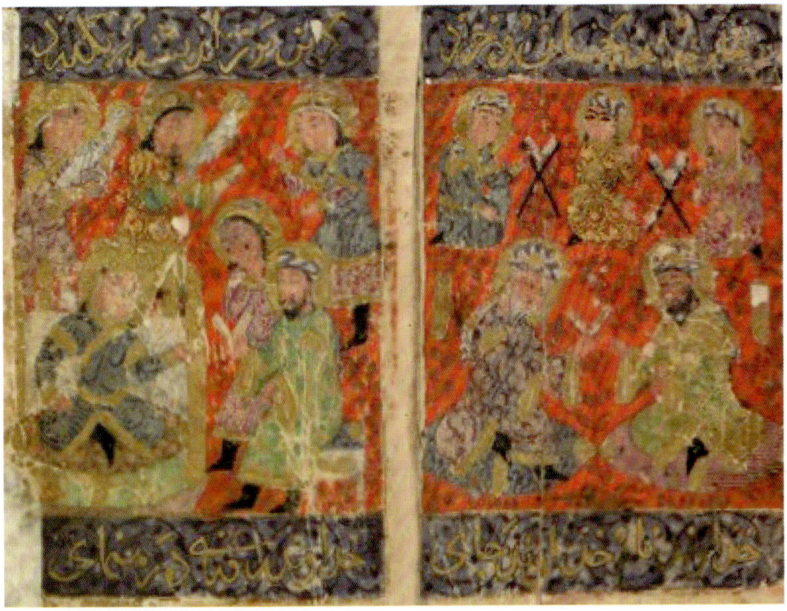

Figure 7.11: Frontpiece from Kalila wa Dimna, 13th century, possibly created in Baghdad

Source: Topkapı Sarayı Kütüphanesi, Istanbul, MH 363.

BIBLIOGRAPHY

Abisaab, Rula Jurdi. *Converting Persia: Religion and Power in the Safavid Empire.* New York: I. B. Tauris, 2004.

Abulafia, D. *The Great Sea: A Human History of the Mediterranean.* Oxford: New York, Oxford University Press, 2011.

Ahmed, Feridun bin. *Risale-i Sipehsalar.* Translated by Mithat Bahari Beytur. Istanbul: Eles, 2006.

Ahmed, S. Z. *The Zenith of an Empire: The Glory of the Suleiman the Magnificent and Lawgiver*. Connecticut: A.E.R. Publications, 2001.

Akın, Günkut. "The Muezzin Mahfili and Pool of the Selimiye Mosque in Edirne." *Muqarnas* 12 (1995): 63-83. DOI: 10.2307/1523224.

Akın, E. "Mustafa Ali's Epic Deeds of Artists: A Study on the earliest Ottoman text about the calligraphers and painters of the Islamic World." PhD diss., The Ohio State University, 2007. ProQuest (AAT 3268899).

Alberti, Leon Batista. *On the Art of Building in Ten Books.* Translated by Joseph Rykwert, Neil Leach, and Robert Tavernor. Cambridge, MA: The MIT Press, 1988.

Algar, Ayla Esen. *Architecture, Art and Sufism in Ottoman Turkey.* Berkeley: University of California Press, 1992.

Ali, Mustafa. *Epic Deeds of Artists.* Edited and translated by Esra Akın-Kivanç. Leiden: Brill, 2011.

And, Metin. *Turkish Miniature Painting: The Ottoman Period.* Istanbul: Dost Publications, 1987.

Arabshah, Ahmed Ibn. *Tamerlane or Timur the Great Amir.* Gujarat, India: Isha Books, 2013.

Arseven, C. E. *Türk Sanatı.* Istanbul: Türk Ocaklari Merkez Nesriyati, 1928.

Atasoy, Nurhan. *A Garden for the Sultan – Gardens and Flowers in the Ottoman Culture.* Istanbul: Kitap Yayınevi, 2011.

Atasoy, Nurhan and Julian Raby. *Iznik: The Pottery of Ottoman Turkey.* Edited by Yanni Petsopoulos. London: Thames and Hudson, 1989.

Atıl, Esin. "Ottoman Miniature Painting under Sultan Mehmed II." *Ars Orientalis* 5, no. 9 (1973): 103-20.

Atıl, Esin. *Süleymanname: The Illustrated History of Süleyman the Magnificent.* Washington, DC: National Gallery of Art, 1986.

Aykut, Nezihi. "Hasan-Beyzade Tarihi." PhD diss., Istanbul University, 1980.

Ayverdi, E. H. *Fatih Devri Mimari Eserleri.* Istanbul: publisher, 1953.

Avcı, Ismail. "Divan Şiirinde İskender-i Zülkarneyn" ("Alexander the Great in Divan Poetry"). *Uluslararası Sosyal Araştırmalar Dergisi* (*The Journal of International Social Research*) 29 (2014): 47-69. www.sosyalarastirmalar.com

Babinger, Franz. *Mehmed the Conqueror and His Time*. 2nd ed.Edited by W. C. Hickman. Translated R. Manheim. Princeton: Princeton University Press, 1992.

Bailey, John, Peri Bearman, Oleg Grabar, Gülru Necipoğlu and Andras Riedlmayer. *Muqarnas: An annual on the visual culture of Islamic world*. Cambridge, MA: Brill, 2007.

Bakhtin, M. M. *The Dialogic Imagination: Four Essays*. Edited by Michael Holquist. Translated by Caryl Emerson and Michael Holquist. Austin: University of Texas Press, 1981.

Ball, Warwick. *Sultans of Rome: The Turkish World Expansion*. Northampton, MA: Olive Branch Press, 2013.

Baron, Hans. *The Crisis of the Early Italian Renaissance*. Princeton: Princeton University Press, 1966.

Barrie, Thomas. *The Sacred In-Between: The Mediating Roles of Architecture*. New York: Routledge, 2010.

Başbakanlık Arşivi. Muhimme Defteri 10, no. 391, 253, 19B. 979. Istanbul.

Basbakanlik Arşivi. Muhimme Defteri 22, no. 171. *On Altıncı*, 18 (1935): 22-24. Istanbul.

Başbakanlık Arşivi. Muhimme Defteri 58, no. 779:306. Istanbul.

Belozerskaya, Marina. *Rethinking the Renaissance: Burgundian Arts Across Europe*. Cambridge: Cambridge University Press, 2002.

Berrall, Julia S. *The Garden*. London: Thames and Hudson, 1966.

Beuchat, Robin. "**Échange interculturel et transfert de representations** Sur les portraits turcs de Paolo Giovio" ("Intercultural exchange and transfer of representations of Turkish portraits of Paolo Giovio"). Université de Genève,' Arborescences: revue d'études françaises, n° 2, 2012. http://www.erudit.org/apropos/utilisation.html

Bisaha, Nancy. *Creating East and West: Renaissance Humanists and the Ottoman Turks*. Philadelphia: University of Pennsylvania Press, 2006.

Blessing, Patricia. "Seljuk Past and Timurid Present: Tile Decoration of the

Yeşil Külliye in Bursa," *Gesta* 56, no. 2 (2017): 225-50. https://doi.org/10.1086/692804

Bosnavî Suûdi. *Hafiz Serhi*. Vol. 1. Istanbul: Matbaa-yı Âmire, 1288 [1877].

Bosworth, C. E. J. Deny and M. J. Siddiq. "Tughra." In *The Encyclopedia of Islam*, vol. X, edited by P. J. Bearman, T. Bianquis, C. E. Bosqorth, E. van Donzel and W. P. Heinrichs. Leiden: Brill (2000): 595-98. http://www.tugra.org/en/hakkinda.asp

Brewster, David P. "The Study of Sufism: Towards a methodology." http://doi.org/10.1016/0048-721X(76)90047-6

Broomhall, Marshall. *Islam in China: A Neglected Problem*. London: Morgan & Scott Ltd., 1910.

Brotton, Jerry. *The Renaissance: A Very Short Introduction*. New York: Oxford University Press, 2006.

Brotton, Jerry. *The Renaissance Bazaar: From the Silk Road to Michelangelo*. New York: Oxford University Press, 2002. Kindle.

Bruschi, Arnaldo H. "Religious Architecture in Renaissance Italy from Brunelleschi to Michelangelo." In *The Renaissance from Brunelleschi to Michelangelo*, edited by Henry Millon and V. Lampugnani, 123-81. Rizzoli, Milan: 1997.

Burioni, Matteo. "Vasari's Rinascita: History, Anthropology or Art Criticism." In *Renaissance Perceptions of Continuity and Discontinuity in Europe, ca. 1300-1550*, edited by H. Schnitker, P. Péporte, and A. C. Lee, 115-127. Leiden: Brill, 2008.

Burckhardt, Titus. *Art of Islam: Language and Meaning*. Indiana: World Wisdom Inc., 2009.

Burke, Peter. *The Italian Renaissance: Culture and Society in Italy*. Princeton: Princeton University Press, 2014.

Can, Şefik. *Fundamentals of Rumi's Thought: A Mevlevi Sufi Perspective*. Clifton, NJ: Tughra Books, 2009.

Canby, Sheila R. *The Shahnama of Shah Tahmasp: The Persian Book of Kings*. New York: The Metropolitan Museum of Art, 2014.

Cantay, Tanju. "XVI. Yuzyil Turk mimarisinde bazi tasarim ve cizim esaslari." In *II. Uluslararasi Turk ve Islam Bilim ve Teknoloji Tarihi Kongresi Bildirileri*, vol. 2. Istanbul: Istanbul Teknik Universitesi Yayini, 1986.

Casale, Giancarlo. "Yüzyila Ait Türkçe Dünya Haritasinda Avrupa Düsüncesi." Translated by Sirin Tekeli. In *Harp Ve Sulh: Avrupa Ve Osmanlilar*, edited by Dejanirah Couto, 57-82. Istanbul: Kitap Yayinev, 2010.

Casale, Giancarlo. "Seeing the Past: Maps and Ottoman Historical Consciousness." In *Writing History at the Ottoman Court: Editing the Past, Fashioning the Future*, edited by Erdem H. Cipa and Emine Fetvaci. Indianapolis: Indiana University Press, 2013. Kindle.

Casale, Giancarlo. *The Ottoman Age of Exploration*. New York: Oxford University Press, 2010.

Çelebi, Celâlzâde Mustafa. *Tabakatü'l- Memâlik ve Derecâtü'l- Mesâlik* (*Kanunî'nin Tarihçisinden Muhteşem Çağ*). Edited by Ayhan Yılmaz. Istanbul: Kariyer Yayınları, 2011.

Çelebi, Evliya. *An Ottoman Traveller: Selections from the Book of Travels by Evliya Celebi*. Translated by Robert Dankoff and Sooyong Kim. London: Eland Publishing, 2011.

Çelebi, Evliya. *Seyahatname*. 10 vols. Istanbul: Ikdam Matbaası, 1896-1930.

Cimok, Fatih. The *Book of Rustem Pasha Tiles*. Istanbul: A Turizm Yayinlari, 2001.

Clark, Emma. *The Art of the Islamic Garden.* Wiltshire, UK: Crowood Press, 2011.

Clark, Emma. "The Symbolism of the Islamic Garden." Islamic Arts &

Architecture. Design, October 2, 2011. http://islamic-arts.org/2011/the-symbolism-of-the-islamic-garden/

Clot, André. *Suleiman the Magnificent.* London: Saqi, 2005.

Clouston, W. A. *On the Magical Elements in Chaucer's Squire's Tale.* London: Chaucer Society, 1888-90.

Contadini, Anna, and Claire Norton, eds. *The Renaissance and the Ottoman World.* Farnham: Ashgate Publishing Limited, 2013.

'Contemplation, Constructed Space, and Senses.' YouTube Video. Lecture by Phoebe Crisman with an introduction by Kim Tanzer, April 6, 2013, posted by University of Virginia Contemplative Sciences Center, August 19, 2013. Accessed May 5, 2015, http://www.youtube.com/watch?v=6FASJrighYE

Coomaraswamy, Ananda. "Notes on the Philosophy of Persian art." *Ars Islamica* 15/16 (1951): 125-8.

Corbin, Henry. *Alone with the* Alone: *Creative Imagination in the Sufism of Ibn Arabi.* Translated by Ralph Manheim. Princeton: Princeton University Press, 1998.

Corbin, Henry. *Spiritual Body and Celestial Earth: From Mazdean Iran to Shi'ite Iran.* Translated by Nancy Pearson. Princeton: Princeton University Press, 1977.

Corbin, Henry. *The Man of Light in Iranian Sufism.* Translated by Nancy Pearson. New York: Omega Publications, 1994.

Cunningham, Lawrence S., John J. Reich, and Lois Fichner-Rathus. *Culture and Values: A Survey of the Humanities, Volume II.* Boston: Clark Baxter, 2010.

Çağaptay, Suna. "Prousa/Bursa, a city within the city: chorography,

conversion and choreography." Academia.edu, February 9, 2018. https://cambridge.academia.edu/SunaCagaptay

Damalı, Atom. *History of Ottoman coins = Osmanlı sikkeleri tarihi: Volume 1.* Istanbul: Nilufer Damalı Eğitim, 2010.

Darling, L. "The Renaissance and the Middle East." In *A Companion to the Worlds of the Renaissance,* edited by G. Ruggiero, 55-69. Malden, MA: Blackwell Publishing, 2007.

Davies, J. G. *Temples, Churches and Mosques.* Oxford: Basil Blackwell, 1982.

Denny, Walter B. *The Ceramics of the Mosque of Rustem Pasha and the Environment of Change.* New York: Garland, 1977.

Denny, Walter B. *Iznik: The Artistry of Ottoman Ceramics.* London: Thames and Hudson, 2010.

Dickie, James. "The Iconography of the Prayer Rug." *Oriental Art* 18 (1972): 41-49.

Duggan, T. M. P. "The Çinili Köşk." http://www.hurriyetdailynews.com/the-cinili-kosk-or-ampquotkasr-i-kashiampquot----the-tiled-topkapi-royal-palace-pavilion.aspx?pageID=438&n=the-cinili-kosk-or-quotkasr-i-kashiquot----the-tiled-topkapi-royal-palace-pavilion-2003-02-23

Ekinci, Öznur Üzgün-İbrahim. "Newroz Piroz Boe." *Rengin Öğrenci Kültür Sanat ve Düsün Dergisi* 5 (2001): 10.

Ergin, Nina. "The Soundscape of Sixteenth-Century Istanbul Mosques: Architecture and Qur'an Recital." *Journal of the Society of Architectural Historians* 67, no. 2 (2008): 204-21. doi: 10.1525/jsah.2008.67.2.204.

Eryılmaz, Fatma Sinem. "From Adam to Süleyman: Visual Representations of Authority in Arifi's Shahnama-yi Al-i 'Osman." In *Writing History at the Ottoman Court: Editing the Past, Fashioning the Future*, edited by H. Erdem and Emine Fetvaci, 100-25. Indiana: Indiana University Press, 2013.

Erzen, Jale Nejdet. "Reading Mosques: Meaning and Architecture in Islam." *The Journal of Aesthetics and Art Criticism* 69, no. 1 (2011): 125-31. http://jstor.org/stable/42635843.

Esin, Emel. "Influences de l'art nomade et de l'architecture de Turkistan." In *1st I.C.T.A.*, Ankara, 1961.

Esin, Emel. *Türklerde Maddi Kültürün Oluşumu*. Istanbul: Kabalcı Yayınları, 1971.

Etlin, Richard. "Aesthetic and the Spatial Sense of Self." *Journal of Aesthetics and Art Criticism* 56, no. 1 (1998): 1-19. http://www.jstor.org/stable/431943.

Fatih Mehmet II Vakfiyeleri, "Türkçe Vakıf Vesikası." Ankara: Vakıflar Umum Müdürlüğü, 1938.

Ferdowsi, Abdelqasem. *Shahnameh: The Persian Book of Kings*. Translated by Dick Davis. New York: Mage Publishers, 2006. Kindle.

Fergusson, James. *The Illustrated History of Architecture*. 2 vols. London: John Murray, 1855.

Finocchio, Ross. "Mannerism: Bronzino (1503–1572) and his Contemporaries." In *Heilbrunn Timeline of Art History*. New York: The Metropolitan Museum of Art, October 2003. http://www.metmuseum.org/toah/hd/zino/hd_zino.htm.

Fleischer, C. H. *Bureaucrat and Intellectual in the Ottoman Empire: The Historian Mustafa Ali, 1541-1600*. Princeton: Princeton University Press, 1986.

Fletcher, Banister. *A History of Architecture on the Comparative Method*. London: BT Batsford, 1924.

Freely, John. *The Grand Turk: Sultan Mehmed II – Conqueror of Constantinople and Master of an Empire*. New York: The Overlook Press, 2009.

Frembgen, Jurgen Wasim. "Calligraphy from Ottoman Dervish Lodges." In *Art*. Islamic Art and Architecture, September 5, 2013. http://islamic-arts.org/2013/calligraphy-from-ottoman-dervish-lodges/.

Froissart, Jean. *Collection des chroniques nationales françaises: Chroniques de Froissart*. Edited by J. A. Buchon. 14 vols. Paris: 1824–26).

"The Genuine Article with Gordon Elliot: IZNIK TILES: Art Renaissance after 300 hundred years." YouTube Video. Produced by Gordon Elliot, posted by Pablo Gandulfo for the Iznik Foundation, March 15, 2012. http://www.youtube.com/watch?v=CU6rvX3UHvY.

Glencross, Andrew. "Historical Consciousness in International Relations Theory: A Hidden Disciplinary Dialogue." Paper prepared for the Millennium Conference, Aberdeen, Scotland, October, 2010. https://millenniumjournal.files.wordpress.com/2010/09/glencross-andrew-historical-consciousness-in-ir-theory-a-hidden-disciplinary-dialogue.pdf.

Glück, Heinrich. *Türkische Kunst.* Budapest and Istanbul: Instituts in Konstantinopel, 1917.

Golombek, Lisa and Donald Silber. *The Architecture of Iran and Turan.* 2 vols. Princeton: Princeton University Press, 1988.

Golombek, Lisa. "The Draped Universe of Islam." In *Content and Context of Visual Arts in Islam*, edited by Priscilla P. Soucek, 25-38. University Park, PA: The Pennsylvania State University Press, 1988. https://s3.amazonaws.com/files.digication.com/M05f7bff842e90d2d36e67917cdac3d50

Golombek, Lisa and Donald Wilber. *The Timurid Architecture of Iran and Turan.* Princeton: Princeton University Press, 1988.

Golombek, Lisa and Maria Subtelny, eds. *Timurid Art and Culture: Iran and Central Asia in the Fifteenth Century*. Leiden: Brill, 1992.

Gombrich E. H. "The Renaissance Conception of Artistic Progress and its Consequences." In *Norm and Form: Studies in the Art of the Renaissance,* 1-10. London: Phaidon Press, 1966.

Goodwin, G. *A History of Ottoman Architecture.* London: Thames and Hudson, 1971.

Goody, Jack. *Renaissances: The One or the Many?* New York: Cambridge University Press, 2010.

Grabar, Oleg. *The Dome of the Rock.* Cambridge, MA: Harvard University Press, 2006.

Grabar, Oleg. "An Exhibition of High Ottoman Art." *Muqarnas* 6 (1989): 1-11. http://www.jstor.org/discover/10.2307/1602275?uid=2134&uid=369538981&uid=2&uid=70&uid=3&uid=369538971&uid=60&sid=21101985671661.

Grabar, Oleg. *The Formation of Islamic Art.* New Haven, CT: Yale University Press, 1973.

Greenblatt, Stephen. *Renaissance Self-Fashioning: From More to Shakespeare.* Chicago: University of Chicago Press, 1980.

Grossman, Heather E. and Alicia Walker, eds. *Mechanisms of Exchange: Transmission in Medieval Art and Architecture of the Mediterranean, ca. 1000-1500.* Leiden: Brill, 2013.

Grousset, Rene. *The Empire of the Steppes: A History of Central Asia.* New Brunswick, NJ: Rutgers University Press, 1970.

Grupico, Theresa. "The Dome in Christian and Islamic Sacred Architecture." *The Forum on Public Policy* 3 (2011): 1-14. http://forumonpublicpolicy.com/vol-2011no3/archive/grupico.pdf

Güler, Zülfi. "Symbols of Anka and Simurg in Sheikh Galib's Diwan." *International Journal of Language Academy* 2/1 (2014): 63-72.

Güler, Zülfi. "Şehy Galib'in Divanı'nda Ayna Sembolü." *Firat Üniversitesi Sosyal Bilimler Dergisi* 14 (1): 2-20.

Gurlitt, Cornelius. *Istanbul'un Mimari Sanatı, Architecture of Constantinople, Die Baukunst Konstantinopels*. Translated by Rezan Kızıltan. Ankara: Enformasyon ve Dokumantasyon Hizmetleri Vakfı, 1999.

Hale, John. *The Civilization of Europe in the Renaissance*. London: Harper Collins Publishers, 1993.

Halman Talat S. *Rapture and Revolution: Essays on Turkish Literature*. Syracuse, NY: Syracuse University Press, 2007.

Halman, Talat S. *Süleyman the Magnificent Poet*. Istanbul: Reyo Ofset, 1987.

Halman, Talat S., ed. *Yunus Emre and His Mystical Poetry*. Indianapolis: Indiana University Press, 1983.

Heilmeyer, Marina. *The Language of Flowers: Symbols and Myths*. Munich: Prestel Publishing, 2006.

Hellemo, Geir Tryggve. "Ottoman Sensoriness: Nature as a Source of Religious Cognition in Istanbul in the Mid-Sixteenth Century." In *Transcendence and Sensoriness: Perceptions, Revelation and the Arts (Studies in Religion and the Arts),* edited by Svein Aage Christoffersen and Geir Tryggve Hellemo. Translated by Frances E. Hopenwasser and Leif Stubbe Teglbjaerg, 131-95. Leiden: Brill, 2015.

Hillenbrand, R. "The Use of Space in Timurid Painting." In *Timurid Art and Culture: Iran and Central Asia in the Fifteenth Century*, edited by Lisa Golombek and Maria Subtelny, 92-95. Leiden: Brill, 1992.

Horata, Osman. "Mevlāna ve Divan Şairleri." Hacettepe Üniversitesi Edebiyat Fakültesi Dergisi (2008): 47-48. http://akademik.semazen.net/article_detail.php?id=417

Horne, Charles F. *Sacred Books and Early Literature of the East: Medieval Arabic, Moorish, and Turkish Vol. VI*. New York: Kessinger Publishing, LLC, 1997.

Howard, Deborah. *Venice and the East, The Impact of the Islamic World in Venetian Architecture 1100-1500*. New Haven, CT: Yale University Press, 2000.

Howard, Deborah. "Venice between East and West: Marc'antonio Barbaro and Palladio's Church of the Redentore." *The Journal of the Society of Architectural Historians* 62, no. 3 (2003): 306-25.

Inalcık, Halil. "The place of Ottoman-Turkish Empire in History." *Cultura Turcica*, Ankara: 1964.

Iznik Foundation. "Iznik Vakıf Çinileri." Accessed November 5, 2016. http://www.iznik.com/about-the-iznik-foundation

Jardine, Lisa. *Worldly Goods: A New History of the Renaissance*. New York: W. W. Norton & Company, Inc., 1996.

Jardine, Lisa and Jerry Brotton. *Global Interests: Renaissance Art between East and West*. London: Reaktion Books, 2000.

Juten, Oda. *"Toruko-Minzoku-to-Isuramu"-ni- Kansuru- Kyoudou-Kenkyu Houkokusho* (Report of joint research on "Turk and Islam"). Tokyo: Tokyo-Gaikokugo-University, 1974.

Kafesçioğlu, Çiğdem. "Representing the City: Constantinople and its Images." In *Constantinopolis/Istanbul: Cultural Encounter, Imperial Vision, and the Construction of the Ottoman Capital*, edited by Çiğdem Kafesçioğlu, 143-177. University Park, PA: The Pennsylvania State University Press, 2009.

Kangal, Selmin, ed. *The Sultan's Portrait: Picturing the House of Osman*. Translated by Priscilla Mary Işın. Istanbul: İşBank, 2000.

Kastritsis, Dimitris. *Sons of Bajezid: Empire Building and Representation in the Ottoman Civil War of 1402-13*. Leiden: Brill, 2007.

Kelleher, Patrick J. *The Holy Crown of Hungary*. Rome: American Academy in Rome, 1951.

Keskin, Mustafa Çağhan. "Timurid Tile Style in Anatolia and Footprints of Masters of Tabriz." 1st International Conference on Architecture & Urban Design, Tirana, Albania, April 2012. http://archnet.org/system/publications/contents/10066/original/DTP102451.pdf?1427898487.

Khan, M. Muhsin, trans. *The Translation of the Meanings of Summarized Sahih Al-Bukhari*. Lahore: Kazi Publications Inc., 1995.

Kingery, W. D. and P. B. Vandiver. *Ceramic Masterpieces: Art, Structure and Technology*. New York: The Free Press, 1986.

Kostof, Spiro. *A History of Architecture: Settings and Rituals*. New York: Oxford, 1985.

Kraidy, Marwan. *Hybridity, Or the Cultural Logic of Globalization*. Philadelphia: Temple University Press, 2005.

Krisciunas, Kevin, "The Legacy of Ulugh Beg." *Bulletin of the Association for the Advancement of Central Asian Research* 5 (1992): 3-6. http://vlib.iue.it/carrie/texts/carrie_books/paksoy-2/cam6.html.

Kritovoulos. *History of Mehmed the Conqueror*. Translated by Charles T. Brigg. Westport, CT: Greenwood Press Publishers, 1970.

Kuban, Doğan. *Ottoman Architecture*. Suffolk: Antique Collectors Club Distributors, 2010.

Kuban, Doğan. "The Style of Sinan's Domed Structures." *Muqarnas* 4 (1987): 72-97.

Kunt, Metin and Christine Woodhead, eds. *Süleyman the Magnificent and His Age: The Ottoman Empire in the Early Modern World*. London: Longman, 1995.

Kunz, George Frederick. *The Curious Lore of Precious Stones*. New York: Dover Publications, 1971.

Kürkçüoğlu, Kemal Edip. *Süleymaniye Vakfiyesi*. Ankara: Vakıflar Umum Müdürlüğü, 1962.

Leach, Katheirne. *Documents and Debates: Sixteenth Century Europe*. Hong Kong: MacMillan Education, 1980.

Lethaby, W. R. *Architecture, nature, and magic*. New York: Cosimo Classics, 2005.

Levi, Scott Cameron and Ron Sela, eds. *Islamic Central Asia: an Anthology of Historical Sources*. Indianapolis: Indiana University Press, 2010.

Lewis, Raphaela. *Everyday Life on Ottoman Turkey*. Batsford: Dorset, 1988.

Libbrecht, Ulrich. "Comparative Philosophy: A Methodological Approach." In *Worldviews and Cultures: Philosophical Reflections from an Intercultural Perspective*, edited by Nicole Note, Raul Fornet-Betancout, Josef Estermann, and Diederik Aerts, 31-68. Brussels: Springer, 2009.

Lokman, Seyyid Huseyin. "Sürname-i Hümayun." Topkapı Palace Museum, H.1344.

Lowenthal, David. *The Past is a Foreign Country.* Cambridge: Cambridge University Press, 1985.

MacClean, Gerald, ed. *Re-Orienting the Renaissance: Cultural Exchanges With the East*. New York: Palgrave Macmillan, 2005.

Mack, Rosamond E. *Bazaar to Piazza: Islamic Trade and Italian Art, 1300-1600.* Berkeley: University of California, 2002.

Madison, D. Soyini. *Critical Ethnography: Method, Ethics, and Performance.* Los Angeles: Sage Publications, 2012.

Magoulias, Harry J., ed. *Decline and Fall of Byzantium to the Ottoman Turks by Doukas: An Annotated Translation of 'Historia Turco-Byzantina.'* Detroit: Wayne State University Press, 1975.

Mantran, R. "Les inscriptions arabes de Brousse." *Bulletin d'Etudes Orientales* 14 (1952-4): 87-114.

Manuel, Frank. *The Shapes of Philosophical History.* Stanford: Stanford University Press, 1965.

Martin, Charles A. "Hagia Sophia and the Great Imperial Mosques." *Art Bulletin* 12 (1930): 321–44.

Matthews, Henry. "Rethinking Ottoman Architecture." In *Oriental Occidental:*

Geography, Identity, Space, edited by Sibel Bozdoğan and Ülker Berke Copur, 361-363. Washington: ACSA International Conference, 2001.

Meckien, Riuchard. "Cultural Memory: The Link between Past, Present, and Future." Institute of Advanced Studies of the University of Sao Paulo. http://www.iea.usp.br/en/news/cultural-memory-the-link-between-past-present-and-future

Mehmed, Ramazanzade. *Tarih-i Nişancı Mehmed Paşa.* Istanbul: Tabhane-yi Amire, 1862.

Menage, V. L. "The 'Map of Hajji Ahmed' and its makers." *Bulletin of the School of Oriental and African Studies* 21 (1958): 291-314.

Menemencioğlu, N. and Fahir Iz, eds. *The Penguin Book of Turkish Verse.* Suffolk, UK: Penguin Books, 1978.

Mensiz, Ercan. "Ottoman Sultan Tugras." Accessed November 14, 2015. http://www.tugra.org/en/hakkinda.asp

Melikoff, I. "La fleur de la souffrance. Recherche sur le sens symbolique de Lâle dans ka poésie mystique turco-iranienne." *Journal Asiatique* 205 (1967): 341-60.

Mensiz, Ercan. "Ottoman Sultan Tugras." Accessed November 14, 2015. http://www.tugra.org/en/hakkinda.asp

Michelsen, Leslie. *Ferozkoh: Tradition and Continuity in Afghan Art (English Edition).* Qatar: A&C Black, 2013.

Monfasani, John. *George of Trebizond: A Biography and a Study of His Rhetoric and Logic.* Leiden: Brill, 1976.

Morewedge, Parviz, ed., *Neoplatonism and Islamic Thought.* Albany, NY: State University of New York Press, 1992.

Morkoç, Selen B. "Reading Architecture from the text: The Ottoman Story of the Four Marble Columns." Accessed February 9, 2018. https://www.academia.edu/27608699/Reading_Architecture_from_Text_The_Story_of_the_Four_Marble_Columns

Mungan, Ihsan. "Hagia Sophia and Mimar Sinan: How to Strengthen the Roof." *Proceeding of the IASS International, Symposium on Shell and Spacial Structures,* 2005, PT.1–2.

Nagel, Alexander and Christopher Wood. "Towards a New Model of Renaissance Anachronism." *Art Bulletin* 87 (2005): 403-32.

Nasr, Sayyed Hussein. *Islamic Art and Spirituality.* Albany, NY: State University of New York Press, 1987.

Nasr, Seyyed Hossein. *The Pilgrimage of Life and the Wisdom of Rumi.* Charlottesville, VA: Foundation for Traditional Studies, 2007.

Necipoğlu, Gülru. *Architecture, Ceremonial, and Power: The Topkapi Palace in the Fifteenth and Sixteenth Centuries (Architectural History Foundation Book).* Cambridge, MA: MIT Press, 1991.

Necipoğlu, Gülru. *The Age of Sinan: Architectural Culture in the Ottoman Empire.* London: Reaktion Books, 2005.

Necipoğlu, Gülru. "Challenging the Past: Sinan and the Competitive Discourse of Early Modern Islamic Architecture." *Muqarnas* 10 (1993): 169–80. http://www.jstor.org/stable/1523183?seq=1#page_scan_tab_contents.

Necipoğlu, Gülru. "Creation of a National Genius: Sinan and the Historiography of

'Classical' Ottoman Architecture." *Muqarnas* 24 (2006): 141-84.http://isites.harvard.edu/fs/docs/icb.topic570061.files//articles/Creation_Genius.pdf.

Necipoğlu, Gülru. "From International Timurid to Ottoman: A Change of Taste in Sixteenth-Century Ceramic Tiles." *Muqarnas* 7 (1991): 136–70. http://isites.harvard.edu/fs/docs/icb.topic570061.files//articles/Necipoglu.%20From%20International%20Timurid%20to%20Ottoman%20A%20Change%20of%20Taste%20in%20Sixteenth-Century%20Ceramic%20Tiles.pdf.

Necipoğlu, Gülru. "From Byzantine Constantinople to Ottoman Kostantiniyye: Creation of a Cosmopolitan Capital and Visual Culture under Sultan Mehmed II." In *From Byzantion to Istanbul: 8000 Years of a Capital*, edited by Nazan Ölçer. Istanbul: Sabanci University, 2010.

Necipoğlu-Kafadar, Gülru. "The Süleymaniye Complex in Istanbul: An Interpretation." *Muqarnas* 3 (1985): 92-117. http://www.jstor.org/stable/1523086?-origin=JSTOR-pdf.

Necipoğlu, Gülru. "Preface.' Sources, Themes, and Cultural Implications of Sinan's Autobiographies.' http://isites.harvard.edu/fs/docs/icb.topic572595.files/chapters_and_prefaces/Necipoglu%20-%20Sources%20Themes%20Cultural%20Implications.pdf

Necipoğlu, Gülru. "The serial portraits of Ottoman sultans in comparative perspective." In *The Sultan's Portrait: Picturing the House of Osman*, edited by Selmin Kangal. Translated by Priscilla Mary Işın. Istanbul: İşBank, 2000. http://isites.harvard.edu/fs/docs/icb.topic572595.files//chapters_and_prefaces/Word%20and%20Image%20in%20Portraits%20of%20the%20Ottoman%20Sultans.pdf

Necipoğlu, Gülru. "Visual Cosmopolitanism and Creative Translation: Artistic Conversations with Renaissance Italy in Mehmed II's Constantinople." *Muqarnas* 29 (2012): 1-82. https://scholar.harvard.edu/files/gnecipoglu/files/m29_necipoglu.pdf

Nicholson, Reynold A. *The Mesnevi of Jalalu'ddin Rumi*, Vols. I and II. Lahore: Islamic Book Service, 1989.

'Nicomachean Ethics of Aristotle,' Book IV. http://www.sacred-texts.com/cla/ari/nico/nico036.htm

Norberg-Schulz, Christian. *Jitsuzon · Kukan · Kenchiku*, (Existence, Space and Architecture). Translated by Kato Kunio. Tokyo: Kajima–Shuppankai, 1973.

Norton, Claire. "Blurring the Boundaries: Intellectual and Cultural Interactions between Eastern and Western: Christian and Muslim Worlds." In *The Renaissance and the Ottoman World*, edited by Anna Contadini and Claire Norton, 3-22. Farnham: Ashgate Publishing Limited, 2013.

O'Connell, Monique and Eric R. Dursteler. *The Mediterranean World: From the Fall of Rome to the Rise of Napoleon.* Baltimore: John Hopkins University Press, 2016.

Ogier, Ghiselinde Busbecq. *The Turkish Letters of Ogier Ghiselin de Busbecq.* Translated by Edward Seymour Forster. Oxford: Oxford University Press, reprinted 1968.

Onay, Ahmet Talay. "Eski Türk Edebiyatında Mazmunlar." *Türkiye Diyanet Vakfı* 77 (1993): 87-88.

Ortaylı, Ilber. *Türklerin Altın Çağı* (The Golden Age of the Turks). Istanbul: Kronik Kitap, 2017.

Ousterhout, Robert. "The East, the West, and the Appropriation of the Past in Early Ottoman Architecture." *Gesta* 43, no. 2 (2004): 165-76. http://www.jstor.org/stable/25067103.

Ousterhout, Robert. "Ethnic Identity and cultural appropriation in early Ottoman Architecture." ND. http://archnet.org/system/publications/contents/4470/original/DPC1020.PDF?1384785510

Önder, Mehmet. *Mevlāna and the Mevlāna Museum.* Edited by Zümrüt Akşit. Istanbul: Akşit Culture and Tourism Publication, 1985.

Öney, Gönül. *Islâm Mimarîsinde Çini.* Istanbul: Ada Yayınları, 1987.

Öz, Tahsin. *Topkapı Sarayı Müzesi Arşivi Kılavuzu II.* Istanbul: Devlet Basımevi, 1938.

Özgüleş, Muzaffer. "Fundamental Developments of 16th Century Ottoman Architecture: Innovations in the Art of Architect Sinan." Science and Technology Policy Studies, Middle East Technical University. Ankara: 2003. http://www.stps.metu.edu.tr/sites/stps.metu.edu.tr/files/0803.pdf

Pamuk, Şevket. *A Monetary History of the Ottoman Empire.* Cambridge: Cambridge University Press, 2000.

Péter, László. "The Holy Crown of Hungary, Visible and Invisible." *The Slavonic and East European Review* 81, no. 3 (2003): 421–510.

Petrosyan, I. E. "An Illustrated Turkish Manuscript of 'Iskender-nāme' by Ahmedi." http://www.islamicmanuscripts.info/reference/articles/Petrosyan-1995-MO-1-2-Iskenderna.PDF

Piotrovsky, M. B. and J. M. Rogers. *Heaven on Earth: Art from Islamic Lands.* Munich: Prestel, 2004.

Popper, Karl R. *The Open Society and its Enemies*, Princeton: Princeton University Press, 2013.

' Qur'an.' Abdullah Yusuf Ali edition.

Raby, Julian. "1560-1650: Maturity and Decline of Iznik Pottery." In *Iznik: The Pottery of Ottoman Turkey,* edited by Y. Petsopoulos, 218-88. London: Thames and Hudson, 1989.

Raby, Julian. "A Sultan of Paradox: Mehmed the Conqueror as a Patron of the Arts." *Oxford Art Journal* 5, no. 1 (1982): 3-8. http://www.jstor.org/stable/1360098.

Raby, Julian. "Development and Growth of Iznik Pottery." In *Iznik: The Pottery of Ottoman Turkey*, edited by Y. Petsopoulos, 76-81. London: Thames and Hudson, 1989.

Raby, Julian. "Mehmed the Conqueror's Greek Scriptorium." *Dumbarton Oaks Papers* 37 (1983): 15-34. http://www.jstor.org/stable/1291474.

Raby, Julian. "The Making of an Iznik Pot." In *Iznik: The Pottery of Ottoman Turkey*, edited by Y. Petsopoulos, 50-74. London: Thames and Hudson, 1989.

Raby, Julian. "Pride and Prejudice: Mehmed the Conqueror and the Italian Portrait Medal." *Studies in the History of Art* 21 (1987): 171-194.

Ramachandran, Ayesha. *The Worldmakers: Global Imagining in Early Modern Europe*. Chicago: The University of Chicago Press, 2015.

Redford, Scott. "The Seljuks of Rum and the Antique." Accessed February 10, 2018. https://www.academia.edu/4245845/The_Seljuks_of_Rum_and_the_Antique

Rice, David Talbot. *Islamic Art*. London: Thames and Hudson, 1991.

Rogers, Michael. "The Arts Under Suleyman the Magnificent." In *Süleyman the Second and His Time*, edited by Halil Inalcik and Cemal Kafadar, 257-294. Istanbul: Isis Press, 2010.

Rogers, J. M. and R. M. Ward. *Suleyman the Magnificent*. London: British Museum Publications, 1990.

Rose, Gillian. *Visual Methodologies: An Introduction to Researching with Visual Materials*. London: Sage Publications Ltd., 2016.

Rubin, P. "What Men Saw: Vasari's Life of Leonardo da Vinci and the image of the Renaissance artist." *Art History* 13 (March 1990): 34-46.

Ruggiero, Guido, ed. *A Companion to the Worlds of the Renaissance.* Malden: MA: Blackwell Publishing, 2007.

Rumi. *Divan-i Kabir* Vol. I. Translated by Bediuzzaman Furuzanfar. Tehran: Darneshgah-e, Tehran, 1957.

Rumi. *The Essential Rumi.* Translated by Coleman Barks and John Moyne. New York: Harper One, 2004.

Rumi. *Selected Poems.* Translated by Coleman Barks and John Moyne. New York: Penguin, 2004.

Rüsen, Jörn. "Historical Consciousness: Narrative Structure, Moral Function and Ontogenic Development." In *Theorizing Historical Consciousness,* edited by Peter Siexas, 63-77. London: University of Toronto Press, 2004.

Rüsen, Jörn. *Historische Orientierung.* Köln: Böhlau, 1994.

Rüsen, Jörn, ed. *Western Historical Thinking: An Intercultural Debate*. New York: Berghahn Books, 2002.

Rüsen, Jörn. "What is Historical Consciousness? - A Theoretical Approach to Empirical Evidence." Translated by Wolfgang Gebhard. Paper presented at Canadian Historical Consciousness in an International Context: Theoretical Frameworks, University of British Columbia, Vancouver, BC, 2001.

Sa'i, Mustafa. *Sinan's Autobiographies: Five Sixteenth Century Texts*. Introductory Notes, Critical Editions, and Translations by Howard Crane and Esra Akin, edited by Gülru Necipoğlu. Leiden: Brill, 2006.

Said, Edward. *Orientalism*. London: Penguin Books, 1995.

Sanderson, John. *The Travels of John Sanderson in the Levant, 1584-1602*. Edited by William Foster. London: Hakluyt Society, 1931.

Sanstead, Lee. 'The Meaning of Michelangelo's David.' Accessed February 19, 2017. http://www.sandstead.com/essays/david.html.

Saoud, R. "Muslim Architecture under Ottoman Patronage (1326-1924)." Foundation for Science Technology and Civilisation. Manchester 2004: 1-5. Accessed September 15, 2016. http://www.muslimheritage.com/uploads/OttomanArchitecture.pdf

Saoud, R. 'Sinan: A Great Ottoman Architect and Urban Designer.' Foundation for Science Technology and Civilisation. Manchester: June 2007: 1-15. Accessed September 15, 2016. http://www.muslimheritage.com/uploads/Mimar_Sinan_Great_Ottoman_Architect.pdf

Savory, Roger. *Iran Under the Safavids*. Cambridge: Cambridge University Press, 2007.

Sayılı, Aydın, Lamaan Ball, and Salim Ayduz. "Turkish Contributions to Scientific Work in Islam." Foundation for Science, Technology and Civilisation. (September 2004): 1-18. Accessed September 15, 2015. http://www.muslimheritage.com/uploads/TurkishScience.pdf

Schimmel, Annemarie. *Rumi's World: The Life and Work of the Great Sufi Poet*. Boston: Shambala, 2001.

Schimmel, Annemarie. "Turk and Hindu: A Poetical Image and Its Application to Historical Fact." In *Islam and Cultural Change in the Middle Ages*, edited by Speros Vryonis, 107-26. Wiesbaden: Otto Harrassowitz, 1975.

Schuon, Frithjof. *The Essential Frithjof Schuon*. Edited by Seyyed Hossein Nasr. Bloomington, IN: World Wisdom Inc., 2005.

Seherr-Thoss, S. P. *Design and Color in Islamic Architecture*. Washington, D.C.: Vendome Press, 1968.

Selaniki, Mustafa Efendi. *Tarih-i Selaniki*. Edited by Mehmet Ipsirli. 2 vols. Istanbul: Türk Tarih Kurum Basımevi, 1989.

Sewell, Brian. "Sinan: The Architect of a Forgotten Renaissance." *Cornucopia* 1992/93.

Shalem, Avinoam. "The Four Faces of the Ka'ba in Mecca." In *Architecture and Pilgrimage, 1000-1500: Southern Europe and Beyond*, edited by Paul Davies, Deborah Howard, and Wendy Pullan, 39-58. Surrey, England: Ashgate Publishing Limited, 2013.

Sinan, Mimar. *Sinan's Autobiographies: Five Sixteenth-Century Texts.* Edited by Gülru Necipoğlu. Translated by Howard Crane and Esra Akın. Leiden: Brill, 2006.

Stanford Encyclopedia of Philosophy. https://plato.stanford.edu/entries/eternity/

Strathem, Paul. *The Medici: Godfathers of the Renaissance*. Pimlico: Florence, 2005.

Subtelny, Maria Eva. "Socioeconomic Bases of Cultural Patronage under the Later Timurids." *International Journal of Middle East Studies* 20 (1988): 479-505. doi:10.1017/S0020743800053861

Sûdi, Bosnavi. *Hafiz Serhi*, Vol. 1. Istanbul: Matbaa-yı Amire, 1871.

Takikawa, Mio. "Hagia Sophia and Sinan's Mosques: Structure and Decoration in Süleymaniye Mosque and Selimiye Mosque." https://seijo.repo.nii.ac.jp/?action=repository_uri&item_id=3340&file_id=22&file_no=1

Tarnas, Richard. *The Passion of the Western Mind: Understanding the Ideas That Have Shaped Our World View*. New York: Ballantine Books, 1991.

Taşköprülüzade. *Es-Sekaiku n-Nu'maniye fi Ulema'i d-Devletil-Osmaniye* (Crimson Peonies of the Ottoman State's Ulema). Edited by A. S. Furat. Istanbul: Iz Yayıncılık, 1985.

"TCF: Turkish Cultural Foundation." Accessed November 15, 2015. http://www.turkishculture.org/traditional-arts/tugra-sultanic-cipher-116.htm

Texier, Charles. Description de l'Asie Mineure, faite par ordre du gouvernement francais de 1833 a 1837. Paris: Ministere de l'instruction, 1862.

Trutty-Coohill, Patricia. "Agathos in Michelangelo's Sistine Ceiling." *AGATHOS: An International Review of the Humanities and Social Sciences* 1 (2010): 7-21.

Tursun Beg. *Tarih-i Ebu'l-Feth*. Edited by Mertol Tulum. Istanbul: Istanbul Fetih Cemiyeti, 1977.

Tursun Beg. *The History of Mehmed the Conqueror*. Edited by H. Inalcık and R. Murphey. Minneapolis-Chicago: Bibliotheca Islamica, 1978.

Uzunçarşılı, I. H. "Tuğra ve pençeler ile ferman ve buyuruldulara dair." *Belleten* 17/18 (1941): 101-57.

Vakıflar Genel Müdürlüğü, Defter 635/1. (Republic of Turkey, Prime Ministry, Directorate Generals of Foundations).

Vakıflar Genel Müdürlüğü. Defter 648. (Republic of Turkey, Prime Ministry, Directorate Generals of Foundations).

Vasari, Giorgio. Preface to Part III, *The Lives of the Painters, Sculptors and Architects*, 4 vols. Edited by William Gaunt. New York: Dent, 1963.

Vasari, Giorgio. *Le vite de' piu eccellenti pittori, scultori ed architetti,* Torino, Letteratura italiana Einaudi, 1986. http://www.letteraturaitaliana.net/pdf/Volume_5/t129.pdf.

Vasari, Giorgio. *Vasari's Lives of the Artists*. Translated by Jonathan Foster. New York: Dover Publications, 2005. Kindle edition.

Vasari, Giorgio. Preface to *The Lives of the Painters, Sculptors and Architects*. Accessed May 5, 2016. http://members.efn.org/~acd/vite/VasariPreface.html

Vasari, Giorgio. *The Lives of the Painters, Sculptors and Architects*. Accessed March 27, 2016. https://ebooks.adelaide.edu.au/v/vasari/giorgio/lives/part2.12.html

Vasari, Giorgio. PART 1 of *The Lives of the Painters, Sculptors and Architects*. Accessed May 5, 2016. http://members.efn.org/~acd/vite/VasariGioPisano.htm1

Vasari, Giorgio. Preface to Part II, *The Lives of the Painters, Sculptors and Architects*. Accessed May 5, 2016. http://members.efn.org/~acd/vite/VasariPreface2.html

Vasari, Giorgio. PART III of *The Lives of the Painters, Sculptors and Architects*. Accessed May 5, 2016. http://members.efn.org/~acd/vite/VasariMichelangelo7.html

Vasari, Giorgio. PART III of *The Lives of the Painters, Sculptors and Architects*. Accessed May, 5, 2016. http://members.efn.org/~acd/vite/VasariMichelangelo3.html

Vasari, Giorgio. PART III of *The Lives of the Painters, Sculptors and Architects*. Accessed May 5, 2016. http://members.efn.org/~acd/vite/VasariLeo.html

Vasari, Giorgio. Part III of *The Lives of the Painters, Sculptors and Architects*. Accessed May 5, 2016. http://members.efn.org/~acd/vite/VasariTorrigiano.html

Warner, A. G. and E. Warner, trans. *The Shahnama of Firdausi*. London: K.Paul, Trench, Trübner, 1905.

Willis, Michael D. "Tiles from the Mosque of Rustem Pasa in Istanbul." *Artibus Asiae* 48 (1987): 278-84. http://www.jstor.org/stable/3249874

Woodhead, Christine, ed. *The Ottoman World*. London: Routledge, 2012.

Yeni Cep Lügat, Envar Neşriyat, Istanbul, 2000.

Yerasimos, S. *Constantinople: Istanbul's Historical Heritage*. Paris: H. F. Ullmann Publishing, 2012.

Zuwiyya, David Z. *Islamic Legends Concerning Alexander the Great*. Albany, NY: State University of New York Press, 2001.

Index

I

L

M

N

O

P

Q

R